BOB MARLEY in Comics

Writer
Gaëts

Text
Sophie Blitman

Cover art
Bast

nbm GRAPHIC NOVELS

Nantier • Beall • Minoustchine
NEW YORK

ISBN 9781681122496
© 2018 Editions Petit as Petit
© 2019 NBM for the English translation
Library of Congress Control Number: 2019948631
Translation by Montana Kane
Lettering by Ortho
Layout design by Mary Delavigne

Printed in Turkey
1st printing December 2019

This book is also available wherever e-books are sold;
ISBN 9781681122502.

nbm
GRAPHIC NOVELS
Comics Biographies

From Nesta to Robert

Artist: Olivier Desvaux

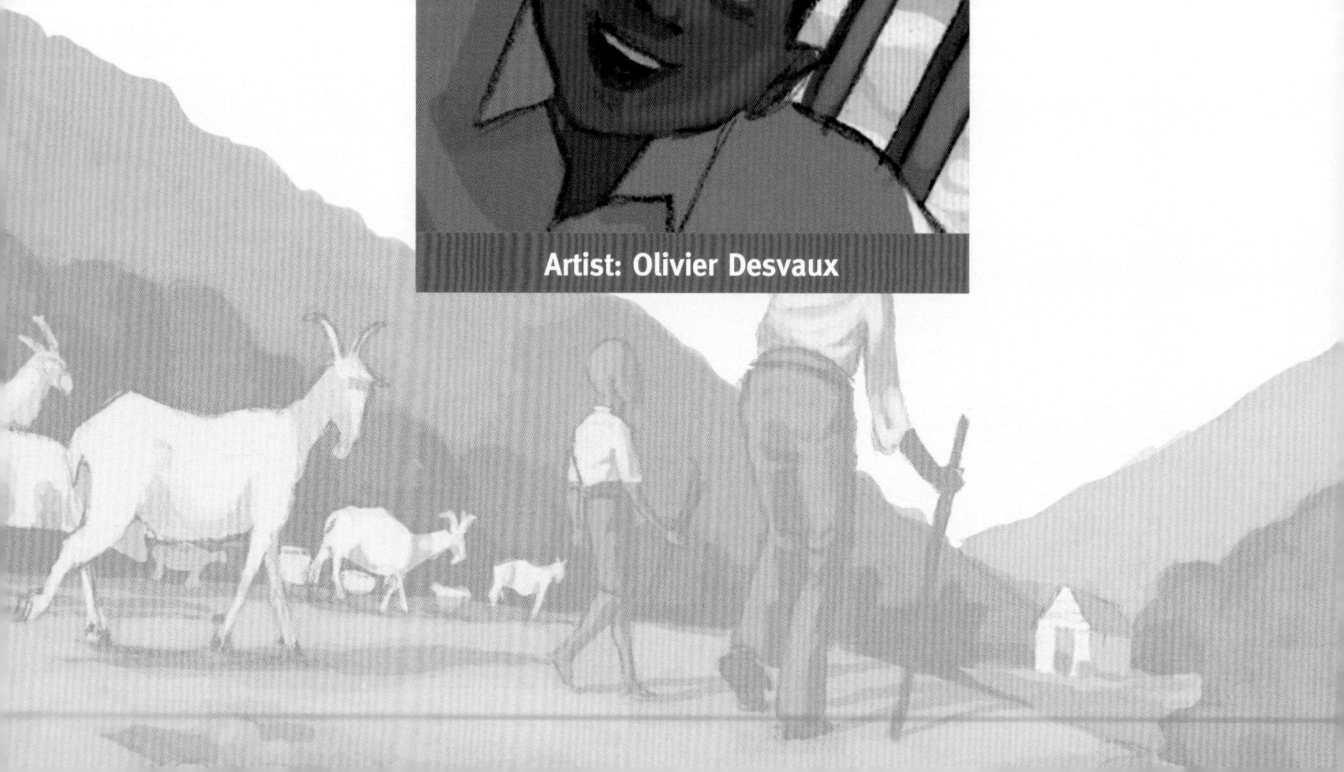

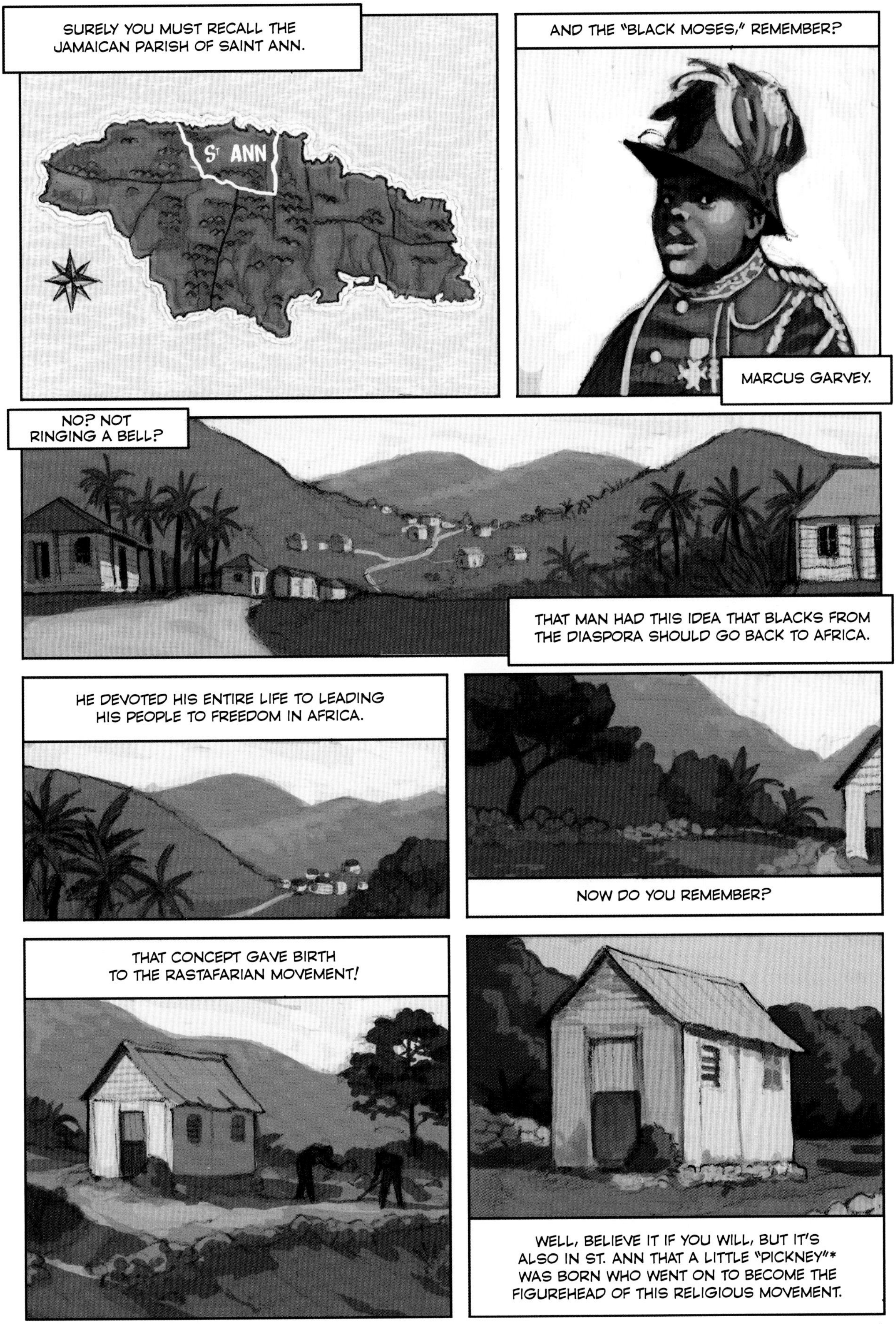
SURELY YOU MUST RECALL THE JAMAICAN PARISH OF SAINT ANN.
ST ANN
AND THE "BLACK MOSES," REMEMBER?
MARCUS GARVEY.
NO? NOT RINGING A BELL?
THAT MAN HAD THIS IDEA THAT BLACKS FROM THE DIASPORA SHOULD GO BACK TO AFRICA.
HE DEVOTED HIS ENTIRE LIFE TO LEADING HIS PEOPLE TO FREEDOM IN AFRICA.
NOW DO YOU REMEMBER?
THAT CONCEPT GAVE BIRTH TO THE RASTAFARIAN MOVEMENT!
WELL, BELIEVE IT IF YOU WILL, BUT IT'S ALSO IN ST. ANN THAT A LITTLE "PICKNEY"* WAS BORN WHO WENT ON TO BECOME THE FIGUREHEAD OF THIS RELIGIOUS MOVEMENT.

*MEANS "KID" IN JAMAICAN PATOIS.

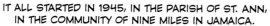

IT ALL STARTED IN 1945, IN THE PARISH OF ST. ANN,
IN THE COMMUNITY OF NINE MILES IN JAMAICA.

THAT WOMAN WITH THE BIG BELLY IS CEDELLA MALCOLM.

THE MAN IN FRONT OF THE HORSE IS NORVAL MARLEY.

AND THAT'S OMERIAH MALCOLM. HE OWNS JUST ABOUT EVERYTHING IN THE DISTRICT.

CEDELLA MALCOLM MARRIED NORVAL, A WHITE JAMAICAN ARMY CAPTAIN, AT THE AGE OF 17.

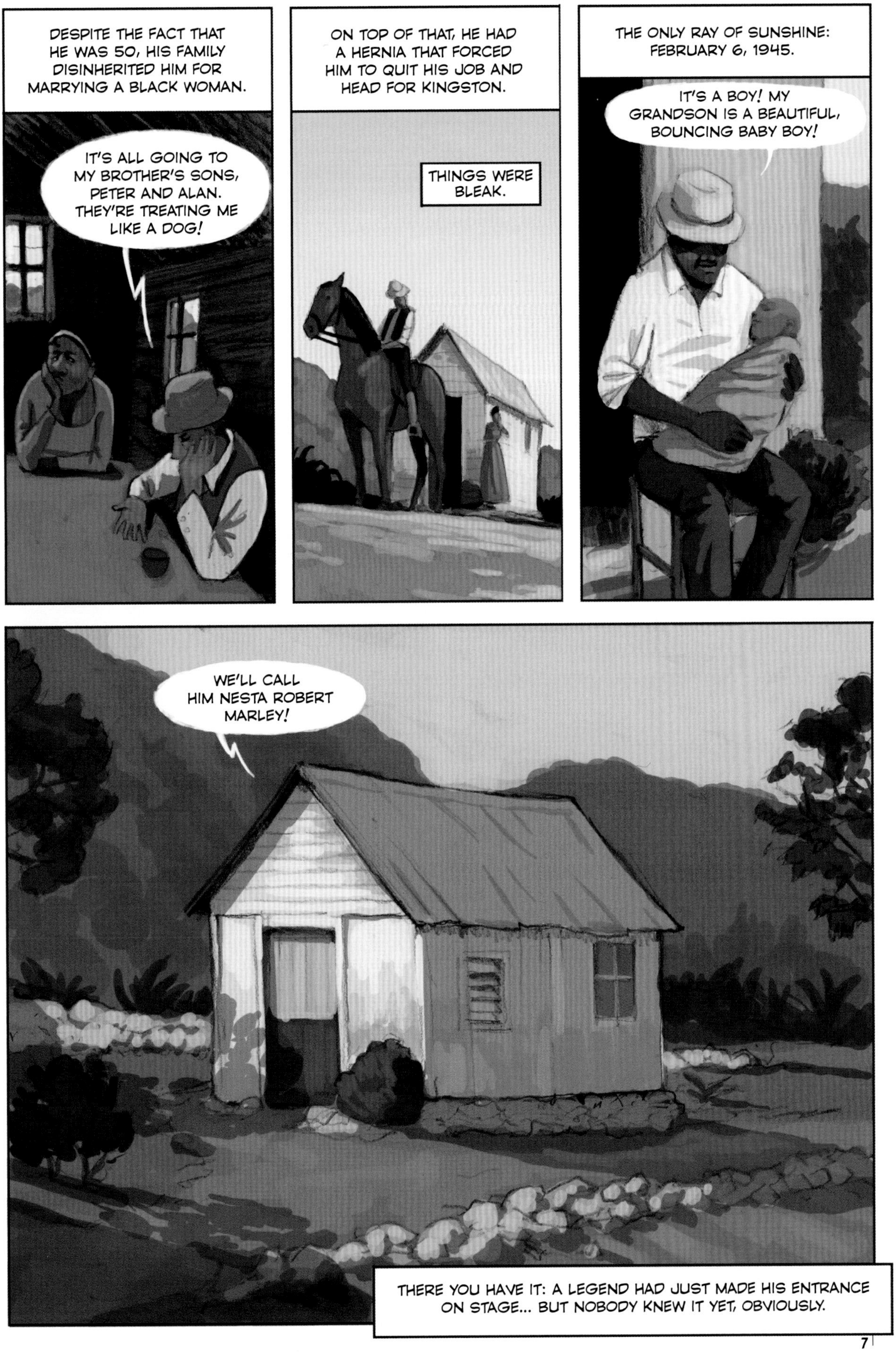

DESPITE THE FACT THAT HE WAS 50, HIS FAMILY DISINHERITED HIM FOR MARRYING A BLACK WOMAN.
IT'S ALL GOING TO MY BROTHER'S SONS, PETER AND ALAN. THEY'RE TREATING ME LIKE A DOG!
ON TOP OF THAT, HE HAD A HERNIA THAT FORCED HIM TO QUIT HIS JOB AND HEAD FOR KINGSTON.
THINGS WERE BLEAK.
THE ONLY RAY OF SUNSHINE: FEBRUARY 6, 1945.
IT'S A BOY! MY GRANDSON IS A BEAUTIFUL, BOUNCING BABY BOY!
WE'LL CALL HIM NESTA ROBERT MARLEY!
THERE YOU HAVE IT: A LEGEND HAD JUST MADE HIS ENTRANCE ON STAGE... BUT NOBODY KNEW IT YET, OBVIOUSLY.

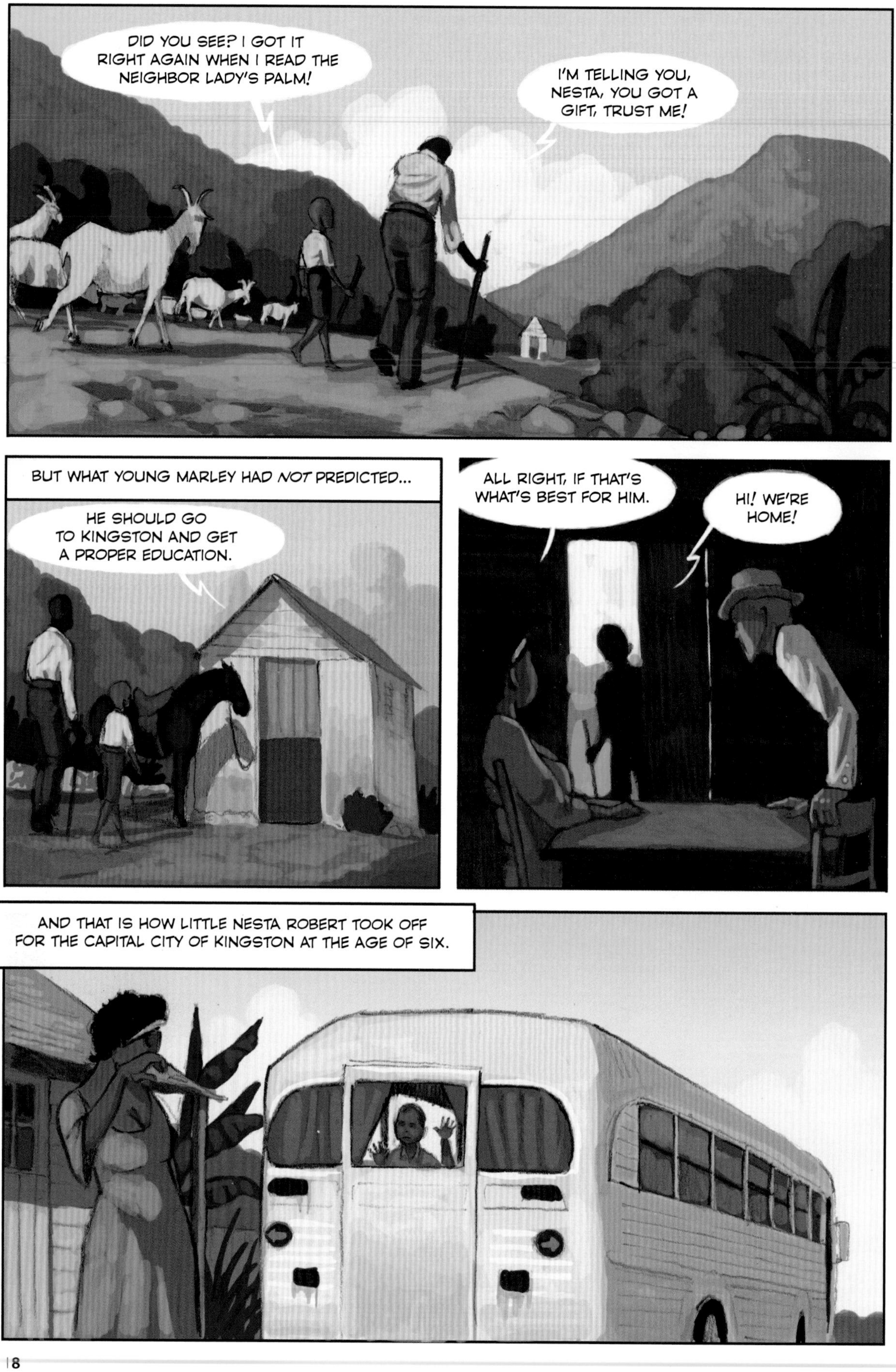
DID YOU SEE? I GOT IT RIGHT AGAIN WHEN I READ THE NEIGHBOR LADY'S PALM!
I'M TELLING YOU, NESTA, YOU GOT A GIFT, TRUST ME!
BUT WHAT YOUNG MARLEY HAD *NOT* PREDICTED...
HE SHOULD GO TO KINGSTON AND GET A PROPER EDUCATION.
HI! WE'RE HOME!
ALL RIGHT, IF THAT'S WHAT'S BEST FOR HIM.
AND THAT IS HOW LITTLE NESTA ROBERT TOOK OFF FOR THE CAPITAL CITY OF KINGSTON AT THE AGE OF SIX.

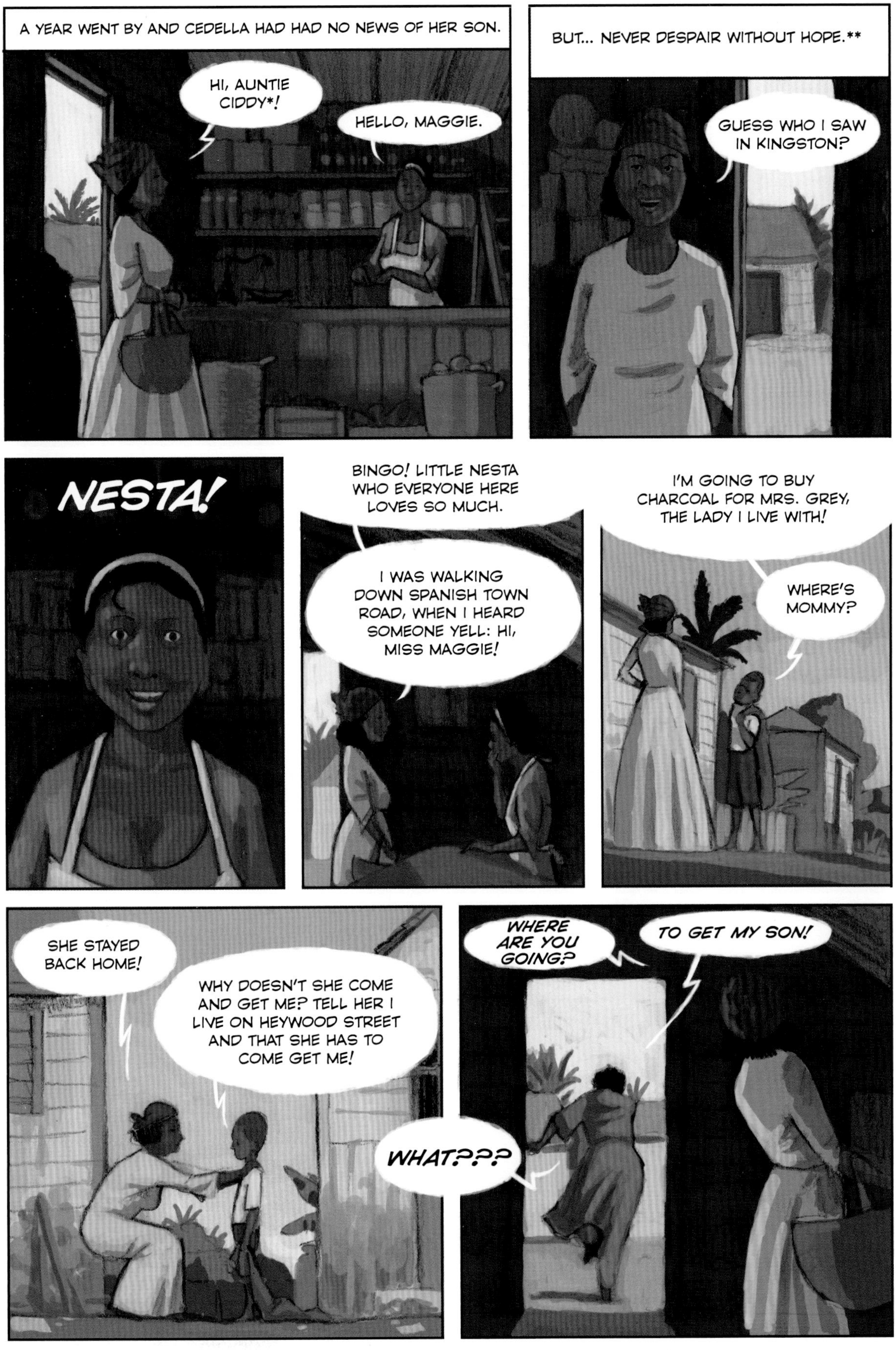
A YEAR WENT BY AND CEDELLA HAD HAD NO NEWS OF HER SON.
HI, AUNTIE CIDDY*!
HELLO, MAGGIE.
BUT... NEVER DESPAIR WITHOUT HOPE.**
GUESS WHO I SAW IN KINGSTON?
NESTA!
BINGO! LITTLE NESTA WHO EVERYONE HERE LOVES SO MUCH.
I WAS WALKING DOWN SPANISH TOWN ROAD, WHEN I HEARD SOMEONE YELL: HI, MISS MAGGIE!
I'M GOING TO BUY CHARCOAL FOR MRS. GREY, THE LADY I LIVE WITH!
WHERE'S MOMMY?
SHE STAYED BACK HOME!
WHY DOESN'T SHE COME AND GET ME? TELL HER I LIVE ON HEYWOOD STREET AND THAT SHE HAS TO COME GET ME!
WHAT???
WHERE ARE YOU GOING?
TO GET MY SON!

*IN ST. ANN, EVERYONE CALLED CEDELLA AUNTIE CIDDY.
** SENECA.

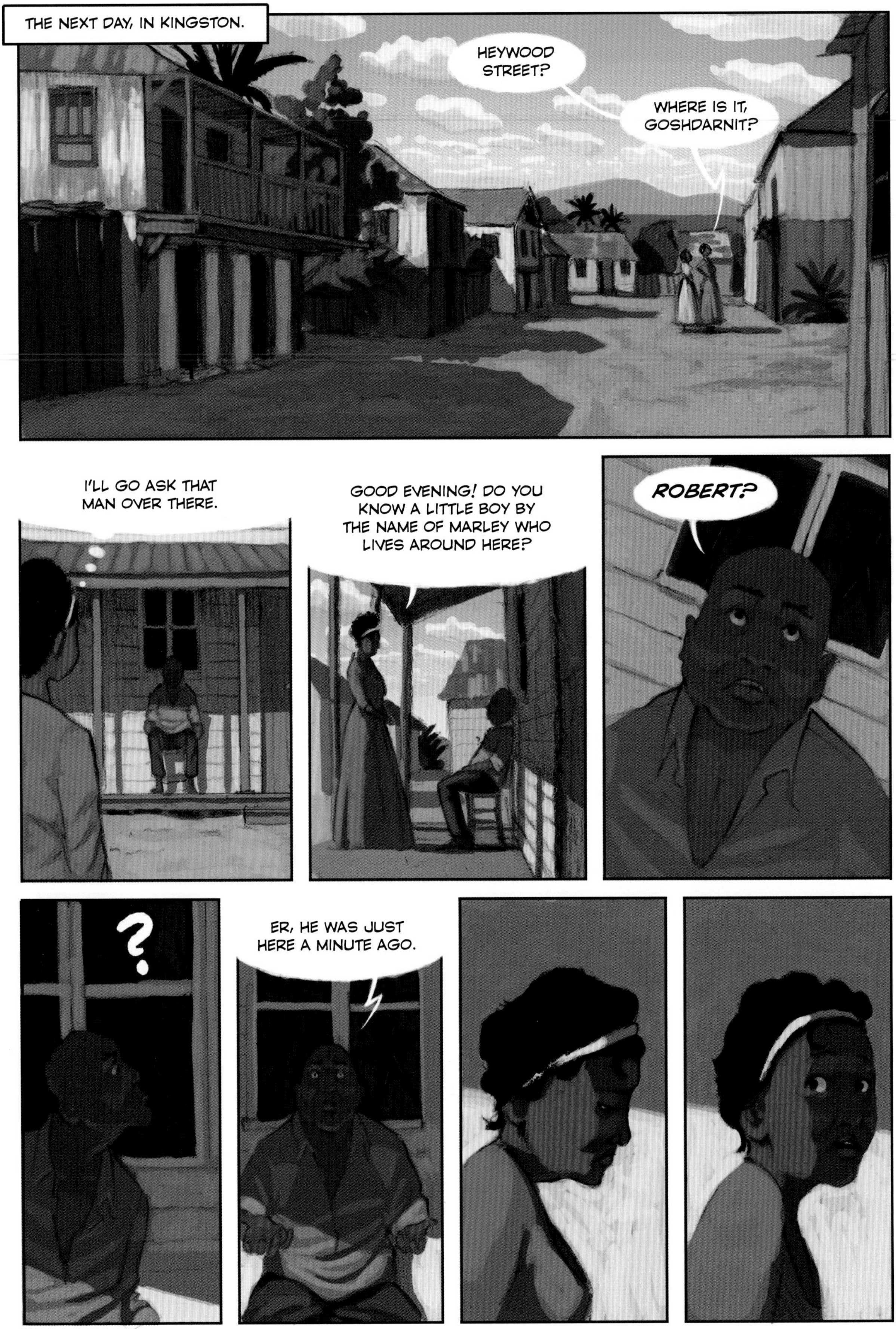

THE NEXT DAY, IN KINGSTON.
HEYWOOD STREET?
WHERE IS IT, GOSHDARNIT?
I'LL GO ASK THAT MAN OVER THERE.
GOOD EVENING! DO YOU KNOW A LITTLE BOY BY THE NAME OF MARLEY WHO LIVES AROUND HERE?
ROBERT?
?
ER, HE WAS JUST HERE A MINUTE AGO.

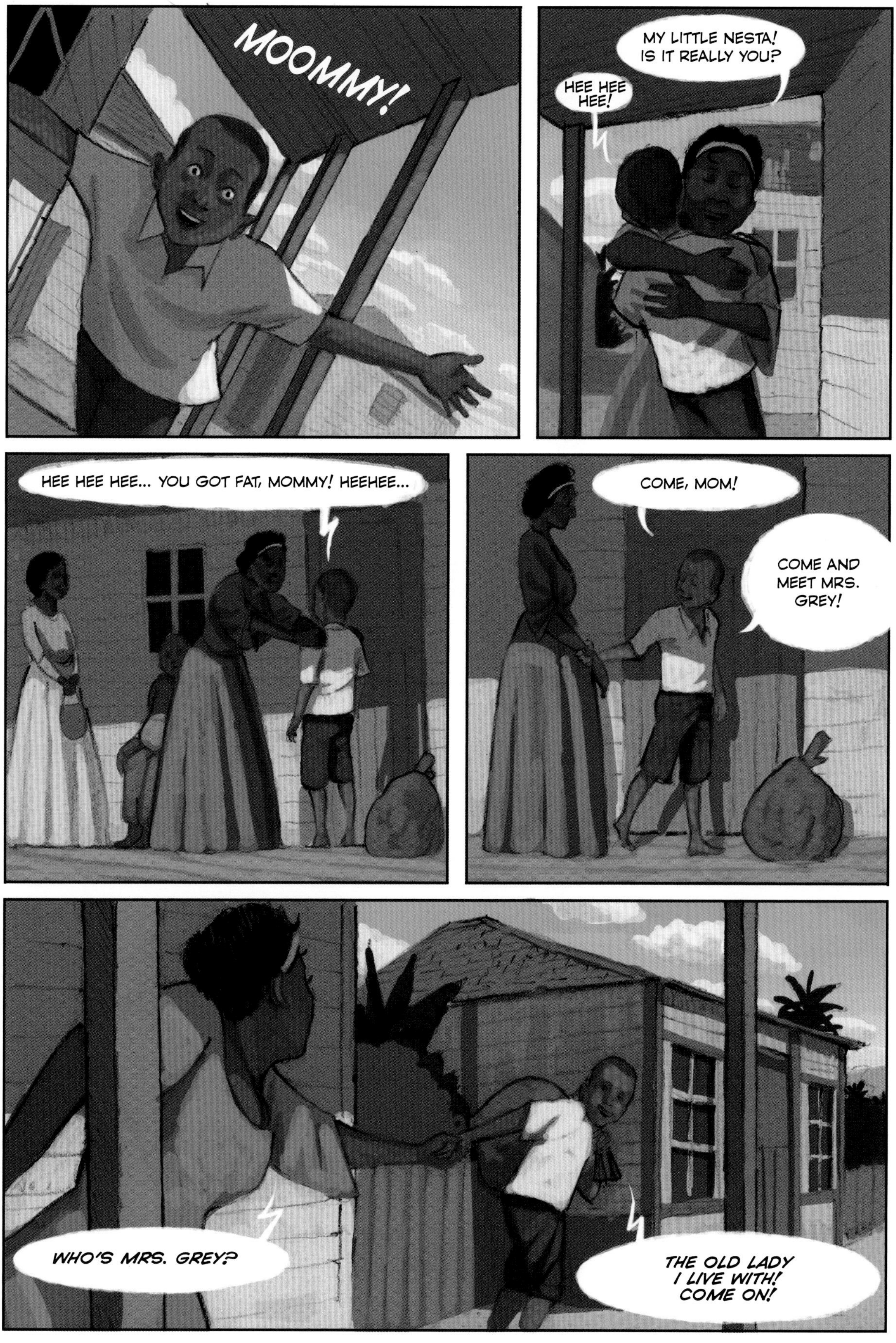
MOOMMY!
MY LITTLE NESTA! IS IT REALLY YOU?
HEE HEE HEE!
HEE HEE HEE... YOU GOT FAT, MOMMY! HEEHEE...
COME, MOM!
COME AND MEET MRS. GREY!
WHO'S MRS. GREY?
THE OLD LADY I LIVE WITH! COME ON!

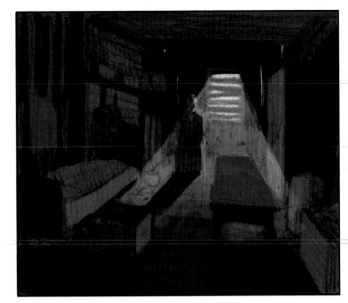

OH, SO YOU'RE ROBERT'S MOTHER!

I'M A FRIEND OF NORVAL'S FAMILY. HE BROUGHT ME THE CHILD SO I WOULD RAISE HIM AND MAKE HIM MY HEIR.

WHY ON EARTH HAVE YOU NEVER COME TO SEE ROBERT?

I HAD NO IDEA WHERE HE WAS...

I WANNA GO HOME, MOM. CAN WE LEAVE?

NESTA HELPS ME OUT WITH THE GROCERIES, THE COAL, AND OTHER ERRANDS. SEEING AS HOW I'M SICK AND ALL, IT WAS HARD SENDING HIM TO SCHOOL...

I'M GOING TO MISS THAT PICKNEY!

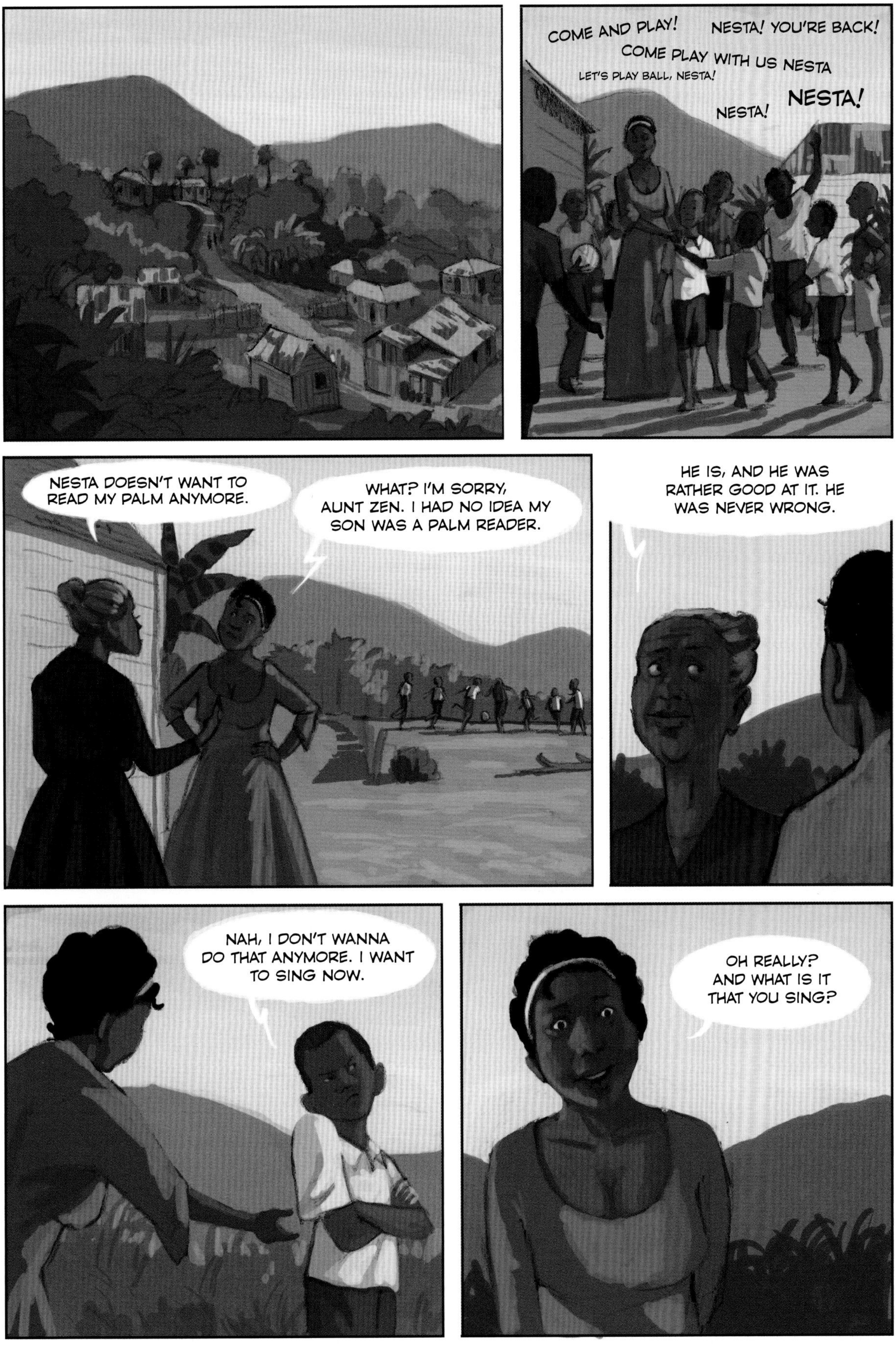
COME AND PLAY!
NESTA! YOU'RE BACK!
COME PLAY WITH US NESTA
LET'S PLAY BALL, NESTA!
NESTA!
NESTA!
NESTA DOESN'T WANT TO READ MY PALM ANYMORE.
WHAT? I'M SORRY, AUNT ZEN. I HAD NO IDEA MY SON WAS A PALM READER.
HE IS, AND HE WAS RATHER GOOD AT IT. HE WAS NEVER WRONG.
NAH, I DON'T WANNA DO THAT ANYMORE. I WANT TO SING NOW.
OH REALLY? AND WHAT IS IT THAT YOU SING?

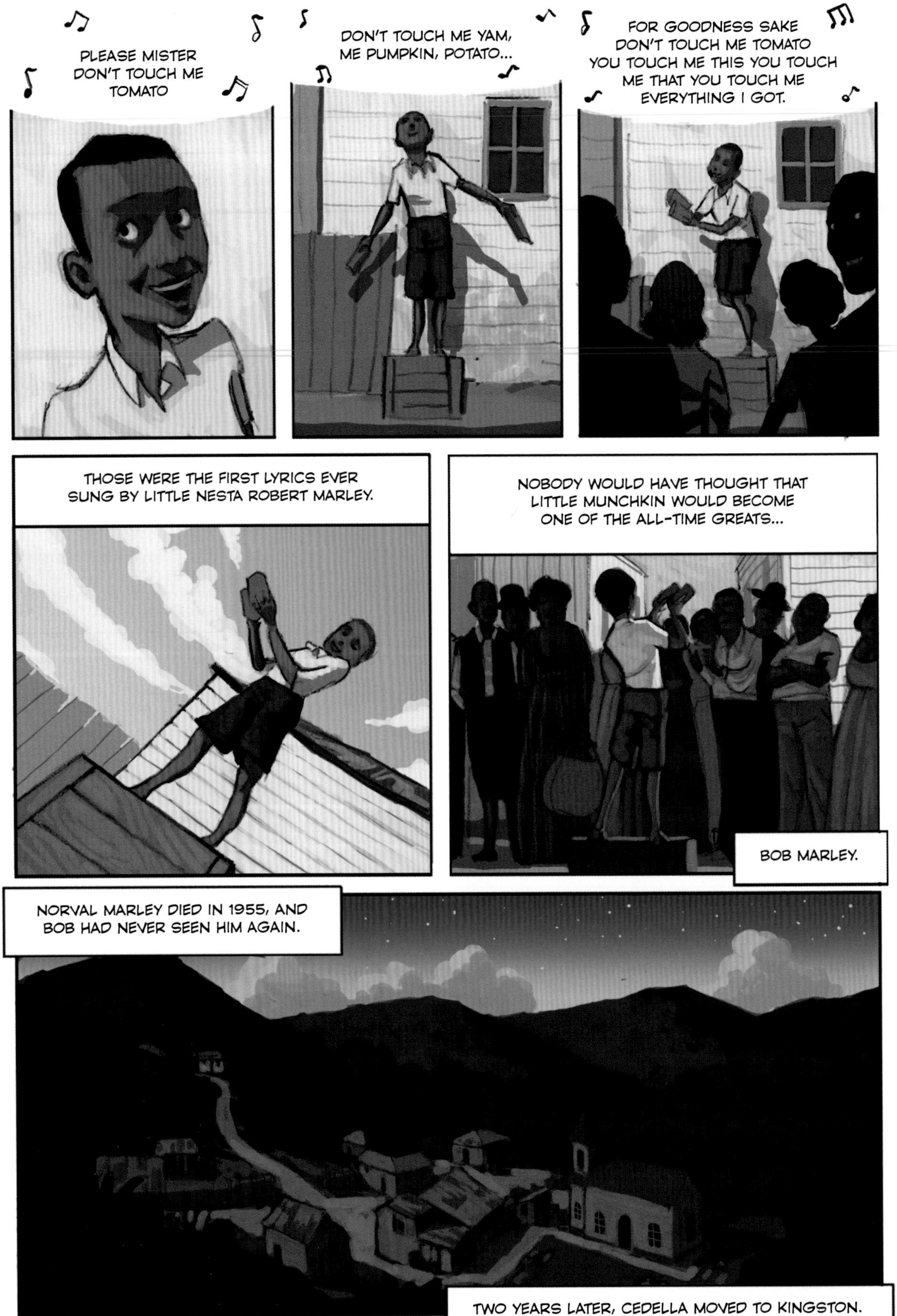
PLEASE MISTER DON'T TOUCH ME TOMATO
DON'T TOUCH ME YAM, ME PUMPKIN, POTATO...
FOR GOODNESS SAKE DON'T TOUCH ME TOMATO YOU TOUCH ME THIS YOU TOUCH ME THAT YOU TOUCH ME EVERYTHING I GOT.
THOSE WERE THE FIRST LYRICS EVER SUNG BY LITTLE NESTA ROBERT MARLEY.
NOBODY WOULD HAVE THOUGHT THAT LITTLE MUNCHKIN WOULD BECOME ONE OF THE ALL-TIME GREATS...
BOB MARLEY.
NORVAL MARLEY DIED IN 1955, AND BOB HAD NEVER SEEN HIM AGAIN.
TWO YEARS LATER, CEDELLA MOVED TO KINGSTON.

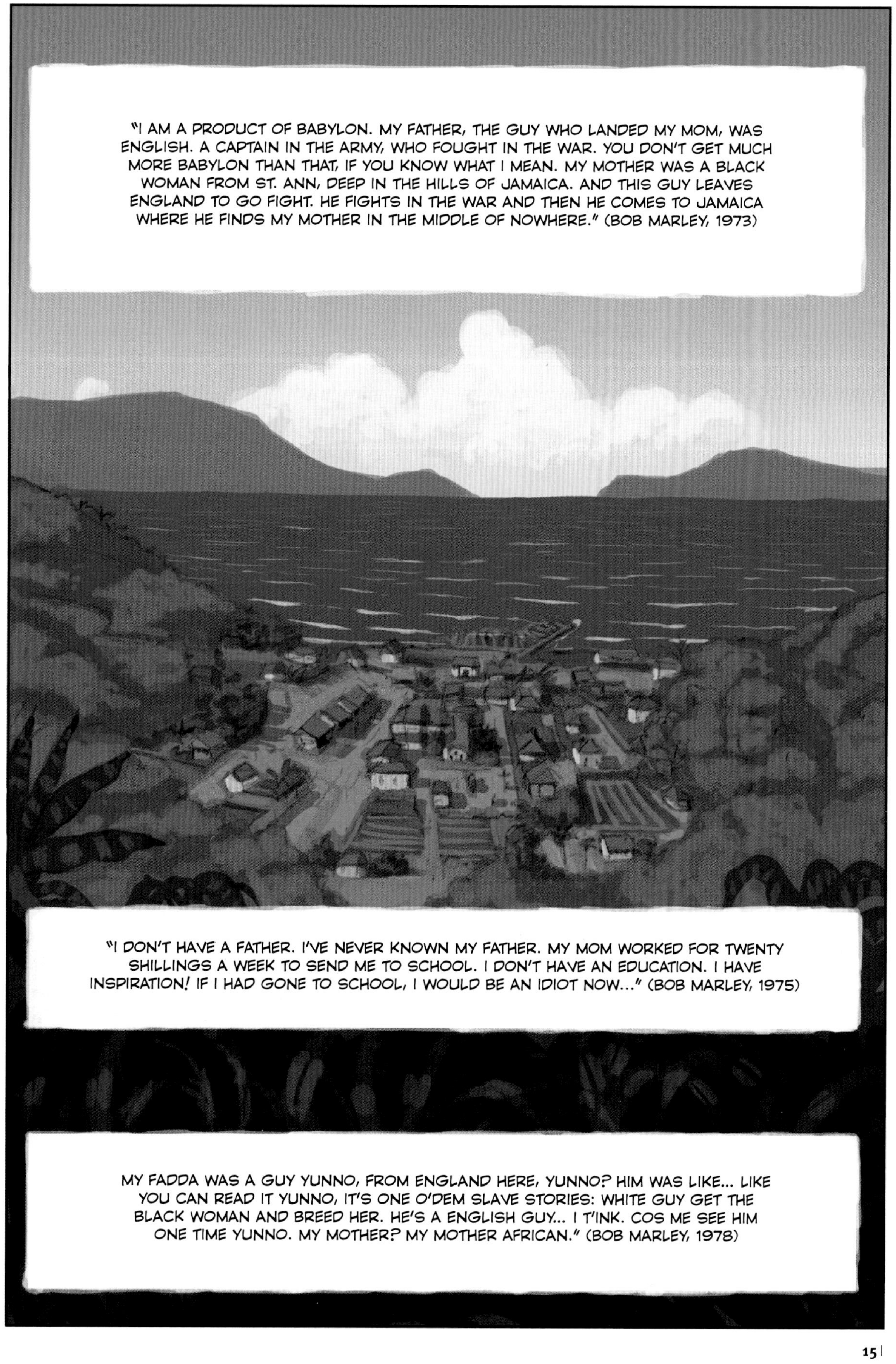
"I AM A PRODUCT OF BABYLON. MY FATHER, THE GUY WHO LANDED MY MOM, WAS ENGLISH. A CAPTAIN IN THE ARMY, WHO FOUGHT IN THE WAR. YOU DON'T GET MUCH MORE BABYLON THAN THAT, IF YOU KNOW WHAT I MEAN. MY MOTHER WAS A BLACK WOMAN FROM ST. ANN, DEEP IN THE HILLS OF JAMAICA. AND THIS GUY LEAVES ENGLAND TO GO FIGHT. HE FIGHTS IN THE WAR AND THEN HE COMES TO JAMAICA WHERE HE FINDS MY MOTHER IN THE MIDDLE OF NOWHERE." (BOB MARLEY, 1973)
"I DON'T HAVE A FATHER. I'VE NEVER KNOWN MY FATHER. MY MOM WORKED FOR TWENTY SHILLINGS A WEEK TO SEND ME TO SCHOOL. I DON'T HAVE AN EDUCATION. I HAVE INSPIRATION! IF I HAD GONE TO SCHOOL, I WOULD BE AN IDIOT NOW..." (BOB MARLEY, 1975)
MY FADDA WAS A GUY YUNNO, FROM ENGLAND HERE, YUNNO? HIM WAS LIKE... LIKE YOU CAN READ IT YUNNO, IT'S ONE O'DEM SLAVE STORIES: WHITE GUY GET THE BLACK WOMAN AND BREED HER. HE'S A ENGLISH GUY... I T'INK. COS ME SEE HIM ONE TIME YUNNO. MY MOTHER? MY MOTHER AFRICAN." (BOB MARLEY, 1978)

The Rude Boys of Trench Town

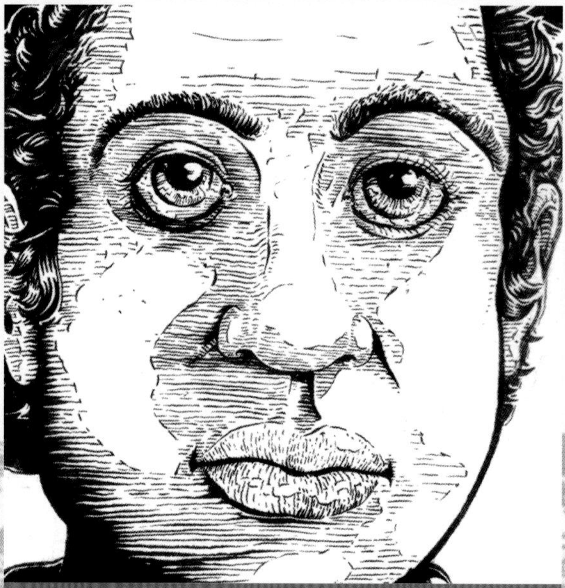

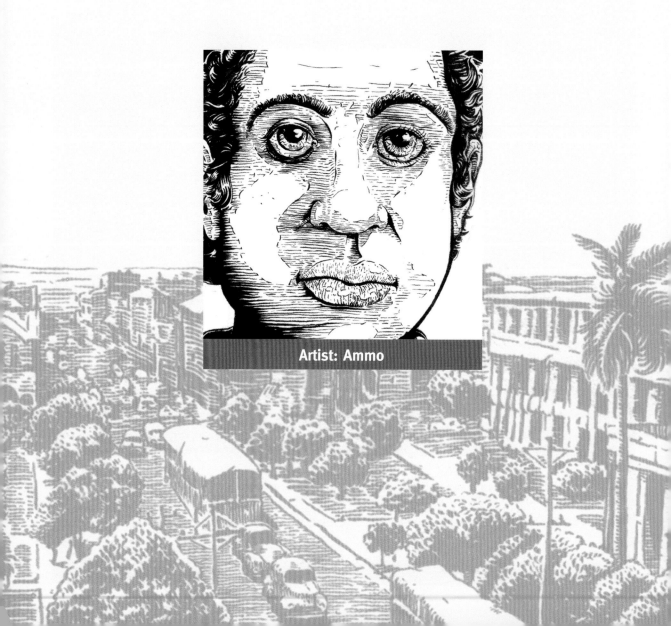

Artist: Ammo

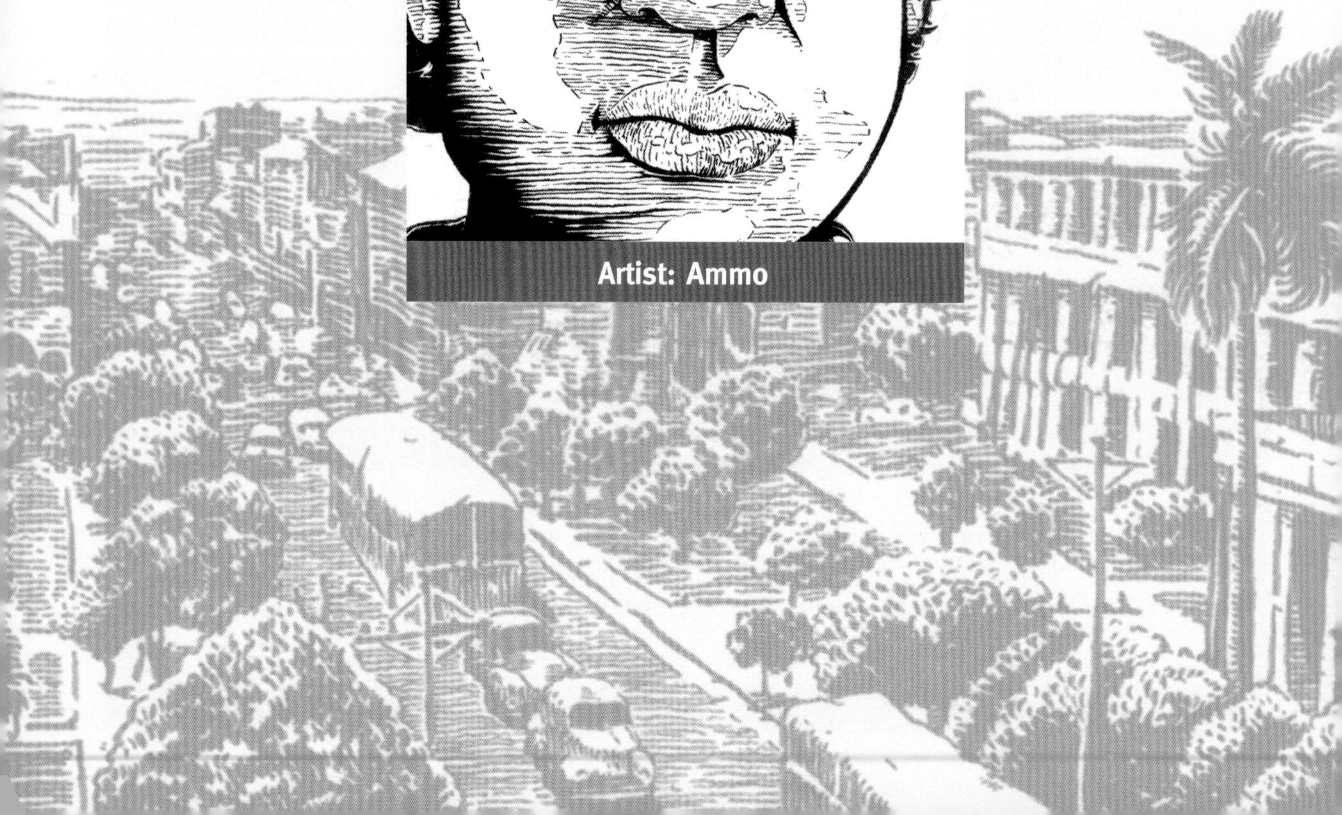

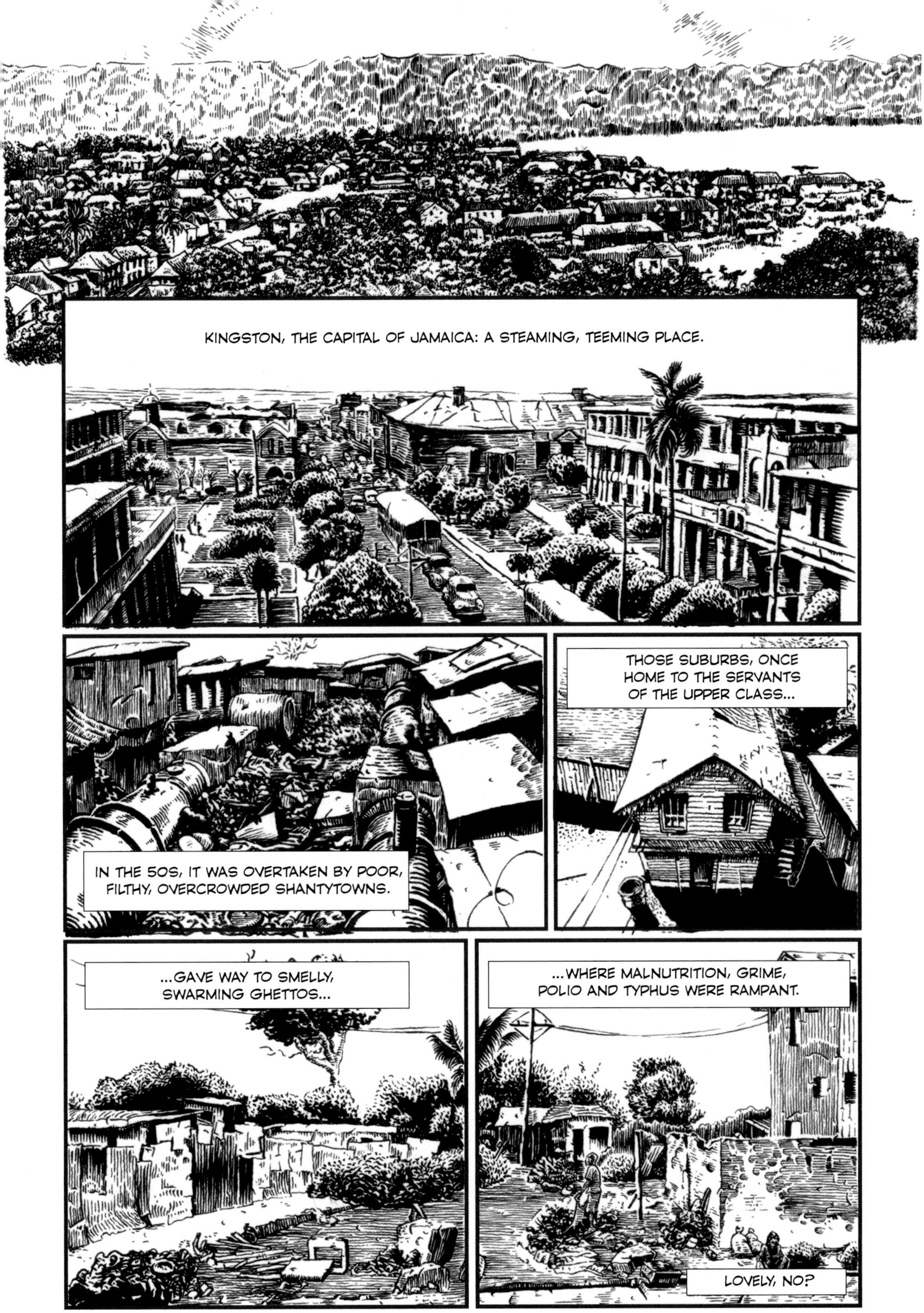
KINGSTON, THE CAPITAL OF JAMAICA: A STEAMING, TEEMING PLACE.
IN THE 50S, IT WAS OVERTAKEN BY POOR, FILTHY, OVERCROWDED SHANTYTOWNS.
THOSE SUBURBS, ONCE HOME TO THE SERVANTS OF THE UPPER CLASS...
...GAVE WAY TO SMELLY, SWARMING GHETTOS...
...WHERE MALNUTRITION, GRIME, POLIO AND TYPHUS WERE RAMPANT.
LOVELY, NO?

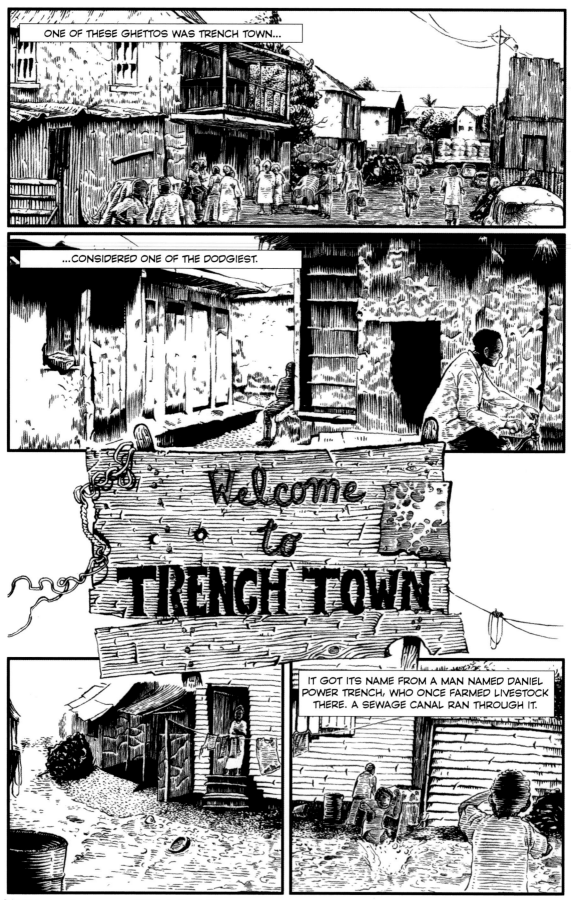

ONE OF THESE GHETTOS WAS TRENCH TOWN...

...CONSIDERED ONE OF THE DODGIEST.

Welcome to TRENCH TOWN

IT GOT ITS NAME FROM A MAN NAMED DANIEL POWER TRENCH, WHO ONCE FARMED LIVESTOCK THERE. A SEWAGE CANAL RAN THROUGH IT.

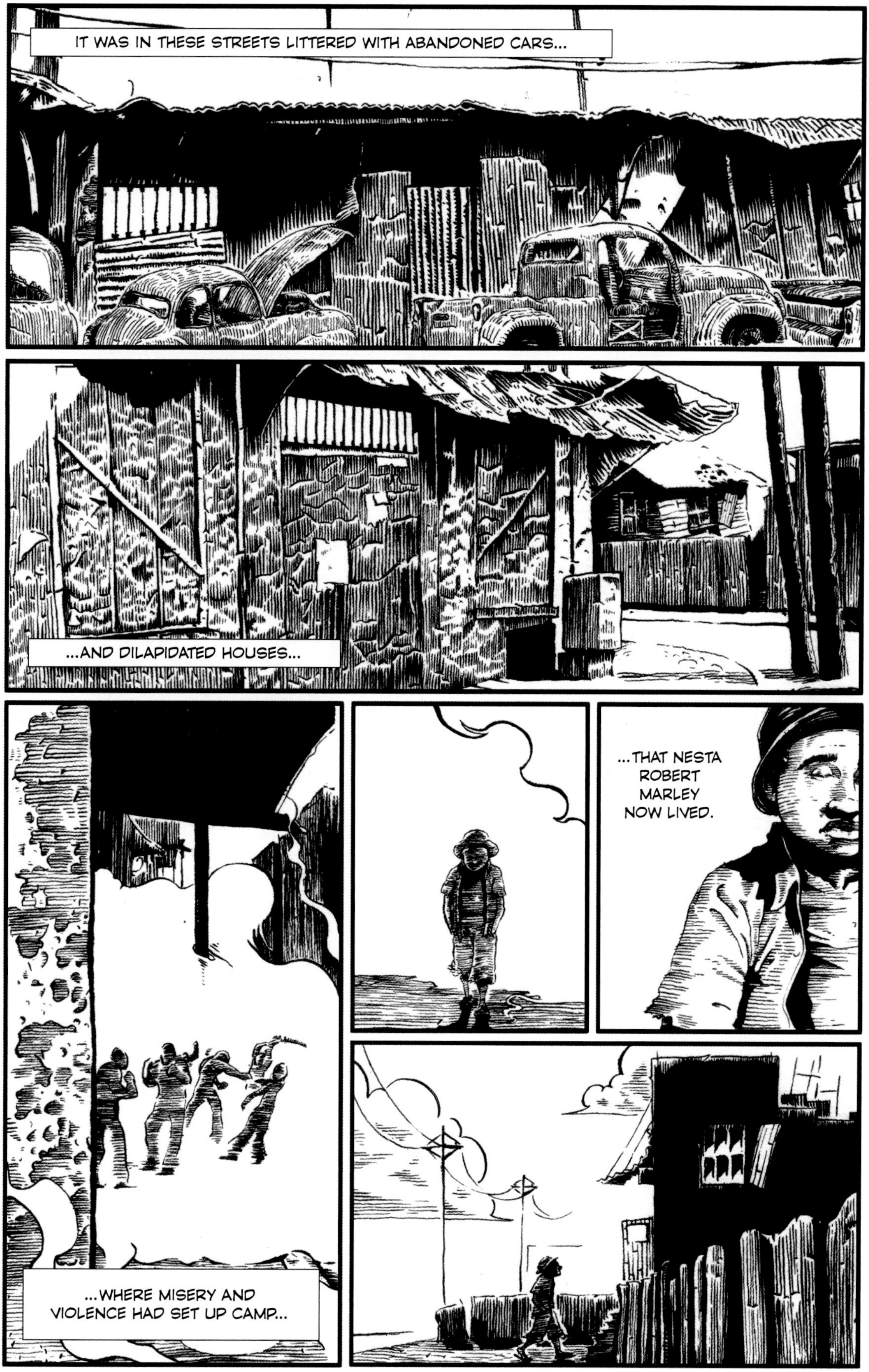
IT WAS IN THESE STREETS LITTERED WITH ABANDONED CARS...
...AND DILAPIDATED HOUSES...
...WHERE MISERY AND VIOLENCE HAD SET UP CAMP...
...THAT NESTA ROBERT MARLEY NOW LIVED.

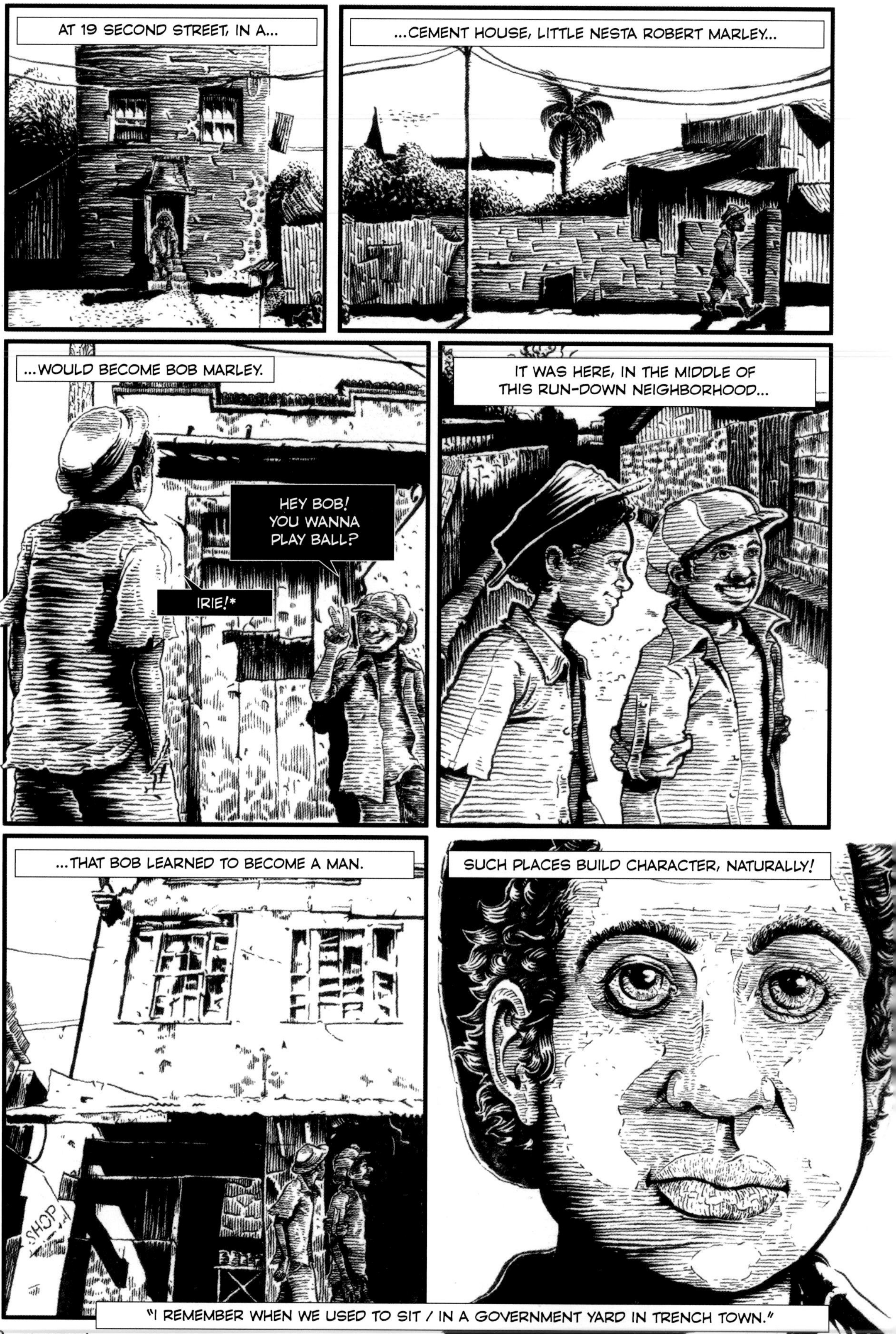
AT 19 SECOND STREET, IN A...
...CEMENT HOUSE, LITTLE NESTA ROBERT MARLEY...
...WOULD BECOME BOB MARLEY.
HEY BOB! YOU WANNA PLAY BALL?
IRIE!*
IT WAS HERE, IN THE MIDDLE OF THIS RUN-DOWN NEIGHBORHOOD...
...THAT BOB LEARNED TO BECOME A MAN.
SHOP
SUCH PLACES BUILD CHARACTER, NATURALLY!
"I REMEMBER WHEN WE USED TO SIT / IN A GOVERNMENT YARD IN TRENCH TOWN."

*ALRIGHT!

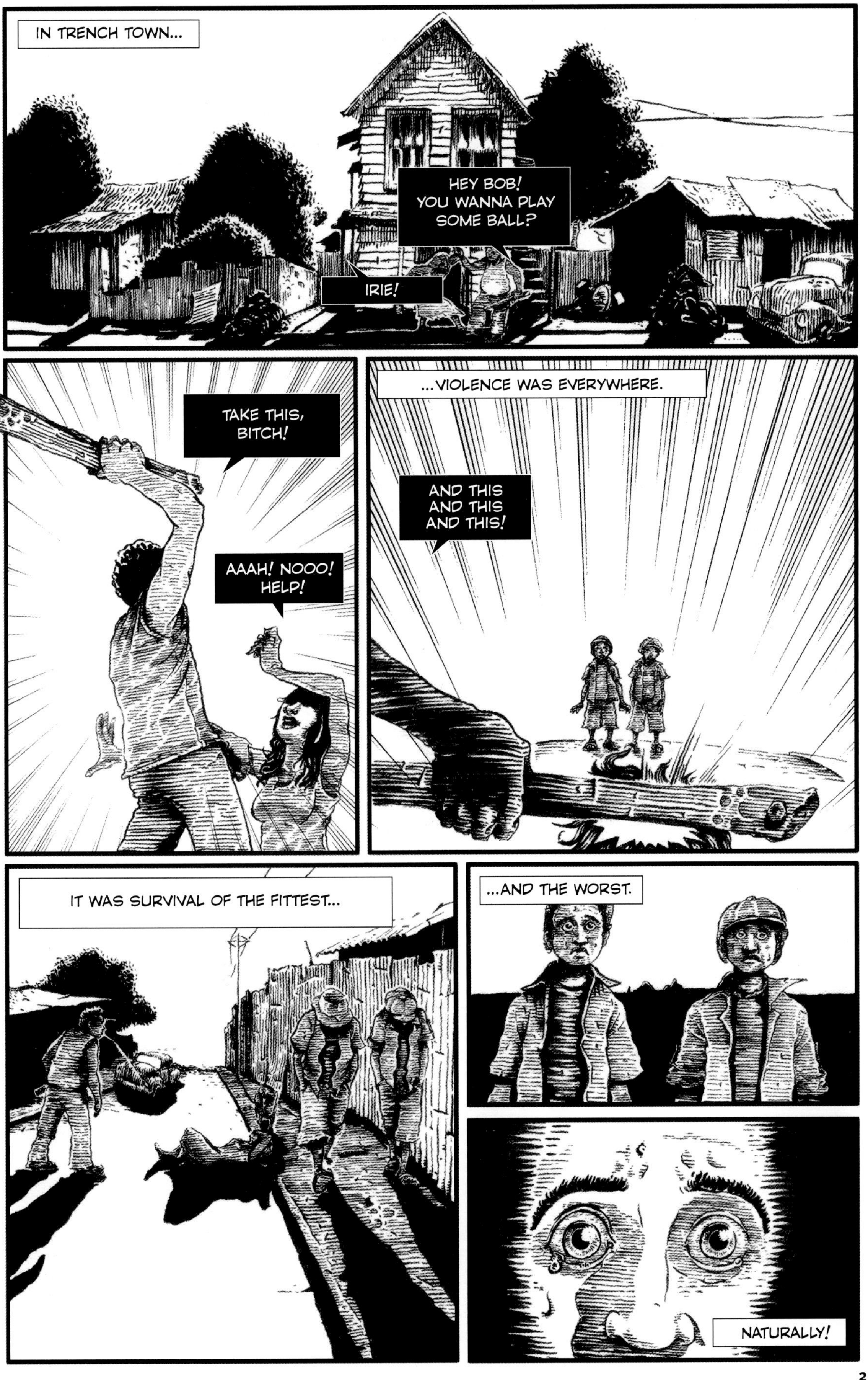
IN TRENCH TOWN...
HEY BOB! YOU WANNA PLAY SOME BALL?
IRIE!
TAKE THIS, BITCH!
AAAH! NOOO! HELP!
...VIOLENCE WAS EVERYWHERE.
AND THIS AND THIS AND THIS!
IT WAS SURVIVAL OF THE FITTEST...
...AND THE WORST.
NATURALLY!

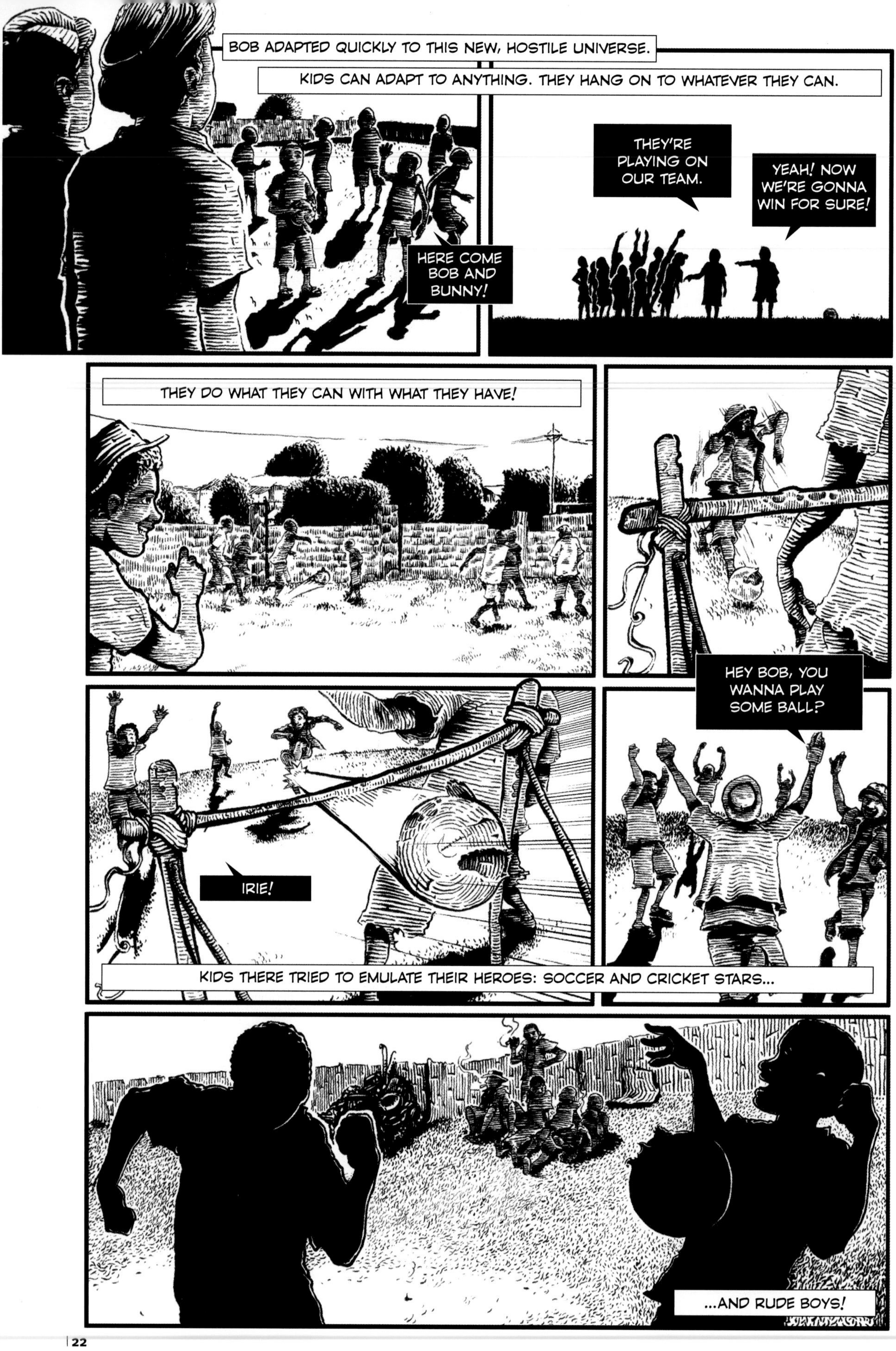

BOB ADAPTED QUICKLY TO THIS NEW, HOSTILE UNIVERSE.
HERE COME BOB AND BUNNY!
KIDS CAN ADAPT TO ANYTHING. THEY HANG ON TO WHATEVER THEY CAN.
THEY'RE PLAYING ON OUR TEAM.
YEAH! NOW WE'RE GONNA WIN FOR SURE!
THEY DO WHAT THEY CAN WITH WHAT THEY HAVE!
IRIE!
HEY BOB, YOU WANNA PLAY SOME BALL?
KIDS THERE TRIED TO EMULATE THEIR HEROES: SOCCER AND CRICKET STARS...
...AND RUDE BOYS!

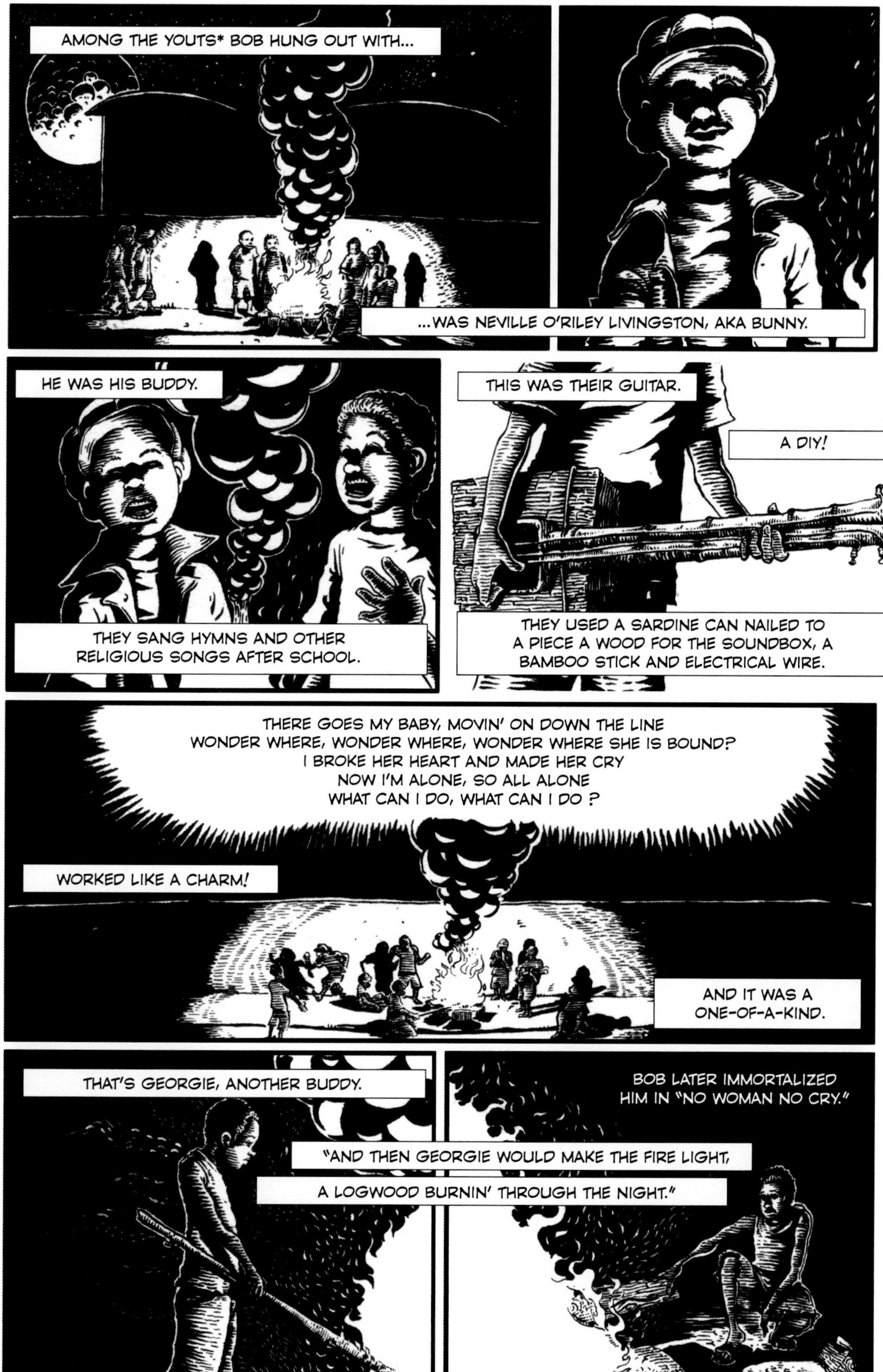
AMONG THE YOUTS* BOB HUNG OUT WITH...
...WAS NEVILLE O'RILEY LIVINGSTON, AKA BUNNY.
HE WAS HIS BUDDY.
THEY SANG HYMNS AND OTHER RELIGIOUS SONGS AFTER SCHOOL.
THIS WAS THEIR GUITAR.
A DIY!
THEY USED A SARDINE CAN NAILED TO A PIECE A WOOD FOR THE SOUNDBOX, A BAMBOO STICK AND ELECTRICAL WIRE.
THERE GOES MY BABY, MOVIN' ON DOWN THE LINE
WONDER WHERE, WONDER WHERE, WONDER WHERE SHE IS BOUND?
I BROKE HER HEART AND MADE HER CRY
NOW I'M ALONE, SO ALL ALONE
WHAT CAN I DO, WHAT CAN I DO ?
WORKED LIKE A CHARM!
AND IT WAS A ONE-OF-A-KIND.
THAT'S GEORGIE, ANOTHER BUDDY.
BOB LATER IMMORTALIZED HIM IN "NO WOMAN NO CRY."
"AND THEN GEORGIE WOULD MAKE THE FIRE LIGHT,
A LOGWOOD BURNIN' THROUGH THE NIGHT."

*BOB'S LIFE-LONG FRIENDS.

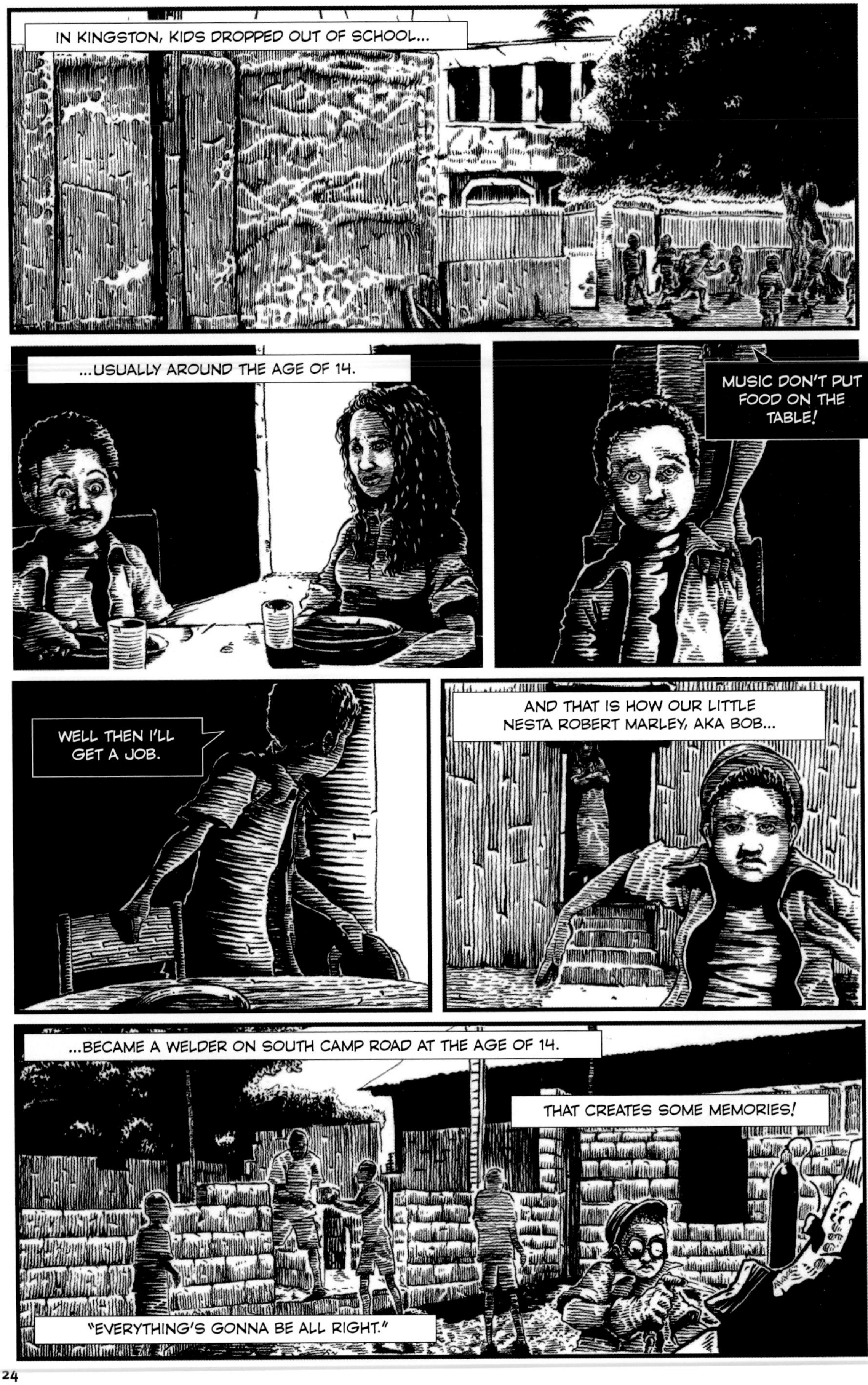
IN KINGSTON, KIDS DROPPED OUT OF SCHOOL...
...USUALLY AROUND THE AGE OF 14.
MUSIC DON'T PUT FOOD ON THE TABLE!
WELL THEN I'LL GET A JOB.
AND THAT IS HOW OUR LITTLE NESTA ROBERT MARLEY, AKA BOB...
...BECAME A WELDER ON SOUTH CAMP ROAD AT THE AGE OF 14.
THAT CREATES SOME MEMORIES!
"EVERYTHING'S GONNA BE ALL RIGHT."

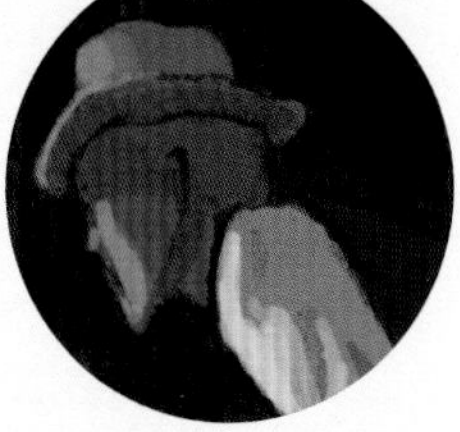

Growing Up Between Worlds

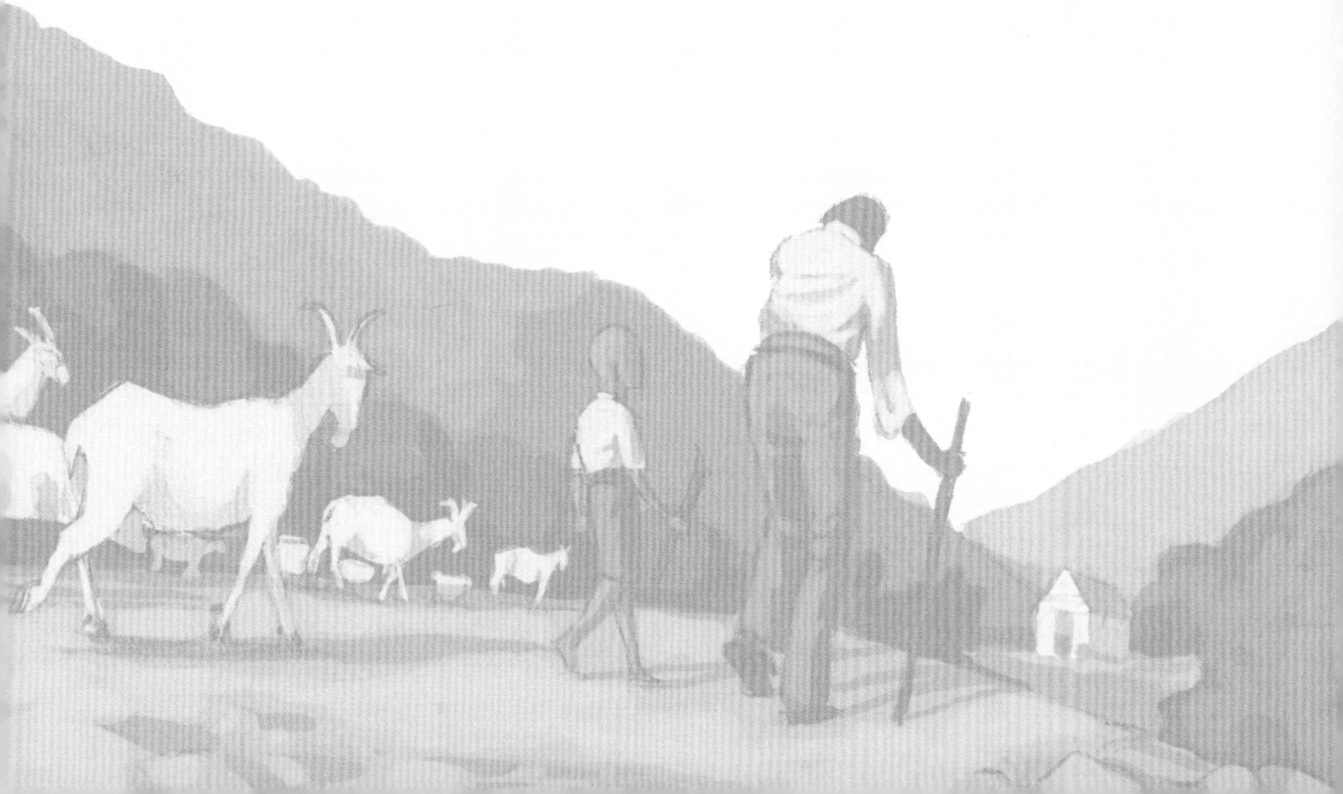

Born of a black country girl and a white father he never really knew, Nesta Robert Marley grew up in the Jamaican countryside before eventually moving to a shantytown in the capital city of Kingston. This mixed background, in every sense of the term, would have a lasting influence on the singer.

February 1945. While Europe was still ravaged by war (the U.S. hadn't landed in Normandy yet but D-Day was near), an entirely different kind of drama was taking place in Jamaica, where Bob Marley was born on February 6 in the parish of St. Ann. Though slavery had been abolished a century ago, racial segregation persisted in this British colony where voices were now rising in support of black pride. One of the men behind this movement was Marcus Garvey, who was known as "the prophet," and who also happened to be born in St. Ann. Other famous people had also been associated with that region, since the northern coast of Jamaica was also where Christopher Columbus dropped anchor on his second voyage. But let us leave those caravels behind and return to Bob, or rather Nesta, since that was his original first name. He was a country child who grew up in the family home and shepherded the goats of his grandfather, Omeriah Malcolm, a descendant of slaves who had become a big farmer in the region. It was rumored that he had inherited a predisposition for magic from his ancestors, which he seemed to have then passed on to young Nesta, who enjoyed reading palms and whose predictions were, more often than not, right on the money. But what he loved more than anything was to sing. In fact, he composed his first songs right there in Nine Miles. Later, many songs would evoke his family home, be it the little bed in his room perched atop a hillock in "Is This Love," or the fire burning in the courtyard in "Catch a Fire," or the big sycamore tree in "Time Will Tell."

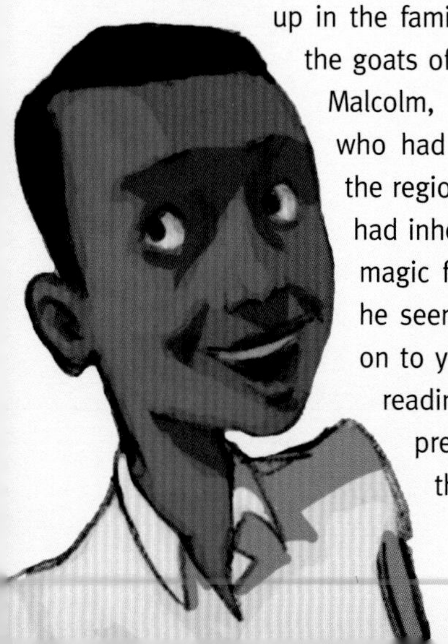

So that's the setting: hardly the lap of luxury, but peaceful. Not so when it came to family life, though. Cedella Malcolm, a young black country girl, was only 17 when she met Norval Marley, a white man in his fifties—or so he claimed, but it's highly likely he was actually older than that. For his job as a foreman, Norval rode his horse across land owned by the British Crown to monitor those working there. An absent father, he eventually abandoned his son, who later described him as "the guy who "get" his mother." However, Norval Marley should be given credit for defying one of the taboos of colonial Jamaica: his marriage to Cedella sparked such anger in his English family that they actually disowned him. That doesn't excuse his behavior, of course, and young Nesta's bitterness is all the more understandable given that he was only 6 when his father took him to the Jamaican capital of Kingston. Not to live with him, but so that he could go to school there. Or at least that was the plan, if it weren't for Mrs. Grey, the family friend to whom Norval entrusted his son, who was an

Cedella Malcolm　　　　**Norval Marley**　　　　**Omeriah Malcom**

old lady and much too thrilled to have a young boy in her service to worry about his education. Nesta stayed there one year, until the day his mother, who didn't know where he was that whole time, finally came to get him. As for his father, he completely vanished from Bob's life, and when he died in 1955, Bob hadn't seen him in years. All Bob Marley inherited from his father was his name and a mixed-race skin color that made life difficult for him: it was too light for some, too dark for others. As the artist would later say, "My father was white and my mother black, you know. Them call me half-caste, or whatever. Well, me don't dip on nobody's side... Me dip on God's side... who give me this talent." That duality made Bob Marley unique, but there was also the duality of having roots in both the countryside and the city: while he never denied his rural background ("I'm just a farmer," he was fond of saying), his years in Kingston marked

What he loved more than anything was to sing.

him just as much. After the year he spent with old Mrs. Grey, Cedella and Nesta moved to the southern part of the capital, in the Trenchtown neighborhood. With solid constructions that featured communal courtyards with kitchens and bathrooms (the infamous tenement yards), the neighborhood was initially conceived for the middle class. However, the lack of a proper sewage system and the rapid population growth quickly turned it into a shantytown. And, it was in that violent and dangerous environment, that Nesta Robert Marley grew up.

Reggae in the Ghetto

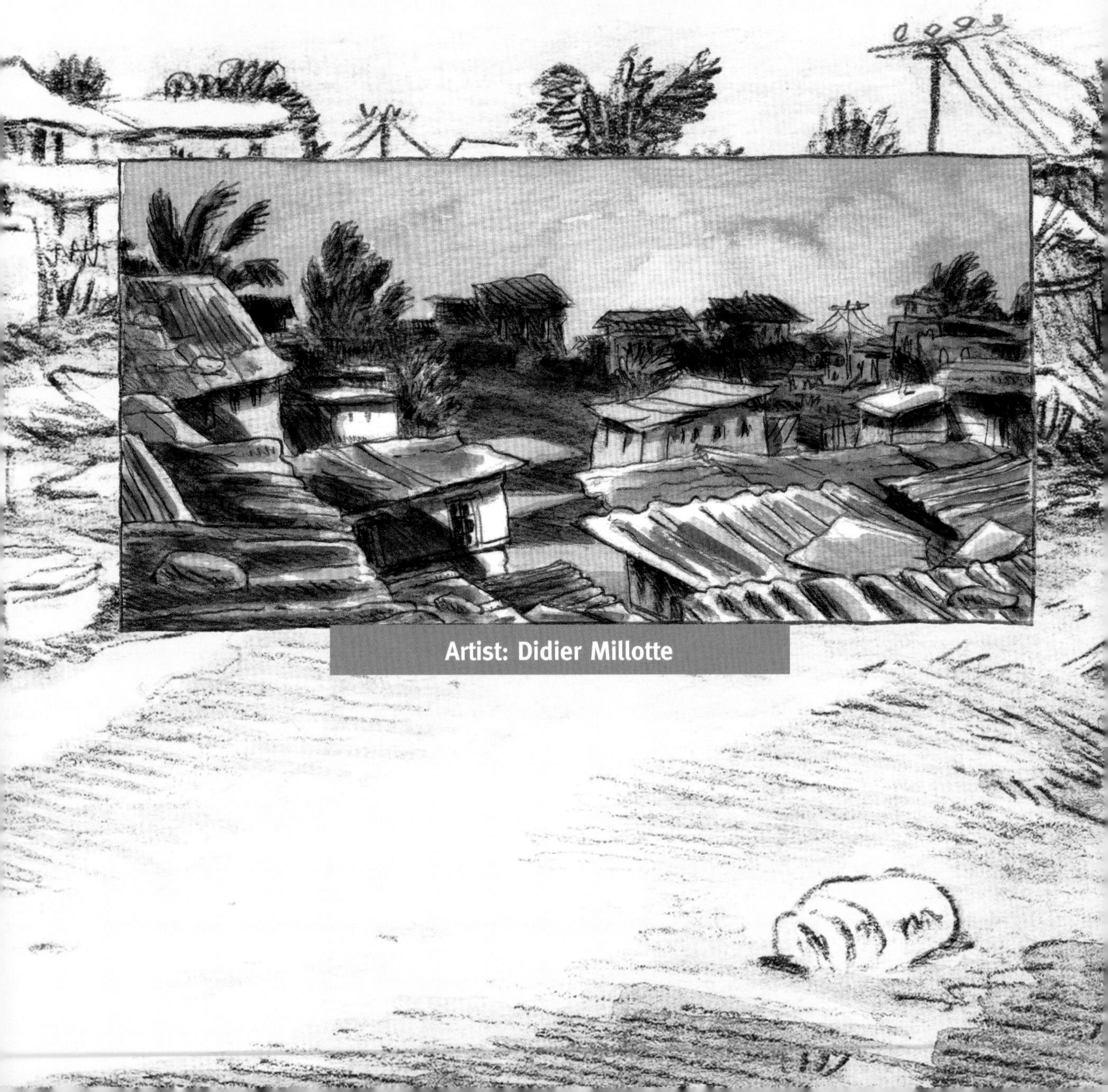

Artist: Didier Millotte

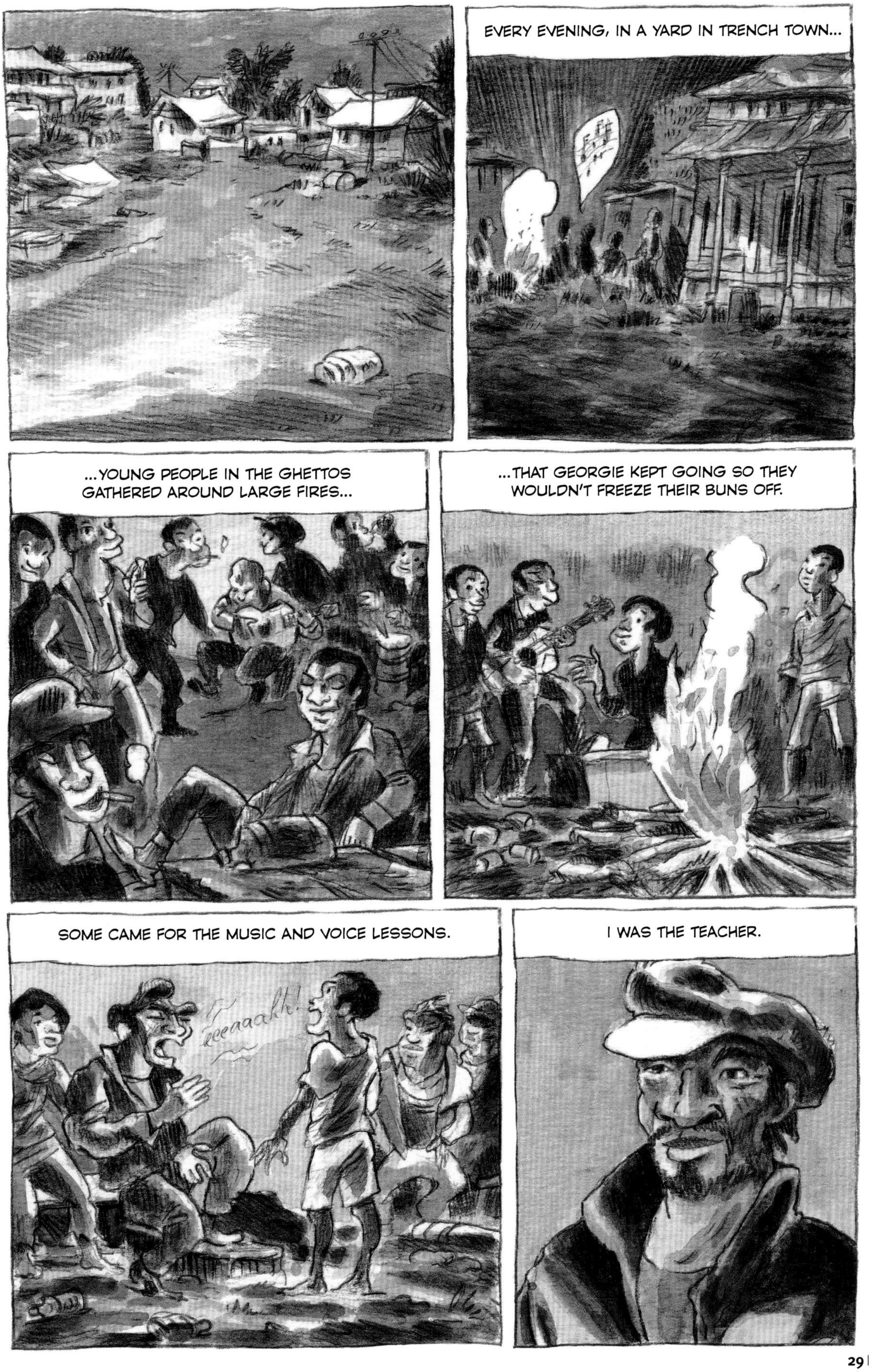
EVERY EVENING, IN A YARD IN TRENCH TOWN...
...YOUNG PEOPLE IN THE GHETTOS GATHERED AROUND LARGE FIRES...
...THAT GEORGIE KEPT GOING SO THEY WOULDN'T FREEZE THEIR BUNS OFF.
SOME CAME FOR THE MUSIC AND VOICE LESSONS.
eeeaaahh!
I WAS THE TEACHER.

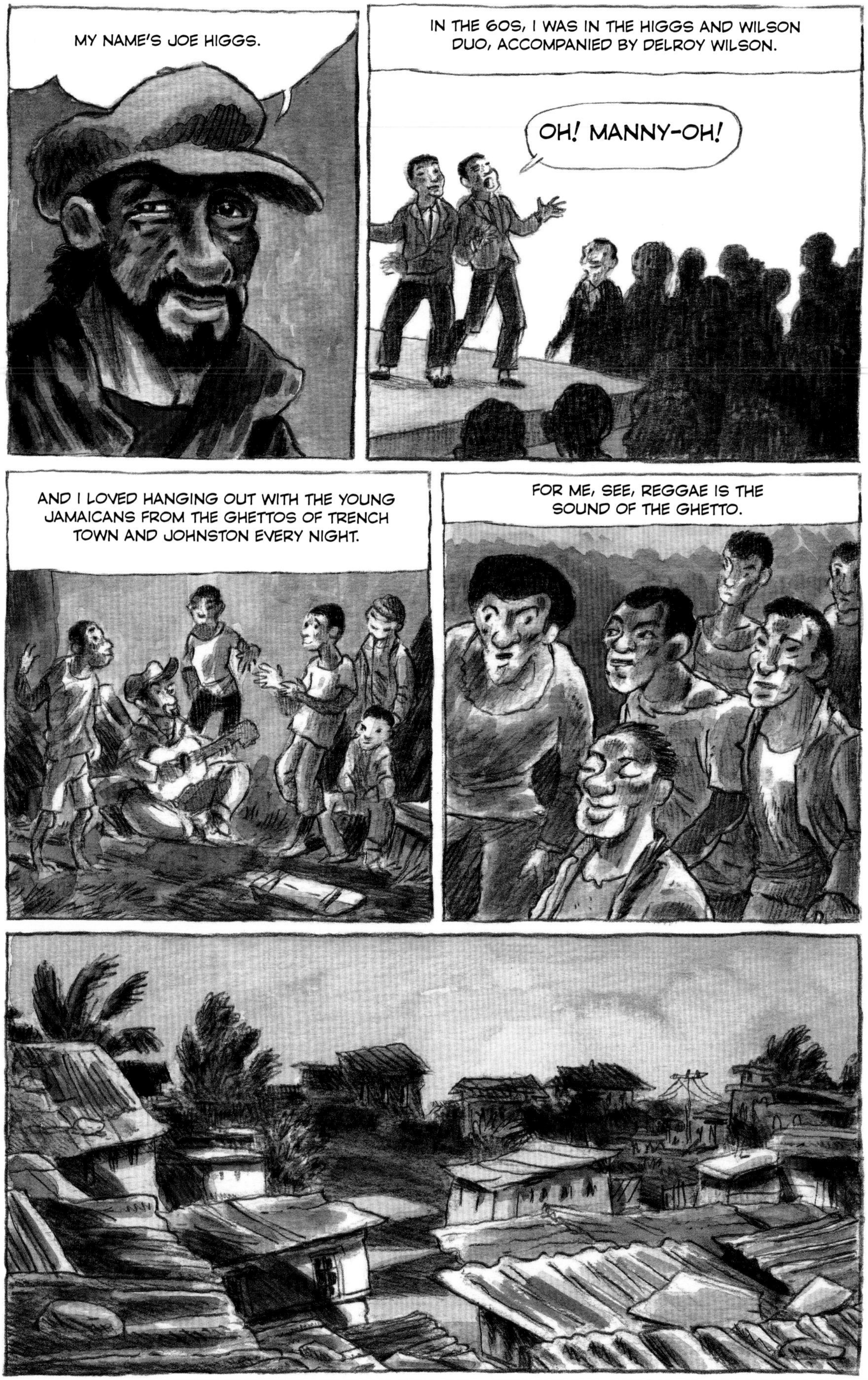
MY NAME'S JOE HIGGS.
IN THE 60S, I WAS IN THE HIGGS AND WILSON DUO, ACCOMPANIED BY DELROY WILSON.
OH! MANNY-OH!
AND I LOVED HANGING OUT WITH THE YOUNG JAMAICANS FROM THE GHETTOS OF TRENCH TOWN AND JOHNSTON EVERY NIGHT.
FOR ME, SEE, REGGAE IS THE SOUND OF THE GHETTO.

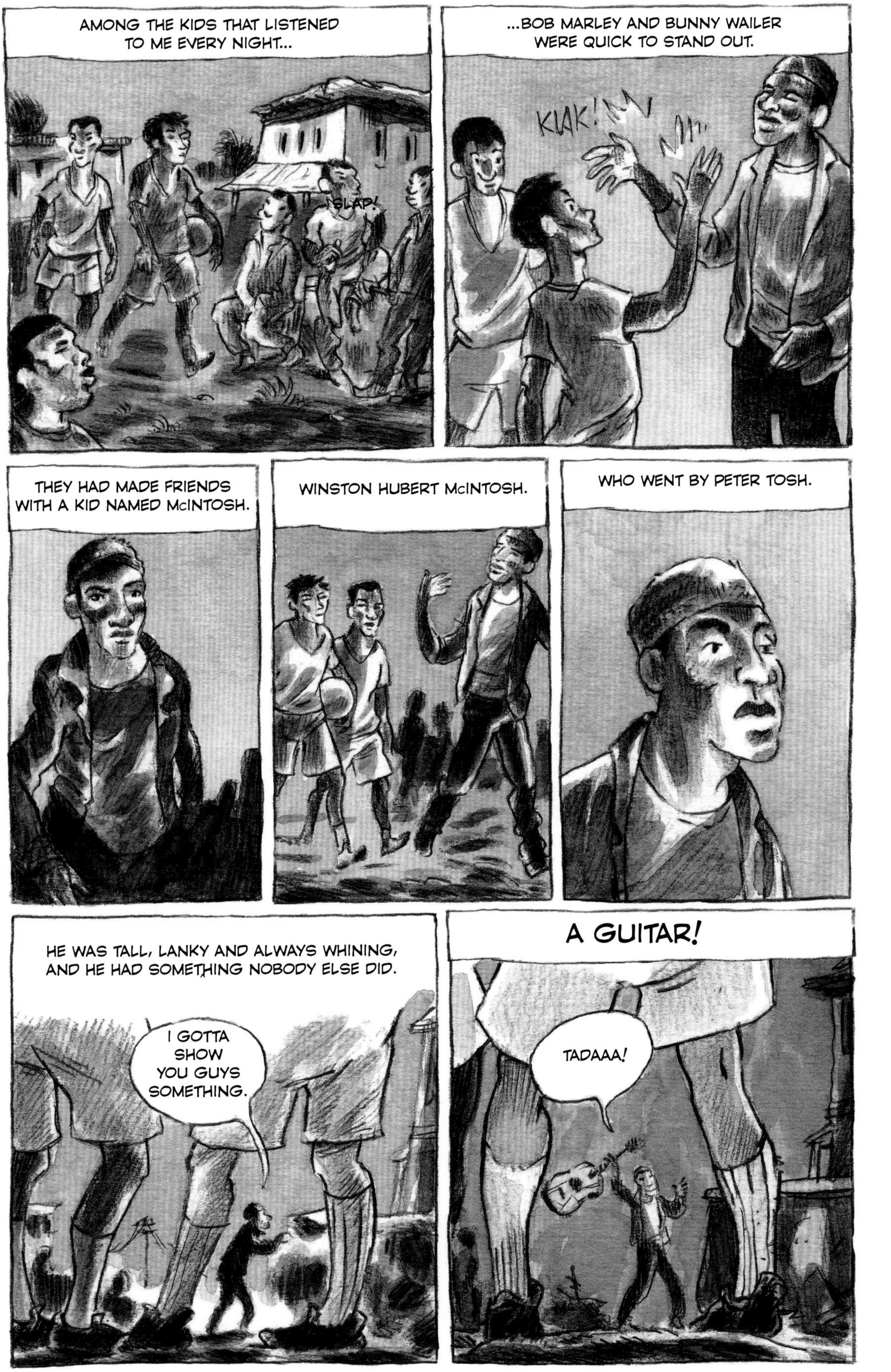
AMONG THE KIDS THAT LISTENED TO ME EVERY NIGHT...
SLAP!
...BOB MARLEY AND BUNNY WAILER WERE QUICK TO STAND OUT.
KLAK!
THEY HAD MADE FRIENDS WITH A KID NAMED McINTOSH.
WINSTON HUBERT McINTOSH.
WHO WENT BY PETER TOSH.
HE WAS TALL, LANKY AND ALWAYS WHINING, AND HE HAD SOMETHING NOBODY ELSE DID.
I GOTTA SHOW YOU GUYS SOMETHING.
A GUITAR!
TADAAA!

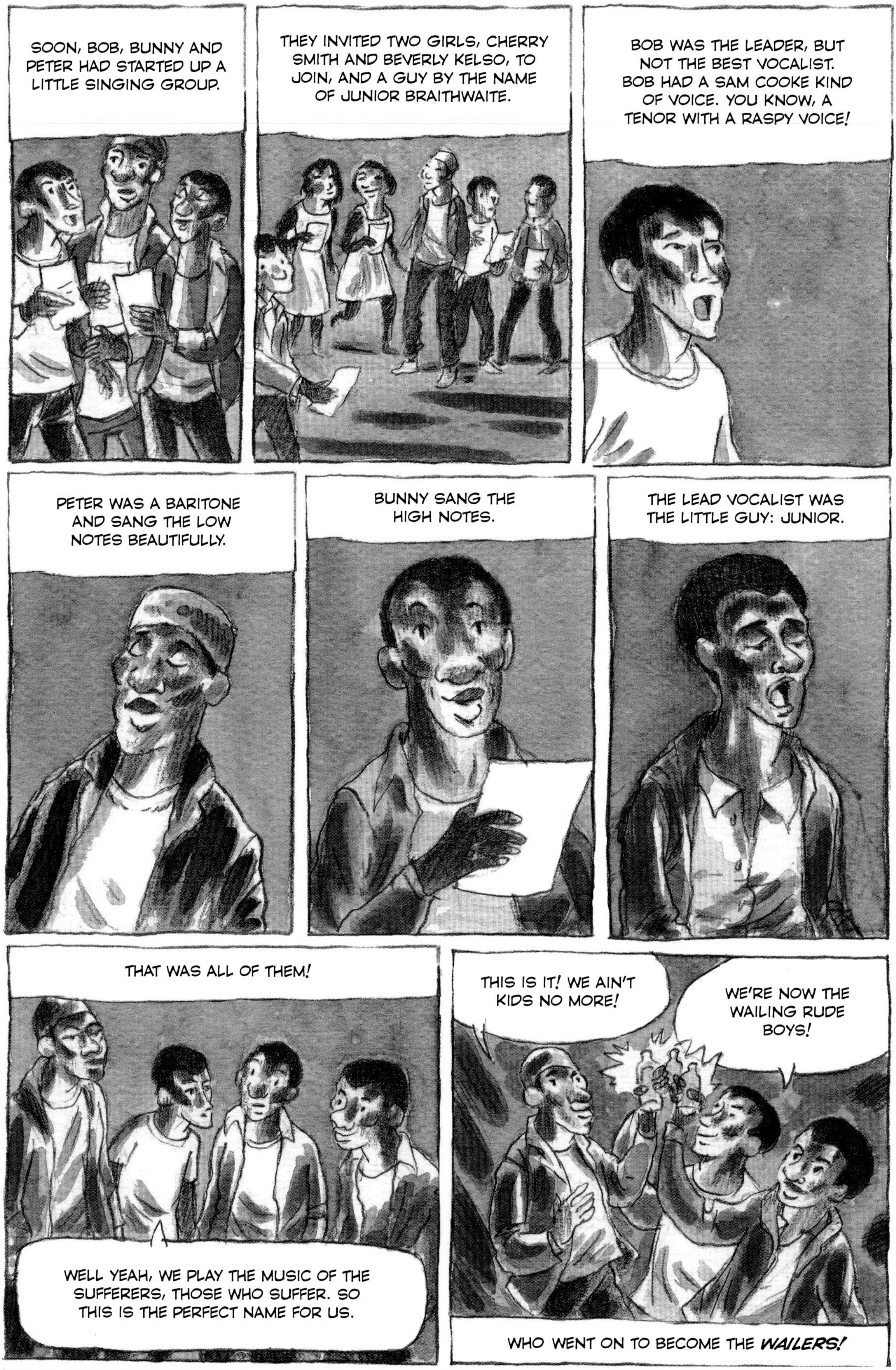
SOON, BOB, BUNNY AND PETER HAD STARTED UP A LITTLE SINGING GROUP.
THEY INVITED TWO GIRLS, CHERRY SMITH AND BEVERLY KELSO, TO JOIN, AND A GUY BY THE NAME OF JUNIOR BRAITHWAITE.
BOB WAS THE LEADER, BUT NOT THE BEST VOCALIST. BOB HAD A SAM COOKE KIND OF VOICE. YOU KNOW, A TENOR WITH A RASPY VOICE!
PETER WAS A BARITONE AND SANG THE LOW NOTES BEAUTIFULLY.
BUNNY SANG THE HIGH NOTES.
THE LEAD VOCALIST WAS THE LITTLE GUY: JUNIOR.
THAT WAS ALL OF THEM!
WELL YEAH, WE PLAY THE MUSIC OF THE SUFFERERS, THOSE WHO SUFFER. SO THIS IS THE PERFECT NAME FOR US.
THIS IS IT! WE AIN'T KIDS NO MORE!
WE'RE NOW THE WAILING RUDE BOYS!
WHO WENT ON TO BECOME THE WAILERS!

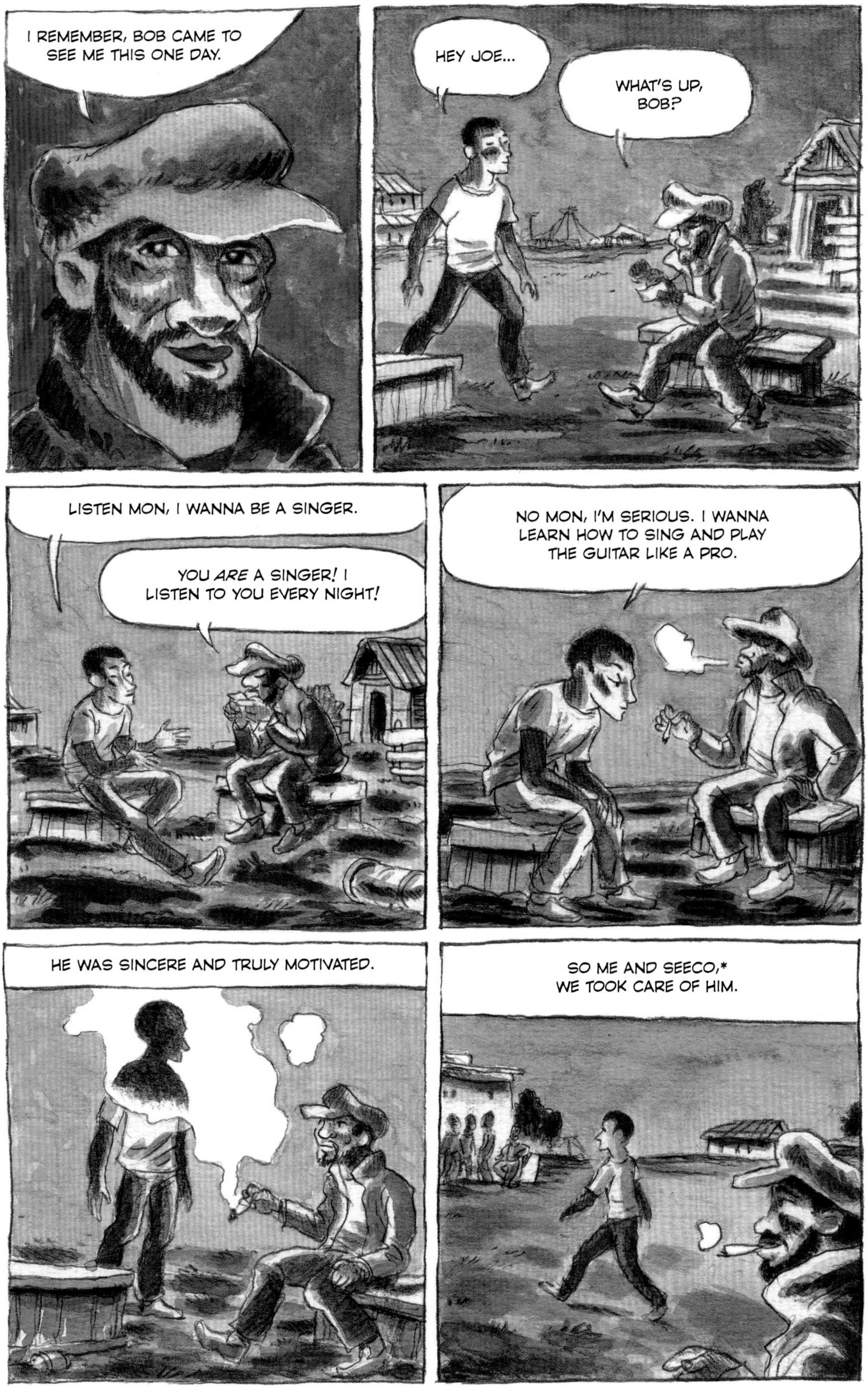
I REMEMBER, BOB CAME TO SEE ME THIS ONE DAY.
HEY JOE...
WHAT'S UP, BOB?
LISTEN MON, I WANNA BE A SINGER.
YOU *ARE* A SINGER! I LISTEN TO YOU EVERY NIGHT!
NO MON, I'M SERIOUS. I WANNA LEARN HOW TO SING AND PLAY THE GUITAR LIKE A PRO.
HE WAS SINCERE AND TRULY MOTIVATED.
SO ME AND SEECO,* WE TOOK CARE OF HIM.

*ALVIN SEECO PATTERSON.

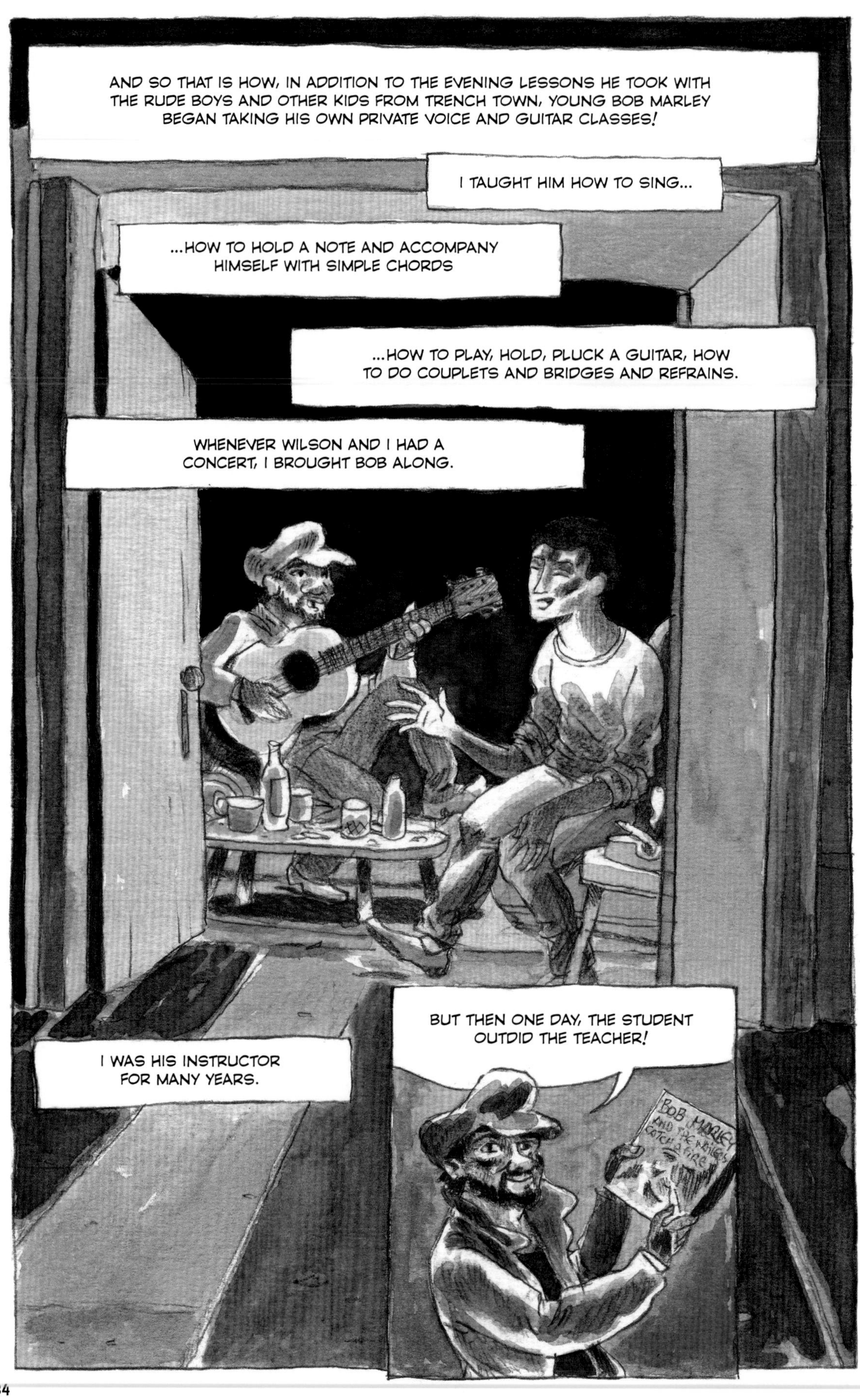
AND SO THAT IS HOW, IN ADDITION TO THE EVENING LESSONS HE TOOK WITH THE RUDE BOYS AND OTHER KIDS FROM TRENCH TOWN, YOUNG BOB MARLEY BEGAN TAKING HIS OWN PRIVATE VOICE AND GUITAR CLASSES!
I TAUGHT HIM HOW TO SING...
...HOW TO HOLD A NOTE AND ACCOMPANY HIMSELF WITH SIMPLE CHORDS
...HOW TO PLAY, HOLD, PLUCK A GUITAR, HOW TO DO COUPLETS AND BRIDGES AND REFRAINS.
WHENEVER WILSON AND I HAD A CONCERT, I BROUGHT BOB ALONG.
I WAS HIS INSTRUCTOR FOR MANY YEARS.
BUT THEN ONE DAY, THE STUDENT OUTDID THE TEACHER!
BOB MARLEY

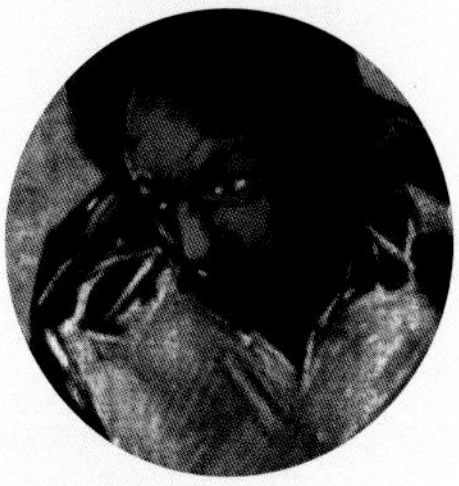

Making friends in Trenchtown

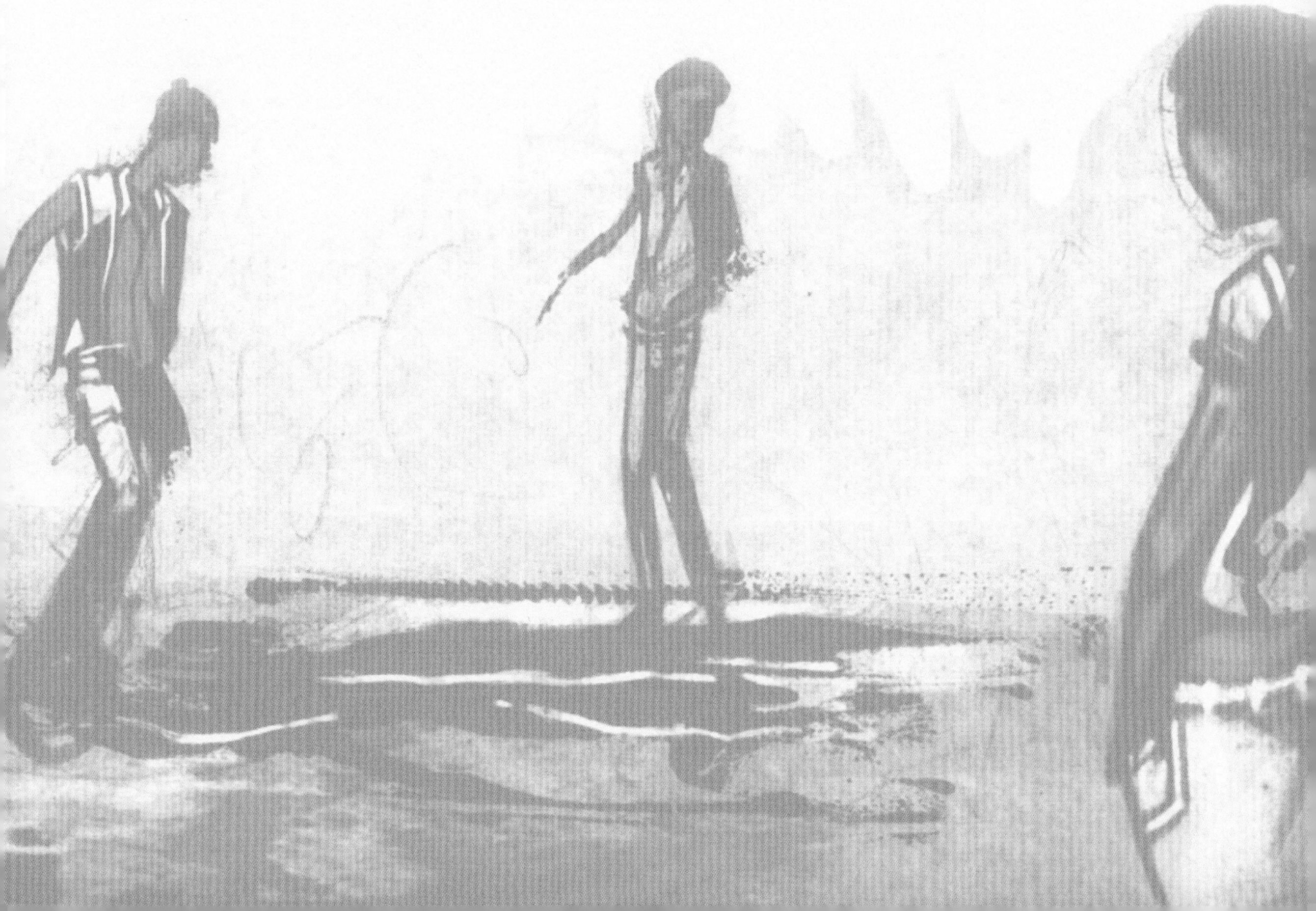

Would Bob Marley have become a singer if he hadn't met Joe Higgs, Bunny Wailer and Peter Tosh? They met in the late 50s in the streets of Trenchtown, where music defied poverty.

In Trenchtown, where he lived with his mother starting in 1957, Bob Marley met Joe Higgs, whom Jimmy Cliff would later call "The father of reggae." When young Nesta arrived in the shantytown, Joe was already known as an experienced singer, even though he himself was only 17. His music was starting to get noticed and in 1960, his first single, "Oh Manny Oh," a duet with Delroy Wilson, made him the star of the ghetto.

At night, the neighborhood kids would come and listen to him sing and play music in his courtyard on Third Street. Nesta was one of them. Early on, Joe Higgs recognized the young boy's potential and set about to teach him the techniques of vocal harmony. It required a lot of hard work as Nesta had to make up for his weak, plaintive voice.

In Trenchtown, the rude boys were nuts about ska.

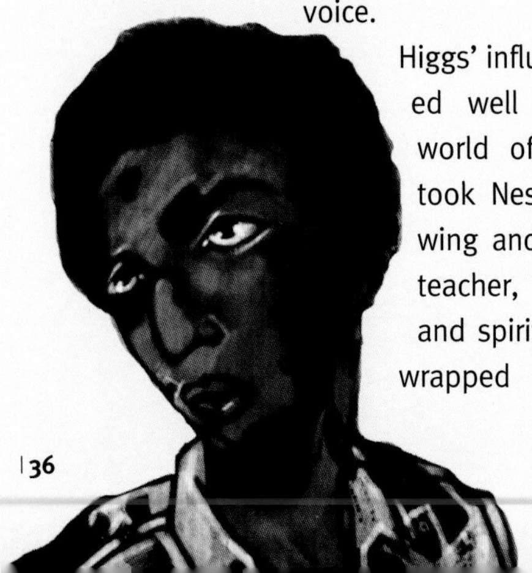

Higgs' influence extended well beyond the world of reggae. He took Nesta under his wing and became his teacher, friend, tutor and spiritual guide all wrapped into one—a multi-faceted role whose importance in his life Bob Marley would later underline. In terms of voice, Nesta's efforts were rewarded: in 1959, he took first prize in a contest at Queens Theater, where he won a whopping... one pound sterling. Not enough to run and open a bank account, perhaps, but for a poor 14-year-old, it was a start. His mother, Cedella, remained levelheaded and insisted that Nesta learn a trade. And so he found himself being a welder by day and a singer by night. His passion and his talent, however, caused the scale to tip most indisputably towards the music side.

He shared that passion for music with Neville O'Riley Livingston, aka Bunny Wailer. The two boys knew each other from before, from their childhood in Nine Miles, but it was in the dusty streets of Trenchtown that their friendship blossomed and the boys became inseparable. Their ears glued to Miami radio, they never got tired of practicing the American R&B hits. When it wasn't that, they were singing hymns and strumming homemade guitars of Bunny's invention: electrical wires for the chords, bamboo sticks for the neck, and a sardine can for the soundbox.

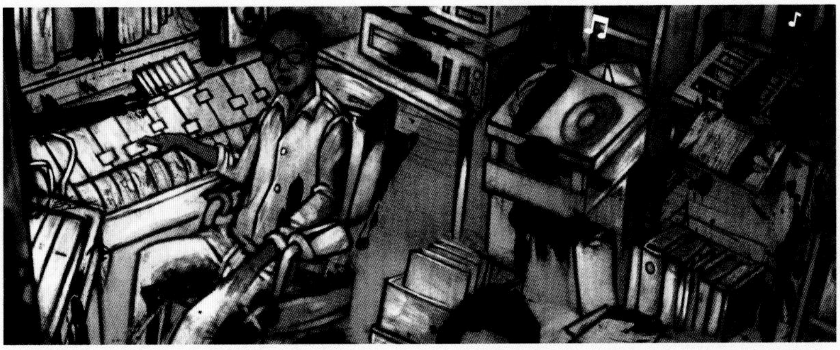

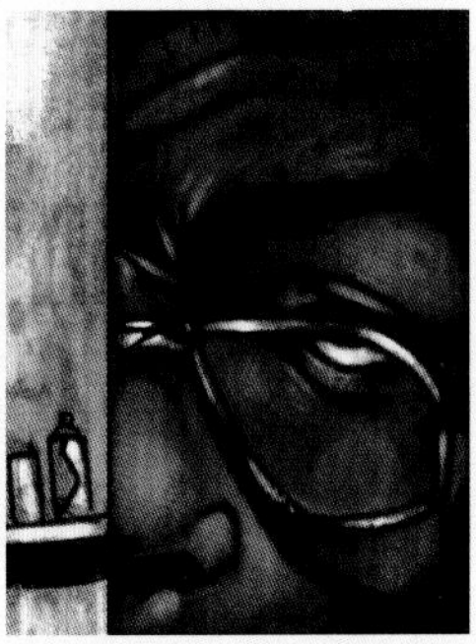

If you can't be rich, you may as well be crafty!

Now joined by Winston Hubert McIntosh, aka Peter Tosh, and Junior Braithwaite (for a few months), they started a little band they first called The Teenagers. But the name seemed a little too innocent for the violent universe of Trenchtown, so they became the Wailing Rude Boys. Then they ditched the part associated with street thugs and shortened the name to The Wailers and focused instead on that blend of pain and pleasure found in Joe Higgs' melodies. And this is how, in between fights with other gangs and frenetic soccer games, a dream began to take shape in the minds of those Trenchtown teens: the dream of becoming the Jamaican Beatles—well, at least when it came to the fame and glory part. Pop music, not so much.

Reggae came primarily from ska and R&B, but it has a slower rhythm—patterned, the Wailers claimed, after the beating of a heart. The bass is actually very present, and the offbeats done on the drums draw their inspiration from the syncopation traditionally found in the beat of African drums. Or at least that's the way Joe Higgs, for whom reggae came from the poverty of the ghetto, saw it. His lyrics used raw language to describe everyday life there: "Everyday my heart is sore, Seeing that I'm so poor, But I shall not give up so easy," he sings in "There's a Reward." While Bob Marley shared that vision of urban life, his rural background led him to also see in the rhythms of reggae the movement of farmers breaking their backs to work the land. As for poverty, it is decidedly present in the music of the man whose feet were "his only carriage," as he describes in "No Woman No Cry." That song, one of Marley's most famous, is much more than just a love song, and recalls the time when they "used to sit in a government yard in Trenchtown." The lyrics pay tribute to another key figure from those days: Georgie Robinson, the one who would "make the fire light" with "logwood burning through the night." Warmth and music are intricately linked here and also function as a metaphor: for Bob Marley, reggae is also "the light that emerges from the darkness," as he sings in "Could You Be Loved": "In the darkness there must come out the light."

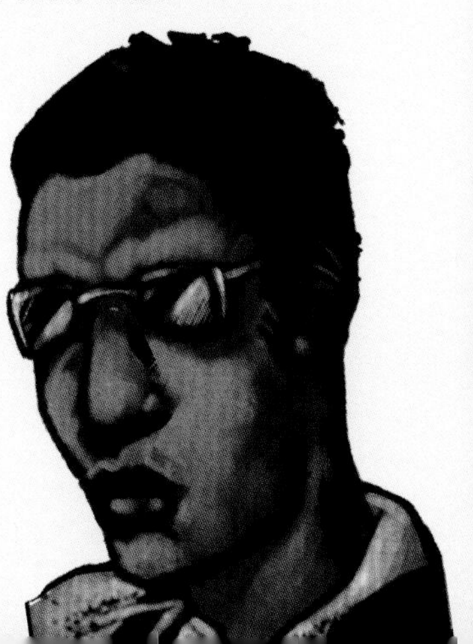

A Ray of Light in the Dark

Artist: Tanguy Pietri

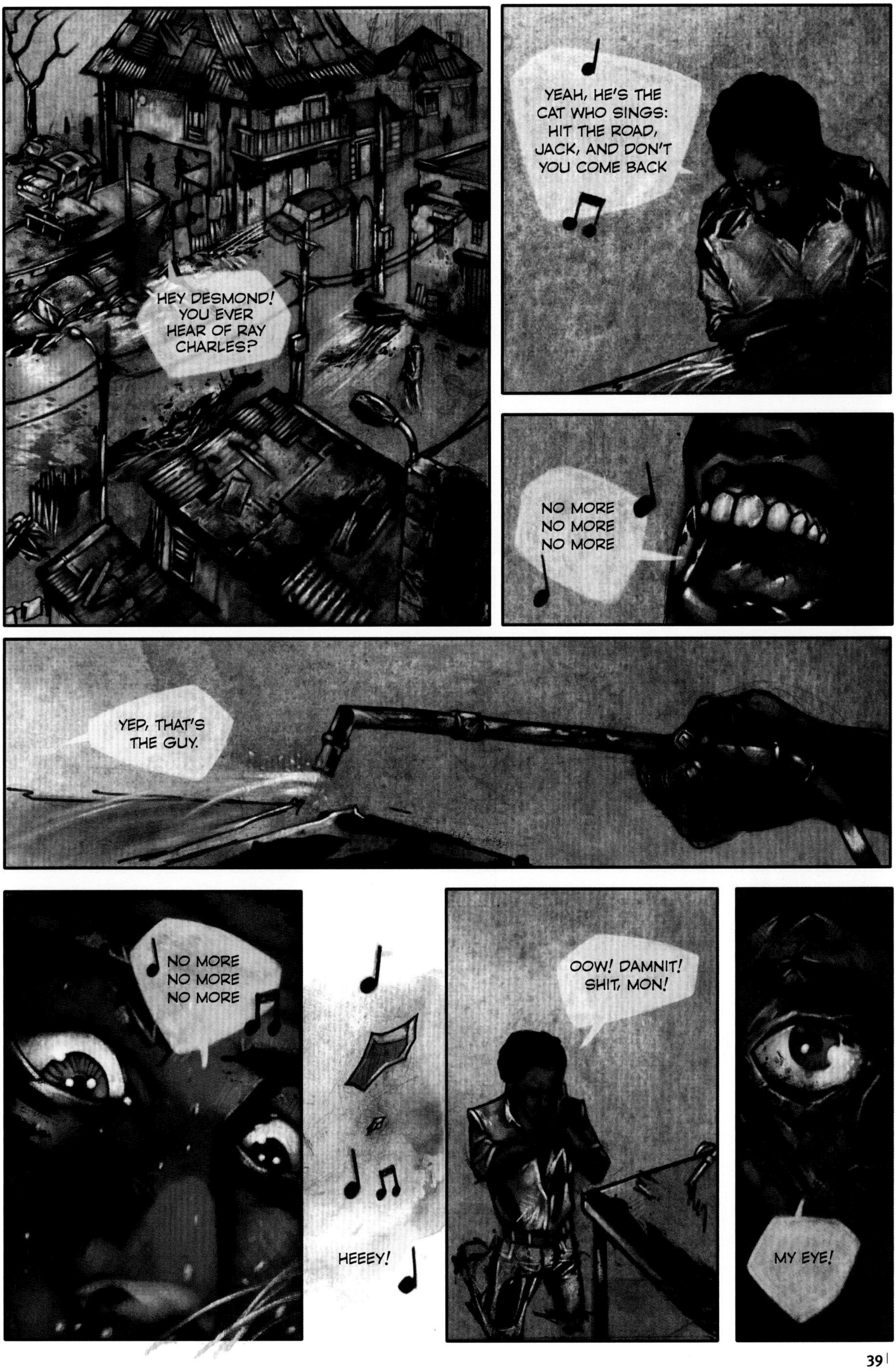
HEY DESMOND! YOU EVER HEAR OF RAY CHARLES?
YEAH, HE'S THE CAT WHO SINGS: HIT THE ROAD, JACK, AND DON'T YOU COME BACK
NO MORE NO MORE NO MORE
YEP, THAT'S THE GUY.
NO MORE NO MORE NO MORE
HEEEY!
OOW! DAMNIT! SHIT, MON!
MY EYE!

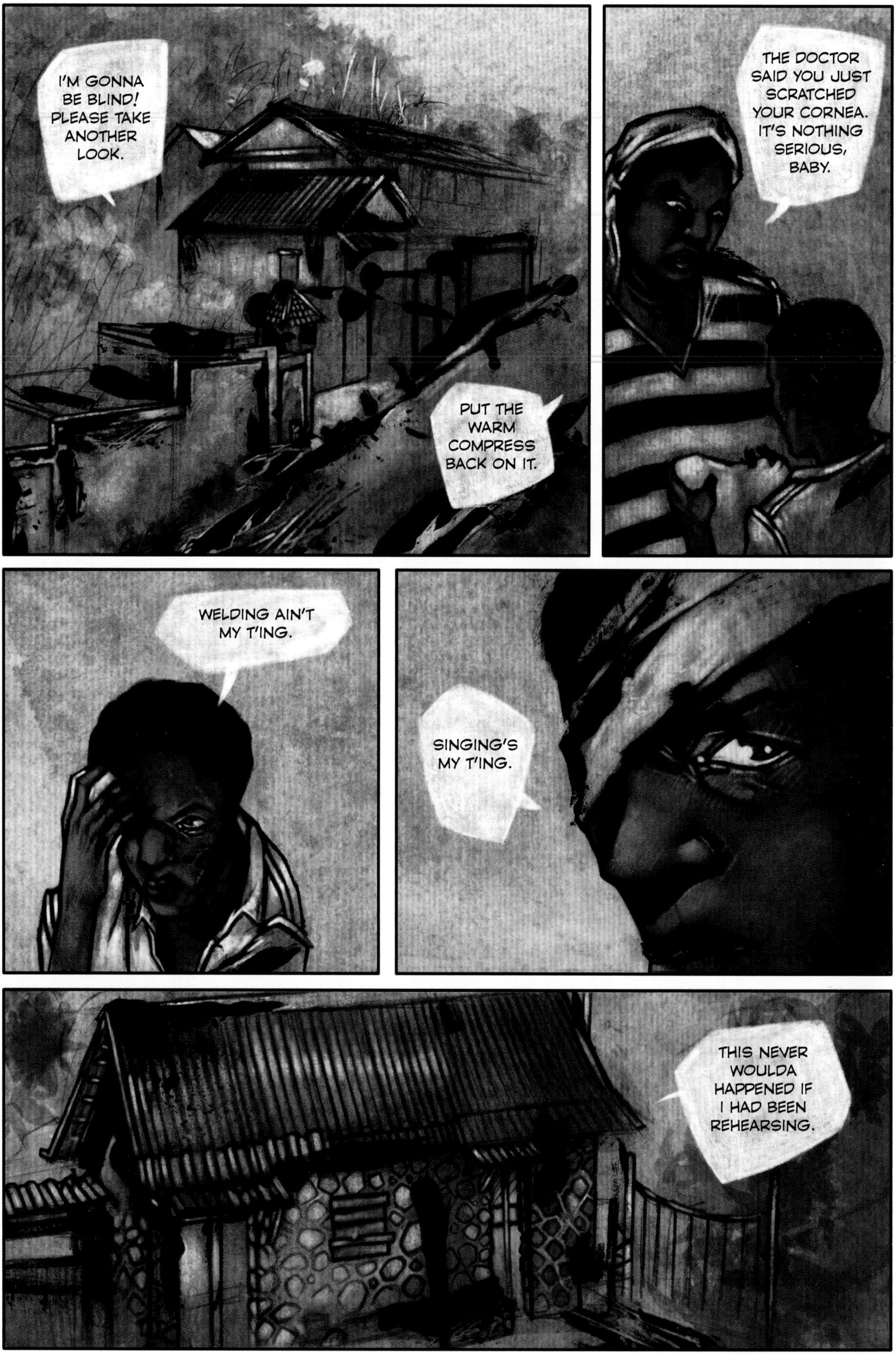
I'M GONNA BE BLIND! PLEASE TAKE ANOTHER LOOK.
PUT THE WARM COMPRESS BACK ON IT.
THE DOCTOR SAID YOU JUST SCRATCHED YOUR CORNEA. IT'S NOTHING SERIOUS, BABY.
WELDING AIN'T MY T'ING.
SINGING'S MY T'ING.
THIS NEVER WOULDA HAPPENED IF I HAD BEEN REHEARSING.

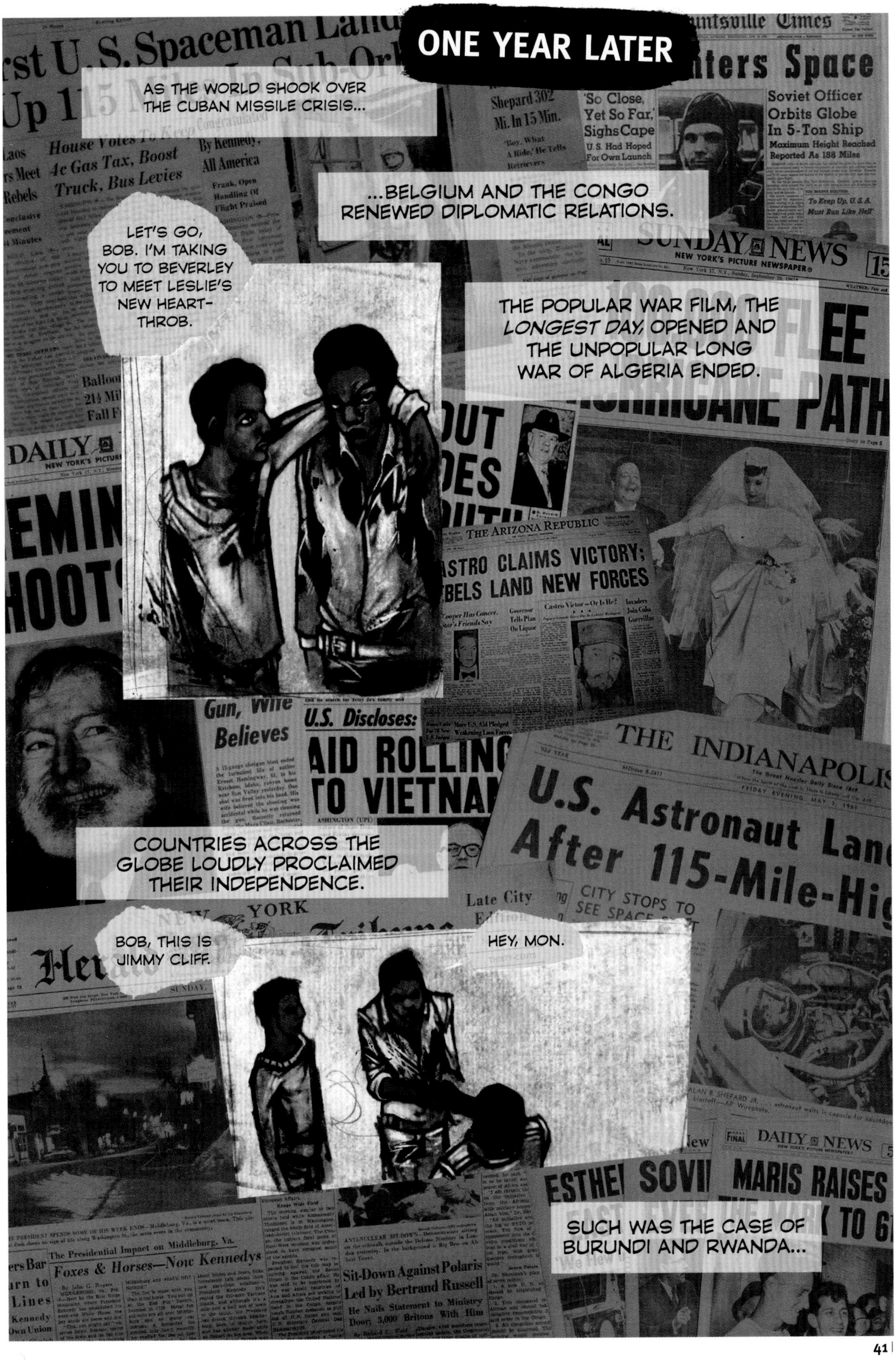
ONE YEAR LATER
AS THE WORLD SHOOK OVER THE CUBAN MISSILE CRISIS...
...BELGIUM AND THE CONGO RENEWED DIPLOMATIC RELATIONS.
LET'S GO, BOB. I'M TAKING YOU TO BEVERLEY TO MEET LESLIE'S NEW HEART-THROB.
THE POPULAR WAR FILM, THE LONGEST DAY, OPENED AND THE UNPOPULAR LONG WAR OF ALGERIA ENDED.
COUNTRIES ACROSS THE GLOBE LOUDLY PROCLAIMED THEIR INDEPENDENCE.
BOB, THIS IS JIMMY CLIFF.
HEY, MON.
SUCH WAS THE CASE OF BURUNDI AND RWANDA...

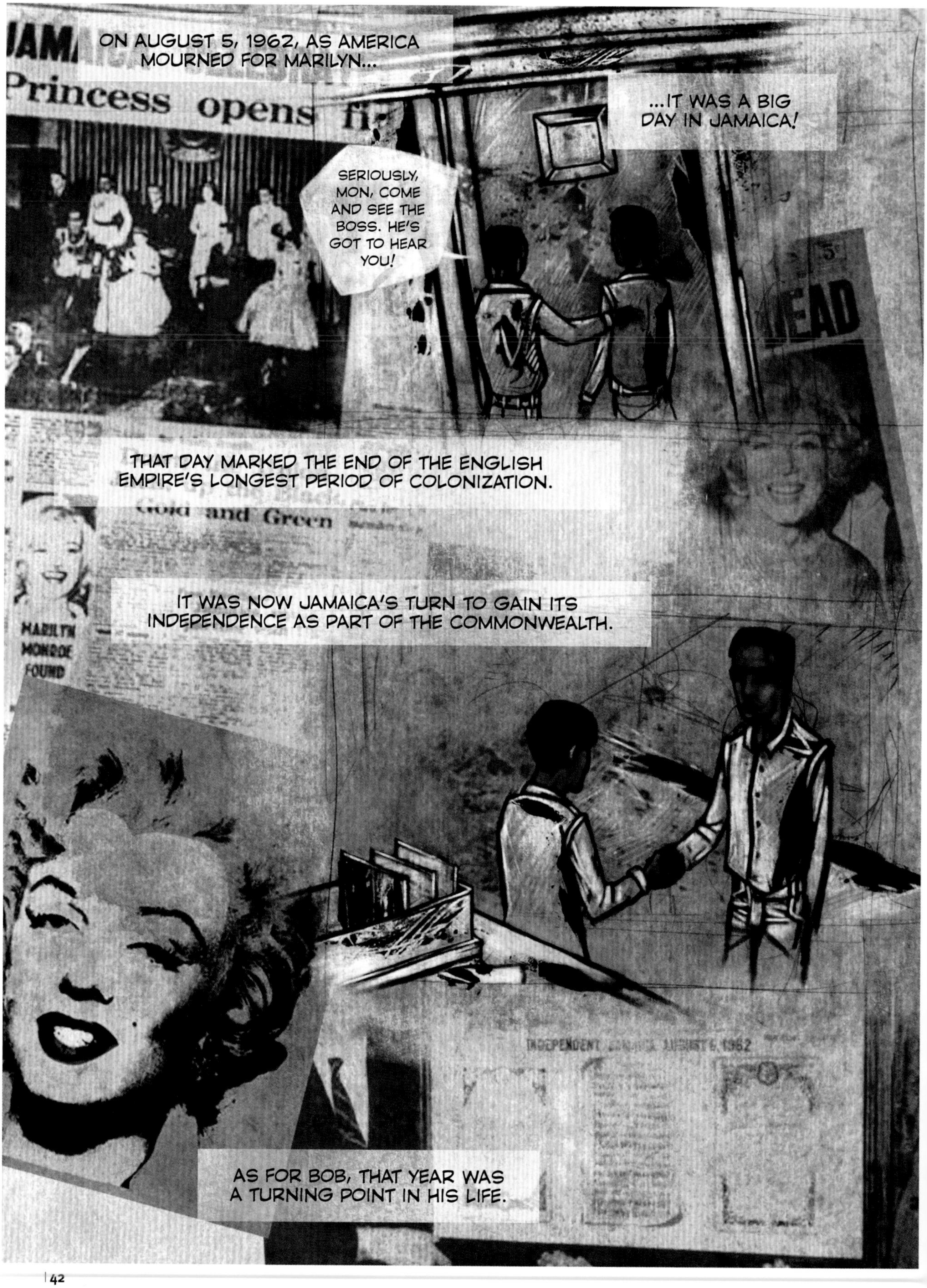
ON AUGUST 5, 1962, AS AMERICA MOURNED FOR MARILYN...
Princess opens
...IT WAS A BIG DAY IN JAMAICA!
SERIOUSLY, MON, COME AND SEE THE BOSS. HE'S GOT TO HEAR YOU!
THAT DAY MARKED THE END OF THE ENGLISH EMPIRE'S LONGEST PERIOD OF COLONIZATION.
Gold and Green
IT WAS NOW JAMAICA'S TURN TO GAIN ITS INDEPENDENCE AS PART OF THE COMMONWEALTH.
MARILYN MONROE FOUND
INDEPENDENT JAMAICA AUGUST 6, 1962
AS FOR BOB, THAT YEAR WAS A TURNING POINT IN HIS LIFE.

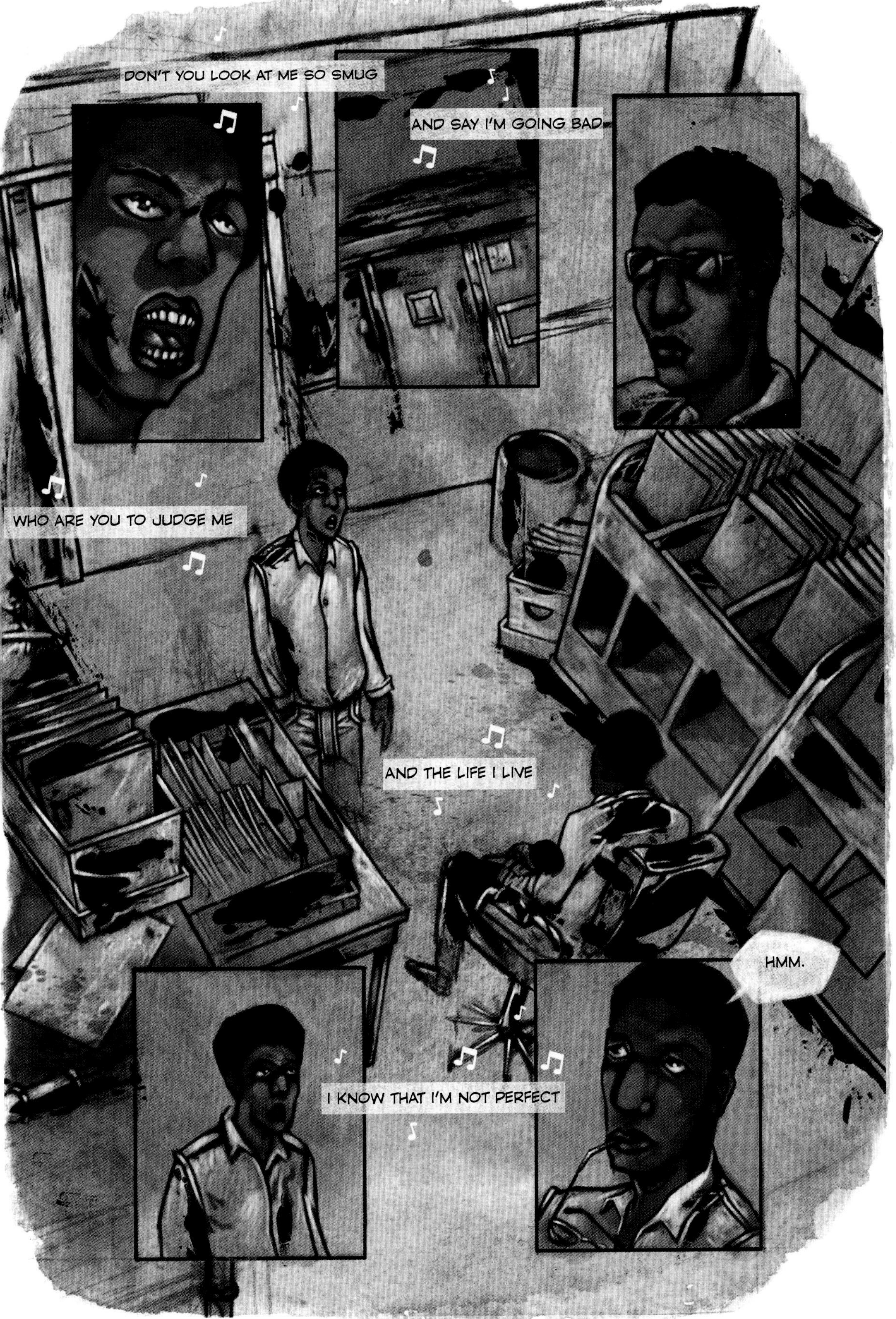
DON'T YOU LOOK AT ME SO SMUG
AND SAY I'M GOING BAD
WHO ARE YOU TO JUDGE ME
AND THE LIFE I LIVE
HMM.
I KNOW THAT I'M NOT PERFECT

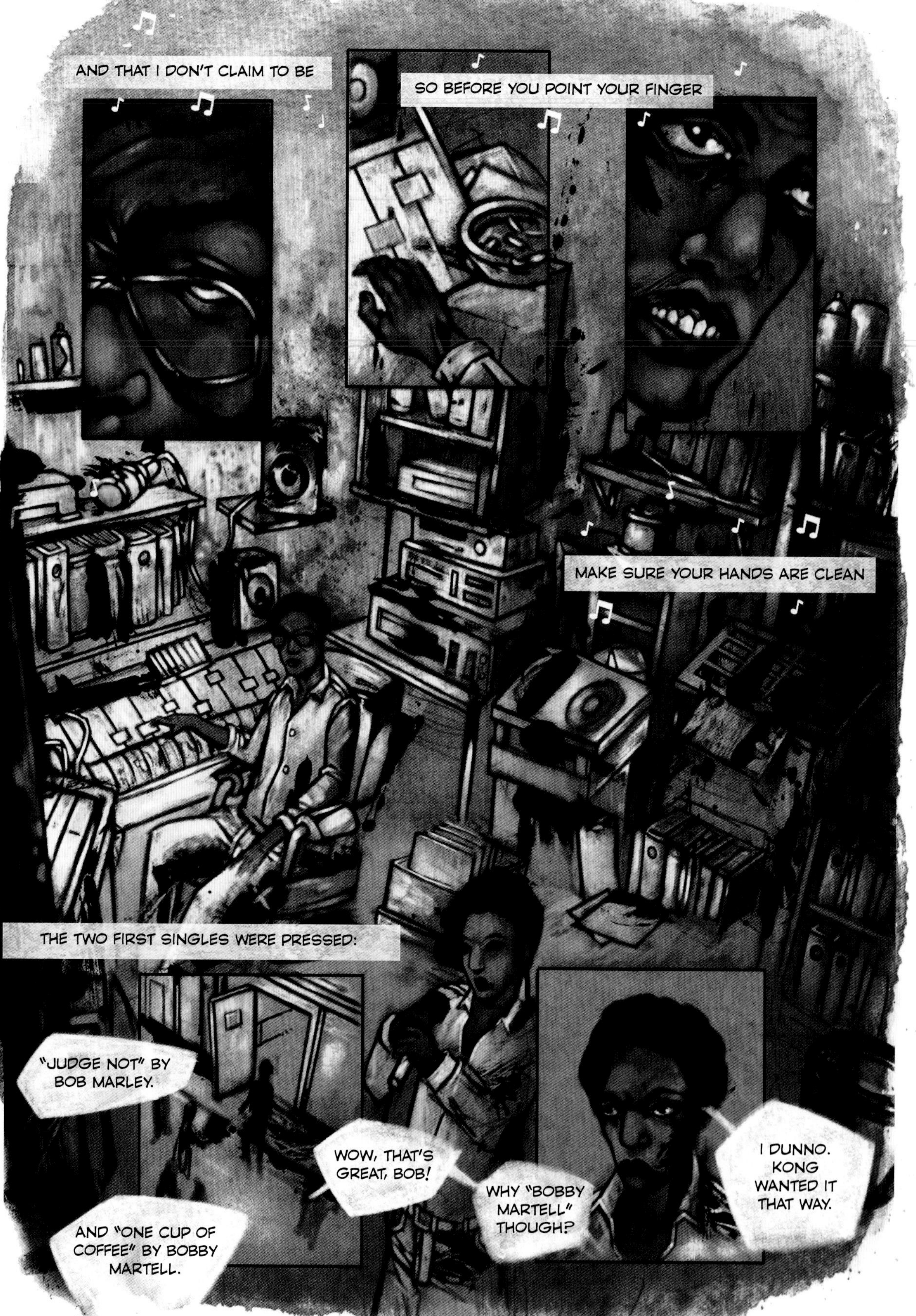
AND THAT I DON'T CLAIM TO BE
SO BEFORE YOU POINT YOUR FINGER
MAKE SURE YOUR HANDS ARE CLEAN
THE TWO FIRST SINGLES WERE PRESSED:
"JUDGE NOT" BY BOB MARLEY.
AND "ONE CUP OF COFFEE" BY BOBBY MARTELL.
WOW, THAT'S GREAT, BOB!
WHY "BOBBY MARTELL" THOUGH?
I DUNNO. KONG WANTED IT THAT WAY.

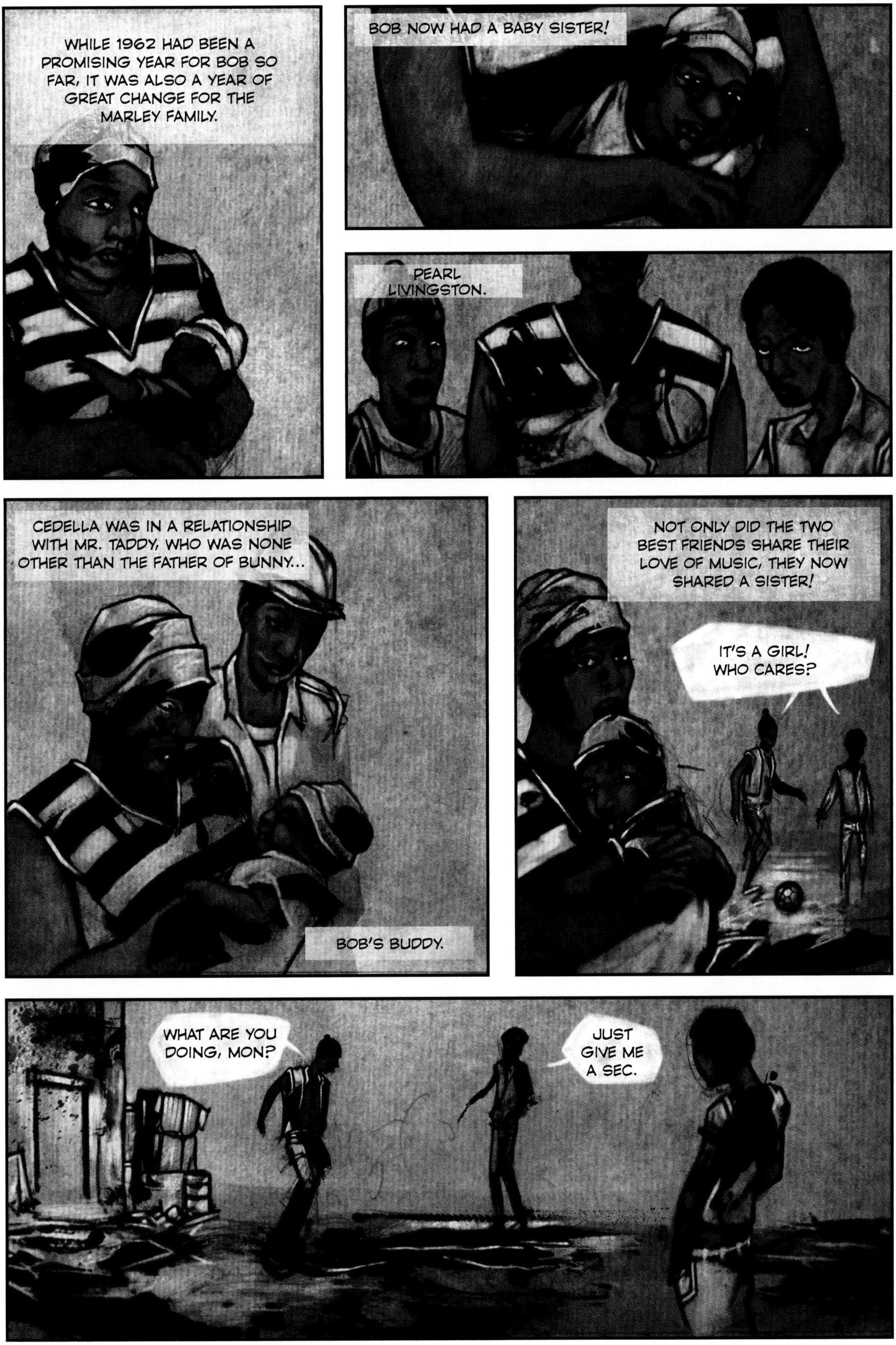
WHILE 1962 HAD BEEN A PROMISING YEAR FOR BOB SO FAR, IT WAS ALSO A YEAR OF GREAT CHANGE FOR THE MARLEY FAMILY.
BOB NOW HAD A BABY SISTER!
PEARL LIVINGSTON.
CEDELLA WAS IN A RELATIONSHIP WITH MR. TADDY, WHO WAS NONE OTHER THAN THE FATHER OF BUNNY...
BOB'S BUDDY.
NOT ONLY DID THE TWO BEST FRIENDS SHARE THEIR LOVE OF MUSIC, THEY NOW SHARED A SISTER!
IT'S A GIRL! WHO CARES?
WHAT ARE YOU DOING, MON?
JUST GIVE ME A SEC.

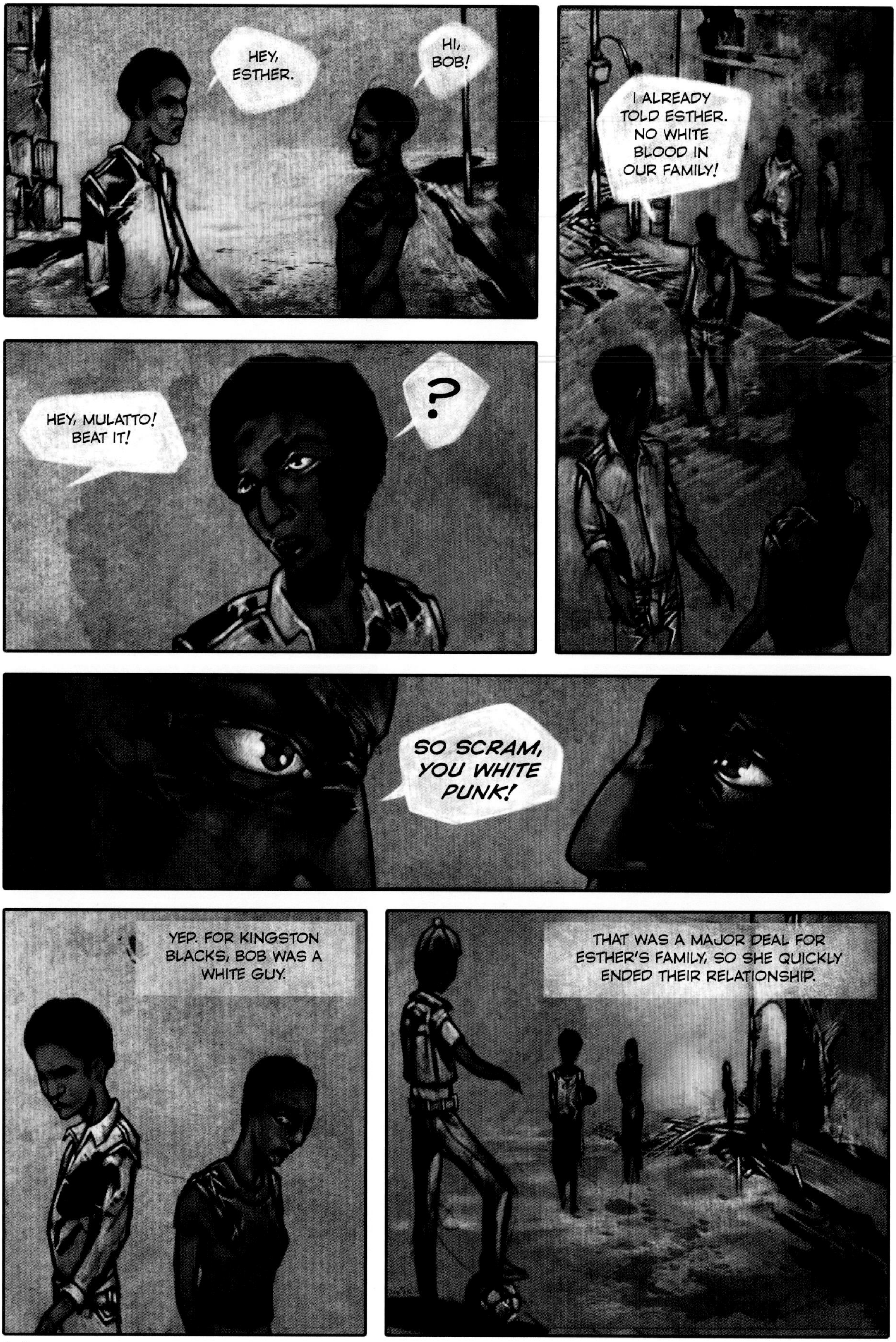
HEY, ESTHER.
HI, BOB!
I ALREADY TOLD ESTHER. NO WHITE BLOOD IN OUR FAMILY!
HEY, MULATTO! BEAT IT!
?
SO SCRAM, YOU WHITE PUNK!
YEP. FOR KINGSTON BLACKS, BOB WAS A WHITE GUY.
THAT WAS A MAJOR DEAL FOR ESTHER'S FAMILY, SO SHE QUICKLY ENDED THEIR RELATIONSHIP.

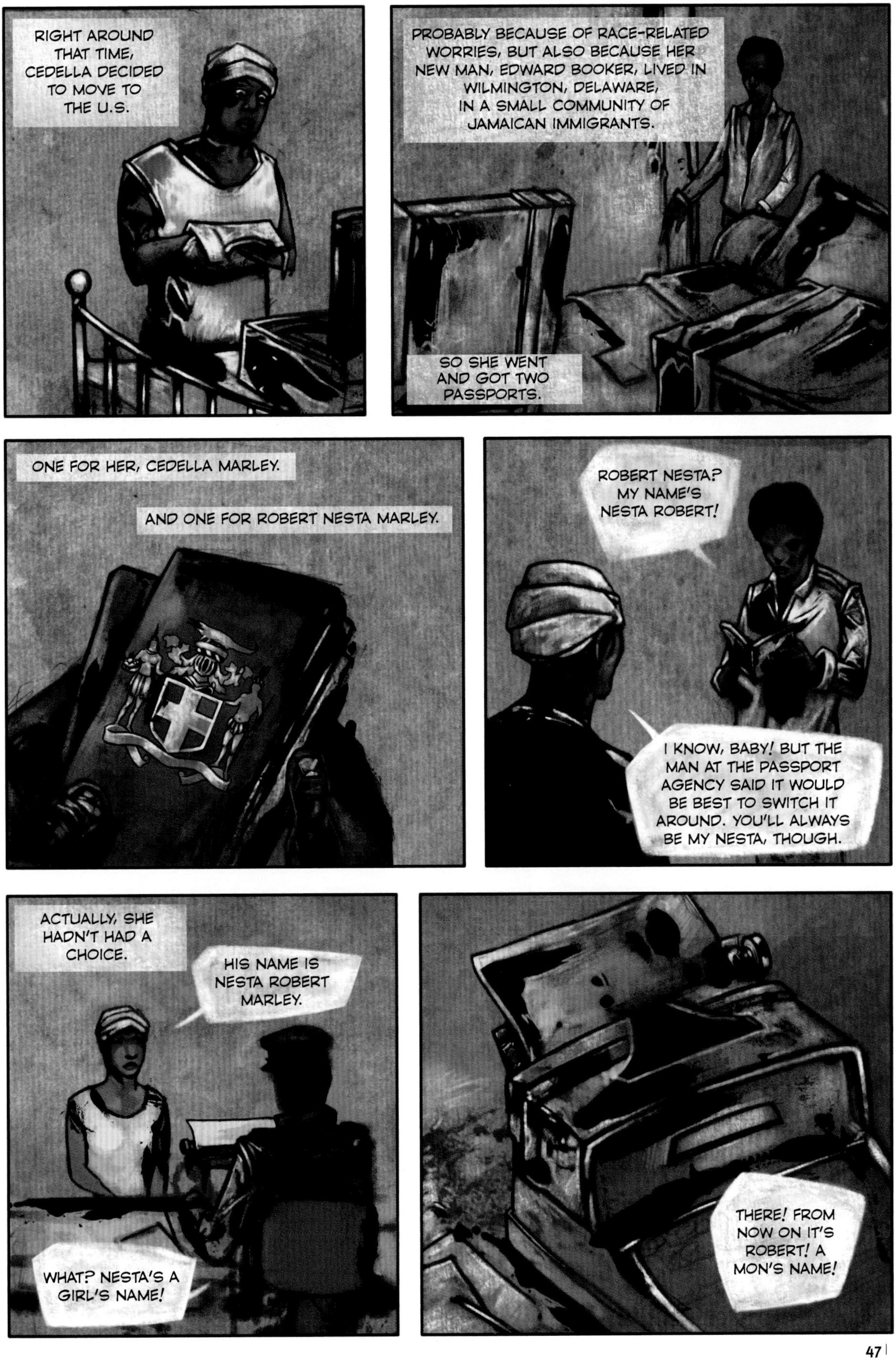
RIGHT AROUND THAT TIME, CEDELLA DECIDED TO MOVE TO THE U.S.
PROBABLY BECAUSE OF RACE-RELATED WORRIES, BUT ALSO BECAUSE HER NEW MAN, EDWARD BOOKER, LIVED IN WILMINGTON, DELAWARE, IN A SMALL COMMUNITY OF JAMAICAN IMMIGRANTS.
SO SHE WENT AND GOT TWO PASSPORTS.
ONE FOR HER, CEDELLA MARLEY.
AND ONE FOR ROBERT NESTA MARLEY.
ROBERT NESTA? MY NAME'S NESTA ROBERT!
I KNOW, BABY! BUT THE MAN AT THE PASSPORT AGENCY SAID IT WOULD BE BEST TO SWITCH IT AROUND. YOU'LL ALWAYS BE MY NESTA, THOUGH.
ACTUALLY, SHE HADN'T HAD A CHOICE.
HIS NAME IS NESTA ROBERT MARLEY.
WHAT? NESTA'S A GIRL'S NAME!
THERE! FROM NOW ON IT'S ROBERT! A MON'S NAME!

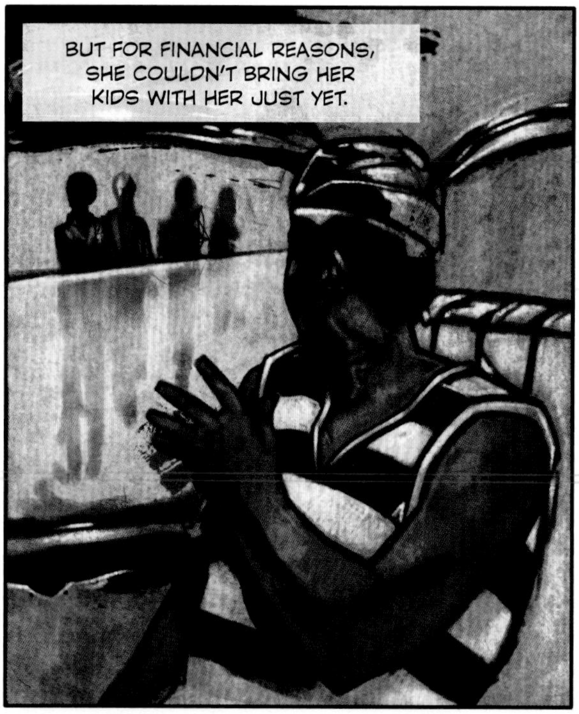
BUT FOR FINANCIAL REASONS, SHE COULDN'T BRING HER KIDS WITH HER JUST YET.
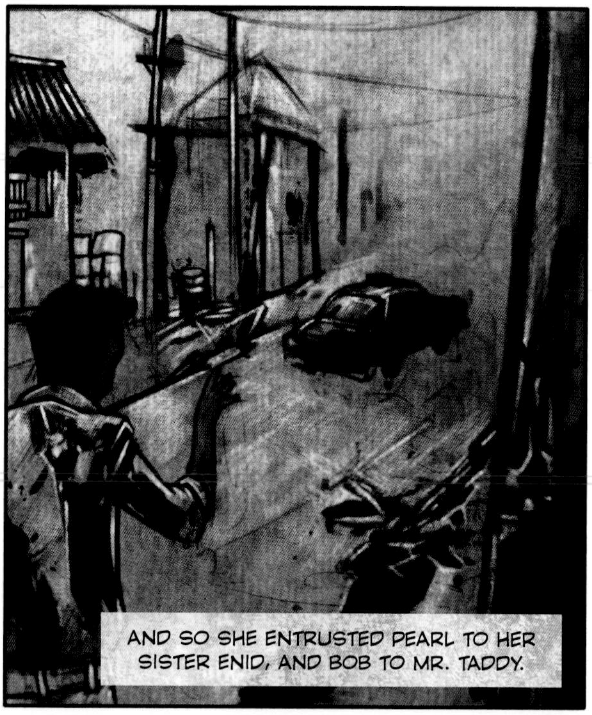
AND SO SHE ENTRUSTED PEARL TO HER SISTER ENID, AND BOB TO MR. TADDY.
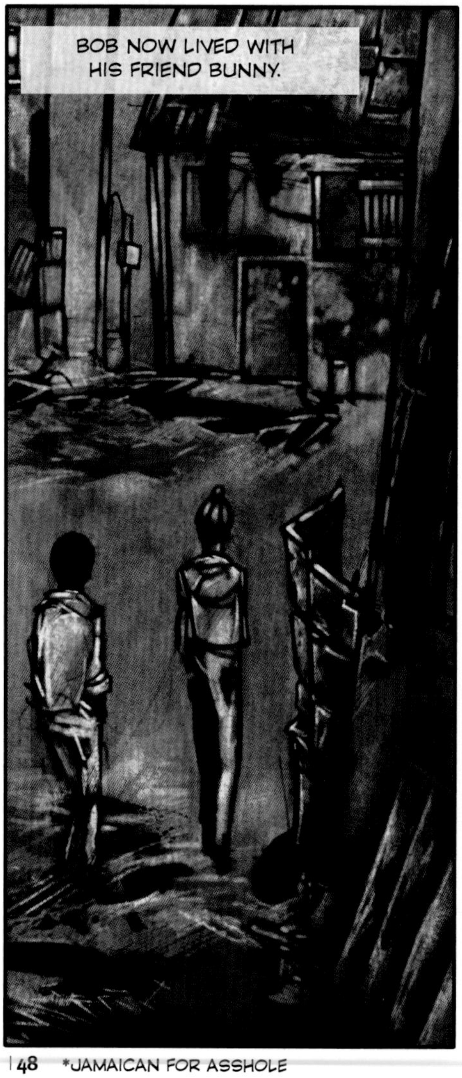
BOB NOW LIVED WITH HIS FRIEND BUNNY.
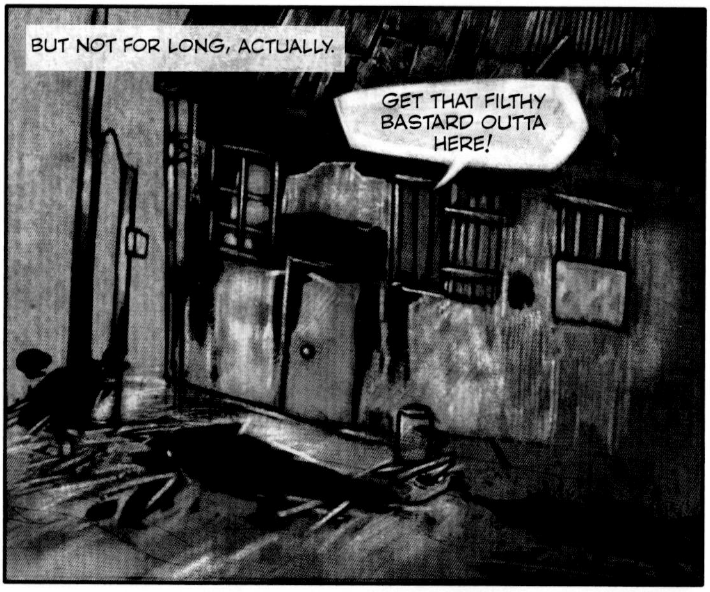
BUT NOT FOR LONG, ACTUALLY.
GET THAT FILTHY BASTARD OUTTA HERE!
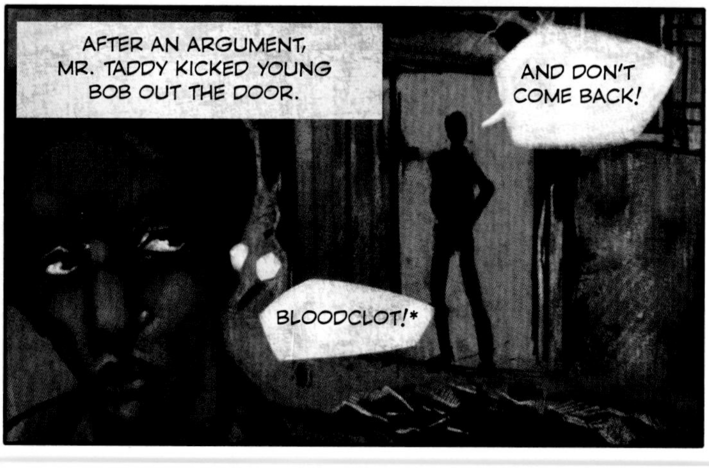
AFTER AN ARGUMENT, MR. TADDY KICKED YOUNG BOB OUT THE DOOR.
AND DON'T COME BACK!
BLOODCLOT!*

 *JAMAICAN FOR ASSHOLE

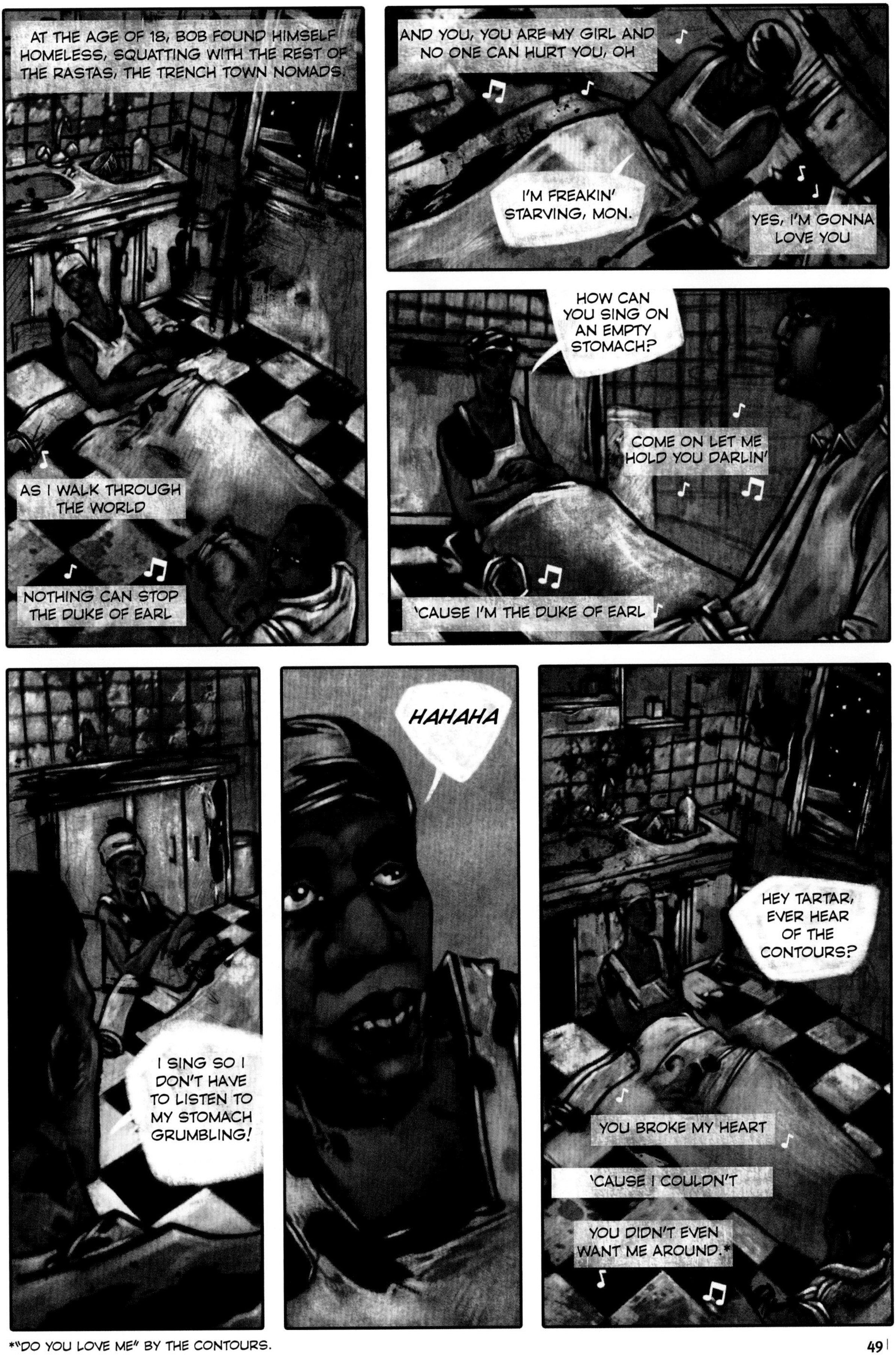
AT THE AGE OF 18, BOB FOUND HIMSELF HOMELESS, SQUATTING WITH THE REST OF THE RASTAS, THE TRENCH TOWN NOMADS.
AS I WALK THROUGH THE WORLD
NOTHING CAN STOP THE DUKE OF EARL
AND YOU, YOU ARE MY GIRL AND NO ONE CAN HURT YOU, OH
I'M FREAKIN' STARVING, MON.
YES, I'M GONNA LOVE YOU
HOW CAN YOU SING ON AN EMPTY STOMACH?
COME ON LET ME HOLD YOU DARLIN'
'CAUSE I'M THE DUKE OF EARL
I SING SO I DON'T HAVE TO LISTEN TO MY STOMACH GRUMBLING!
HAHAHA
HEY TARTAR, EVER HEAR OF THE CONTOURS?
YOU BROKE MY HEART
'CAUSE I COULDN'T
YOU DIDN'T EVEN WANT ME AROUND.*

*"DO YOU LOVE ME" BY THE CONTOURS.

Sound Systems, Ska & Studio One

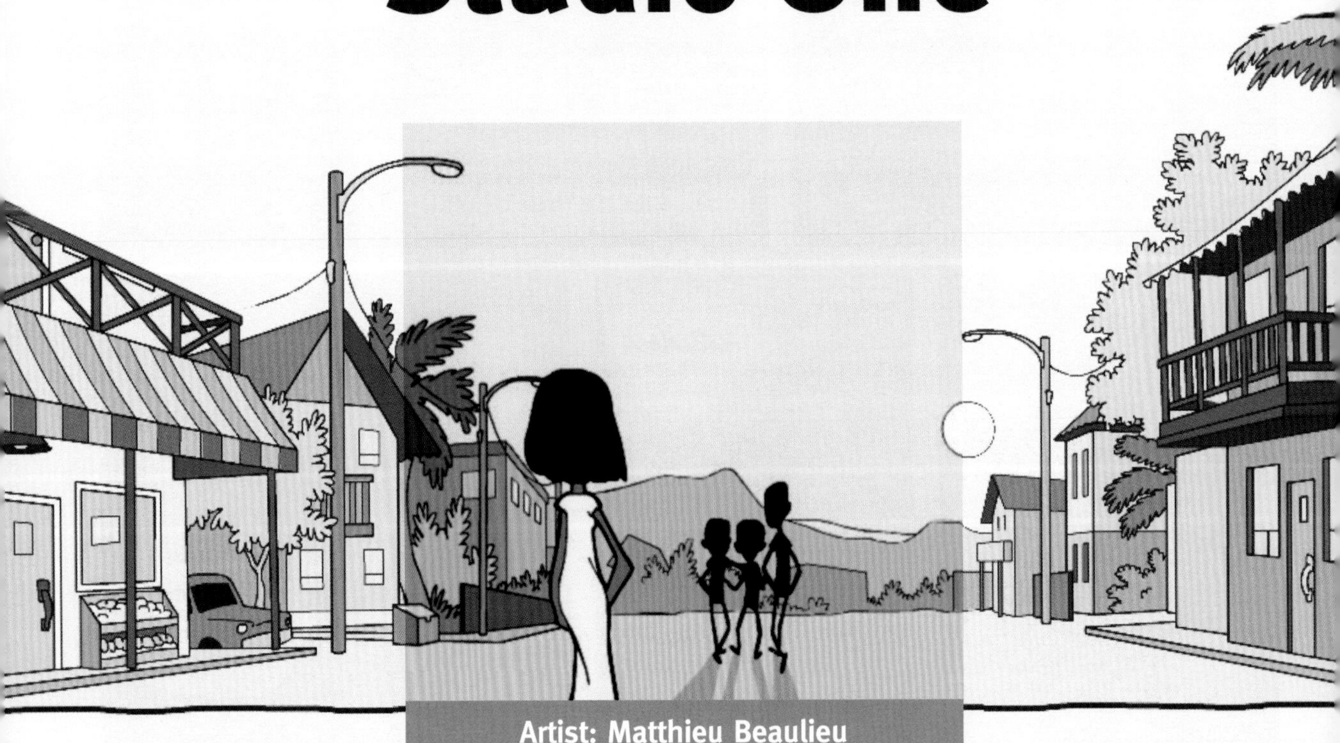

Artist: Matthieu Beaulieu

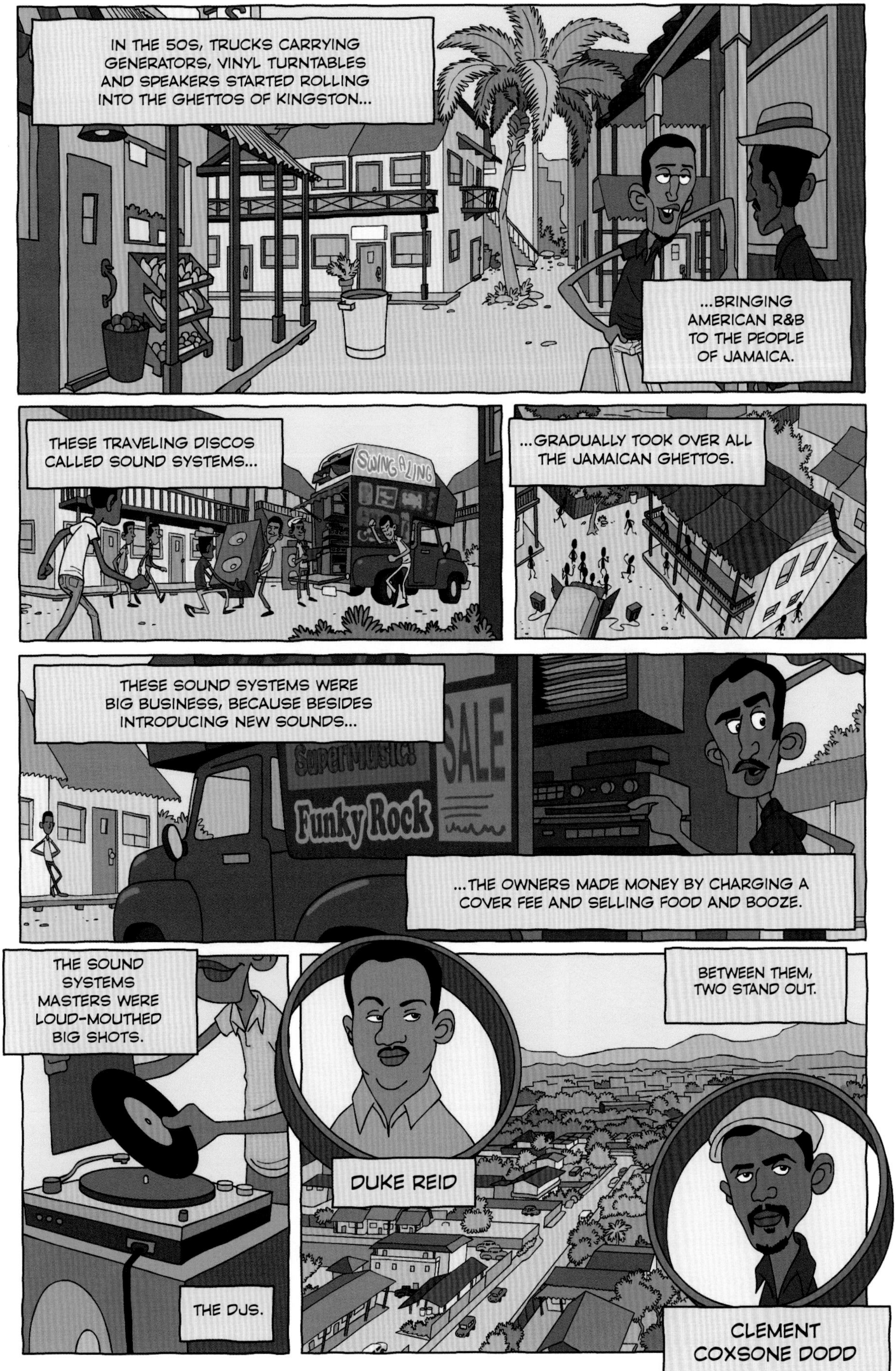
IN THE 50S, TRUCKS CARRYING GENERATORS, VINYL TURNTABLES AND SPEAKERS STARTED ROLLING INTO THE GHETTOS OF KINGSTON...
...BRINGING AMERICAN R&B TO THE PEOPLE OF JAMAICA.
THESE TRAVELING DISCOS CALLED SOUND SYSTEMS...
SWING A LING
...GRADUALLY TOOK OVER ALL THE JAMAICAN GHETTOS.
THESE SOUND SYSTEMS WERE BIG BUSINESS, BECAUSE BESIDES INTRODUCING NEW SOUNDS...
SuperMusic!
Funky Rock
SALE
...THE OWNERS MADE MONEY BY CHARGING A COVER FEE AND SELLING FOOD AND BOOZE.
THE SOUND SYSTEMS MASTERS WERE LOUD-MOUTHED BIG SHOTS.
THE DJS.
BETWEEN THEM, TWO STAND OUT.
DUKE REID
CLEMENT COXSONE DODD

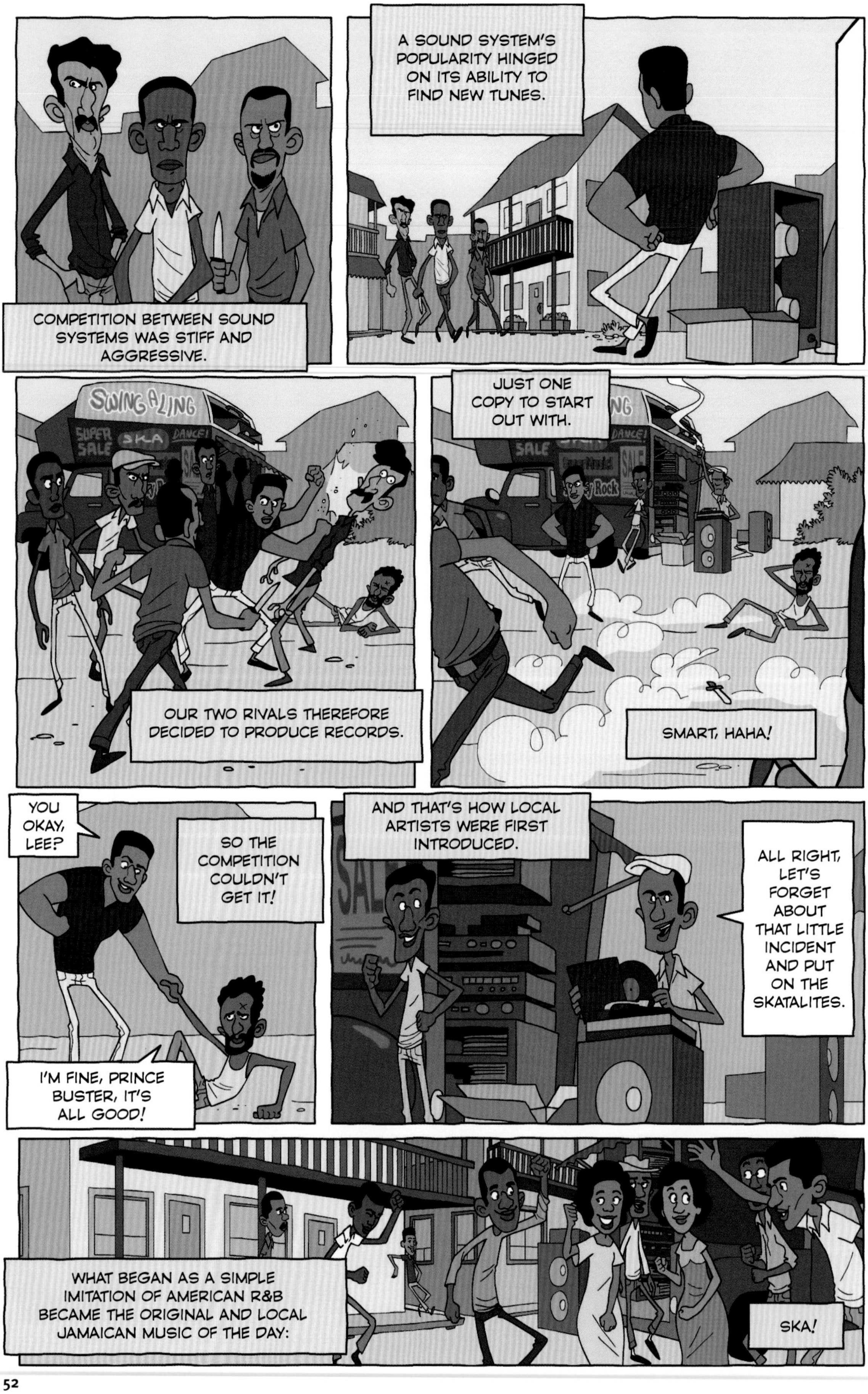
COMPETITION BETWEEN SOUND SYSTEMS WAS STIFF AND AGGRESSIVE.
A SOUND SYSTEM'S POPULARITY HINGED ON ITS ABILITY TO FIND NEW TUNES.
SWING A LING
SUPER SALE
SKA
DANCE!
OUR TWO RIVALS THEREFORE DECIDED TO PRODUCE RECORDS.
JUST ONE COPY TO START OUT WITH.
SMART, HAHA!
YOU OKAY, LEE?
SO THE COMPETITION COULDN'T GET IT!
I'M FINE, PRINCE BUSTER, IT'S ALL GOOD!
AND THAT'S HOW LOCAL ARTISTS WERE FIRST INTRODUCED.
ALL RIGHT, LET'S FORGET ABOUT THAT LITTLE INCIDENT AND PUT ON THE SKATALITES.
WHAT BEGAN AS A SIMPLE IMITATION OF AMERICAN R&B BECAME THE ORIGINAL AND LOCAL JAMAICAN MUSIC OF THE DAY:
SKA!

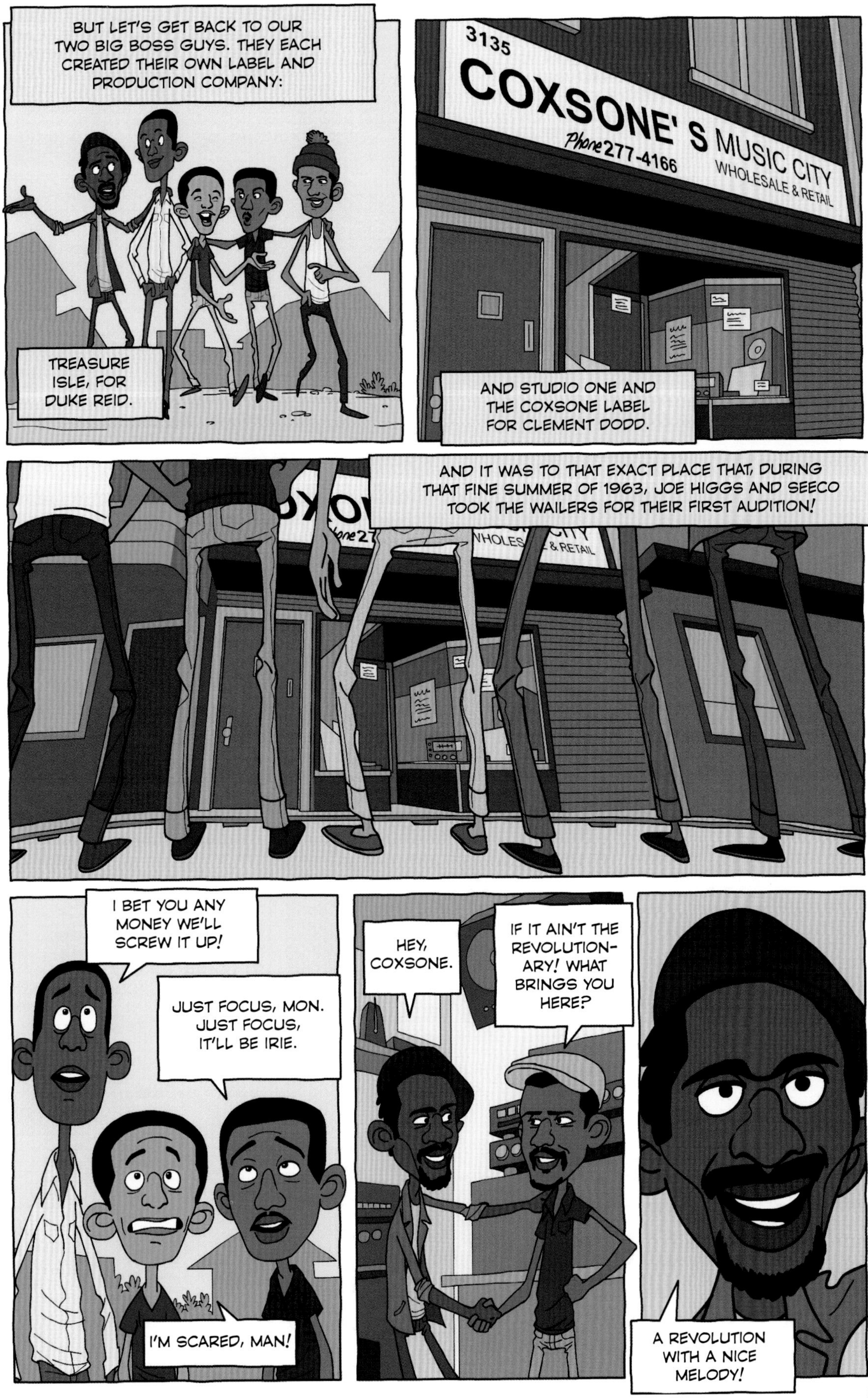
BUT LET'S GET BACK TO OUR TWO BIG BOSS GUYS. THEY EACH CREATED THEIR OWN LABEL AND PRODUCTION COMPANY:
TREASURE ISLE, FOR DUKE REID.
3135 COXSONE'S MUSIC CITY
Phone 277-4166
WHOLESALE & RETAIL
AND STUDIO ONE AND THE COXSONE LABEL FOR CLEMENT DODD.
AND IT WAS TO THAT EXACT PLACE THAT, DURING THAT FINE SUMMER OF 1963, JOE HIGGS AND SEECO TOOK THE WAILERS FOR THEIR FIRST AUDITION!
I BET YOU ANY MONEY WE'LL SCREW IT UP!
JUST FOCUS, MON. JUST FOCUS, IT'LL BE IRIE.
I'M SCARED, MAN!
HEY, COXSONE.
IF IT AIN'T THE REVOLUTION-ARY! WHAT BRINGS YOU HERE?
A REVOLUTION WITH A NICE MELODY!

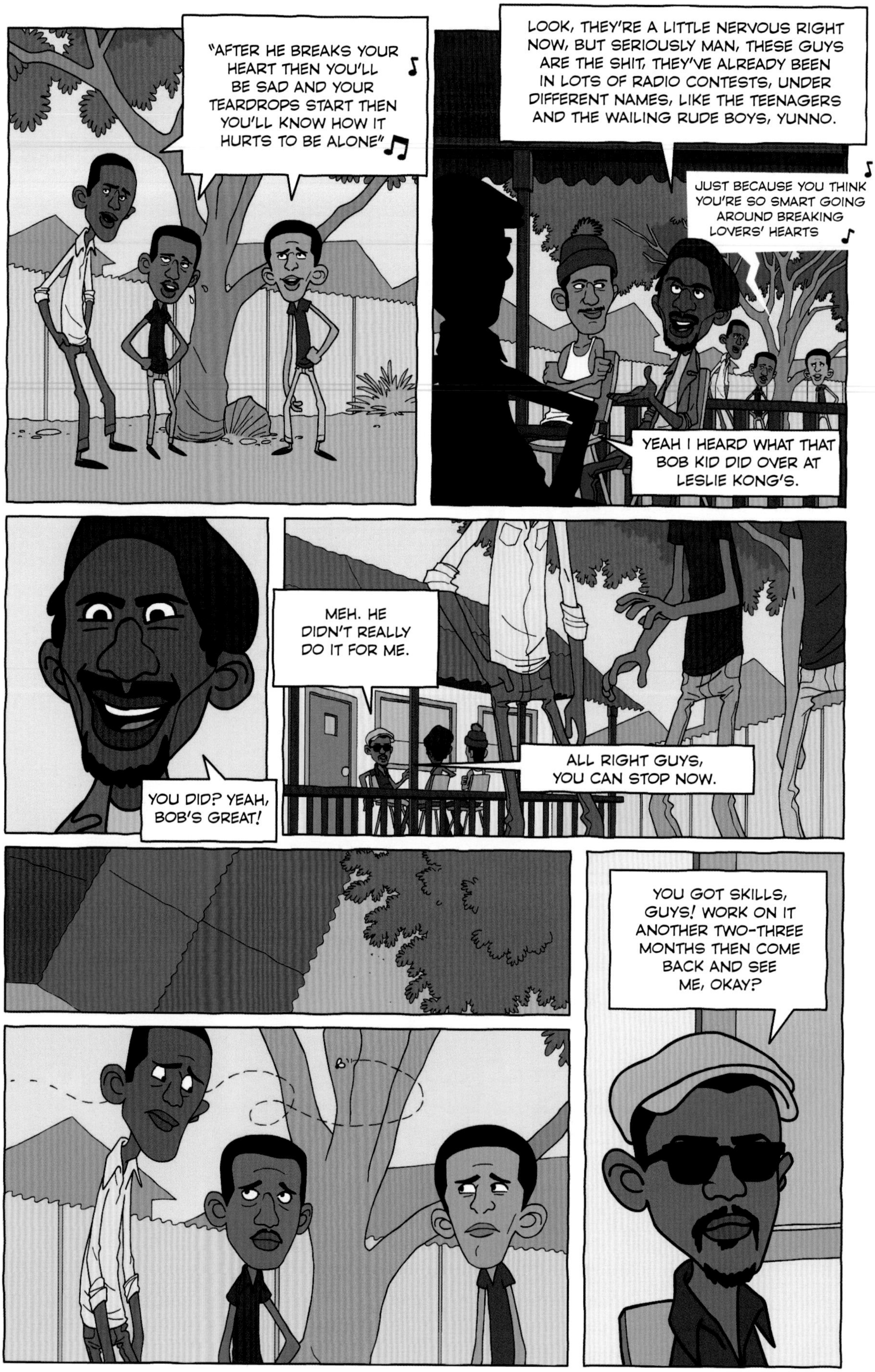
"AFTER HE BREAKS YOUR HEART THEN YOU'LL BE SAD AND YOUR TEARDROPS START THEN YOU'LL KNOW HOW IT HURTS TO BE ALONE"
LOOK, THEY'RE A LITTLE NERVOUS RIGHT NOW, BUT SERIOUSLY MAN, THESE GUYS ARE THE SHIT, THEY'VE ALREADY BEEN IN LOTS OF RADIO CONTESTS, UNDER DIFFERENT NAMES, LIKE THE TEENAGERS AND THE WAILING RUDE BOYS, YUNNO.
JUST BECAUSE YOU THINK YOU'RE SO SMART GOING AROUND BREAKING LOVERS' HEARTS
YEAH I HEARD WHAT THAT BOB KID DID OVER AT LESLIE KONG'S.
YOU DID? YEAH, BOB'S GREAT!
MEH. HE DIDN'T REALLY DO IT FOR ME.
ALL RIGHT GUYS, YOU CAN STOP NOW.
YOU GOT SKILLS, GUYS! WORK ON IT ANOTHER TWO-THREE MONTHS THEN COME BACK AND SEE ME, OKAY?

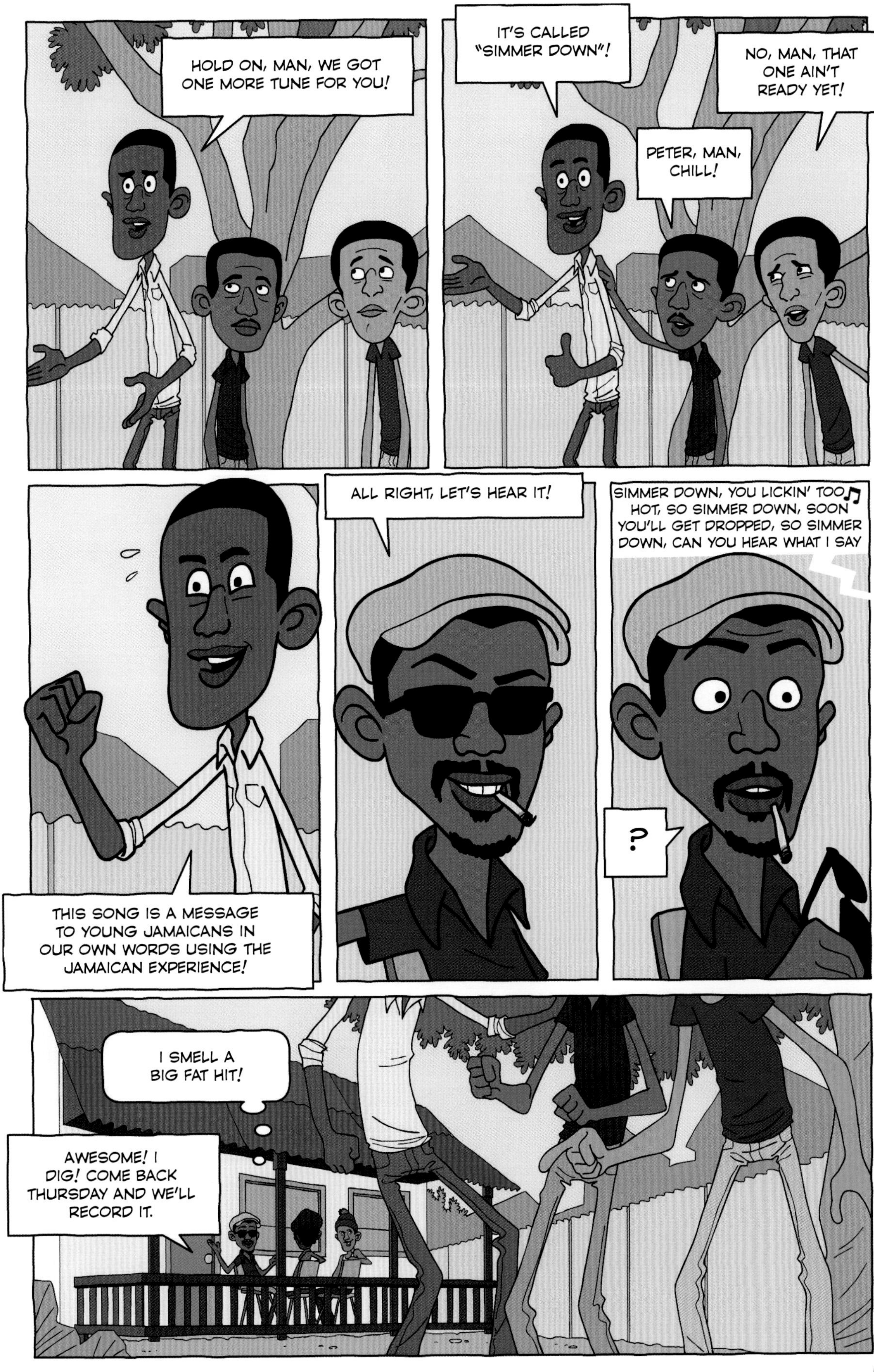

HOLD ON, MAN, WE GOT ONE MORE TUNE FOR YOU!
IT'S CALLED "SIMMER DOWN"!
PETER, MAN, CHILL!
NO, MAN, THAT ONE AIN'T READY YET!
THIS SONG IS A MESSAGE TO YOUNG JAMAICANS IN OUR OWN WORDS USING THE JAMAICAN EXPERIENCE!
ALL RIGHT, LET'S HEAR IT!
SIMMER DOWN, YOU LICKIN' TOO HOT, SO SIMMER DOWN, SOON YOU'LL GET DROPPED, SO SIMMER DOWN, CAN YOU HEAR WHAT I SAY
?
I SMELL A BIG FAT HIT!
AWESOME! I DIG! COME BACK THURSDAY AND WE'LL RECORD IT.

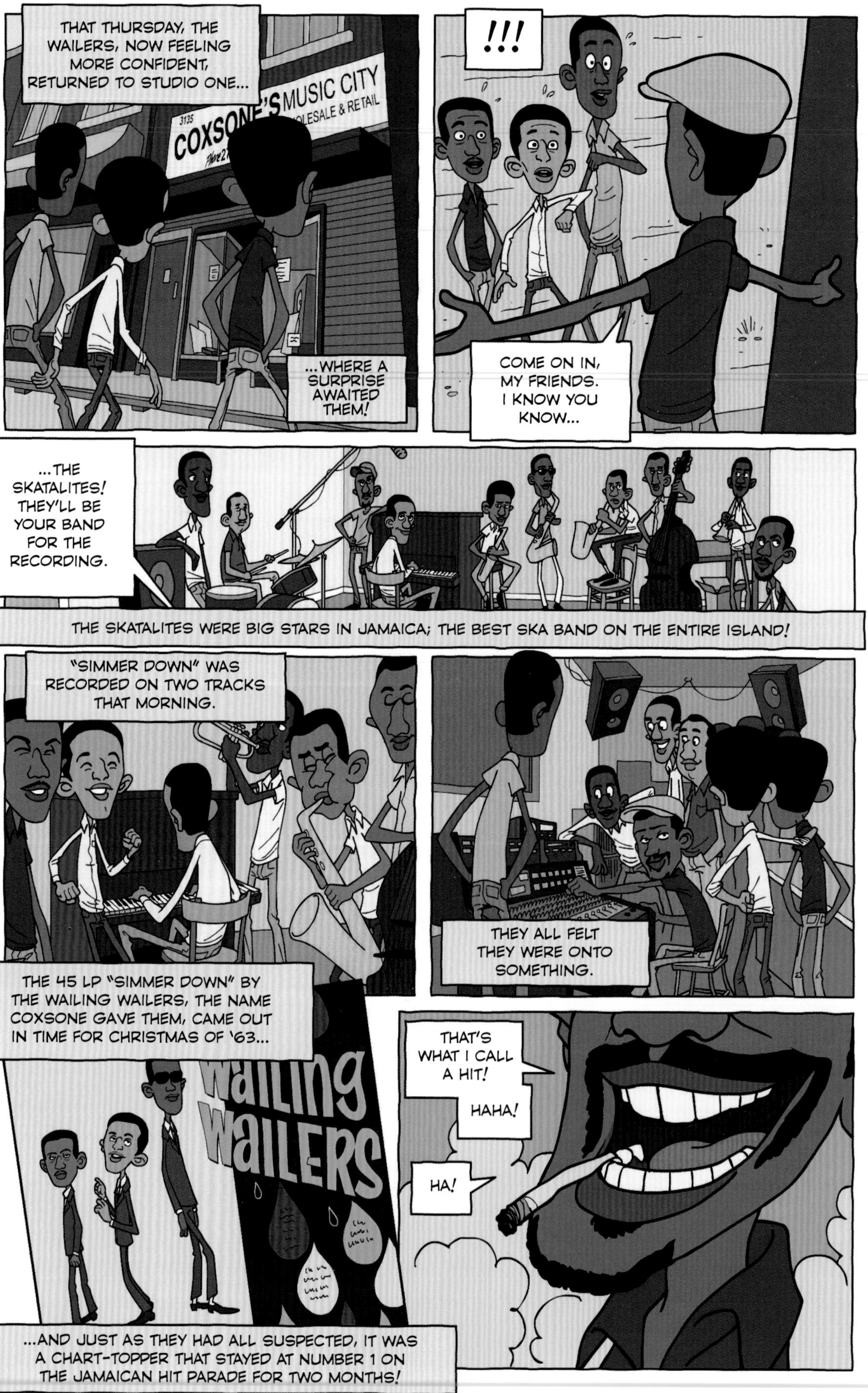

THAT THURSDAY, THE WAILERS, NOW FEELING MORE CONFIDENT, RETURNED TO STUDIO ONE...
COXSONE'S MUSIC CITY
WHOLESALE & RETAIL
...WHERE A SURPRISE AWAITED THEM!
!!!
COME ON IN, MY FRIENDS. I KNOW YOU KNOW...
...THE SKATALITES! THEY'LL BE YOUR BAND FOR THE RECORDING.
THE SKATALITES WERE BIG STARS IN JAMAICA; THE BEST SKA BAND ON THE ENTIRE ISLAND!
"SIMMER DOWN" WAS RECORDED ON TWO TRACKS THAT MORNING.
THEY ALL FELT THEY WERE ONTO SOMETHING.
THE 45 LP "SIMMER DOWN" BY THE WAILING WAILERS, THE NAME COXSONE GAVE THEM, CAME OUT IN TIME FOR CHRISTMAS OF '63...
WAILING WAILERS
THAT'S WHAT I CALL A HIT!
HAHA!
HA!
...AND JUST AS THEY HAD ALL SUSPECTED, IT WAS A CHART-TOPPER THAT STAYED AT NUMBER 1 ON THE JAMAICAN HIT PARADE FOR TWO MONTHS!

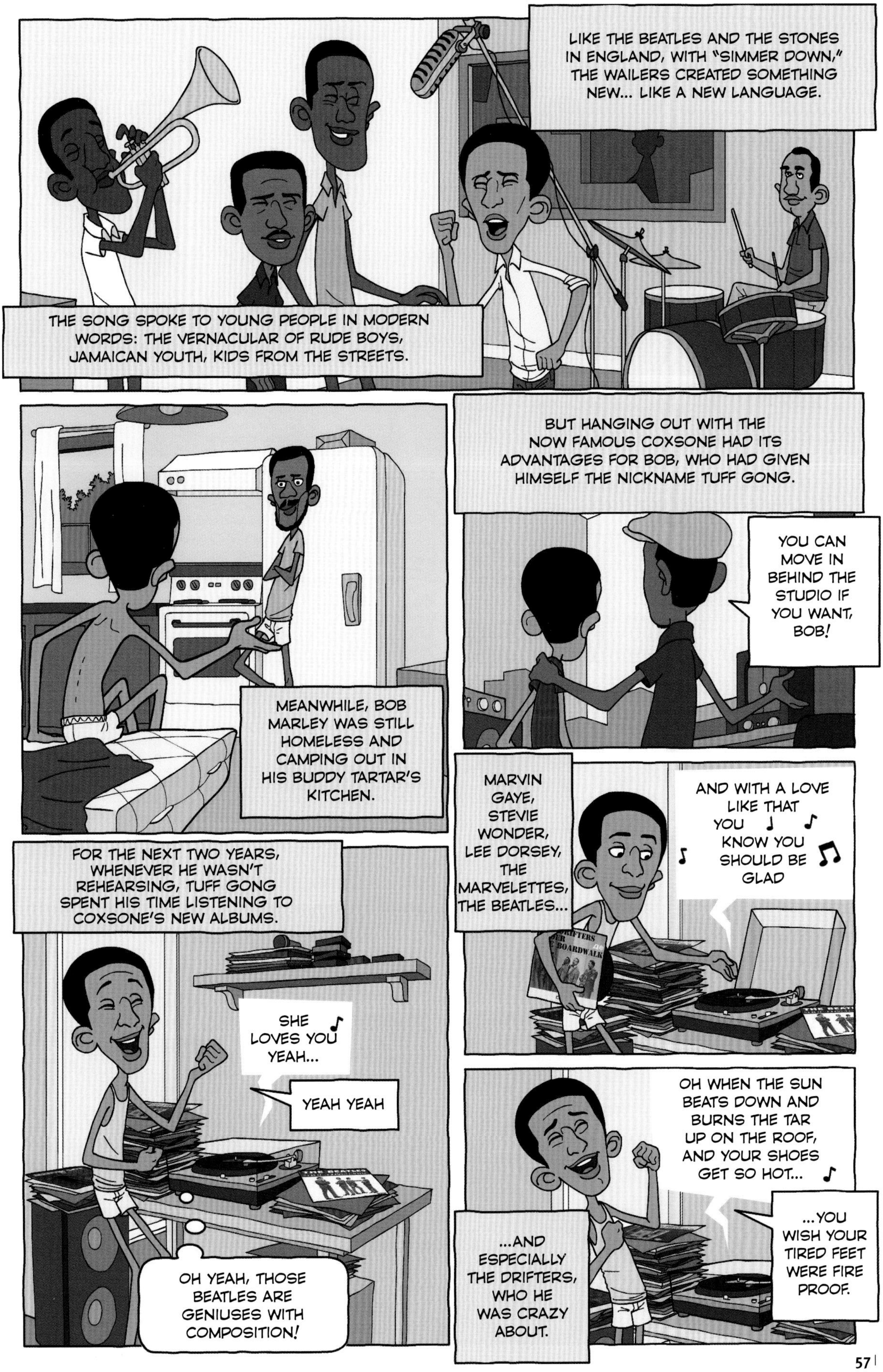
LIKE THE BEATLES AND THE STONES IN ENGLAND, WITH "SIMMER DOWN," THE WAILERS CREATED SOMETHING NEW... LIKE A NEW LANGUAGE.
THE SONG SPOKE TO YOUNG PEOPLE IN MODERN WORDS: THE VERNACULAR OF RUDE BOYS, JAMAICAN YOUTH, KIDS FROM THE STREETS.
MEANWHILE, BOB MARLEY WAS STILL HOMELESS AND CAMPING OUT IN HIS BUDDY TARTAR'S KITCHEN.
BUT HANGING OUT WITH THE NOW FAMOUS COXSONE HAD ITS ADVANTAGES FOR BOB, WHO HAD GIVEN HIMSELF THE NICKNAME TUFF GONG.
YOU CAN MOVE IN BEHIND THE STUDIO IF YOU WANT, BOB!
FOR THE NEXT TWO YEARS, WHENEVER HE WASN'T REHEARSING, TUFF GONG SPENT HIS TIME LISTENING TO COXSONE'S NEW ALBUMS.
SHE LOVES YOU YEAH...
YEAH YEAH
OH YEAH, THOSE BEATLES ARE GENIUSES WITH COMPOSITION!
MARVIN GAYE, STEVIE WONDER, LEE DORSEY, THE MARVELETTES, THE BEATLES...
AND WITH A LOVE LIKE THAT YOU KNOW YOU SHOULD BE GLAD
DRIFTERS UNDER THE BOARDWALK
OH WHEN THE SUN BEATS DOWN AND BURNS THE TAR UP ON THE ROOF, AND YOUR SHOES GET SO HOT...
...AND ESPECIALLY THE DRIFTERS, WHO HE WAS CRAZY ABOUT.
...YOU WISH YOUR TIRED FEET WERE FIRE PROOF.

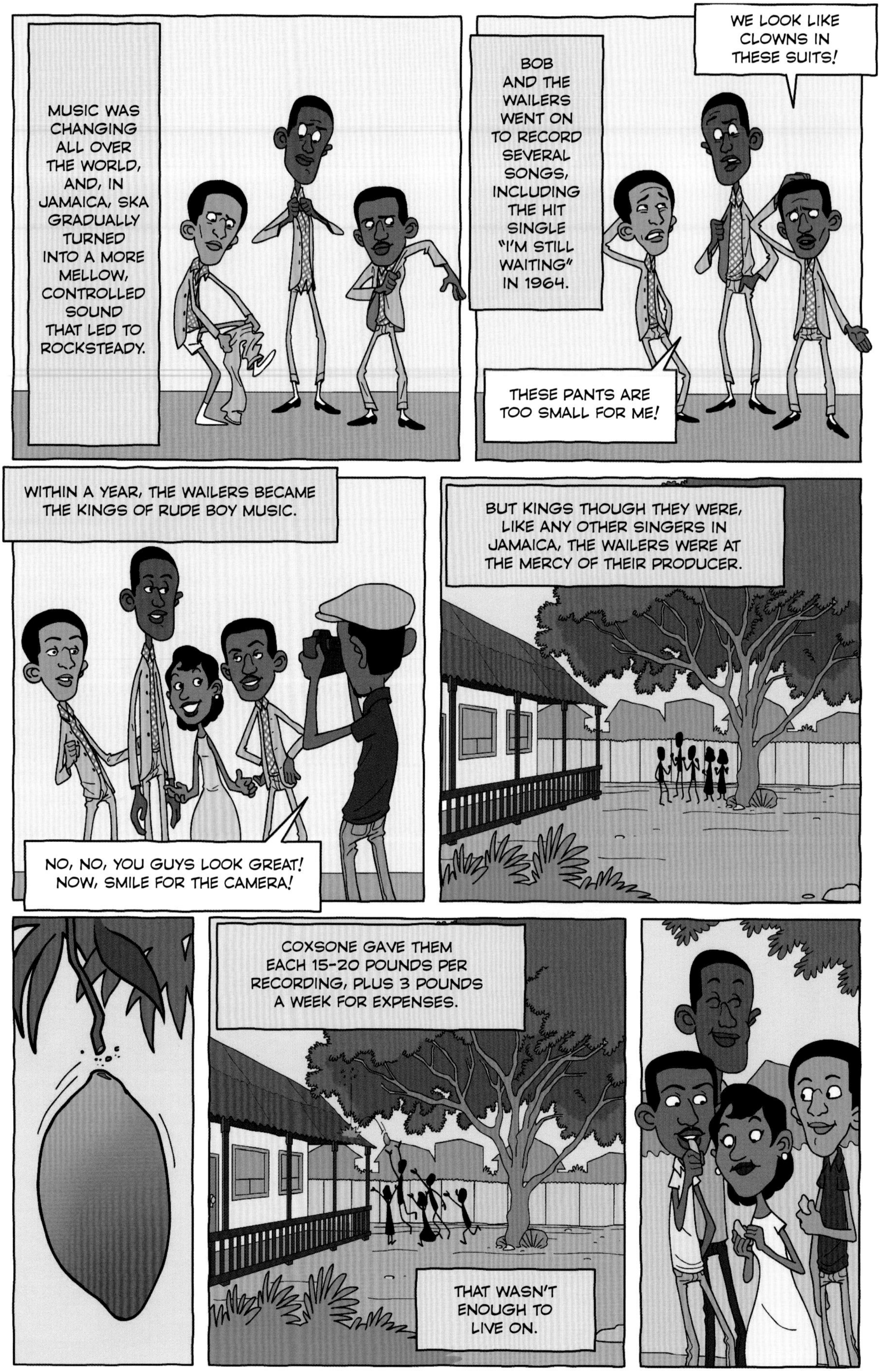
MUSIC WAS CHANGING ALL OVER THE WORLD, AND, IN JAMAICA, SKA GRADUALLY TURNED INTO A MORE MELLOW, CONTROLLED SOUND THAT LED TO ROCKSTEADY.
BOB AND THE WAILERS WENT ON TO RECORD SEVERAL SONGS, INCLUDING THE HIT SINGLE "I'M STILL WAITING" IN 1964.
WE LOOK LIKE CLOWNS IN THESE SUITS!
THESE PANTS ARE TOO SMALL FOR ME!
WITHIN A YEAR, THE WAILERS BECAME THE KINGS OF RUDE BOY MUSIC.
NO, NO, YOU GUYS LOOK GREAT! NOW, SMILE FOR THE CAMERA!
BUT KINGS THOUGH THEY WERE, LIKE ANY OTHER SINGERS IN JAMAICA, THE WAILERS WERE AT THE MERCY OF THEIR PRODUCER.
COXSONE GAVE THEM EACH 15-20 POUNDS PER RECORDING, PLUS 3 POUNDS A WEEK FOR EXPENSES.
THAT WASN'T ENOUGH TO LIVE ON.

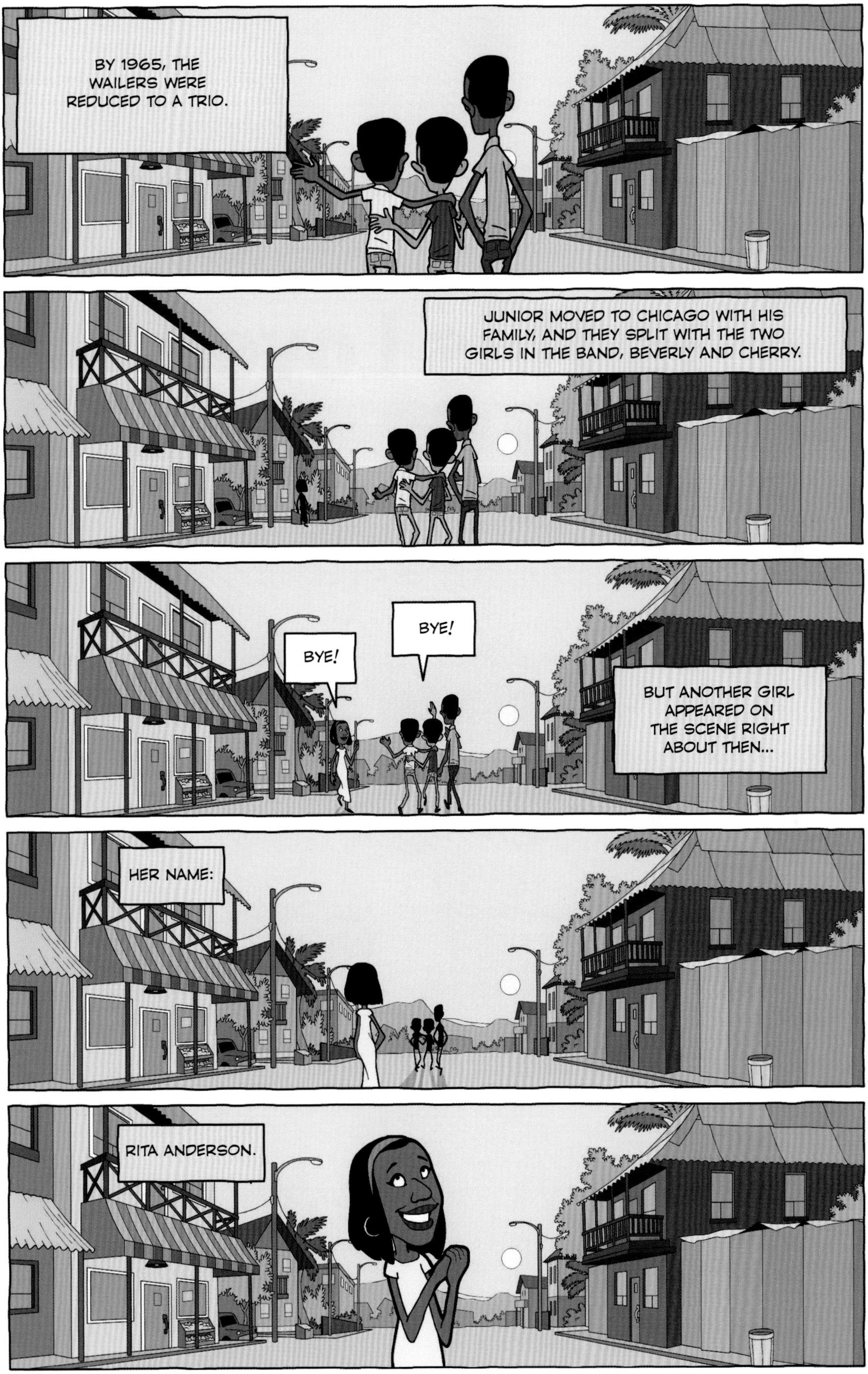
BY 1965, THE WAILERS WERE REDUCED TO A TRIO.
JUNIOR MOVED TO CHICAGO WITH HIS FAMILY, AND THEY SPLIT WITH THE TWO GIRLS IN THE BAND, BEVERLY AND CHERRY.
BYE!
BYE!
BUT ANOTHER GIRL APPEARED ON THE SCENE RIGHT ABOUT THEN...
HER NAME:
RITA ANDERSON.

Is This Love?

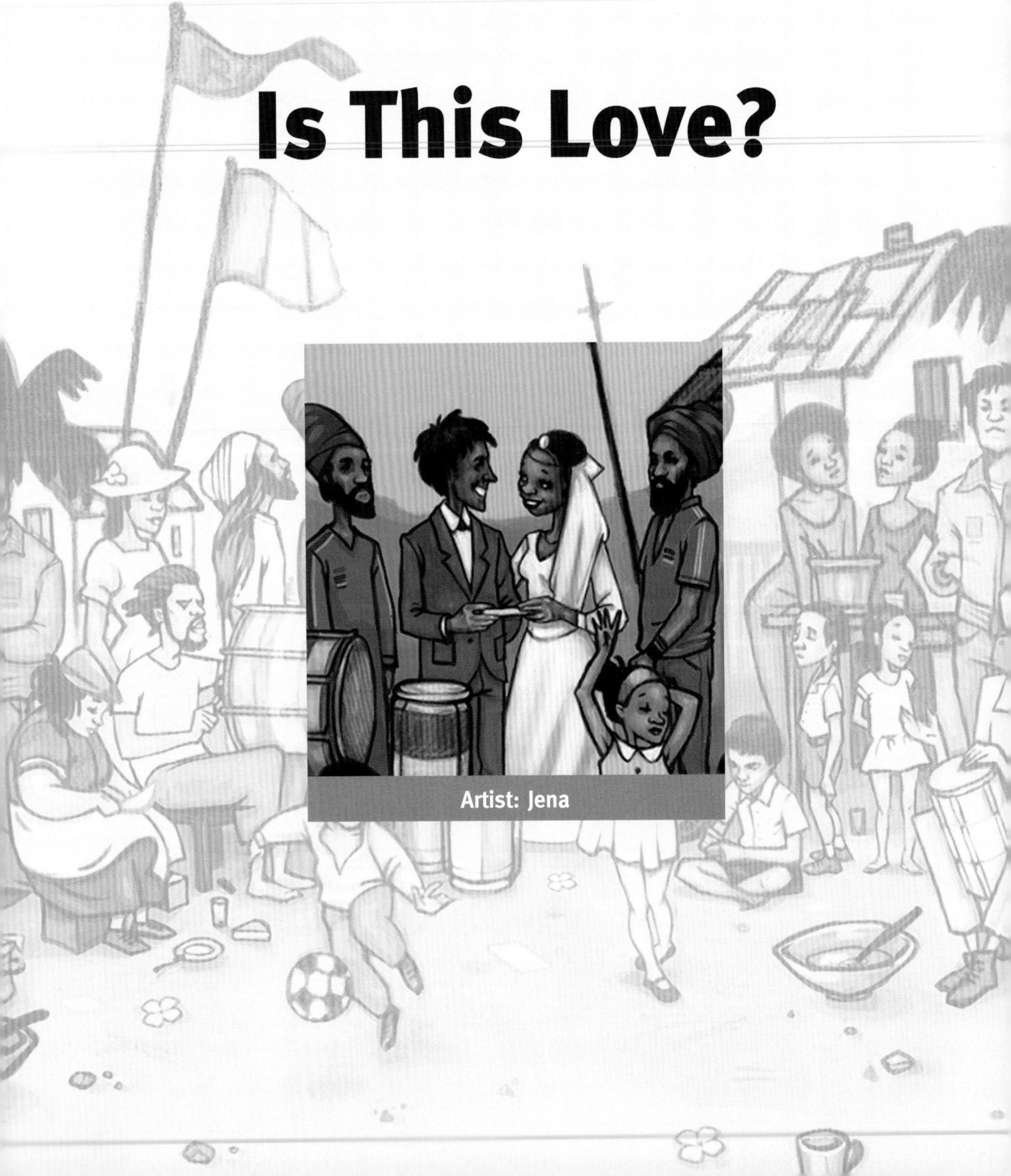

Artist: Jena

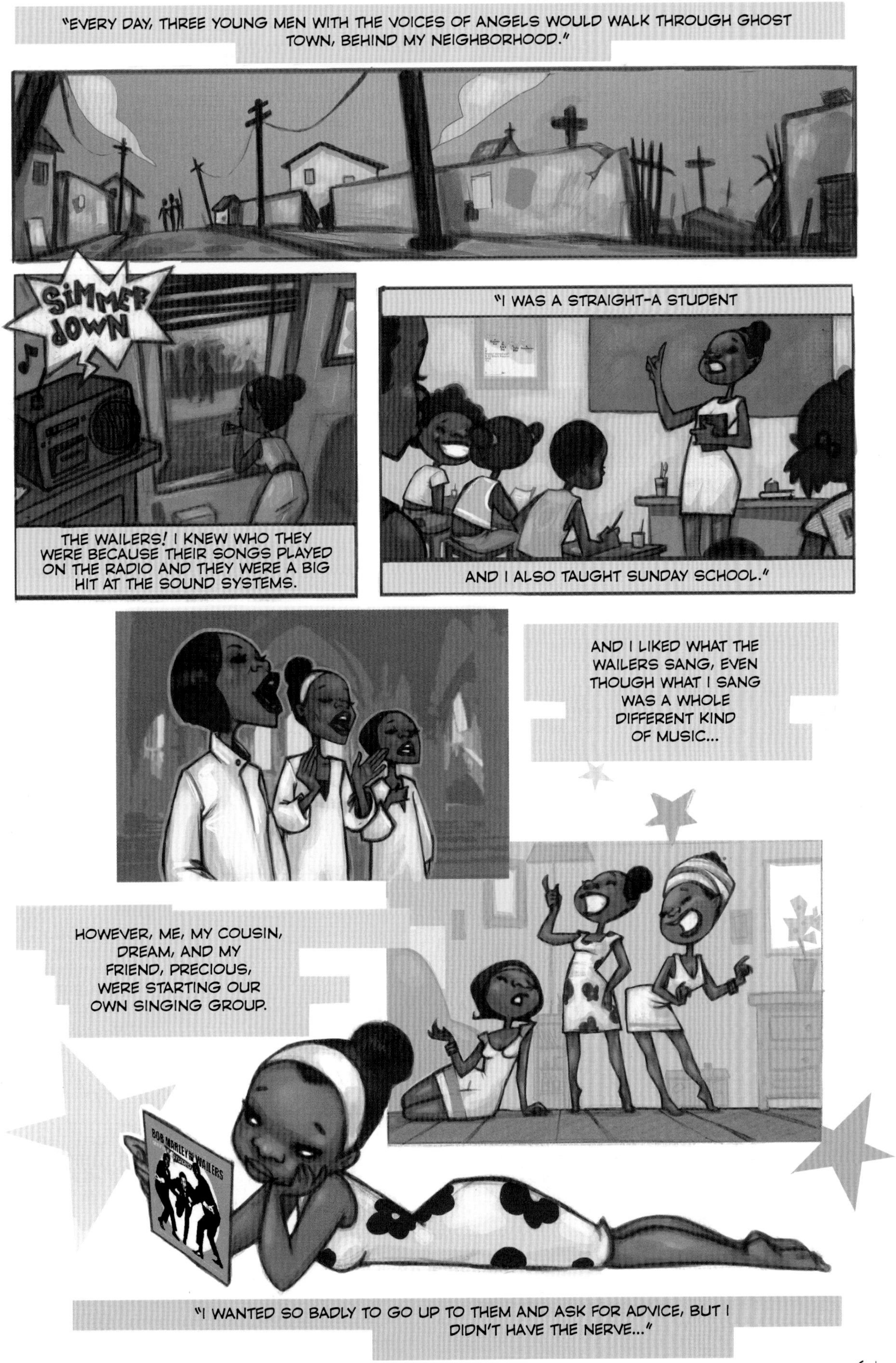
"EVERY DAY, THREE YOUNG MEN WITH THE VOICES OF ANGELS WOULD WALK THROUGH GHOST TOWN, BEHIND MY NEIGHBORHOOD."
SIMMER DOWN
THE WAILERS! I KNEW WHO THEY WERE BECAUSE THEIR SONGS PLAYED ON THE RADIO AND THEY WERE A BIG HIT AT THE SOUND SYSTEMS.
"I WAS A STRAIGHT-A STUDENT
AND I ALSO TAUGHT SUNDAY SCHOOL."
AND I LIKED WHAT THE WAILERS SANG, EVEN THOUGH WHAT I SANG WAS A WHOLE DIFFERENT KIND OF MUSIC...
HOWEVER, ME, MY COUSIN, DREAM, AND MY FRIEND, PRECIOUS, WERE STARTING OUR OWN SINGING GROUP.
"I WANTED SO BADLY TO GO UP TO THEM AND ASK FOR ADVICE, BUT I DIDN'T HAVE THE NERVE..."

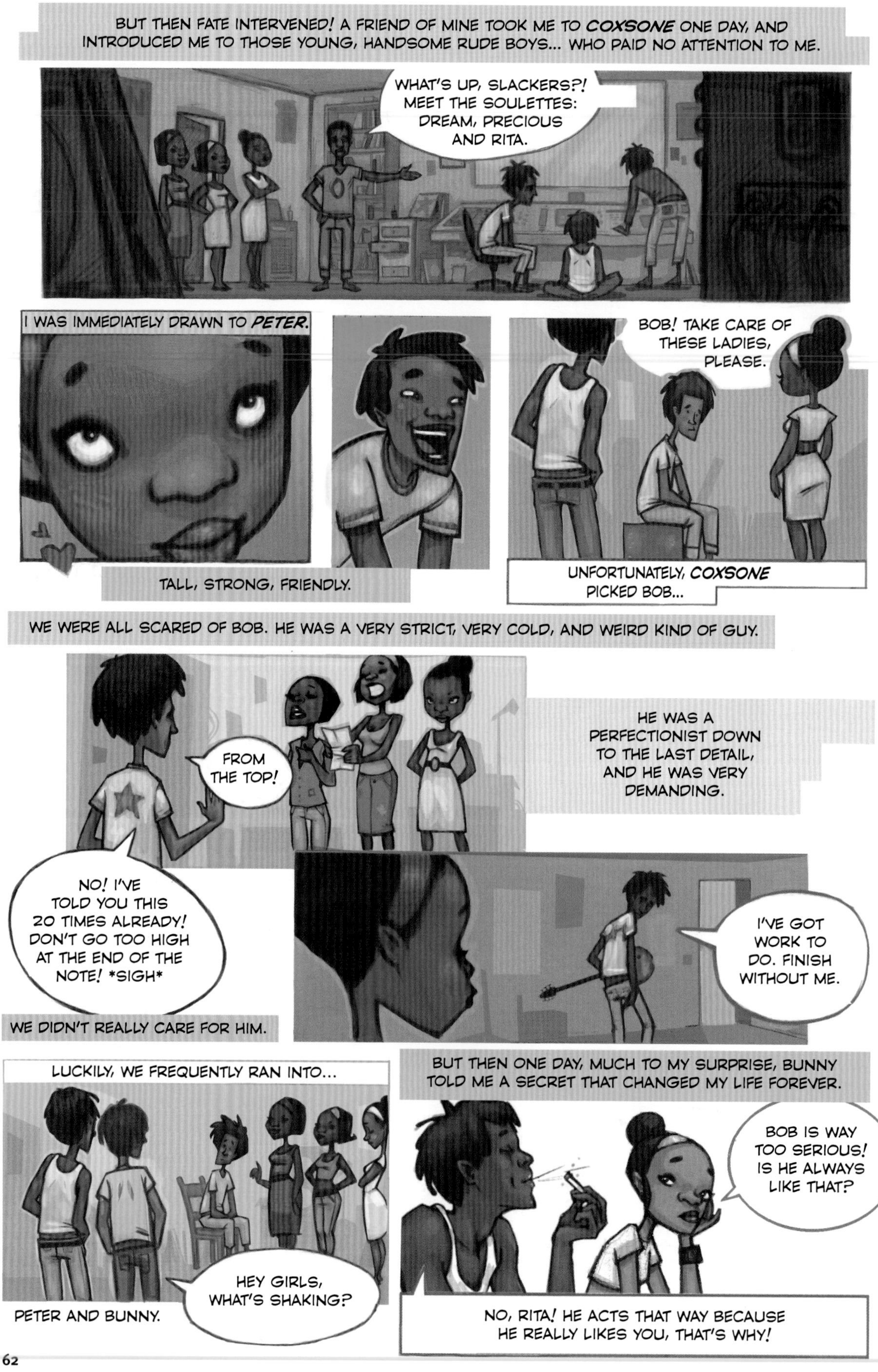
BUT THEN FATE INTERVENED! A FRIEND OF MINE TOOK ME TO COXSONE ONE DAY, AND INTRODUCED ME TO THOSE YOUNG, HANDSOME RUDE BOYS... WHO PAID NO ATTENTION TO ME.
WHAT'S UP, SLACKERS?! MEET THE SOULETTES: DREAM, PRECIOUS AND RITA.
I WAS IMMEDIATELY DRAWN TO PETER.
TALL, STRONG, FRIENDLY.
BOB! TAKE CARE OF THESE LADIES, PLEASE.
UNFORTUNATELY, COXSONE PICKED BOB...
WE WERE ALL SCARED OF BOB. HE WAS A VERY STRICT, VERY COLD, AND WEIRD KIND OF GUY.
FROM THE TOP!
HE WAS A PERFECTIONIST DOWN TO THE LAST DETAIL, AND HE WAS VERY DEMANDING.
NO! I'VE TOLD YOU THIS 20 TIMES ALREADY! DON'T GO TOO HIGH AT THE END OF THE NOTE! *SIGH*
WE DIDN'T REALLY CARE FOR HIM.
I'VE GOT WORK TO DO. FINISH WITHOUT ME.
LUCKILY, WE FREQUENTLY RAN INTO...
HEY GIRLS, WHAT'S SHAKING?
PETER AND BUNNY.
BUT THEN ONE DAY, MUCH TO MY SURPRISE, BUNNY TOLD ME A SECRET THAT CHANGED MY LIFE FOREVER.
BOB IS WAY TOO SERIOUS! IS HE ALWAYS LIKE THAT?
NO, RITA! HE ACTS THAT WAY BECAUSE HE REALLY LIKES YOU, THAT'S WHY!

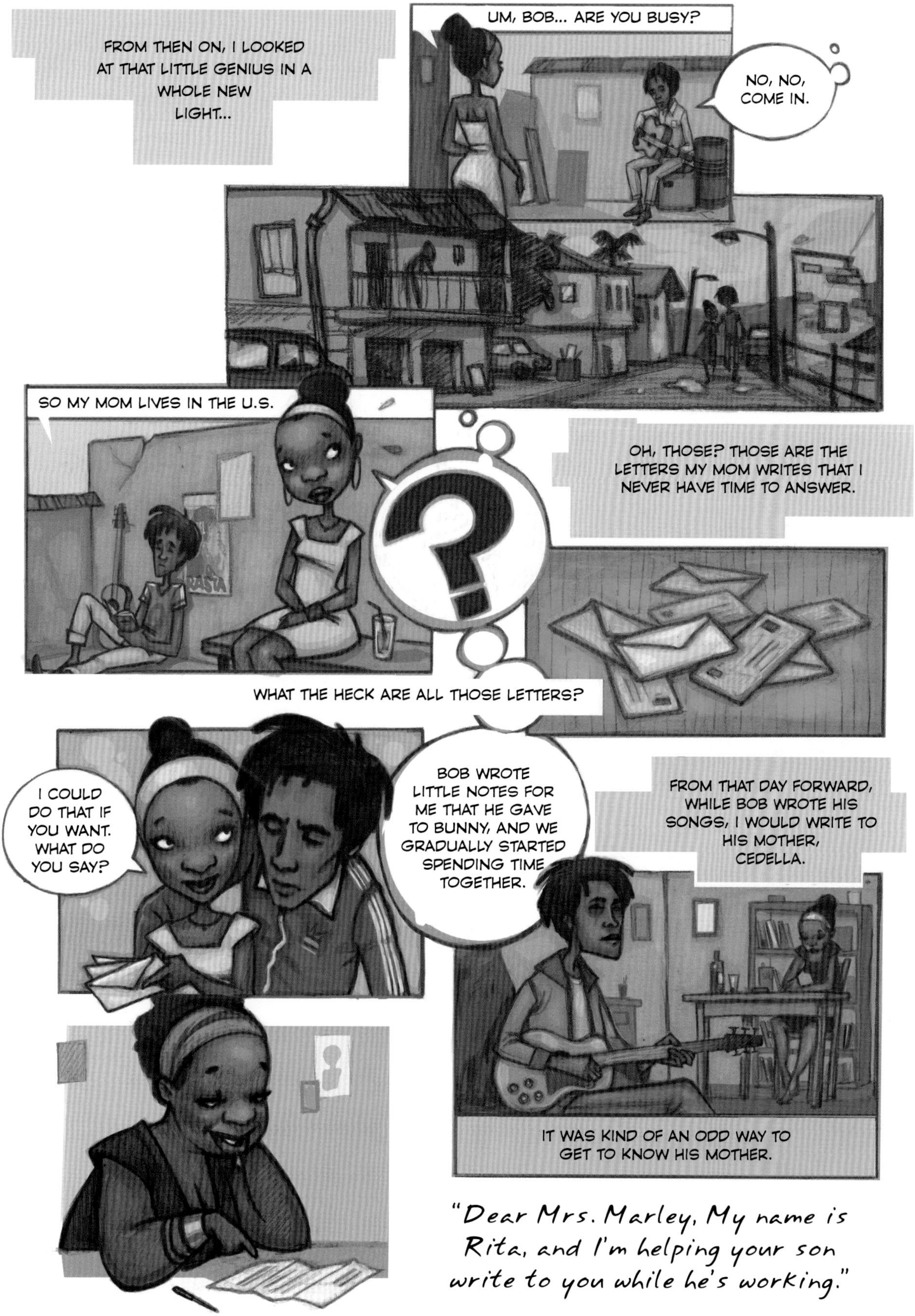

FROM THEN ON, I LOOKED AT THAT LITTLE GENIUS IN A WHOLE NEW LIGHT...
UM, BOB... ARE YOU BUSY?
NO, NO, COME IN.
SO MY MOM LIVES IN THE U.S.
RASTA
WHAT THE HECK ARE ALL THOSE LETTERS?
OH, THOSE? THOSE ARE THE LETTERS MY MOM WRITES THAT I NEVER HAVE TIME TO ANSWER.
I COULD DO THAT IF YOU WANT. WHAT DO YOU SAY?
BOB WROTE LITTLE NOTES FOR ME THAT HE GAVE TO BUNNY, AND WE GRADUALLY STARTED SPENDING TIME TOGETHER.
FROM THAT DAY FORWARD, WHILE BOB WROTE HIS SONGS, I WOULD WRITE TO HIS MOTHER, CEDELLA.
IT WAS KIND OF AN ODD WAY TO GET TO KNOW HIS MOTHER.
"Dear Mrs. Marley, My name is Rita, and I'm helping your son write to you while he's working."

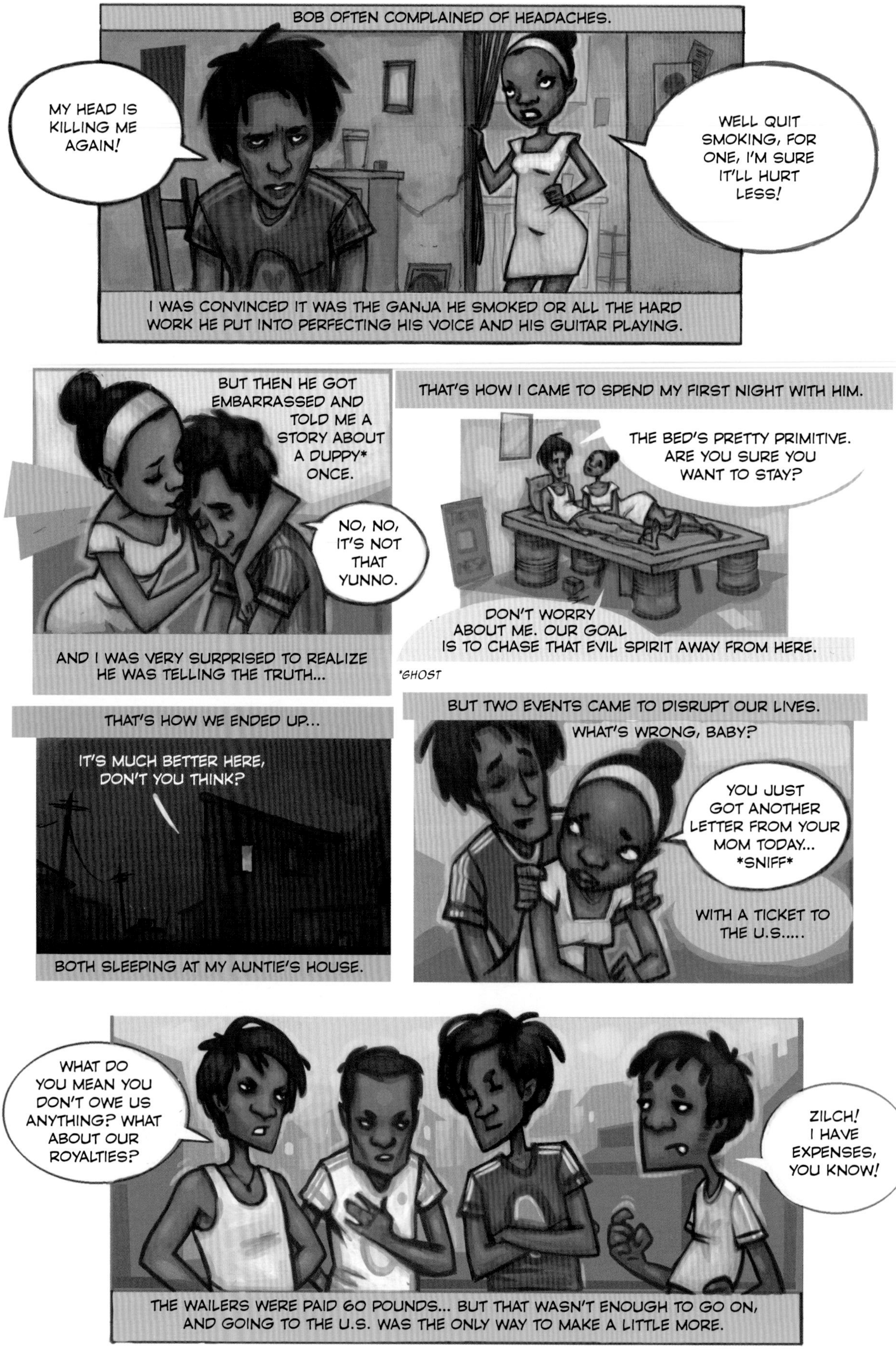

BOB OFTEN COMPLAINED OF HEADACHES.
MY HEAD IS KILLING ME AGAIN!
WELL QUIT SMOKING, FOR ONE, I'M SURE IT'LL HURT LESS!
I WAS CONVINCED IT WAS THE GANJA HE SMOKED OR ALL THE HARD WORK HE PUT INTO PERFECTING HIS VOICE AND HIS GUITAR PLAYING.
BUT THEN HE GOT EMBARRASSED AND TOLD ME A STORY ABOUT A DUPPY* ONCE.
NO, NO, IT'S NOT THAT YUNNO.
AND I WAS VERY SURPRISED TO REALIZE HE WAS TELLING THE TRUTH...
THAT'S HOW I CAME TO SPEND MY FIRST NIGHT WITH HIM.
THE BED'S PRETTY PRIMITIVE. ARE YOU SURE YOU WANT TO STAY?
DON'T WORRY ABOUT ME. OUR GOAL IS TO CHASE THAT EVIL SPIRIT AWAY FROM HERE.
*GHOST
THAT'S HOW WE ENDED UP...
IT'S MUCH BETTER HERE, DON'T YOU THINK?
BOTH SLEEPING AT MY AUNTIE'S HOUSE.
BUT TWO EVENTS CAME TO DISRUPT OUR LIVES.
WHAT'S WRONG, BABY?
YOU JUST GOT ANOTHER LETTER FROM YOUR MOM TODAY... *SNIFF*
WITH A TICKET TO THE U.S.....
WHAT DO YOU MEAN YOU DON'T OWE US ANYTHING? WHAT ABOUT OUR ROYALTIES?
ZILCH! I HAVE EXPENSES, YOU KNOW!
THE WAILERS WERE PAID 60 POUNDS... BUT THAT WASN'T ENOUGH TO GO ON, AND GOING TO THE U.S. WAS THE ONLY WAY TO MAKE A LITTLE MORE.

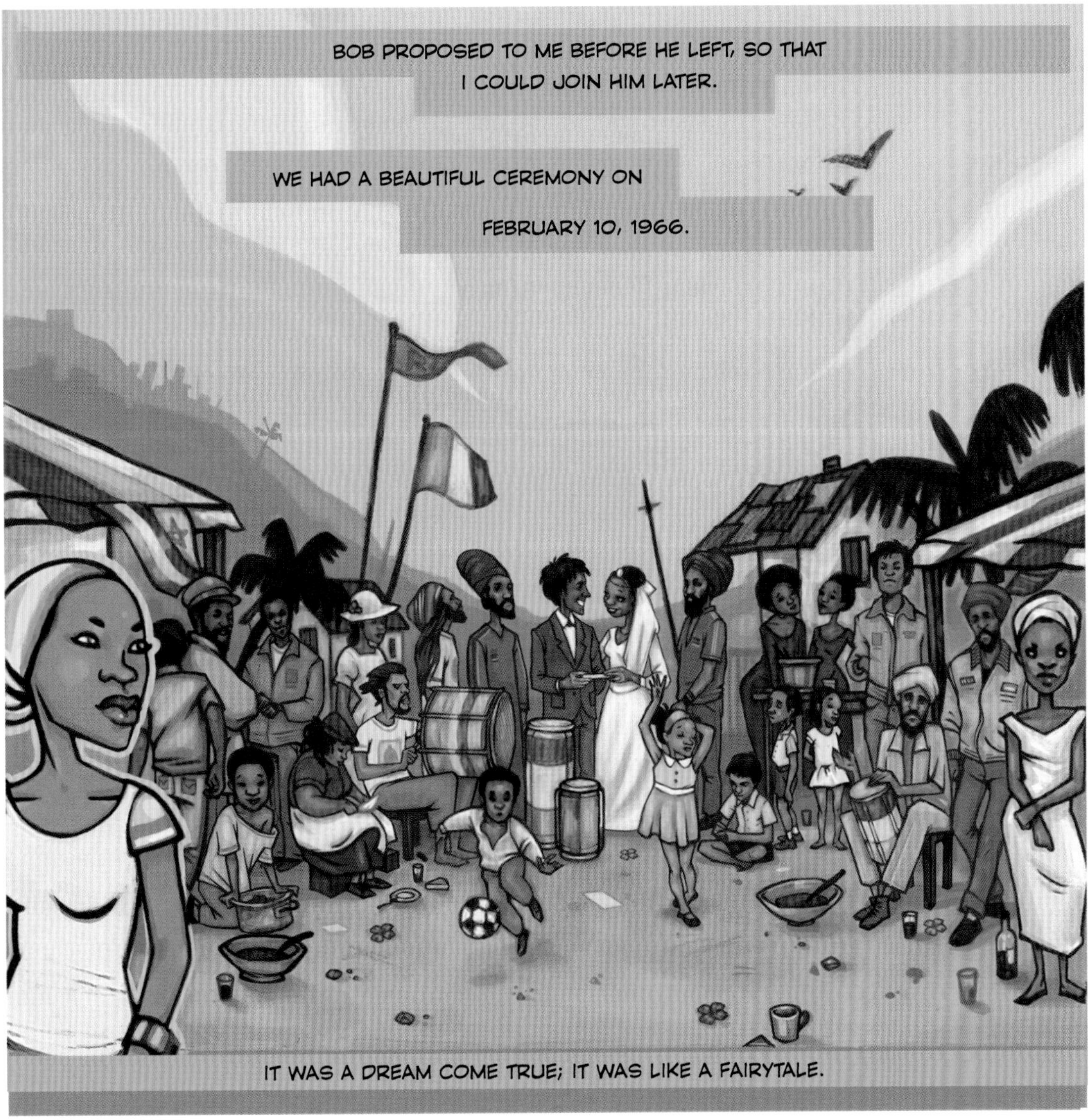
BOB PROPOSED TO ME BEFORE HE LEFT, SO THAT I COULD JOIN HIM LATER.
WE HAD A BEAUTIFUL CEREMONY ON FEBRUARY 10, 1966.
IT WAS A DREAM COME TRUE; IT WAS LIKE A FAIRYTALE.

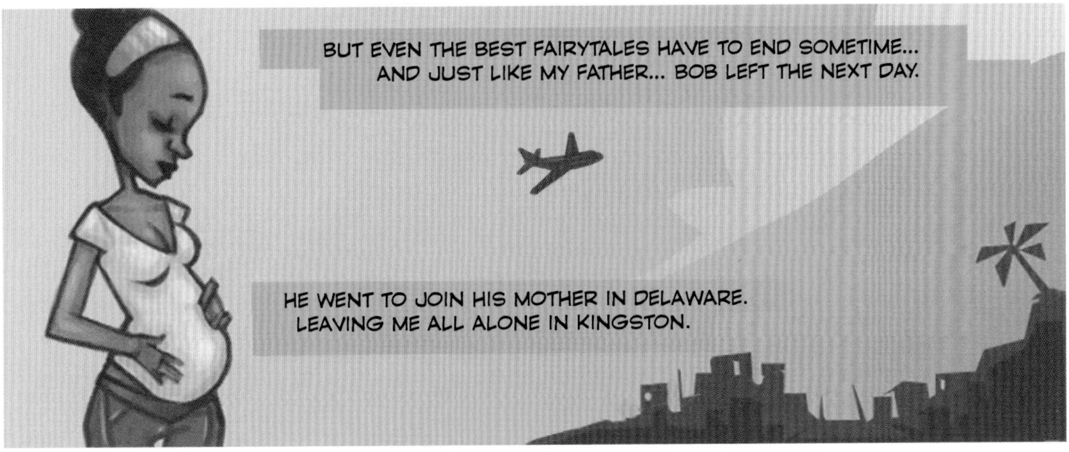
BUT EVEN THE BEST FAIRYTALES HAVE TO END SOMETIME... AND JUST LIKE MY FATHER... BOB LEFT THE NEXT DAY.
HE WENT TO JOIN HIS MOTHER IN DELAWARE. LEAVING ME ALL ALONE IN KINGSTON.

The Roots of the Rasta Movement

Artist: Efix

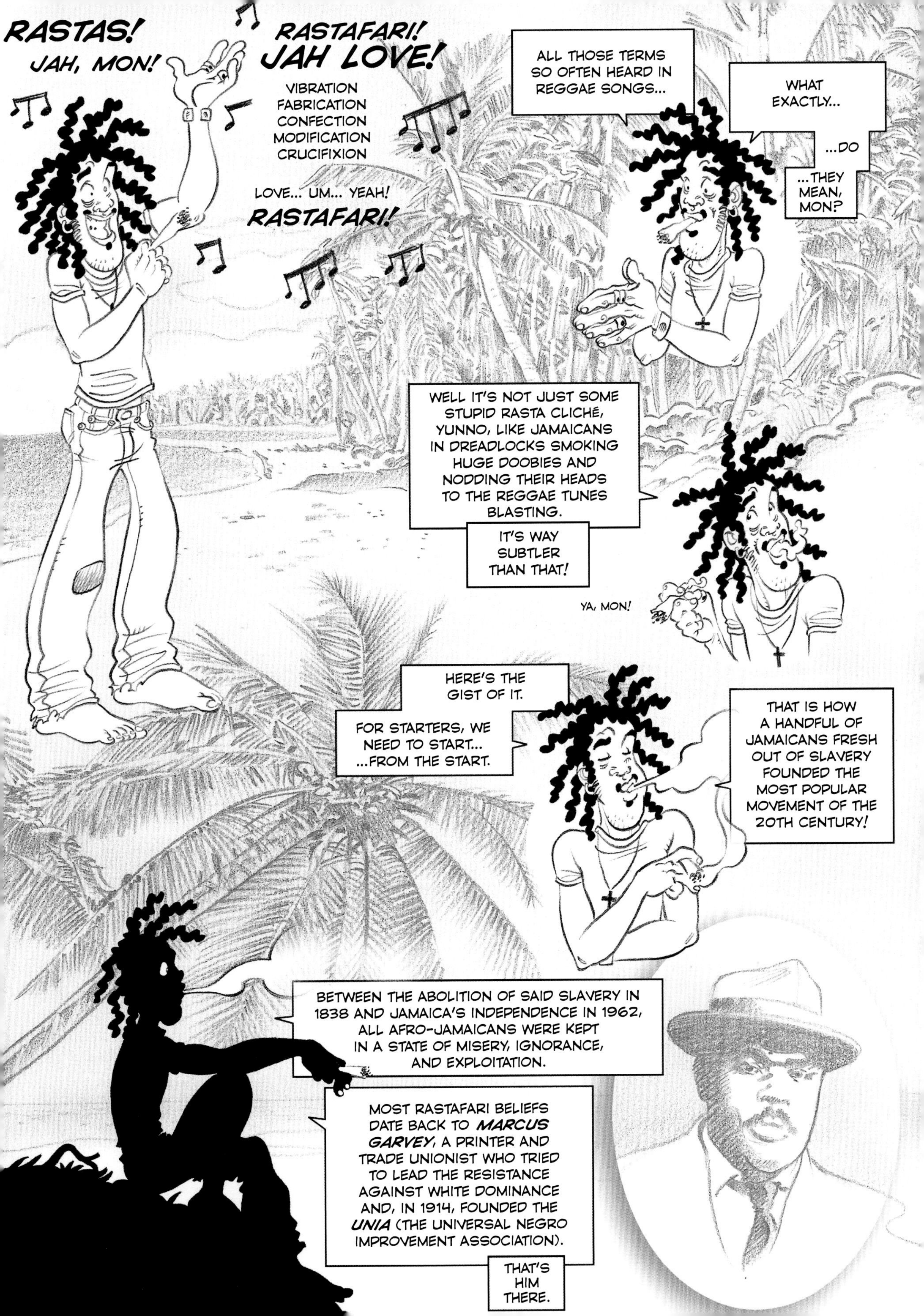

RASTAS!
JAH, MON!
RASTAFARI! JAH LOVE!
VIBRATION
FABRICATION
CONFECTION
MODIFICATION
CRUCIFIXION
LOVE... UM... YEAH!
RASTAFARI!
ALL THOSE TERMS SO OFTEN HEARD IN REGGAE SONGS...
WHAT EXACTLY...
...DO
...THEY MEAN, MON?
WELL IT'S NOT JUST SOME STUPID RASTA CLICHÉ, YUNNO, LIKE JAMAICANS IN DREADLOCKS SMOKING HUGE DOOBIES AND NODDING THEIR HEADS TO THE REGGAE TUNES BLASTING.
IT'S WAY SUBTLER THAN THAT!
YA, MON!
HERE'S THE GIST OF IT.
FOR STARTERS, WE NEED TO START... ...FROM THE START.
THAT IS HOW A HANDFUL OF JAMAICANS FRESH OUT OF SLAVERY FOUNDED THE MOST POPULAR MOVEMENT OF THE 20TH CENTURY!
BETWEEN THE ABOLITION OF SAID SLAVERY IN 1838 AND JAMAICA'S INDEPENDENCE IN 1962, ALL AFRO-JAMAICANS WERE KEPT IN A STATE OF MISERY, IGNORANCE, AND EXPLOITATION.
MOST RASTAFARI BELIEFS DATE BACK TO *MARCUS GARVEY*, A PRINTER AND TRADE UNIONIST WHO TRIED TO LEAD THE RESISTANCE AGAINST WHITE DOMINANCE AND, IN 1914, FOUNDED THE *UNIA* (THE UNIVERSAL NEGRO IMPROVEMENT ASSOCIATION).
THAT'S HIM THERE.

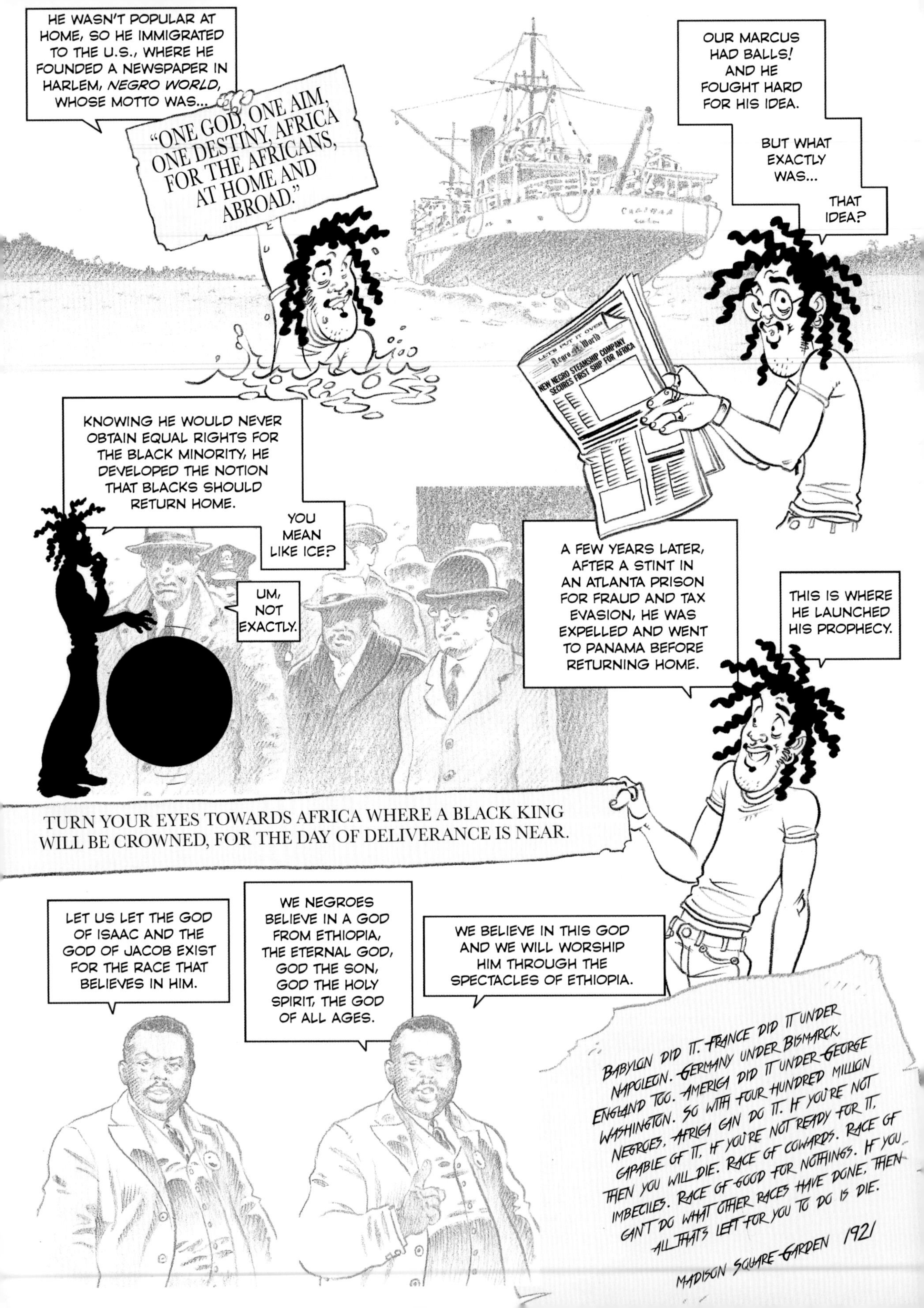
HE WASN'T POPULAR AT HOME, SO HE IMMIGRATED TO THE U.S., WHERE HE FOUNDED A NEWSPAPER IN HARLEM, *NEGRO WORLD*, WHOSE MOTTO WAS...
"ONE GOD, ONE AIM, ONE DESTINY, AFRICA FOR THE AFRICANS, AT HOME AND ABROAD."
OUR MARCUS HAD BALLS! AND HE FOUGHT HARD FOR HIS IDEA.
BUT WHAT EXACTLY WAS...
THAT IDEA?
LET'S PUT IT OVER
Negro World
NEW NEGRO STEAMSHIP COMPANY SECURES FIRST SHIP FOR AFRICA
KNOWING HE WOULD NEVER OBTAIN EQUAL RIGHTS FOR THE BLACK MINORITY, HE DEVELOPED THE NOTION THAT BLACKS SHOULD RETURN HOME.
YOU MEAN LIKE ICE?
UM, NOT EXACTLY.
A FEW YEARS LATER, AFTER A STINT IN AN ATLANTA PRISON FOR FRAUD AND TAX EVASION, HE WAS EXPELLED AND WENT TO PANAMA BEFORE RETURNING HOME.
THIS IS WHERE HE LAUNCHED HIS PROPHECY.
TURN YOUR EYES TOWARDS AFRICA WHERE A BLACK KING WILL BE CROWNED, FOR THE DAY OF DELIVERANCE IS NEAR.
LET US LET THE GOD OF ISAAC AND THE GOD OF JACOB EXIST FOR THE RACE THAT BELIEVES IN HIM.
WE NEGROES BELIEVE IN A GOD FROM ETHIOPIA, THE ETERNAL GOD, GOD THE SON, GOD THE HOLY SPIRIT, THE GOD OF ALL AGES.
WE BELIEVE IN THIS GOD AND WE WILL WORSHIP HIM THROUGH THE SPECTACLES OF ETHIOPIA.
BABYLON DID IT. FRANCE DID IT UNDER NAPOLEON. GERMANY UNDER BISMARCK. ENGLAND TOO. AMERICA DID IT UNDER GEORGE WASHINGTON. SO WITH FOUR HUNDRED MILLION NEGROES, AFRICA CAN DO IT. IF YOU'RE NOT CAPABLE OF IT, IF YOU'RE NOT READY FOR IT, THEN YOU WILL DIE. RACE OF COWARDS. RACE OF IMBECILES. RACE OF GOOD FOR NOTHINGS. IF YOU CAN'T DO WHAT OTHER RACES HAVE DONE, THEN ALL THAT'S LEFT FOR YOU TO DO IS DIE.
MADISON SQUARE GARDEN 1921

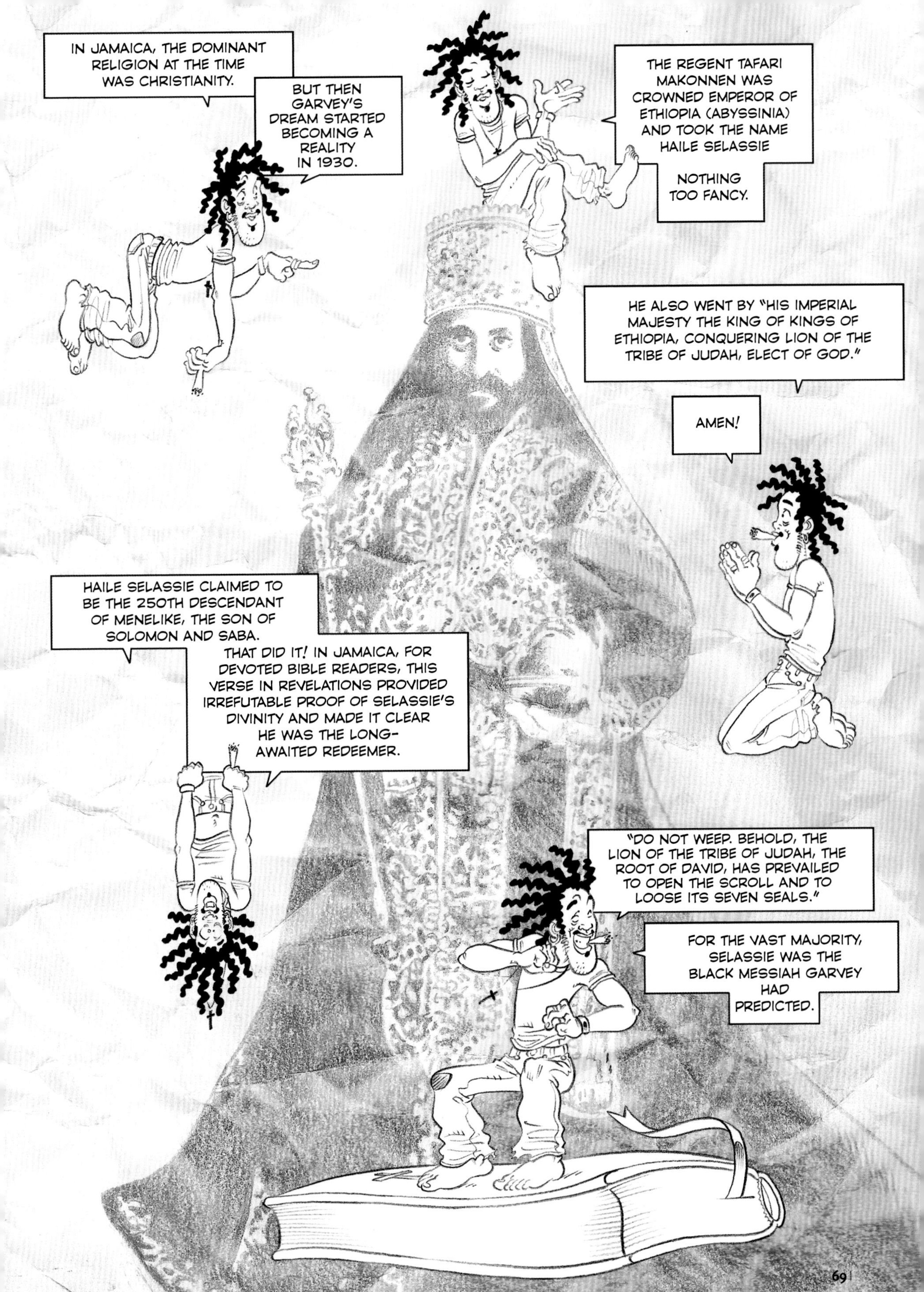
IN JAMAICA, THE DOMINANT RELIGION AT THE TIME WAS CHRISTIANITY.
BUT THEN GARVEY'S DREAM STARTED BECOMING A REALITY IN 1930.
THE REGENT TAFARI MAKONNEN WAS CROWNED EMPEROR OF ETHIOPIA (ABYSSINIA) AND TOOK THE NAME HAILE SELASSIE
NOTHING TOO FANCY.
HE ALSO WENT BY "HIS IMPERIAL MAJESTY THE KING OF KINGS OF ETHIOPIA, CONQUERING LION OF THE TRIBE OF JUDAH, ELECT OF GOD."
AMEN!
HAILE SELASSIE CLAIMED TO BE THE 250TH DESCENDANT OF MENELIKE, THE SON OF SOLOMON AND SABA.
THAT DID IT! IN JAMAICA, FOR DEVOTED BIBLE READERS, THIS VERSE IN REVELATIONS PROVIDED IRREFUTABLE PROOF OF SELASSIE'S DIVINITY AND MADE IT CLEAR HE WAS THE LONG-AWAITED REDEEMER.
"DO NOT WEEP. BEHOLD, THE LION OF THE TRIBE OF JUDAH, THE ROOT OF DAVID, HAS PREVAILED TO OPEN THE SCROLL AND TO LOOSE ITS SEVEN SEALS."
FOR THE VAST MAJORITY, SELASSIE WAS THE BLACK MESSIAH GARVEY HAD PREDICTED.

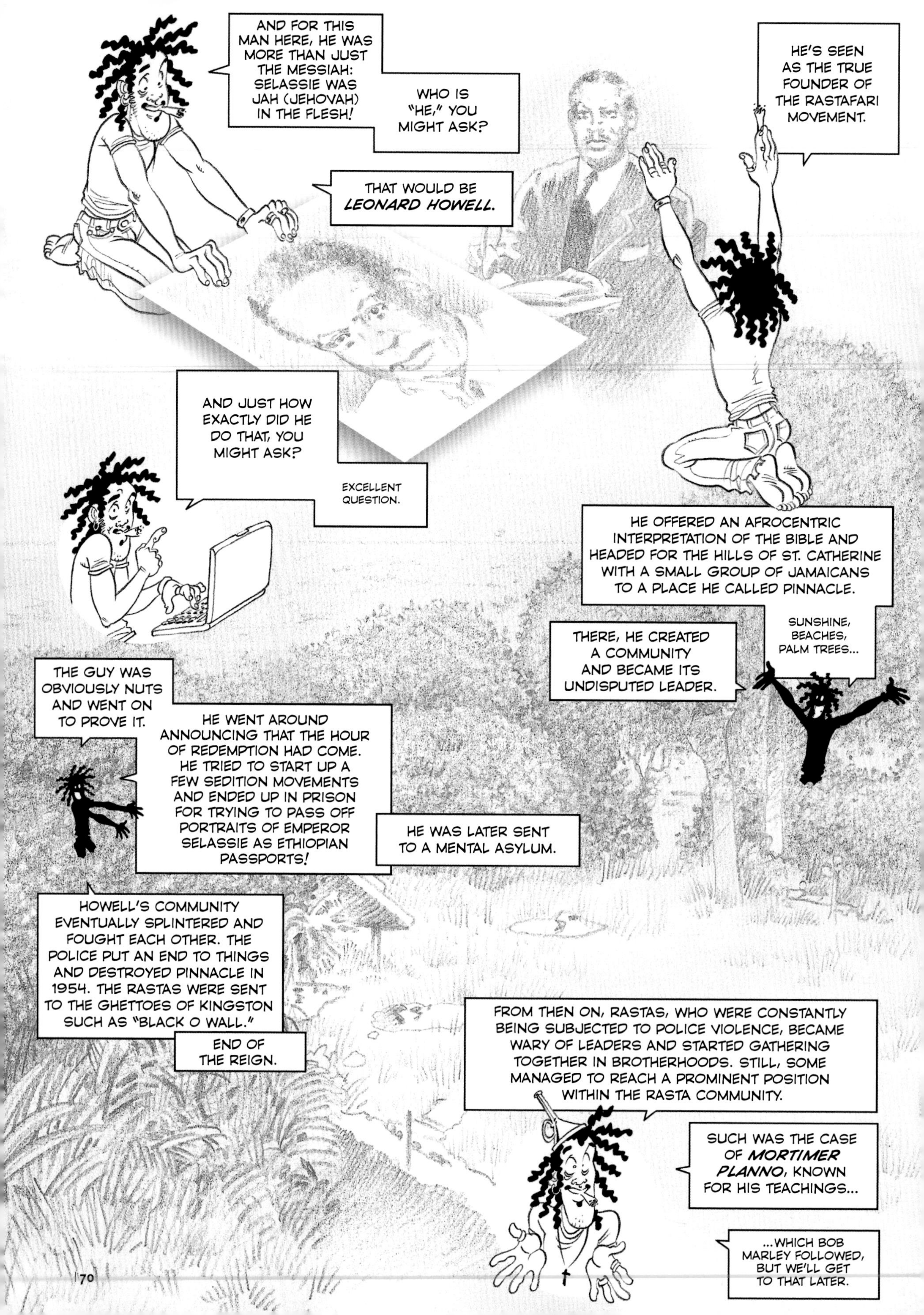
AND FOR THIS MAN HERE, HE WAS MORE THAN JUST THE MESSIAH: SELASSIE WAS JAH (JEHOVAH) IN THE FLESH!
WHO IS "HE," YOU MIGHT ASK?
THAT WOULD BE LEONARD HOWELL.
HE'S SEEN AS THE TRUE FOUNDER OF THE RASTAFARI MOVEMENT.
AND JUST HOW EXACTLY DID HE DO THAT, YOU MIGHT ASK?
EXCELLENT QUESTION.
HE OFFERED AN AFROCENTRIC INTERPRETATION OF THE BIBLE AND HEADED FOR THE HILLS OF ST. CATHERINE WITH A SMALL GROUP OF JAMAICANS TO A PLACE HE CALLED PINNACLE.
SUNSHINE, BEACHES, PALM TREES...
THERE, HE CREATED A COMMUNITY AND BECAME ITS UNDISPUTED LEADER.
THE GUY WAS OBVIOUSLY NUTS AND WENT ON TO PROVE IT.
HE WENT AROUND ANNOUNCING THAT THE HOUR OF REDEMPTION HAD COME. HE TRIED TO START UP A FEW SEDITION MOVEMENTS AND ENDED UP IN PRISON FOR TRYING TO PASS OFF PORTRAITS OF EMPEROR SELASSIE AS ETHIOPIAN PASSPORTS!
HE WAS LATER SENT TO A MENTAL ASYLUM.
HOWELL'S COMMUNITY EVENTUALLY SPLINTERED AND FOUGHT EACH OTHER. THE POLICE PUT AN END TO THINGS AND DESTROYED PINNACLE IN 1954. THE RASTAS WERE SENT TO THE GHETTOES OF KINGSTON SUCH AS "BLACK O WALL."
END OF THE REIGN.
FROM THEN ON, RASTAS, WHO WERE CONSTANTLY BEING SUBJECTED TO POLICE VIOLENCE, BECAME WARY OF LEADERS AND STARTED GATHERING TOGETHER IN BROTHERHOODS. STILL, SOME MANAGED TO REACH A PROMINENT POSITION WITHIN THE RASTA COMMUNITY.
SUCH WAS THE CASE OF MORTIMER PLANNO, KNOWN FOR HIS TEACHINGS...
...WHICH BOB MARLEY FOLLOWED, BUT WE'LL GET TO THAT LATER.

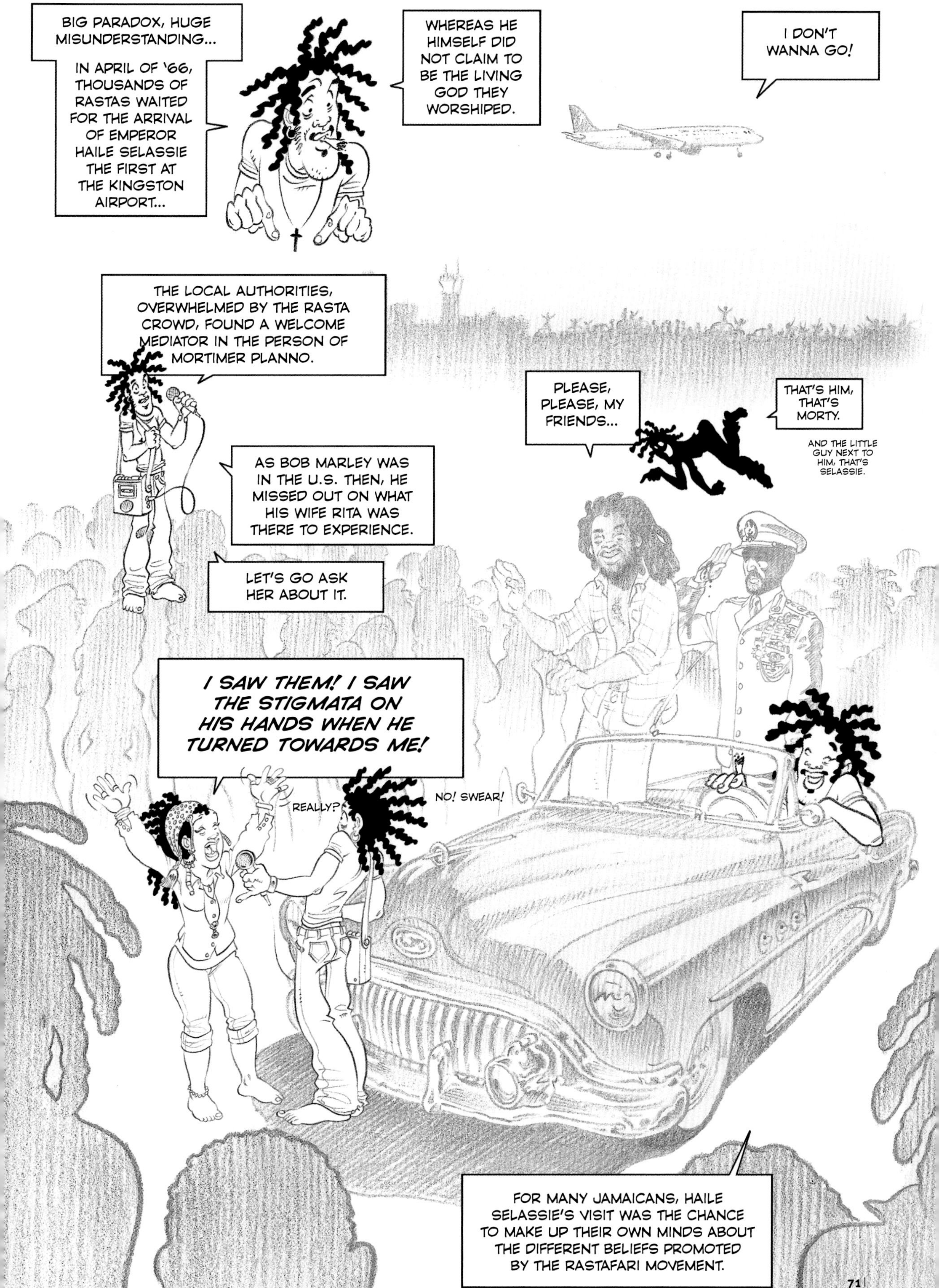

BIG PARADOX, HUGE MISUNDERSTANDING...
IN APRIL OF '66, THOUSANDS OF RASTAS WAITED FOR THE ARRIVAL OF EMPEROR HAILE SELASSIE THE FIRST AT THE KINGSTON AIRPORT...
WHEREAS HE HIMSELF DID NOT CLAIM TO BE THE LIVING GOD THEY WORSHIPED.
I DON'T WANNA GO!
THE LOCAL AUTHORITIES, OVERWHELMED BY THE RASTA CROWD, FOUND A WELCOME MEDIATOR IN THE PERSON OF MORTIMER PLANNO.
PLEASE, PLEASE, MY FRIENDS...
THAT'S HIM, THAT'S MORTY.
AND THE LITTLE GUY NEXT TO HIM, THAT'S SELASSIE.
AS BOB MARLEY WAS IN THE U.S. THEN, HE MISSED OUT ON WHAT HIS WIFE RITA WAS THERE TO EXPERIENCE.
LET'S GO ASK HER ABOUT IT.
I SAW THEM! I SAW THE STIGMATA ON HIS HANDS WHEN HE TURNED TOWARDS ME!
REALLY?
NO! SWEAR!
FOR MANY JAMAICANS, HAILE SELASSIE'S VISIT WAS THE CHANCE TO MAKE UP THEIR OWN MINDS ABOUT THE DIFFERENT BELIEFS PROMOTED BY THE RASTAFARI MOVEMENT.

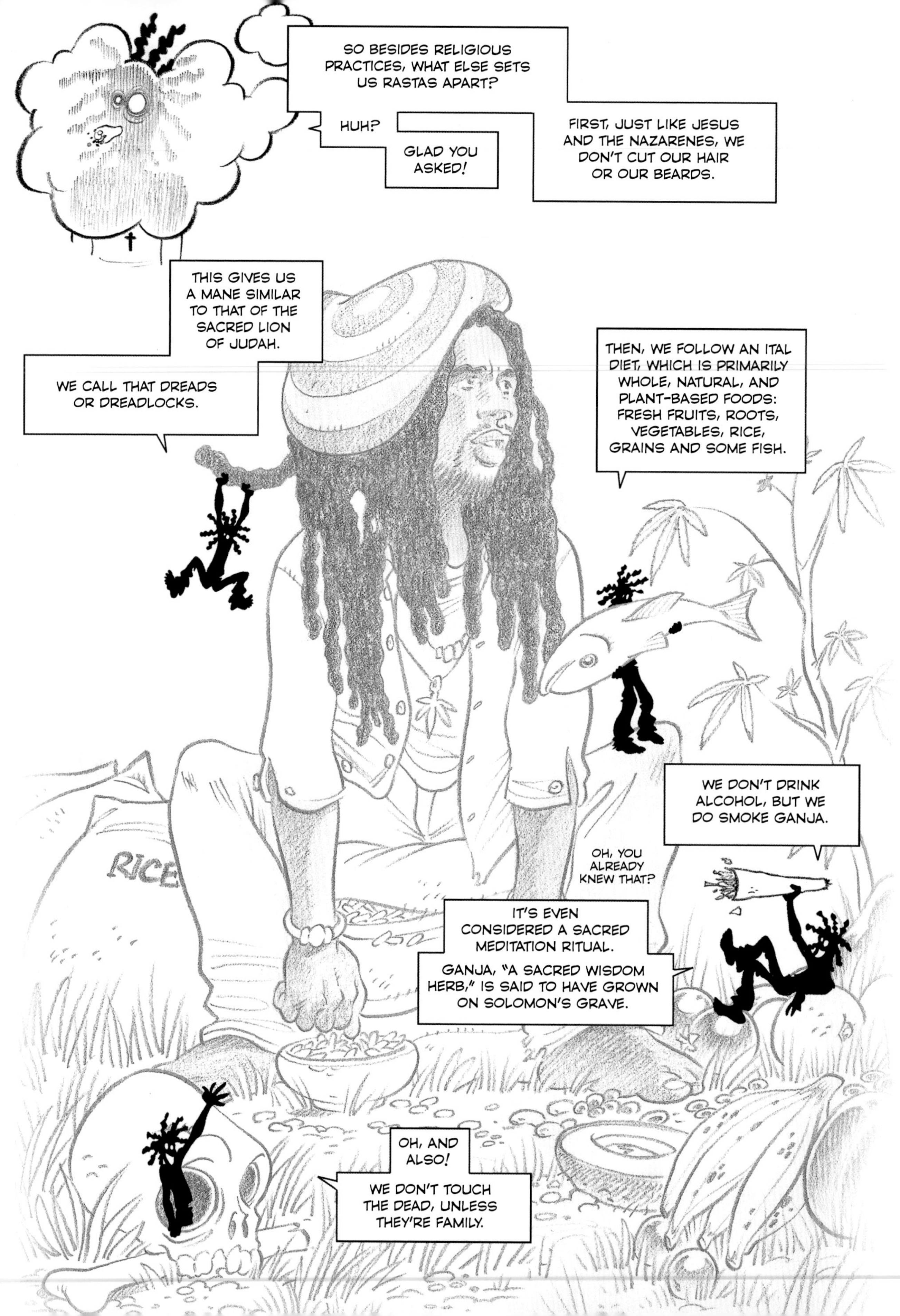

SO BESIDES RELIGIOUS PRACTICES, WHAT ELSE SETS US RASTAS APART?
HUH?
GLAD YOU ASKED!
FIRST, JUST LIKE JESUS AND THE NAZARENES, WE DON'T CUT OUR HAIR OR OUR BEARDS.
THIS GIVES US A MANE SIMILAR TO THAT OF THE SACRED LION OF JUDAH.
WE CALL THAT DREADS OR DREADLOCKS.
THEN, WE FOLLOW AN ITAL DIET, WHICH IS PRIMARILY WHOLE, NATURAL, AND PLANT-BASED FOODS: FRESH FRUITS, ROOTS, VEGETABLES, RICE, GRAINS AND SOME FISH.
RICE
WE DON'T DRINK ALCOHOL, BUT WE DO SMOKE GANJA.
OH, YOU ALREADY KNEW THAT?
IT'S EVEN CONSIDERED A SACRED MEDITATION RITUAL.
GANJA, "A SACRED WISDOM HERB," IS SAID TO HAVE GROWN ON SOLOMON'S GRAVE.
OH, AND ALSO!
WE DON'T TOUCH THE DEAD, UNLESS THEY'RE FAMILY.

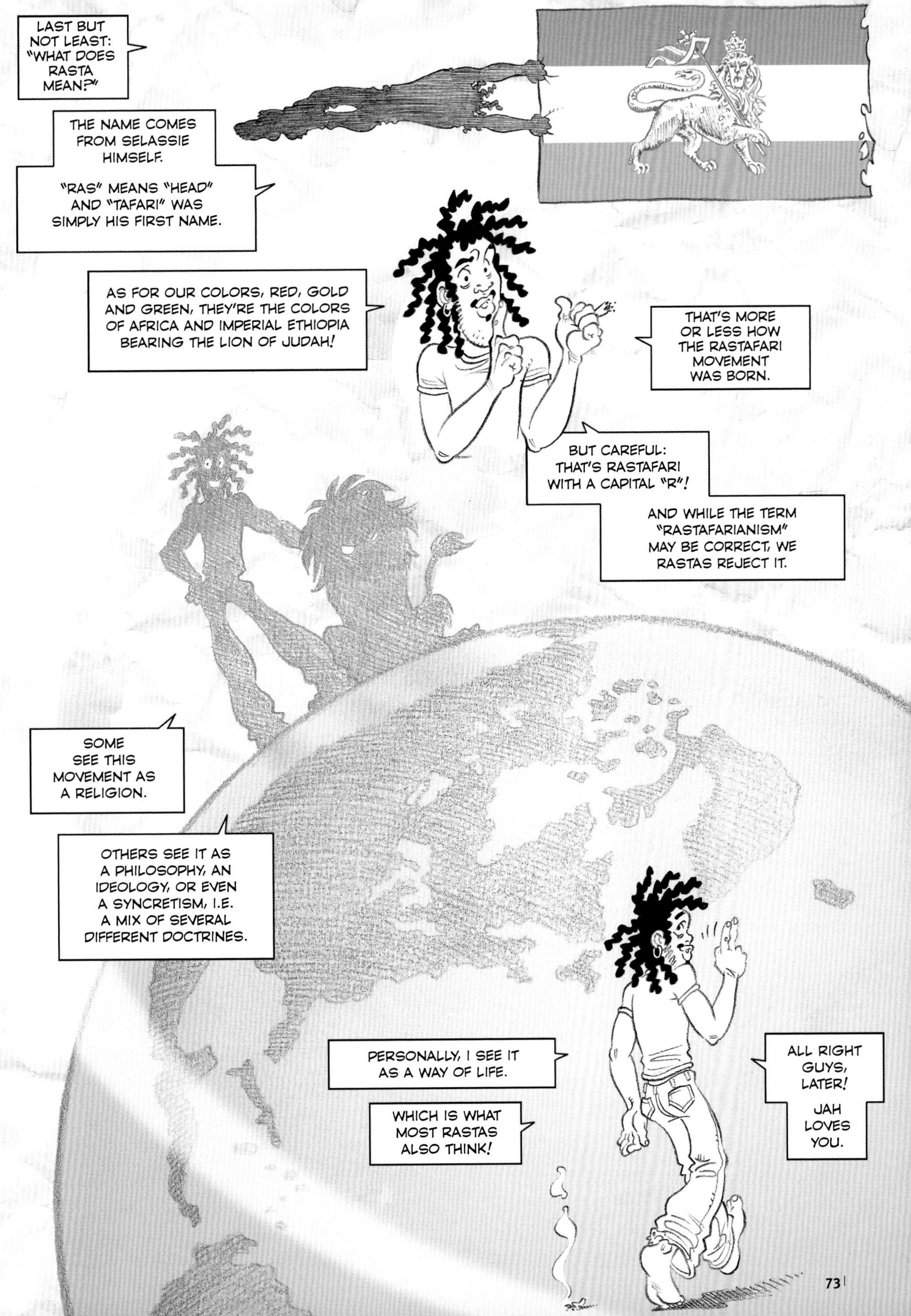
LAST BUT NOT LEAST: "WHAT DOES RASTA MEAN?"
THE NAME COMES FROM SELASSIE HIMSELF.
"RAS" MEANS "HEAD" AND "TAFARI" WAS SIMPLY HIS FIRST NAME.
AS FOR OUR COLORS, RED, GOLD AND GREEN, THEY'RE THE COLORS OF AFRICA AND IMPERIAL ETHIOPIA BEARING THE LION OF JUDAH!
THAT'S MORE OR LESS HOW THE RASTAFARI MOVEMENT WAS BORN.
BUT CAREFUL: THAT'S RASTAFARI WITH A CAPITAL "R"!
AND WHILE THE TERM "RASTAFARIANISM" MAY BE CORRECT, WE RASTAS REJECT IT.
SOME SEE THIS MOVEMENT AS A RELIGION.
OTHERS SEE IT AS A PHILOSOPHY, AN IDEOLOGY, OR EVEN A SYNCRETISM, I.E. A MIX OF SEVERAL DIFFERENT DOCTRINES.
PERSONALLY, I SEE IT AS A WAY OF LIFE.
WHICH IS WHAT MOST RASTAS ALSO THINK!
ALL RIGHT GUYS, LATER!
JAH LOVES YOU.

Tuff Gong in Nine Miles

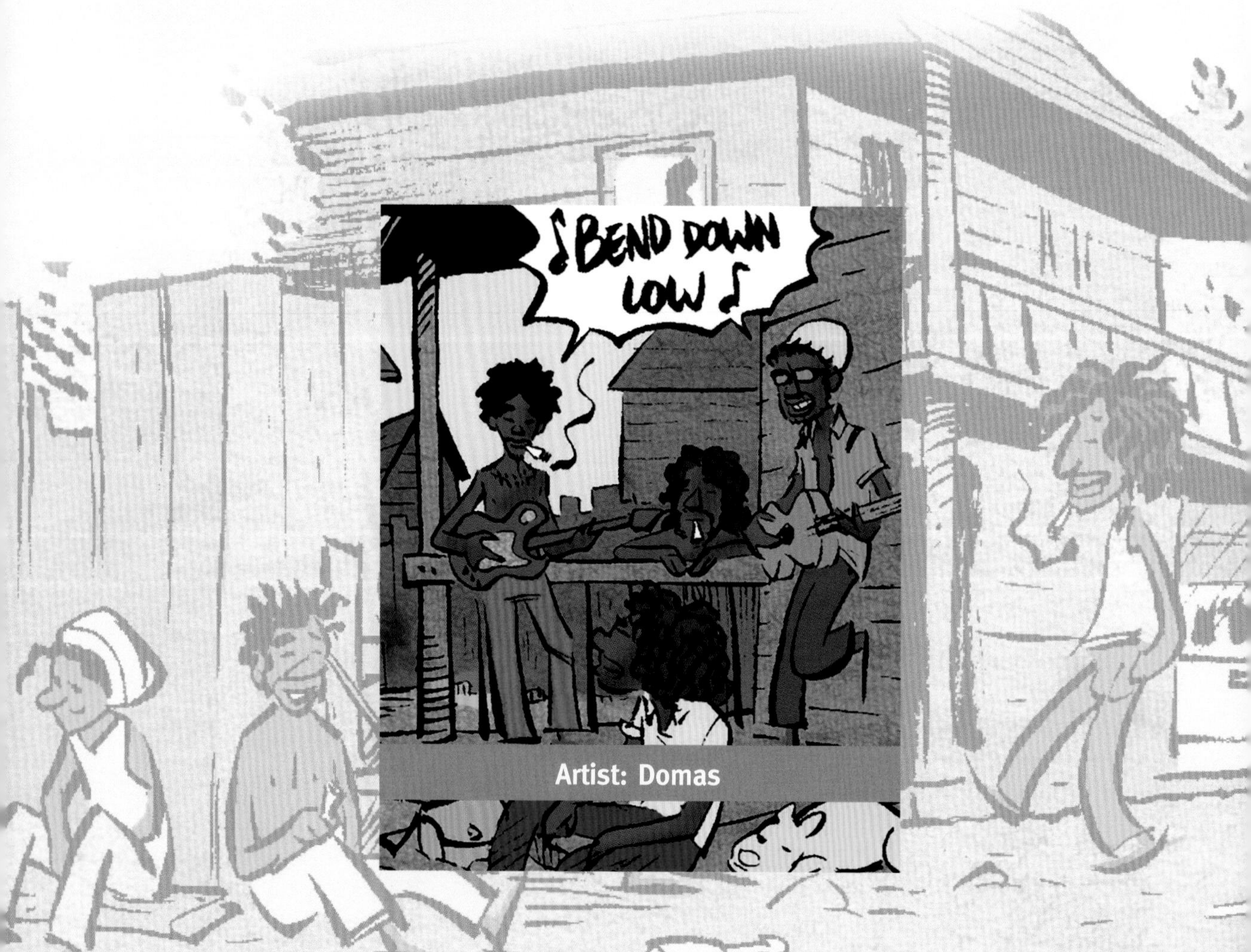

BEND DOWN LOW

Artist: Domas

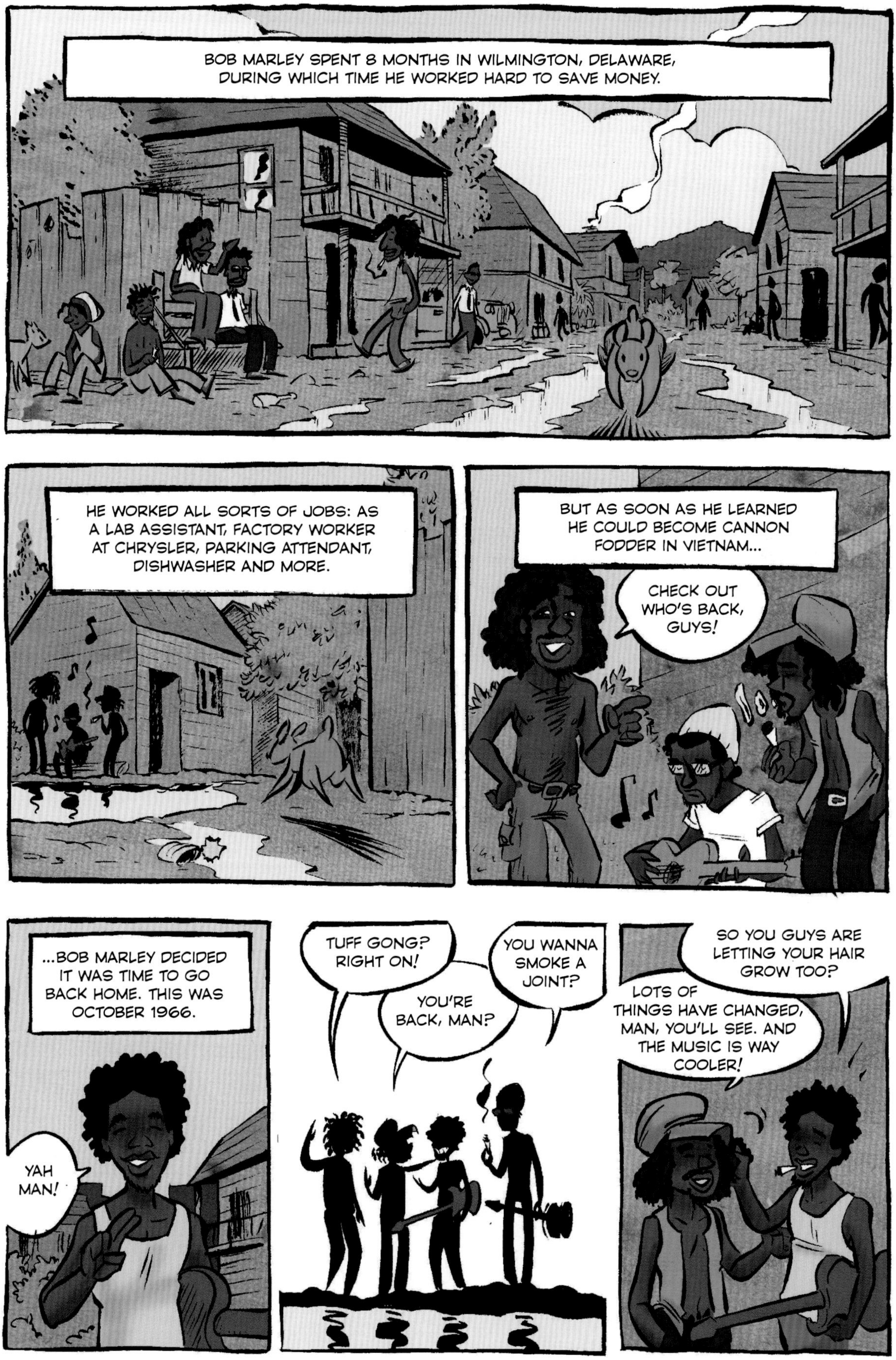
BOB MARLEY SPENT 8 MONTHS IN WILMINGTON, DELAWARE, DURING WHICH TIME HE WORKED HARD TO SAVE MONEY.
HE WORKED ALL SORTS OF JOBS: AS A LAB ASSISTANT, FACTORY WORKER AT CHRYSLER, PARKING ATTENDANT, DISHWASHER AND MORE.
BUT AS SOON AS HE LEARNED HE COULD BECOME CANNON FODDER IN VIETNAM...
CHECK OUT WHO'S BACK, GUYS!
...BOB MARLEY DECIDED IT WAS TIME TO GO BACK HOME. THIS WAS OCTOBER 1966.
YAH MAN!
TUFF GONG? RIGHT ON!
YOU'RE BACK, MAN?
YOU WANNA SMOKE A JOINT?
SO YOU GUYS ARE LETTING YOUR HAIR GROW TOO?
LOTS OF THINGS HAVE CHANGED, MAN, YOU'LL SEE. AND THE MUSIC IS WAY COOLER!

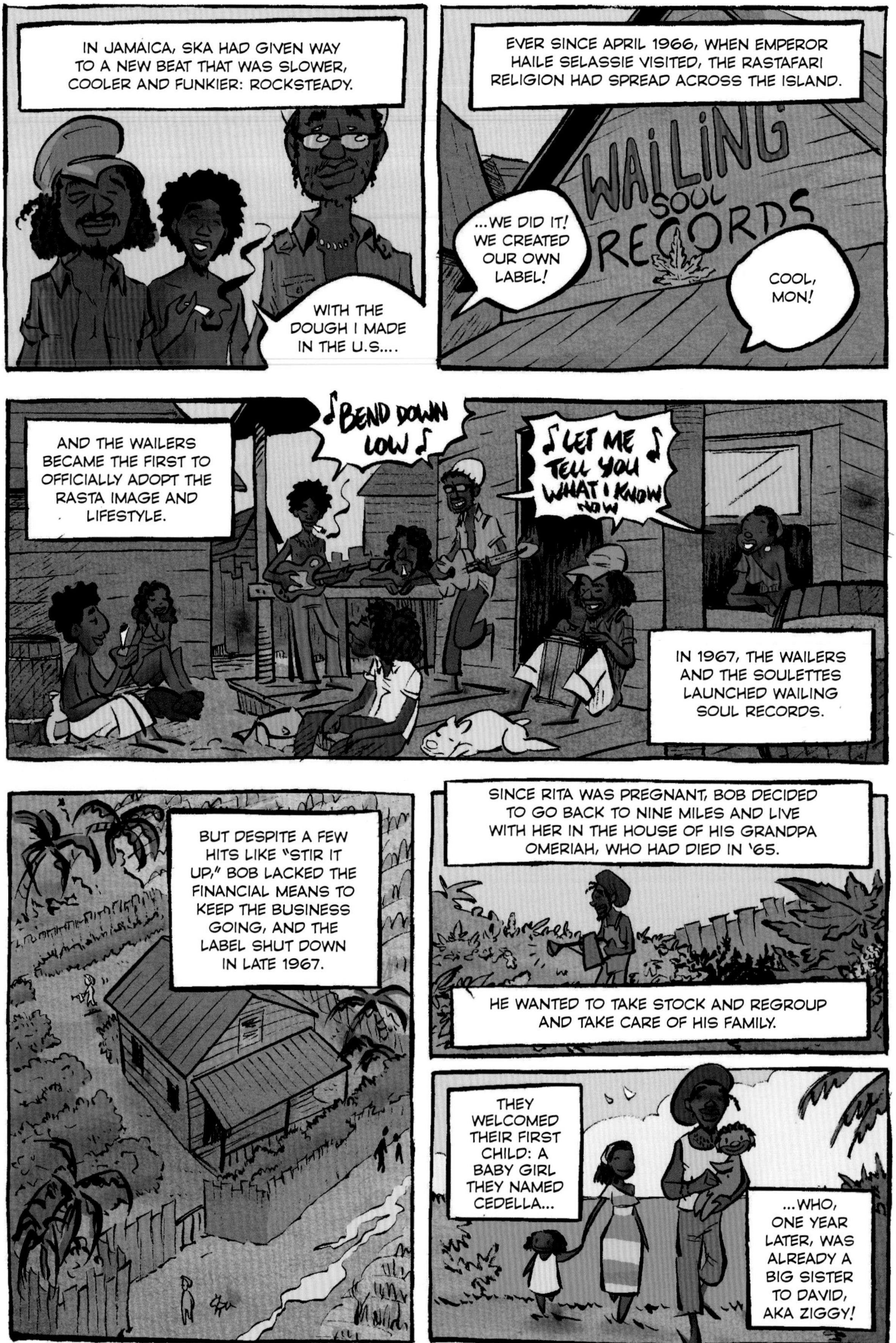
IN JAMAICA, SKA HAD GIVEN WAY TO A NEW BEAT THAT WAS SLOWER, COOLER AND FUNKIER: ROCKSTEADY.
WITH THE DOUGH I MADE IN THE U.S....
EVER SINCE APRIL 1966, WHEN EMPEROR HAILE SELASSIE VISITED, THE RASTAFARI RELIGION HAD SPREAD ACROSS THE ISLAND.
WAILING SOUL RECORDS
...WE DID IT! WE CREATED OUR OWN LABEL!
COOL, MON!
AND THE WAILERS BECAME THE FIRST TO OFFICIALLY ADOPT THE RASTA IMAGE AND LIFESTYLE.
♪BEND DOWN LOW♪
♪LET ME TELL YOU WHAT I KNOW NOW♪
IN 1967, THE WAILERS AND THE SOULETTES LAUNCHED WAILING SOUL RECORDS.
BUT DESPITE A FEW HITS LIKE "STIR IT UP," BOB LACKED THE FINANCIAL MEANS TO KEEP THE BUSINESS GOING, AND THE LABEL SHUT DOWN IN LATE 1967.
SINCE RITA WAS PREGNANT, BOB DECIDED TO GO BACK TO NINE MILES AND LIVE WITH HER IN THE HOUSE OF HIS GRANDPA OMERIAH, WHO HAD DIED IN '65.
HE WANTED TO TAKE STOCK AND REGROUP AND TAKE CARE OF HIS FAMILY.
THEY WELCOMED THEIR FIRST CHILD: A BABY GIRL THEY NAMED CEDELLA...
...WHO, ONE YEAR LATER, WAS ALREADY A BIG SISTER TO DAVID, AKA ZIGGY!

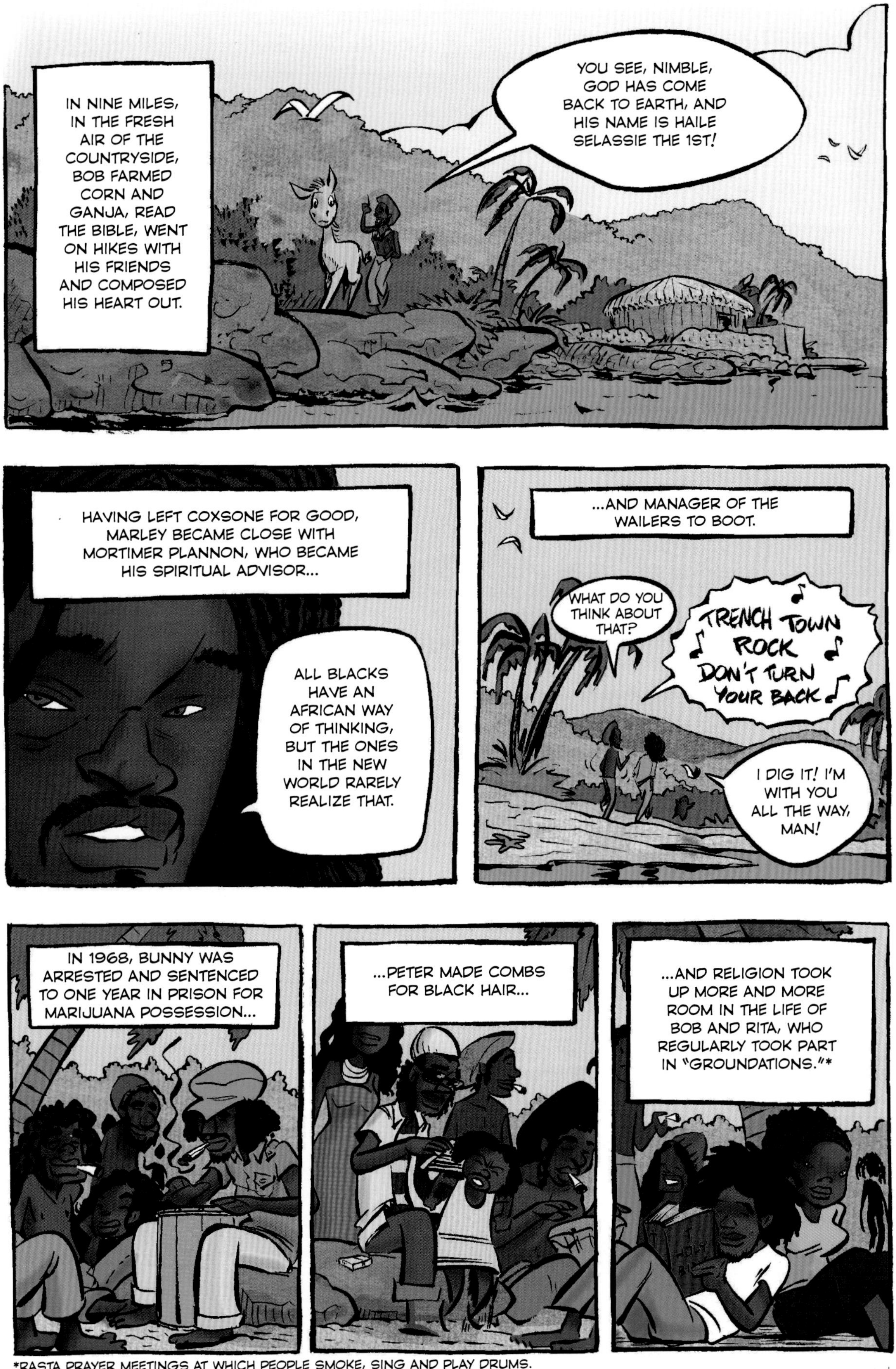
IN NINE MILES, IN THE FRESH AIR OF THE COUNTRYSIDE, BOB FARMED CORN AND GANJA, READ THE BIBLE, WENT ON HIKES WITH HIS FRIENDS AND COMPOSED HIS HEART OUT.
YOU SEE, NIMBLE, GOD HAS COME BACK TO EARTH, AND HIS NAME IS HAILE SELASSIE THE 1ST!
HAVING LEFT COXSONE FOR GOOD, MARLEY BECAME CLOSE WITH MORTIMER PLANNON, WHO BECAME HIS SPIRITUAL ADVISOR...
ALL BLACKS HAVE AN AFRICAN WAY OF THINKING, BUT THE ONES IN THE NEW WORLD RARELY REALIZE THAT.
...AND MANAGER OF THE WAILERS TO BOOT.
WHAT DO YOU THINK ABOUT THAT?
TRENCH TOWN ROCK DON'T TURN YOUR BACK
I DIG IT! I'M WITH YOU ALL THE WAY, MAN!
IN 1968, BUNNY WAS ARRESTED AND SENTENCED TO ONE YEAR IN PRISON FOR MARIJUANA POSSESSION...
...PETER MADE COMBS FOR BLACK HAIR...
...AND RELIGION TOOK UP MORE AND MORE ROOM IN THE LIFE OF BOB AND RITA, WHO REGULARLY TOOK PART IN "GROUNDATIONS."*

*RASTA PRAYER MEETINGS AT WHICH PEOPLE SMOKE, SING AND PLAY DRUMS.

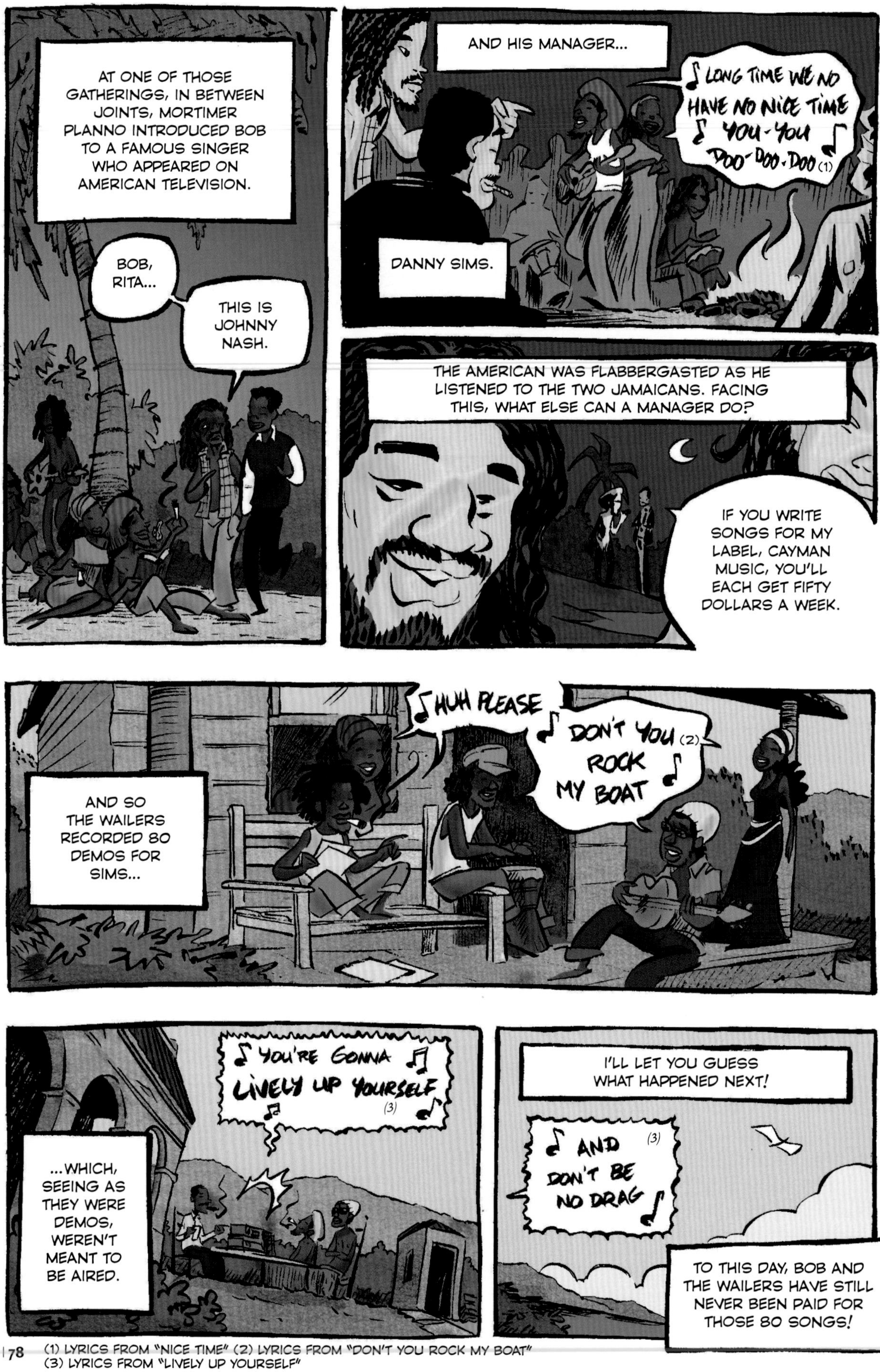
AT ONE OF THOSE GATHERINGS, IN BETWEEN JOINTS, MORTIMER PLANNO INTRODUCED BOB TO A FAMOUS SINGER WHO APPEARED ON AMERICAN TELEVISION.
BOB, RITA...
THIS IS JOHNNY NASH.
AND HIS MANAGER...
♪ LONG TIME WE NO HAVE NO NICE TIME ♪ YOU-YOU ♪ DOO-DOO-DOO (1)
DANNY SIMS.
THE AMERICAN WAS FLABBERGASTED AS HE LISTENED TO THE TWO JAMAICANS. FACING THIS, WHAT ELSE CAN A MANAGER DO?
IF YOU WRITE SONGS FOR MY LABEL, CAYMAN MUSIC, YOU'LL EACH GET FIFTY DOLLARS A WEEK.
AND SO THE WAILERS RECORDED 80 DEMOS FOR SIMS...
♪ HUH PLEASE
♪ DON'T YOU (2) ROCK MY BOAT ♪
...WHICH, SEEING AS THEY WERE DEMOS, WEREN'T MEANT TO BE AIRED.
♪ YOU'RE GONNA ♫ LIVELY UP YOURSELF (3) ♪ ♫
I'LL LET YOU GUESS WHAT HAPPENED NEXT!
♪ AND (3) DON'T BE NO DRAG ♪
TO THIS DAY, BOB AND THE WAILERS HAVE STILL NEVER BEEN PAID FOR THOSE 80 SONGS!

(1) LYRICS FROM "NICE TIME" (2) LYRICS FROM "DON'T YOU ROCK MY BOAT"
(3) LYRICS FROM "LIVELY UP YOURSELF"

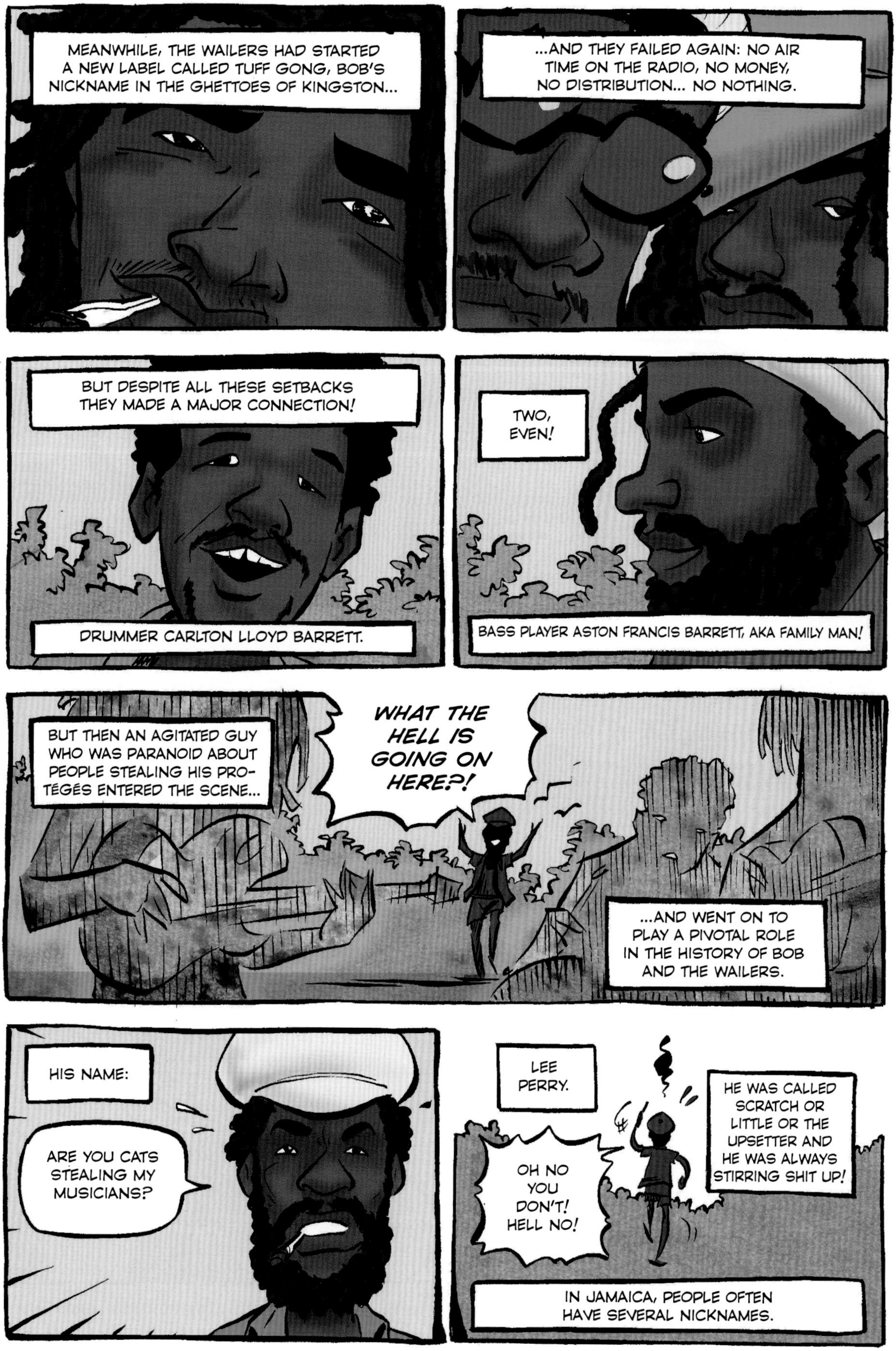
MEANWHILE, THE WAILERS HAD STARTED A NEW LABEL CALLED TUFF GONG, BOB'S NICKNAME IN THE GHETTOES OF KINGSTON...
...AND THEY FAILED AGAIN: NO AIR TIME ON THE RADIO, NO MONEY, NO DISTRIBUTION... NO NOTHING.
BUT DESPITE ALL THESE SETBACKS THEY MADE A MAJOR CONNECTION!
DRUMMER CARLTON LLOYD BARRETT.
TWO, EVEN!
BASS PLAYER ASTON FRANCIS BARRETT, AKA FAMILY MAN!
BUT THEN AN AGITATED GUY WHO WAS PARANOID ABOUT PEOPLE STEALING HIS PROTÉGÉS ENTERED THE SCENE...
WHAT THE HELL IS GOING ON HERE?!
...AND WENT ON TO PLAY A PIVOTAL ROLE IN THE HISTORY OF BOB AND THE WAILERS.
HIS NAME:
ARE YOU CATS STEALING MY MUSICIANS?
LEE PERRY.
HE WAS CALLED SCRATCH OR LITTLE OR THE UPSETTER AND HE WAS ALWAYS STIRRING SHIT UP!
OH NO YOU DON'T! HELL NO!
IN JAMAICA, PEOPLE OFTEN HAVE SEVERAL NICKNAMES.

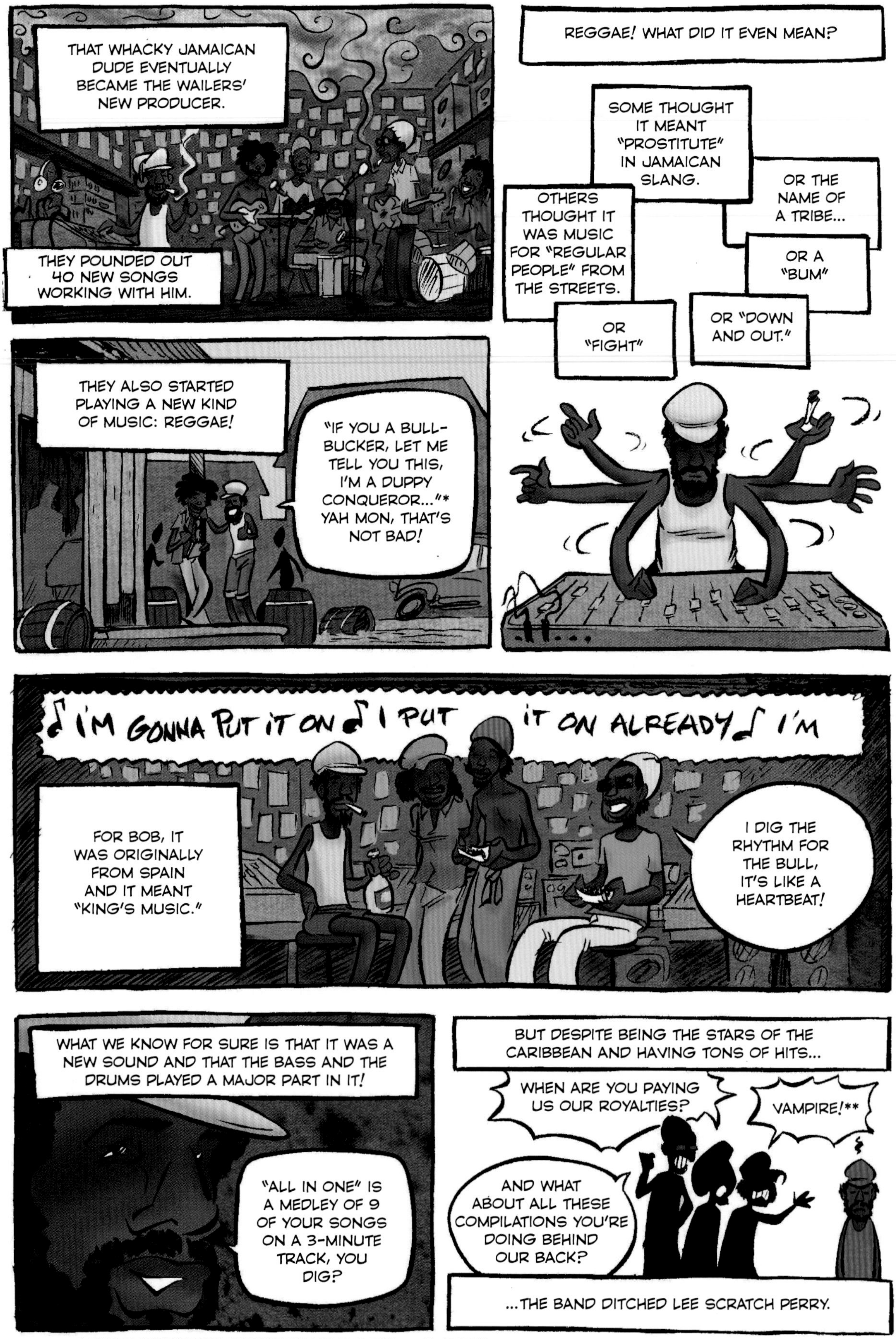
THAT WHACKY JAMAICAN DUDE EVENTUALLY BECAME THE WAILERS' NEW PRODUCER.
THEY POUNDED OUT 40 NEW SONGS WORKING WITH HIM.
REGGAE! WHAT DID IT EVEN MEAN?
SOME THOUGHT IT MEANT "PROSTITUTE" IN JAMAICAN SLANG.
OR THE NAME OF A TRIBE...
OTHERS THOUGHT IT WAS MUSIC FOR "REGULAR PEOPLE" FROM THE STREETS.
OR A "BUM"
OR "FIGHT"
OR "DOWN AND OUT."
THEY ALSO STARTED PLAYING A NEW KIND OF MUSIC: REGGAE!
"IF YOU A BULL-BUCKER, LET ME TELL YOU THIS, I'M A DUPPY CONQUEROR..."* YAH MON, THAT'S NOT BAD!
I'M GONNA PUT IT ON I PUT IT ON ALREADY I'M
FOR BOB, IT WAS ORIGINALLY FROM SPAIN AND IT MEANT "KING'S MUSIC."
I DIG THE RHYTHM FOR THE BULL, IT'S LIKE A HEARTBEAT!
WHAT WE KNOW FOR SURE IS THAT IT WAS A NEW SOUND AND THAT THE BASS AND THE DRUMS PLAYED A MAJOR PART IN IT!
"ALL IN ONE" IS A MEDLEY OF 9 OF YOUR SONGS ON A 3-MINUTE TRACK, YOU DIG?
BUT DESPITE BEING THE STARS OF THE CARIBBEAN AND HAVING TONS OF HITS...
WHEN ARE YOU PAYING US OUR ROYALTIES?
VAMPIRE!**
AND WHAT ABOUT ALL THESE COMPILATIONS YOU'RE DOING BEHIND OUR BACK?
...THE BAND DITCHED LEE SCRATCH PERRY.

* DUPPY CONQUEROR, WRITTEN BY LEE AND BOB ** CROOK

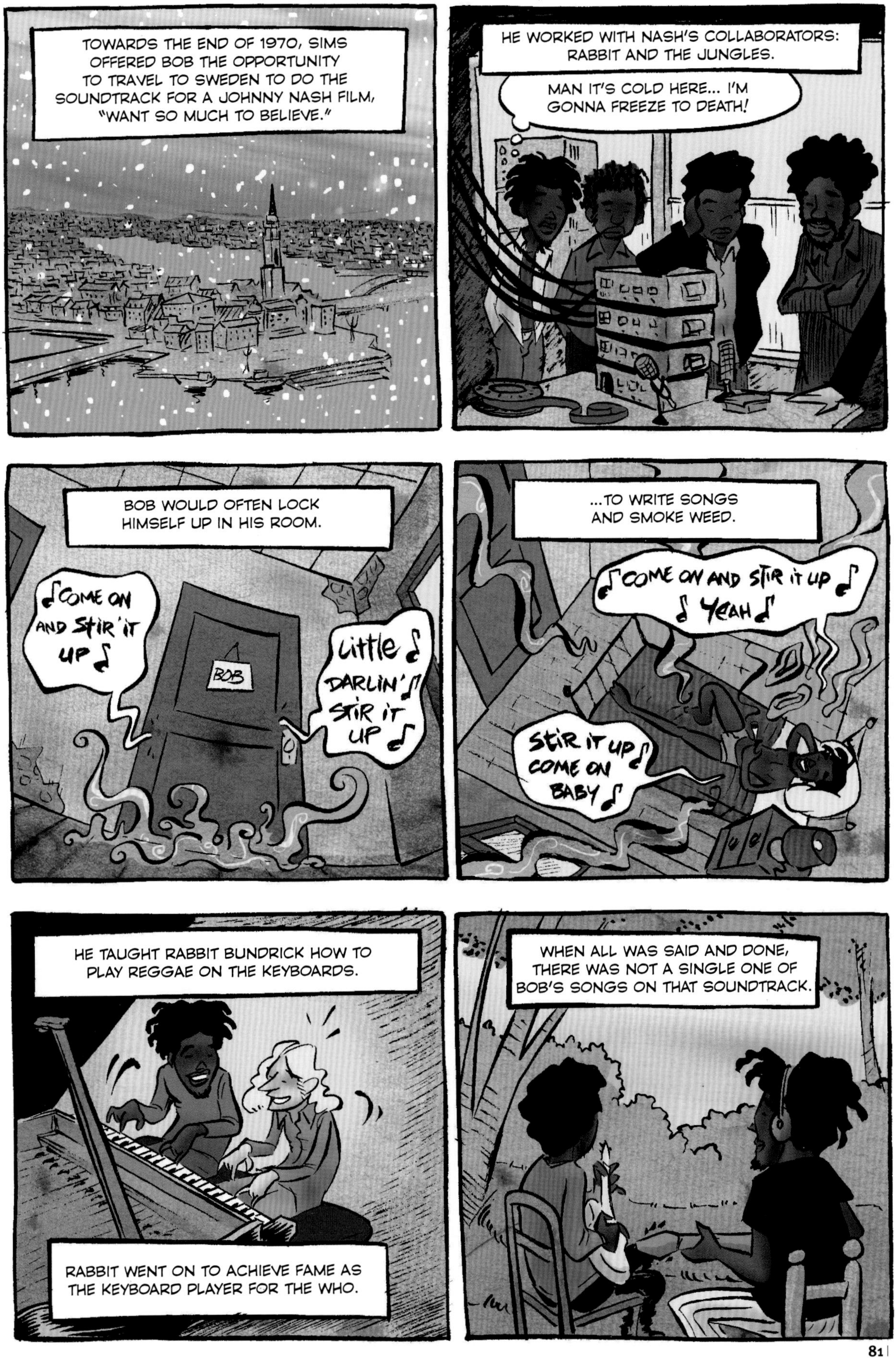

TOWARDS THE END OF 1970, SIMS OFFERED BOB THE OPPORTUNITY TO TRAVEL TO SWEDEN TO DO THE SOUNDTRACK FOR A JOHNNY NASH FILM, "WANT SO MUCH TO BELIEVE."
HE WORKED WITH NASH'S COLLABORATORS: RABBIT AND THE JUNGLES.
MAN IT'S COLD HERE... I'M GONNA FREEZE TO DEATH!
BOB WOULD OFTEN LOCK HIMSELF UP IN HIS ROOM.
COME ON AND STIR IT UP
BOB
LITTLE DARLIN' STIR IT UP
...TO WRITE SONGS AND SMOKE WEED.
COME ON AND STIR IT UP YEAH
STIR IT UP COME ON BABY
HE TAUGHT RABBIT BUNDRICK HOW TO PLAY REGGAE ON THE KEYBOARDS.
RABBIT WENT ON TO ACHIEVE FAME AS THE KEYBOARD PLAYER FOR THE WHO.
WHEN ALL WAS SAID AND DONE, THERE WAS NOT A SINGLE ONE OF BOB'S SONGS ON THAT SOUNDTRACK.

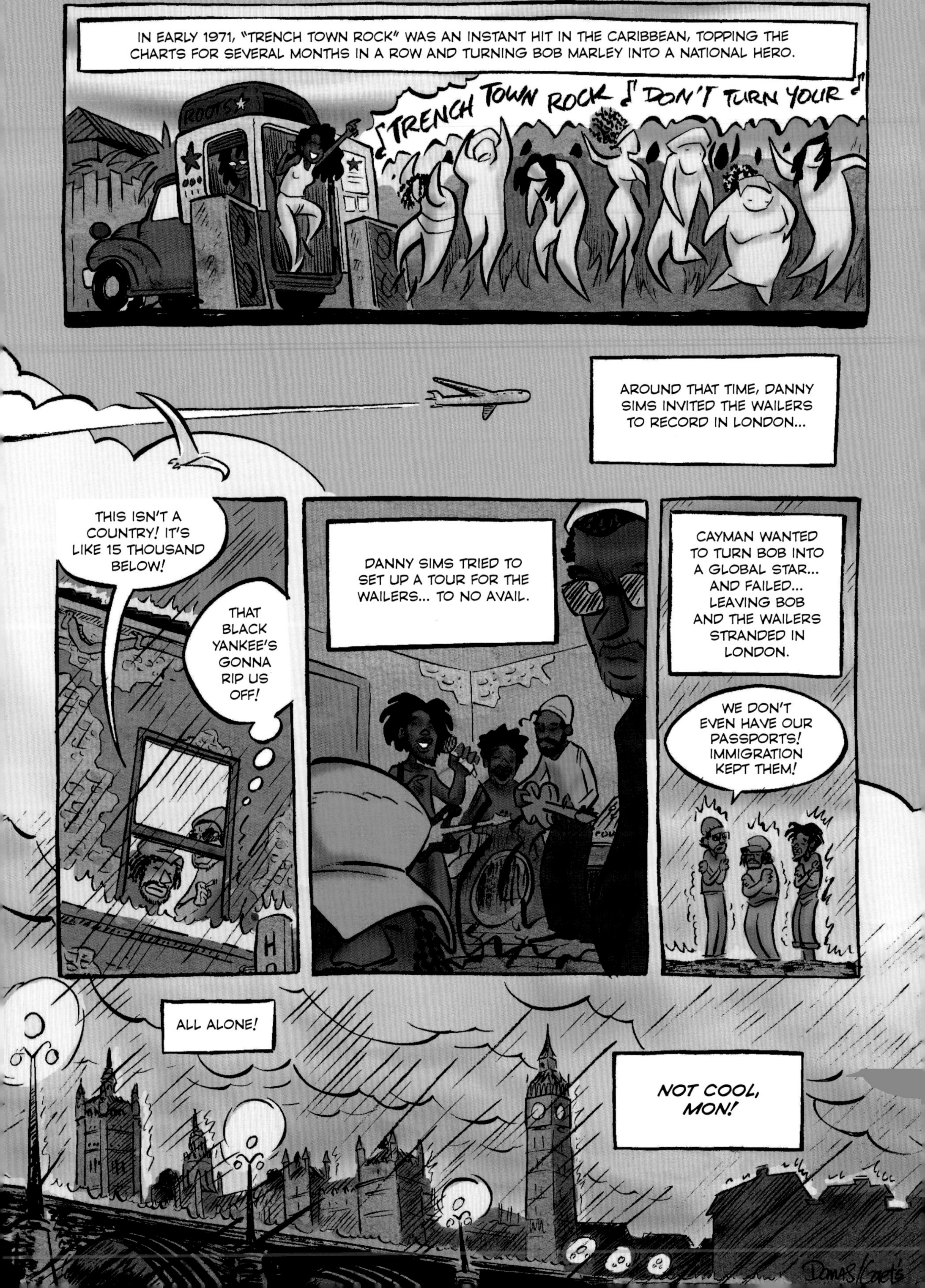
IN EARLY 1971, "TRENCH TOWN ROCK" WAS AN INSTANT HIT IN THE CARIBBEAN, TOPPING THE CHARTS FOR SEVERAL MONTHS IN A ROW AND TURNING BOB MARLEY INTO A NATIONAL HERO.
TRENCH TOWN ROCK DON'T TURN YOUR
ROOTS
AROUND THAT TIME, DANNY SIMS INVITED THE WAILERS TO RECORD IN LONDON...
THIS ISN'T A COUNTRY! IT'S LIKE 15 THOUSAND BELOW!
THAT BLACK YANKEE'S GONNA RIP US OFF!
DANNY SIMS TRIED TO SET UP A TOUR FOR THE WAILERS... TO NO AVAIL.
CAYMAN WANTED TO TURN BOB INTO A GLOBAL STAR... AND FAILED... LEAVING BOB AND THE WAILERS STRANDED IN LONDON.
WE DON'T EVEN HAVE OUR PASSPORTS! IMMIGRATION KEPT THEM!
ALL ALONE!
NOT COOL, MON!

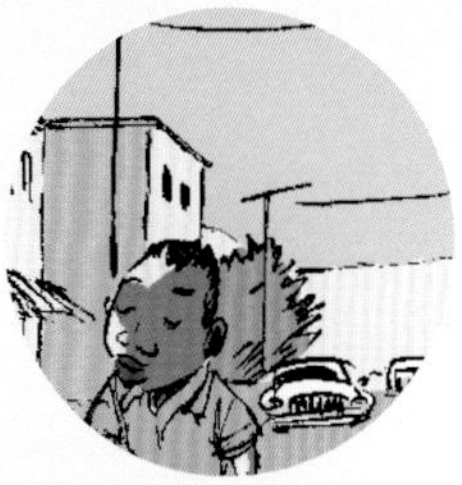

The Path to Success

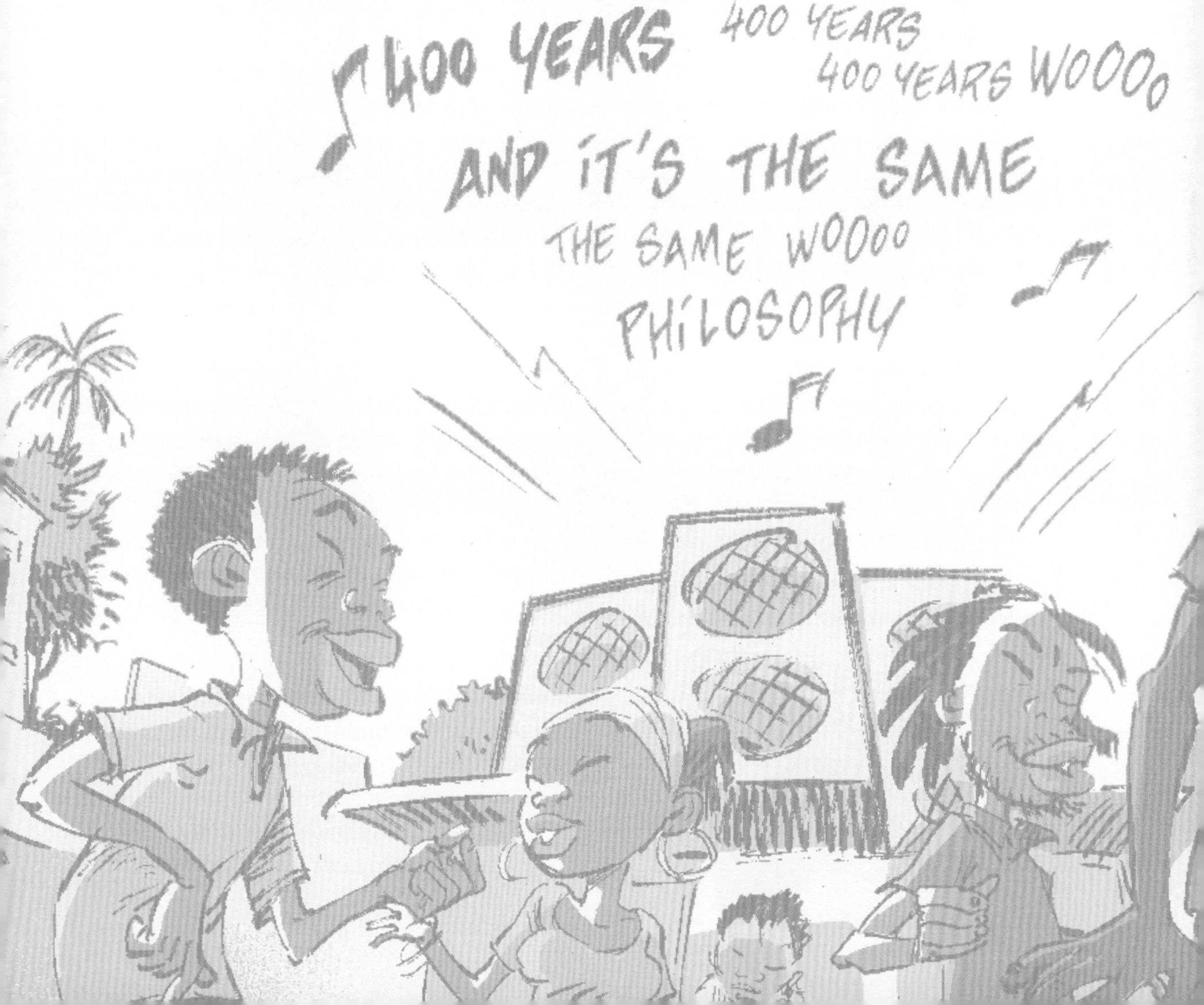
400 YEARS 400 YEARS
400 YEARS WOOOo
AND IT'S THE SAME
THE SAME WOOOO
PHILOSOPHY

After many challenges in his early years, namely commercial flops and misadventures with his producers, Bob Marley found his own path. It was a journey as musical as it was political and spiritual.

As Corneille wisely wrote, "in souls nobly born, valor does not depend upon age." Maybe so, but in 1961, at the age of 16, Bob Marley had not yet achieved fame: "Judge Not," released on the Beverley label, was his first single and a total flop. However, instead of letting that stop him (and given what came later, he was certainly right not to!), the young man went at it again: he tried to do a cover of a country song by Claude Gray, and the following year released the single "One Cup of Coffee," which was also a flop. Strike two! But there was no way in hell he was going to spend the rest of his life as a welder: he had already almost lost an eye while handling a molten piece of metal! Improving as a musician, on the other hand, seemed feasible. Bob Marley and his buddies added background singers to their songs and gradually leaned towards the reggae sound that would become their trademark.

In 1963, Junior Braithwaite, Peter Tosh, Bunny Wailer and Bob Marley auditioned for Studio One.

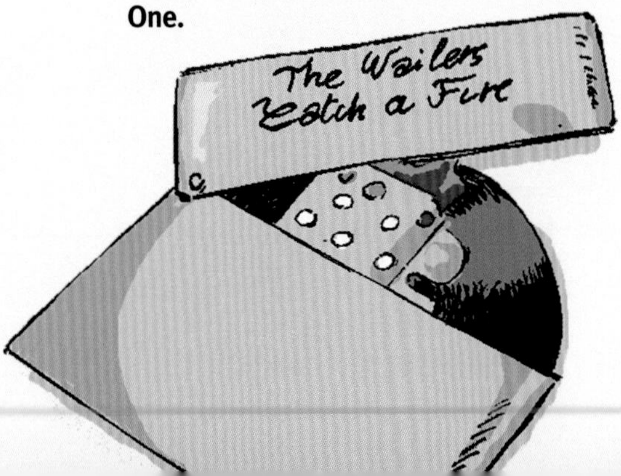
The Wailers
Catch a Fire

It was primarily Peter's voice, with its juvenile timber, that persuaded Clement Coxsone Dod to sign them—or to record an album, to be more specific, since contracts and royalties weren't exactly a priority for Jamaican producers in those days, be it Coxsone, Mortimer Planno, Danny Sims or Lee Scratch Perry. Be that as it may, it was thanks to Studio One that "Simmer Down" saw the light of day, towards the end of 1963. The Wailers were accompanied by a band that later called itself the Skatalites, in reference to the musical genre that was sweeping the island. This time around, the single was a huge hit in Jamaica, selling over 80,000 copies. Other hits followed, namely "Rude Boy," "I'm Still Waiting," and "Put It on." These titles no doubt resonated with the youth of a country in the dawn of its independence, as the lyrics spoke concretely of their angst and daily life. Yet at the same time, those songs offered a message of peace, as with the exhortation for everyone to "get together and feel alright," the famous refrain from "One Love."

However, while The Wailers began to experience success from an artistic standpoint, the same cannot be said of the financial aspect. As it turned out, you could be a local celebrity and still not make a dime... a situation which, incidentally, only made the band more politically minded.

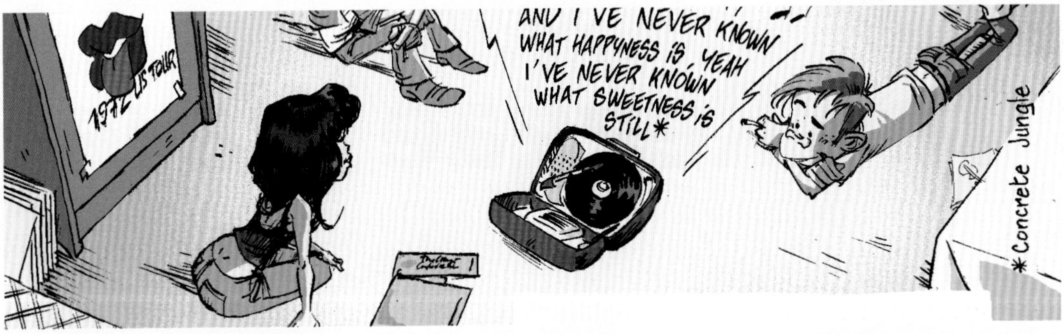
1972 US TOUR
AND I VE NEVER KNOWN WHAT HAPPYNESS IS, YEAH I'VE NEVER KNOWN WHAT SWEETNESS IS STILL*
*Concrete Jungle

Bob Marley could think of only one solution: start his own record label. But that required money... So he decided to move to the U.S., even though he had just met—and married—Rita Anderson. In February of 1966, he went to live with his mother on the East Coast, in Delaware. From Chrysler factories to lab benches at DuPont Chemical, from valet parking to dishwashing, Bob Marley worked a series of odd jobs but never stopped writing songs, to which he sometimes enjoyed giving a double meaning. "Night Shift," for instance, refers to work, of course, but "work" also means sex in Jamaican slang. The song evokes both working the late shift and yearning to be reunited with his wife Rita. That happened not long after, in October of '66: Bob Marley returned to Jamaica to avoid being drafted and sent to Vietnam, where, at the height of the Cold War, the U.S. was beefing up its military presence.

Bob's lyrics started taking on markedly more political and social undertones.

Upon his return, Bob Marley's songs, which he and the Wailers produced themselves, took on more political undertones. Such was the case, for example, of the ambiguous "Freedom Time," which celebrated both their split with Studio One and the end of slavery. The tone became more overtly political in the 70s, in particular with "Them belly full, but we hungry." The "we" is threatening, for, as he warns, "A hungry mob is an angry mob." It was also in the late 60s that Bob Marley's music began taking on religious connotations: because he was in the U.S. at the time, he had missed the Jamaican visit of King Haile Selassie of Ethiopia, the Rastafarians' messenger, but began subscribing to that faith in 1966. Practically speaking, this meant adopting a new look (out with the rocker style and in with the dreads), reading of the Bible diligently, sticking to a vegetarian diet, engaging in regular consumption of marijuana, and taking part in rituals performed to the sound of Nyabinghi drums. He retreated to the countryside for a whole year to try out the Rasta way of life, before returning to city life in the slums of Kingston.

The Reggae Wave

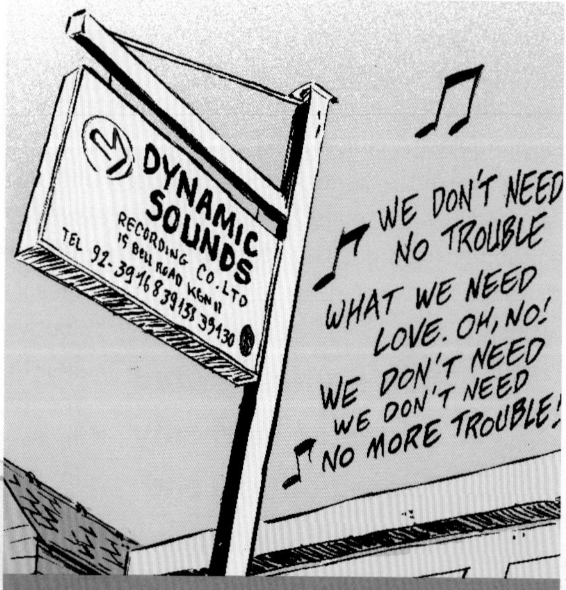

DYNAMIC SOUNDS
RECORDING CO. LTD
15 BELL ROAD KGN 11
TEL 92-39168 39138 39130
WE DON'T NEED
NO TROUBLE
WHAT WE NEED
LOVE. OH, NO!
WE DON'T NEED
WE DON'T NEED
NO MORE TROUBLE!

Artist: Simon Léturgie

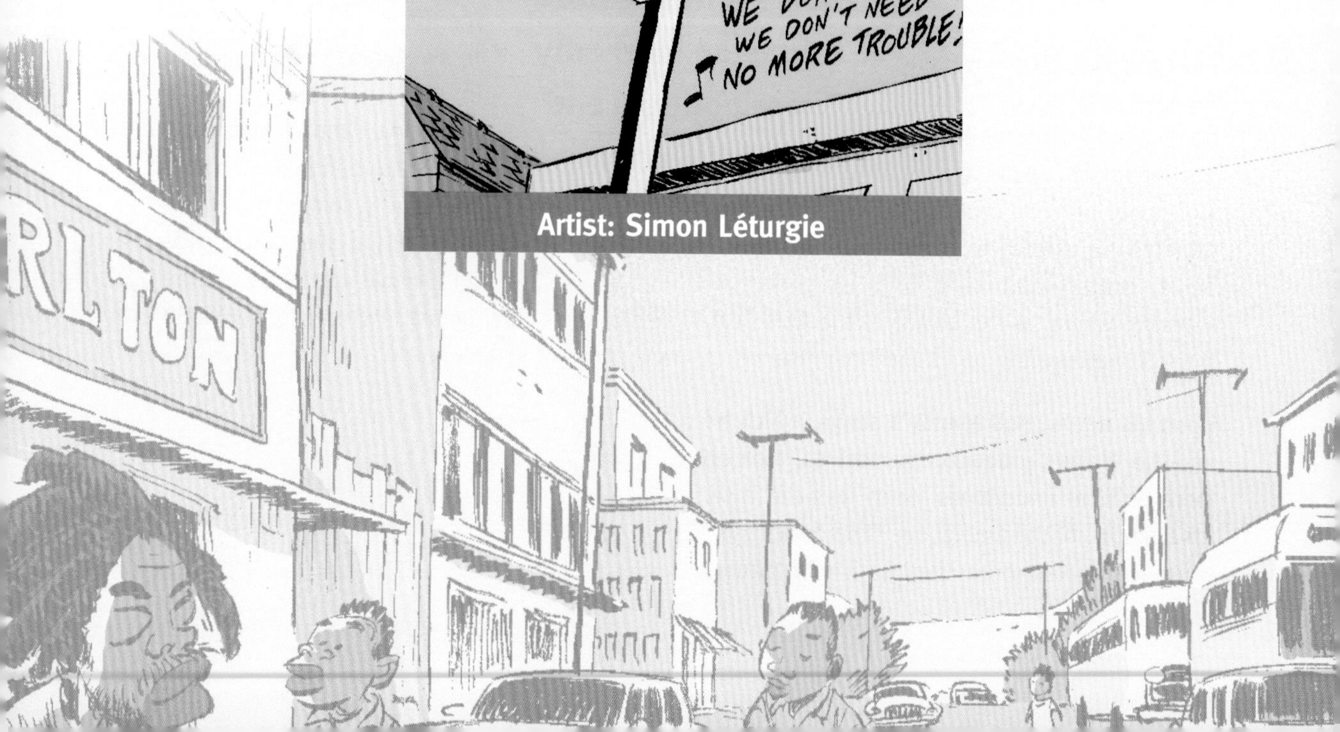

RLTON

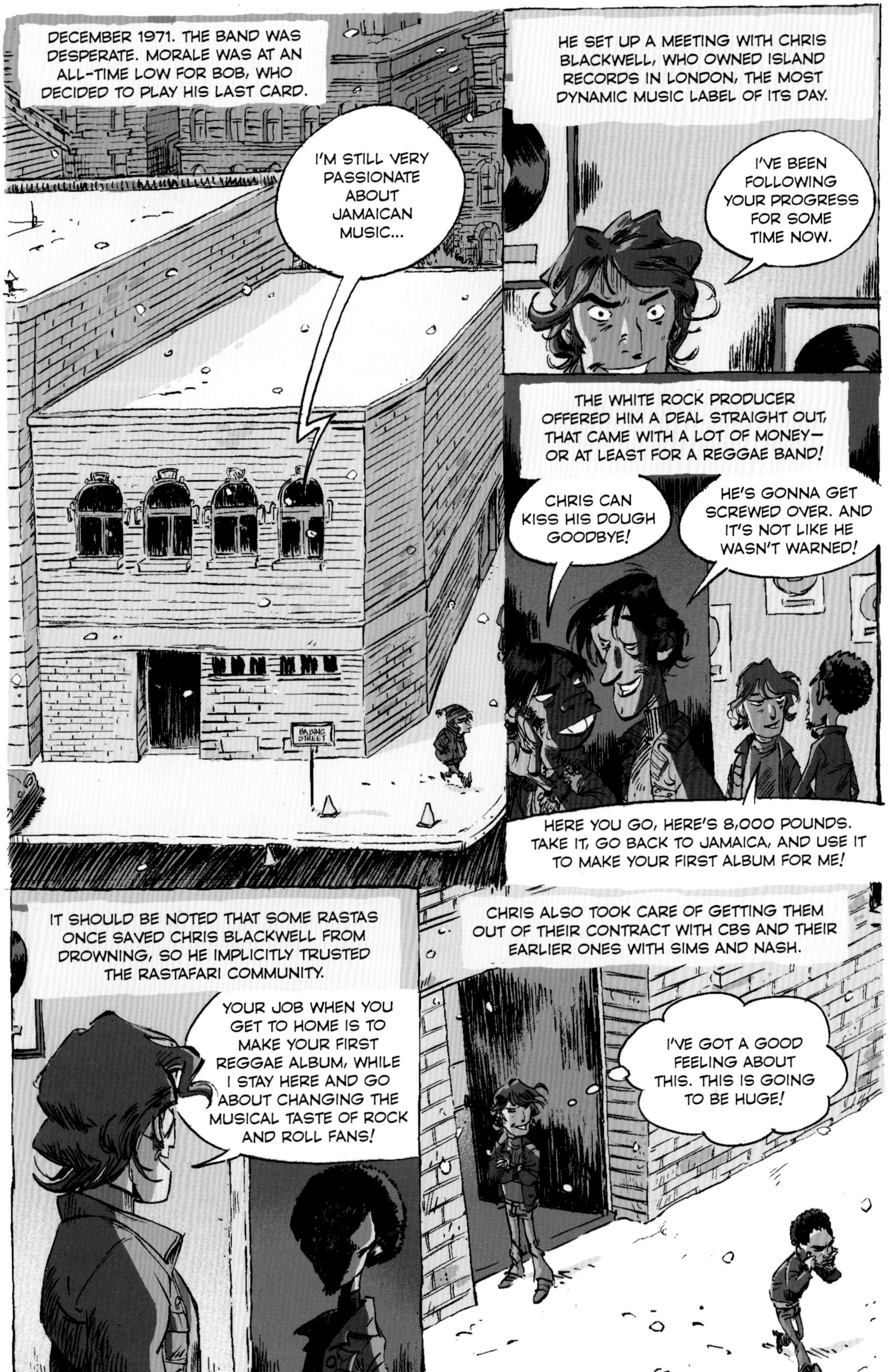
DECEMBER 1971. THE BAND WAS DESPERATE. MORALE WAS AT AN ALL-TIME LOW FOR BOB, WHO DECIDED TO PLAY HIS LAST CARD.
I'M STILL VERY PASSIONATE ABOUT JAMAICAN MUSIC...
BASING STREET
HE SET UP A MEETING WITH CHRIS BLACKWELL, WHO OWNED ISLAND RECORDS IN LONDON, THE MOST DYNAMIC MUSIC LABEL OF ITS DAY.
I'VE BEEN FOLLOWING YOUR PROGRESS FOR SOME TIME NOW.
THE WHITE ROCK PRODUCER OFFERED HIM A DEAL STRAIGHT OUT, THAT CAME WITH A LOT OF MONEY— OR AT LEAST FOR A REGGAE BAND!
CHRIS CAN KISS HIS DOUGH GOODBYE!
HE'S GONNA GET SCREWED OVER. AND IT'S NOT LIKE HE WASN'T WARNED!
HERE YOU GO, HERE'S 8,000 POUNDS. TAKE IT, GO BACK TO JAMAICA, AND USE IT TO MAKE YOUR FIRST ALBUM FOR ME!
IT SHOULD BE NOTED THAT SOME RASTAS ONCE SAVED CHRIS BLACKWELL FROM DROWNING, SO HE IMPLICITLY TRUSTED THE RASTAFARI COMMUNITY.
YOUR JOB WHEN YOU GET TO HOME IS TO MAKE YOUR FIRST REGGAE ALBUM, WHILE I STAY HERE AND GO ABOUT CHANGING THE MUSICAL TASTE OF ROCK AND ROLL FANS!
CHRIS ALSO TOOK CARE OF GETTING THEM OUT OF THEIR CONTRACT WITH CBS AND THEIR EARLIER ONES WITH SIMS AND NASH.
I'VE GOT A GOOD FEELING ABOUT THIS. THIS IS GOING TO BE HUGE!

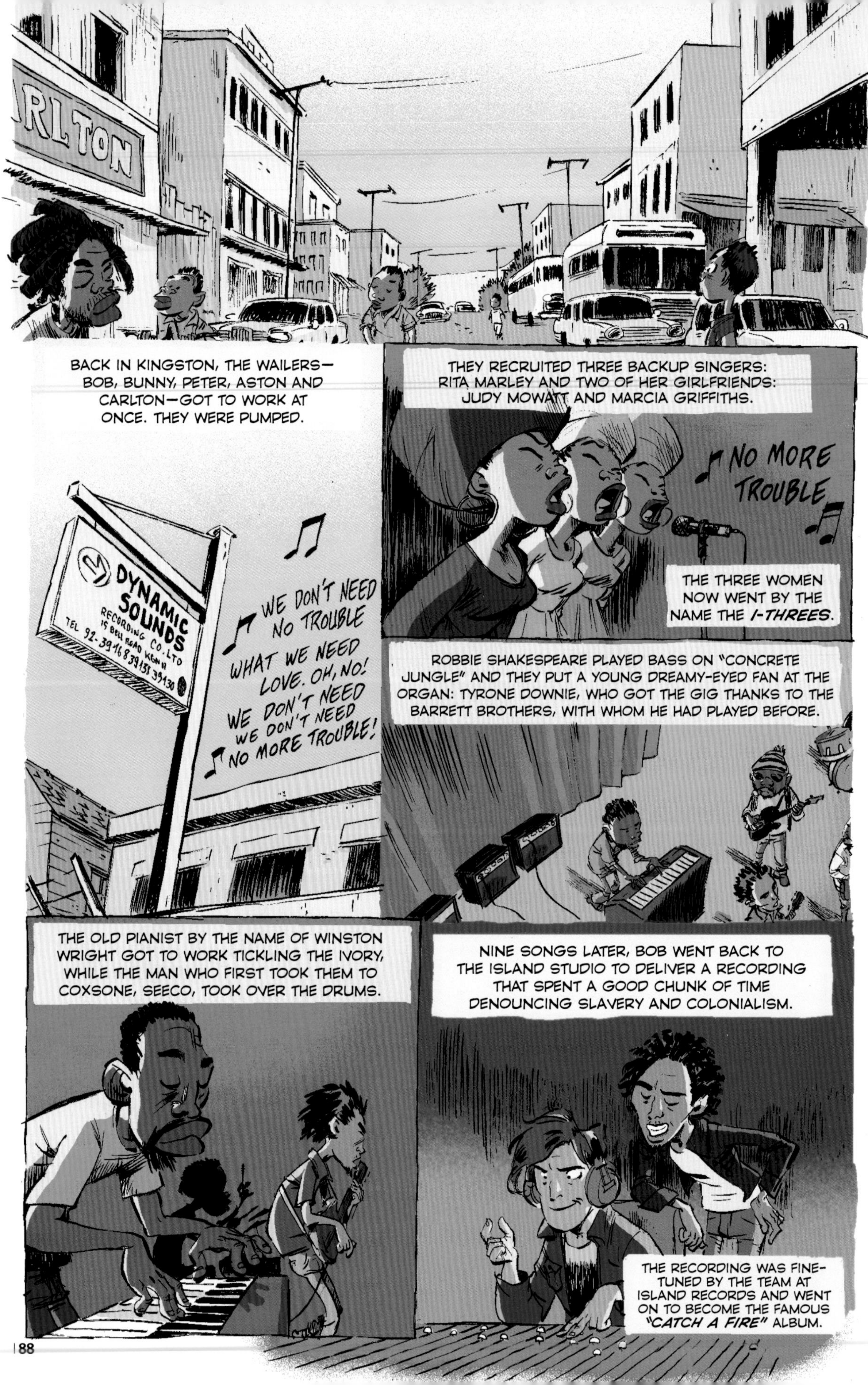
RLTON
BACK IN KINGSTON, THE WAILERS—BOB, BUNNY, PETER, ASTON AND CARLTON—GOT TO WORK AT ONCE. THEY WERE PUMPED.
DYNAMIC SOUNDS
RECORDING CO. LTD
15 BELL ROAD KGN 11
TEL 92-39168 39135 39130
WE DON'T NEED NO TROUBLE
WHAT WE NEED LOVE. OH, NO!
WE DON'T NEED WE DON'T NEED NO MORE TROUBLE!
THEY RECRUITED THREE BACKUP SINGERS: RITA MARLEY AND TWO OF HER GIRLFRIENDS: JUDY MOWATT AND MARCIA GRIFFITHS.
NO MORE TROUBLE
THE THREE WOMEN NOW WENT BY THE NAME THE *I-THREES*.
ROBBIE SHAKESPEARE PLAYED BASS ON "CONCRETE JUNGLE" AND THEY PUT A YOUNG DREAMY-EYED FAN AT THE ORGAN: TYRONE DOWNIE, WHO GOT THE GIG THANKS TO THE BARRETT BROTHERS, WITH WHOM HE HAD PLAYED BEFORE.
THE OLD PIANIST BY THE NAME OF WINSTON WRIGHT GOT TO WORK TICKLING THE IVORY, WHILE THE MAN WHO FIRST TOOK THEM TO COXSONE, SEECO, TOOK OVER THE DRUMS.
NINE SONGS LATER, BOB WENT BACK TO THE ISLAND STUDIO TO DELIVER A RECORDING THAT SPENT A GOOD CHUNK OF TIME DENOUNCING SLAVERY AND COLONIALISM.
THE RECORDING WAS FINE-TUNED BY THE TEAM AT ISLAND RECORDS AND WENT ON TO BECOME THE FAMOUS *"CATCH A FIRE"* ALBUM.

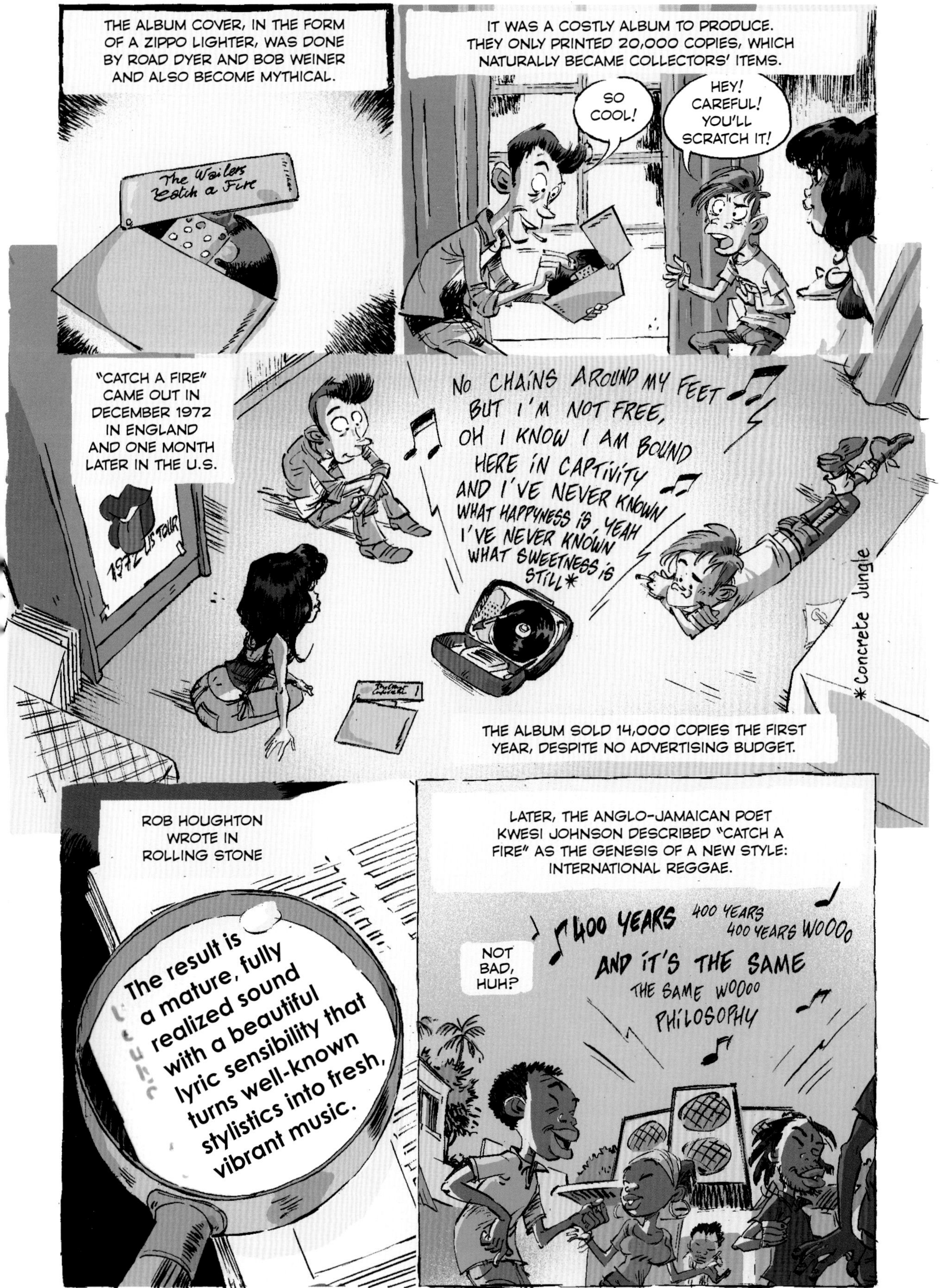

THE ALBUM COVER, IN THE FORM OF A ZIPPO LIGHTER, WAS DONE BY ROAD DYER AND BOB WEINER AND ALSO BECOME MYTHICAL.
The Wailers Catch a Fire
IT WAS A COSTLY ALBUM TO PRODUCE. THEY ONLY PRINTED 20,000 COPIES, WHICH NATURALLY BECAME COLLECTORS' ITEMS.
SO COOL!
HEY! CAREFUL! YOU'LL SCRATCH IT!
"CATCH A FIRE" CAME OUT IN DECEMBER 1972 IN ENGLAND AND ONE MONTH LATER IN THE U.S.
1972 US TOUR
NO CHAINS AROUND MY FEET BUT I'M NOT FREE, OH I KNOW I AM BOUND HERE IN CAPTIVITY AND I'VE NEVER KNOWN WHAT HAPPYNESS IS, YEAH I'VE NEVER KNOWN WHAT SWEETNESS IS STILL*
*Concrete Jungle
THE ALBUM SOLD 14,000 COPIES THE FIRST YEAR, DESPITE NO ADVERTISING BUDGET.
ROB HOUGHTON WROTE IN ROLLING STONE
The result is a mature, fully realized sound with a beautiful lyric sensibility that turns well-known stylistics into fresh, vibrant music.
LATER, THE ANGLO-JAMAICAN POET KWESI JOHNSON DESCRIBED "CATCH A FIRE" AS THE GENESIS OF A NEW STYLE: INTERNATIONAL REGGAE.
NOT BAD, HUH?
400 YEARS 400 YEARS 400 YEARS WOOOo
AND IT'S THE SAME THE SAME WOOOo PHILOSOPHY

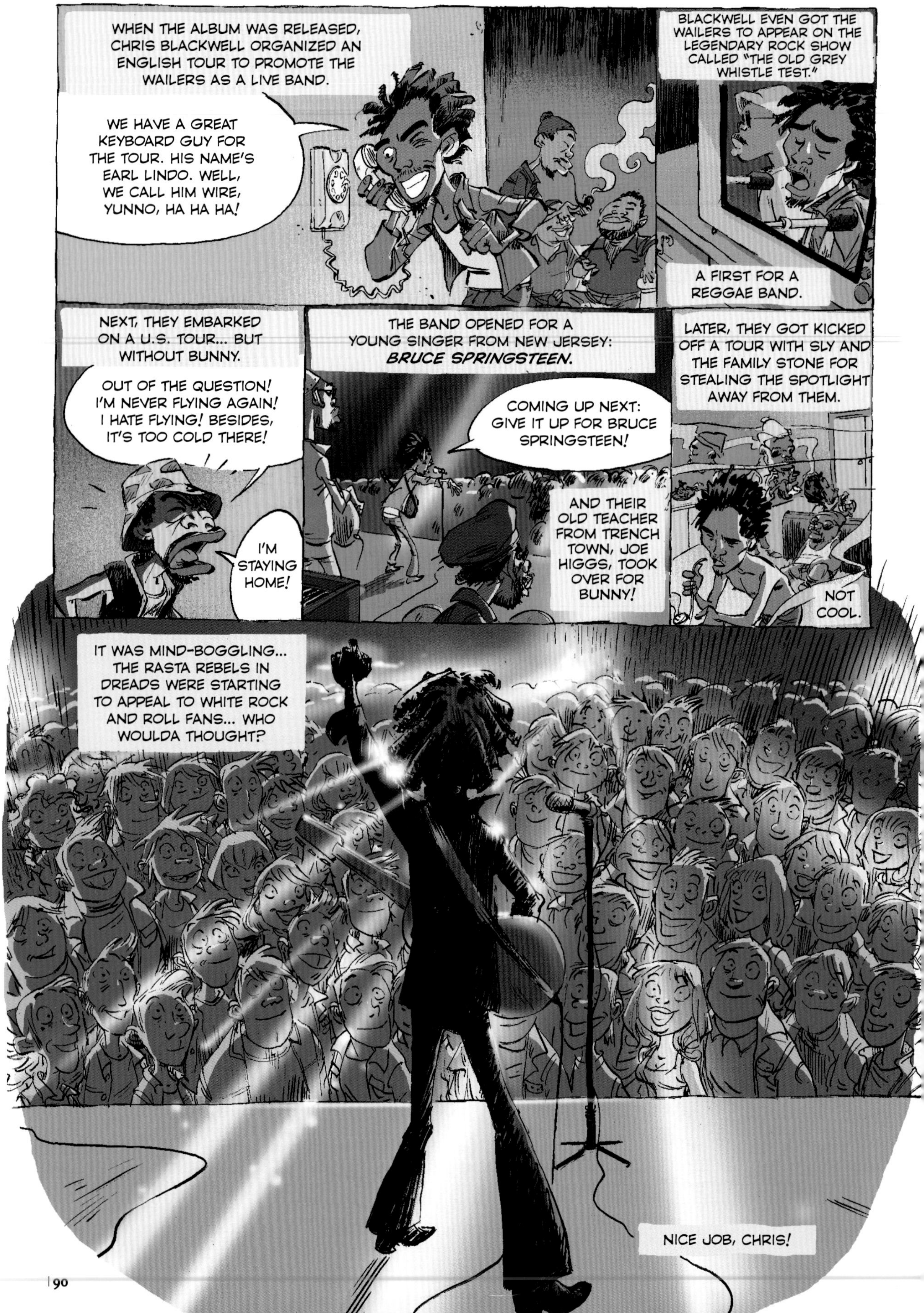

WHEN THE ALBUM WAS RELEASED, CHRIS BLACKWELL ORGANIZED AN ENGLISH TOUR TO PROMOTE THE WAILERS AS A LIVE BAND.
WE HAVE A GREAT KEYBOARD GUY FOR THE TOUR. HIS NAME'S EARL LINDO. WELL, WE CALL HIM WIRE, YUNNO, HA HA HA!
BLACKWELL EVEN GOT THE WAILERS TO APPEAR ON THE LEGENDARY ROCK SHOW CALLED "THE OLD GREY WHISTLE TEST."
A FIRST FOR A REGGAE BAND.
NEXT, THEY EMBARKED ON A U.S. TOUR... BUT WITHOUT BUNNY.
OUT OF THE QUESTION! I'M NEVER FLYING AGAIN! I HATE FLYING! BESIDES, IT'S TOO COLD THERE!
I'M STAYING HOME!
THE BAND OPENED FOR A YOUNG SINGER FROM NEW JERSEY: *BRUCE SPRINGSTEEN.*
COMING UP NEXT: GIVE IT UP FOR BRUCE SPRINGSTEEN!
AND THEIR OLD TEACHER FROM TRENCH TOWN, JOE HIGGS, TOOK OVER FOR BUNNY!
LATER, THEY GOT KICKED OFF A TOUR WITH SLY AND THE FAMILY STONE FOR STEALING THE SPOTLIGHT AWAY FROM THEM.
NOT COOL.
IT WAS MIND-BOGGLING... THE RASTA REBELS IN DREADS WERE STARTING TO APPEAL TO WHITE ROCK AND ROLL FANS... WHO WOULDA THOUGHT?
NICE JOB, CHRIS!

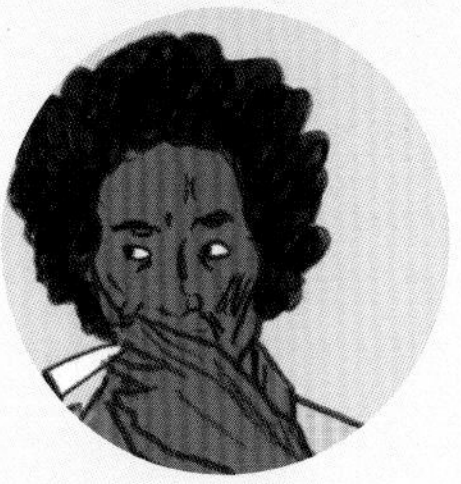

An “ International Reggae”

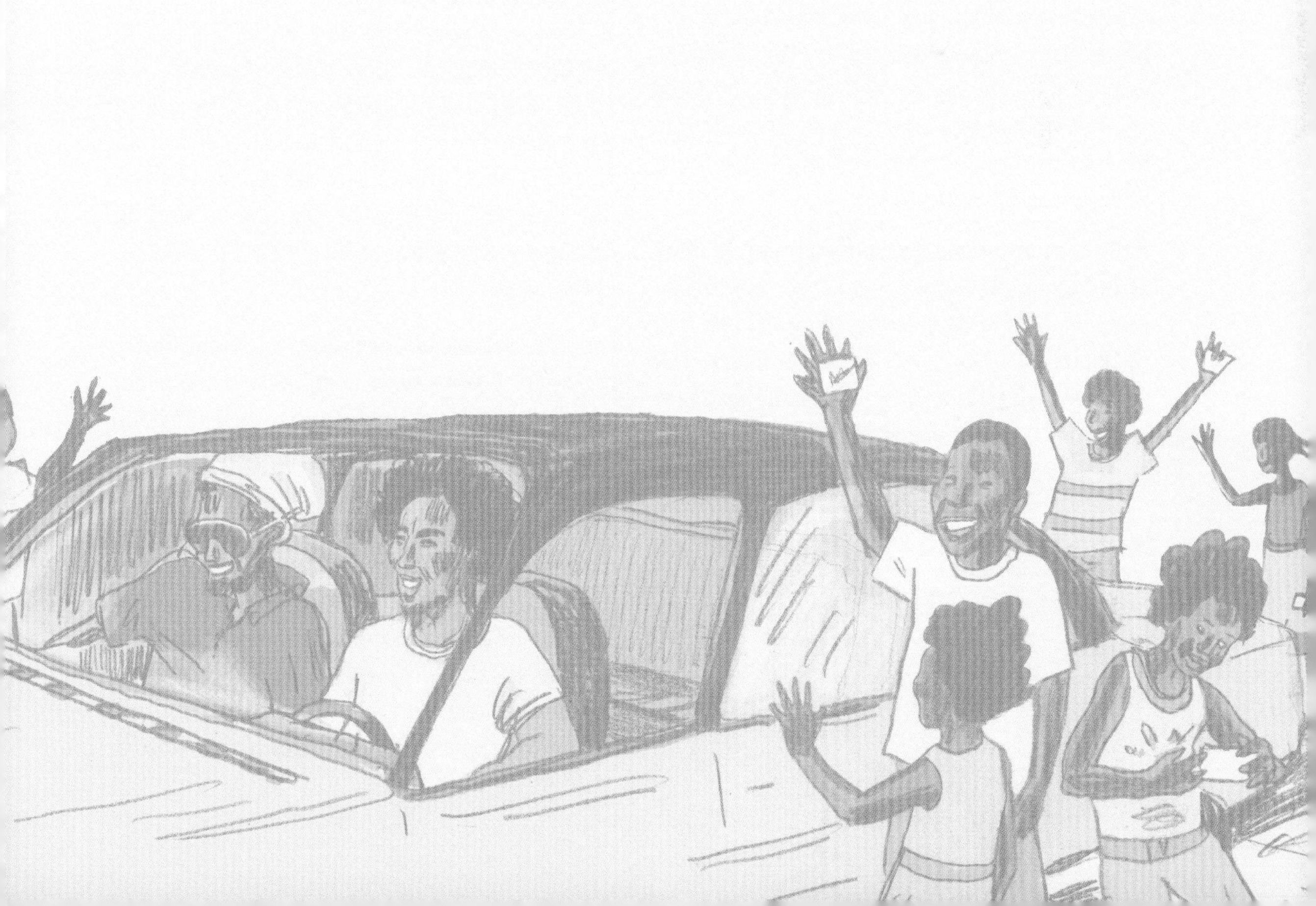

The 1973 *Catch A Fire* album launched Bob Marley's international career. The intuition and marketing savvy of Chris Blackwell, the producer from Island Records, had a lot to do with it.

In the 60s, Bob Marley and the Wailers had a fledgling reputation in Jamaica, but it would take a lot more work before they achieved international fame. It was in the following decade that their career really took off, thanks in particular to their partnership with producer Chris Blackwell. The London-based founder of Island Records had always had a flair for finding emerging talent, and he also had a special fondness for Jamaica, where he had spent part of his childhood. In 1964, he launched the young Millie Small, whose ska song "My Boy Lollipop" was a hit—a hit big enough to give the label an international reputation. Island Records then focused on rock and produced artists like Steve Winwood and Cat Stevens.

But trends come and go, and you need to think ahead. Chris Blackwell could sense that reggae was going to be the next big thing, and he had no intention of missing the boat! Jimmy Cliff was the perfect candidate to embody that new style, especially given that little rebellious touch of his that was sure to be a crowd-pleaser. And so Chris Blackwell signed the singer whose ambition was also to be in the movies.

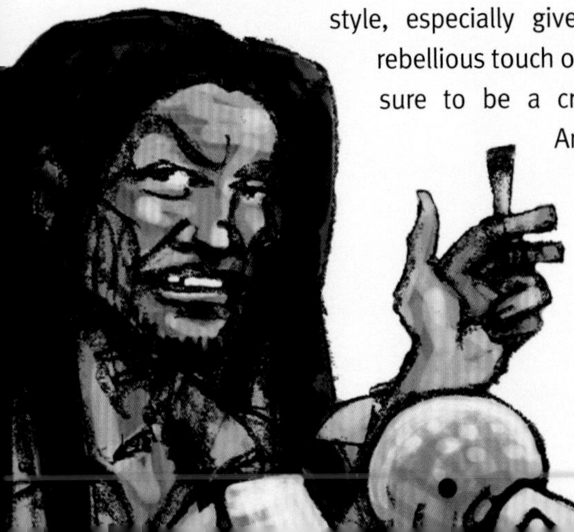

In 1972, *The Harder They Come* came out, a crime thriller inspired by the life of a real criminal from the 40s. Jimmy Cliff played a young Jamaican man from the country who moves to Kingston to try to make it as a musician. Not exactly an Oscar-worthy performance, but the movie helped introduce reggae across the globe and Blackwell wanted to take advantage of that opportunity to release albums. The only hitch: Jimmy Cliff distanced himself from Island Records and opted to sign with a different label. For lack of any better options, Chris Blackwell then turned his attention to The Wailers, whose progress he had been following since day one—a backup plan that would prove to be not such a bad one, in the end!

For the penniless musicians of Trenchtown, the offer couldn't have come at a better time, especially since, as opposed to their previous producers, Island Records paid them for their work up front: 6,000 pounds in cold hard cash! They were to use that money to not just do a compilation of titles, which was what was done back then, but to come up with a whole album. And so the band got to work and a few months later, *Catch A Fire* was birthed. The songs were recorded in Jamaica and then sent to London, where several parts were remixed

and guitar solos were added. The goal: to give the album more of a rock sound so as to make it more pleasing to the American and European musical palate. The result was "a new type of Jamaican music," as poet and musician Linton Kwesi Johnson later said, speaking of what he called "international reggae."

However, no matter how good it is, music alone does not commercial success make, and Chris Blackwell knew that. Luckily, he was an ace at marketing. The producer was known for devoting special attention to album covers and in early 1973, aficionados were thrilled to find an odd-looking package in the form a Zippo lighter in music store bins, which opened onto a vinyl album engulfed in cardboard flames—a reference to the title of the 33LP, *Catch A Fire*. Pretty high concept! "I really believe that if people see something that looks cool, on some unconscious level, they believe that something is going to happen when they listen to the album," Chris Blackwell later explained in an interview with the British daily The Telegraph. But despite that initiative, with just 14,000 albums sold the first year, the audience remained limited. Nonetheless, the road to success was being paved.

Catch A Fire was actually a fairly political album: while love and romance are featured prominently, the nine tracks mainly deal with themes of poverty, injustice and social inequality. With the release of *Trenchtown Rock* the following year, The Wailers became the spokespersons for the disenfranchised. The opening track of the album, "Concrete Jungle," describes the urban violence of the ghettoes. "I've never known happiness, I've never known what sweet caress is," sings Bob Marley, who describes himself as a captive despite having "No chains around my feet." While "Slave Driver" also explores the same theme ("Today they say that we are free, Only to be chained in poverty"), the tone is more threatening towards the slave driver ("The table is turn, baby, now, Catch a fire, so you can get burn, baby, now"). And yet, despite the call to rebellion, there remains an underlying dream: that of universal peace, based on "Make love, not war," as expressed in "No More Trouble."

In the space of just a few months, reggae had gone global.

Villa Rasta

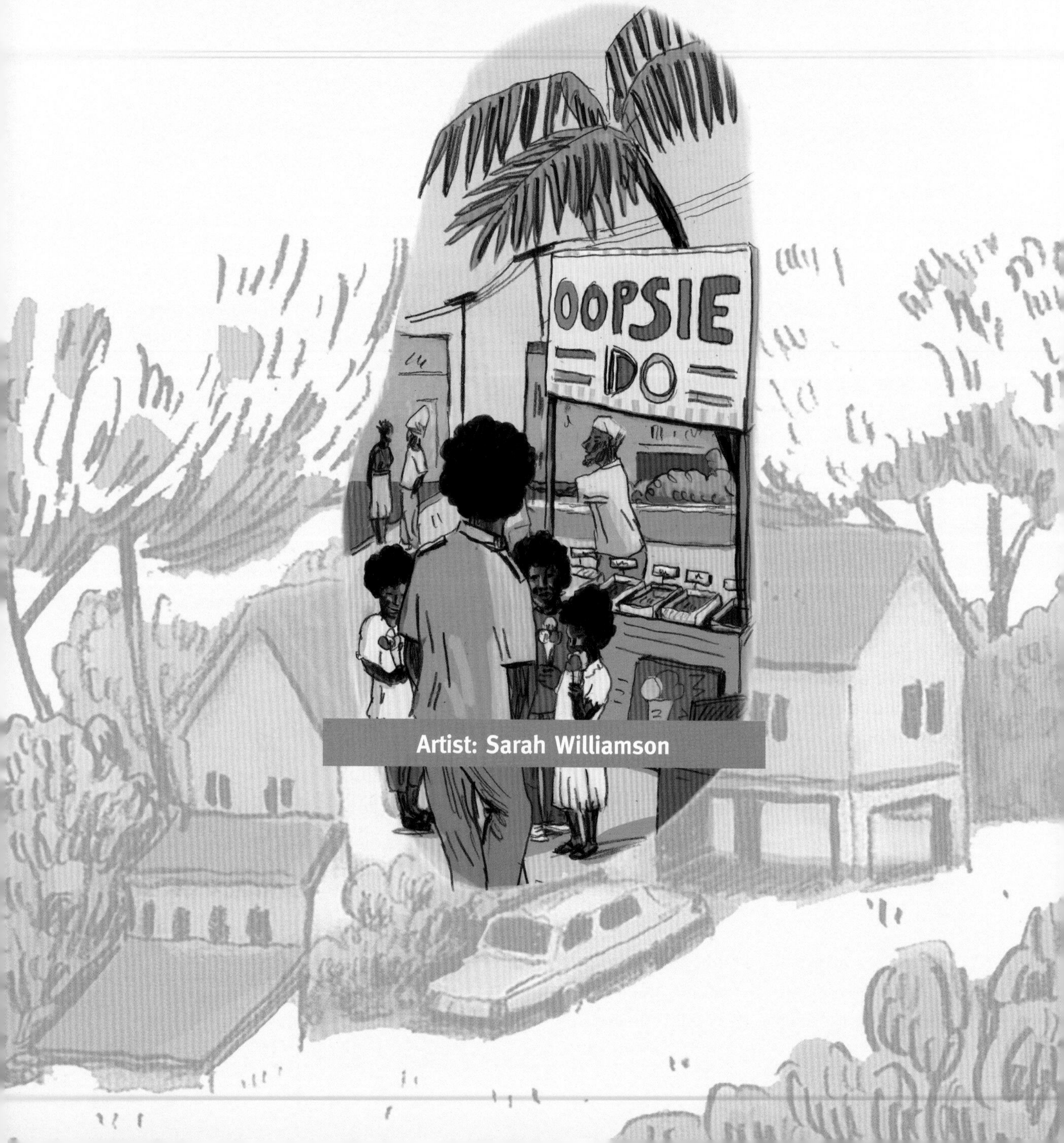

OOPSIE
DO

Artist: Sarah Williamson

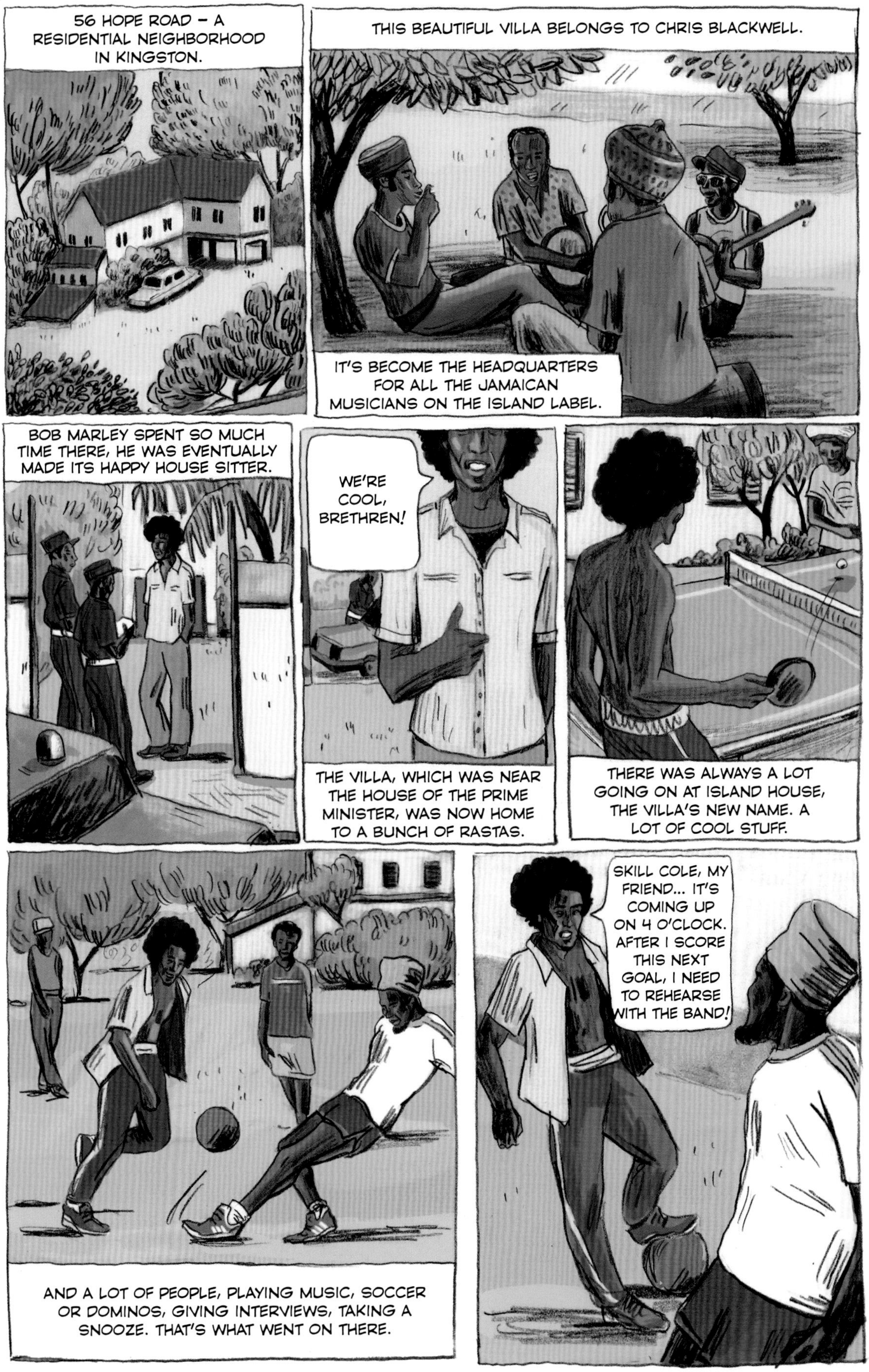
56 HOPE ROAD – A RESIDENTIAL NEIGHBORHOOD IN KINGSTON.
THIS BEAUTIFUL VILLA BELONGS TO CHRIS BLACKWELL.
IT'S BECOME THE HEADQUARTERS FOR ALL THE JAMAICAN MUSICIANS ON THE ISLAND LABEL.
BOB MARLEY SPENT SO MUCH TIME THERE, HE WAS EVENTUALLY MADE ITS HAPPY HOUSE SITTER.
WE'RE COOL, BRETHREN!
THE VILLA, WHICH WAS NEAR THE HOUSE OF THE PRIME MINISTER, WAS NOW HOME TO A BUNCH OF RASTAS.
THERE WAS ALWAYS A LOT GOING ON AT ISLAND HOUSE, THE VILLA'S NEW NAME. A LOT OF COOL STUFF.
AND A LOT OF PEOPLE, PLAYING MUSIC, SOCCER OR DOMINOS, GIVING INTERVIEWS, TAKING A SNOOZE. THAT'S WHAT WENT ON THERE.
SKILL COLE, MY FRIEND... IT'S COMING UP ON 4 O'CLOCK. AFTER I SCORE THIS NEXT GOAL, I NEED TO REHEARSE WITH THE BAND!

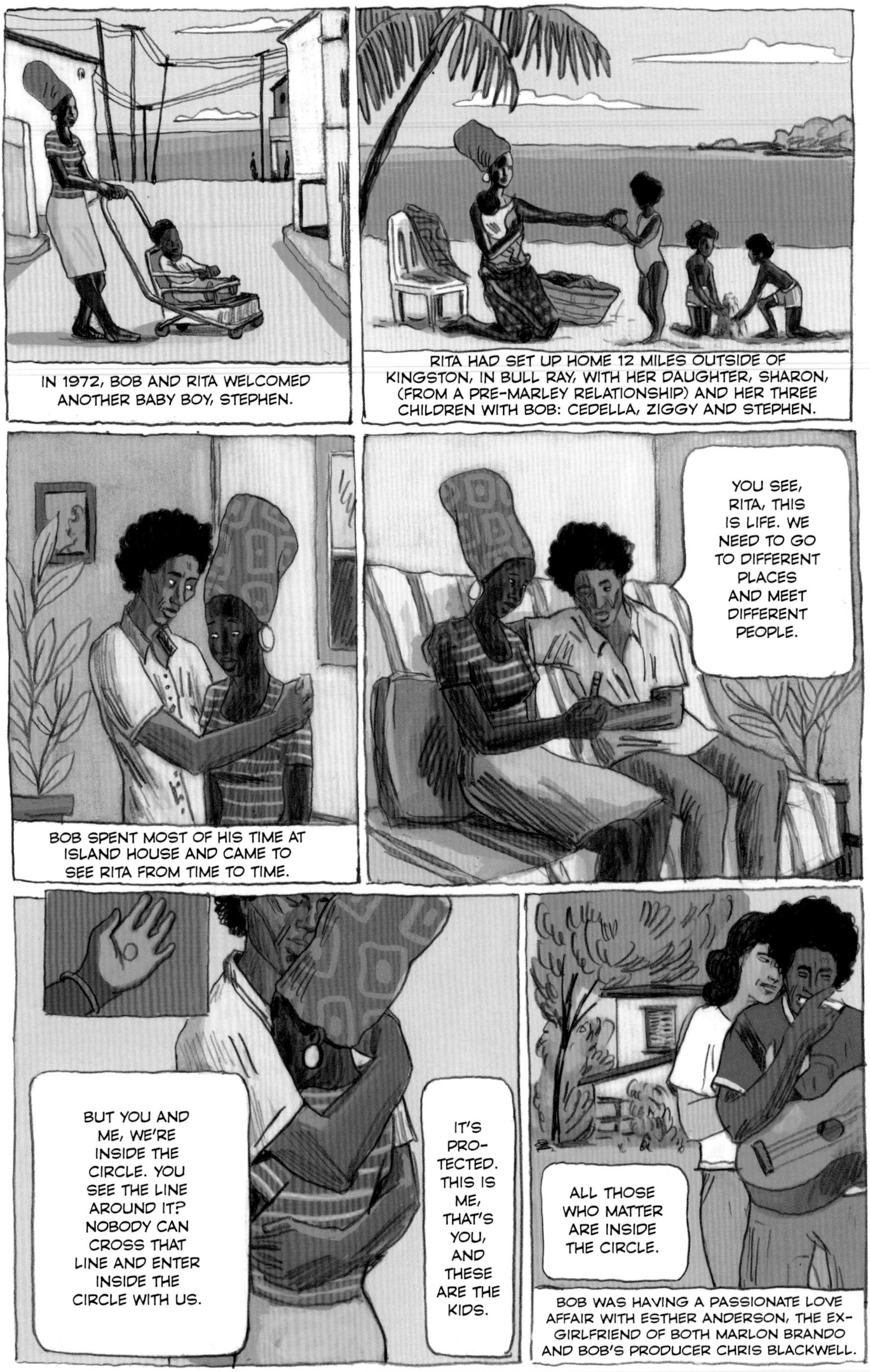
IN 1972, BOB AND RITA WELCOMED ANOTHER BABY BOY, STEPHEN.
RITA HAD SET UP HOME 12 MILES OUTSIDE OF KINGSTON, IN BULL RAY, WITH HER DAUGHTER, SHARON, (FROM A PRE-MARLEY RELATIONSHIP) AND HER THREE CHILDREN WITH BOB: CEDELLA, ZIGGY AND STEPHEN.
BOB SPENT MOST OF HIS TIME AT ISLAND HOUSE AND CAME TO SEE RITA FROM TIME TO TIME.
YOU SEE, RITA, THIS IS LIFE. WE NEED TO GO TO DIFFERENT PLACES AND MEET DIFFERENT PEOPLE.
BUT YOU AND ME, WE'RE INSIDE THE CIRCLE. YOU SEE THE LINE AROUND IT? NOBODY CAN CROSS THAT LINE AND ENTER INSIDE THE CIRCLE WITH US.
IT'S PRO-TECTED. THIS IS ME, THAT'S YOU, AND THESE ARE THE KIDS.
ALL THOSE WHO MATTER ARE INSIDE THE CIRCLE.
BOB WAS HAVING A PASSIONATE LOVE AFFAIR WITH ESTHER ANDERSON, THE EX-GIRLFRIEND OF BOTH MARLON BRANDO AND BOB'S PRODUCER CHRIS BLACKWELL.

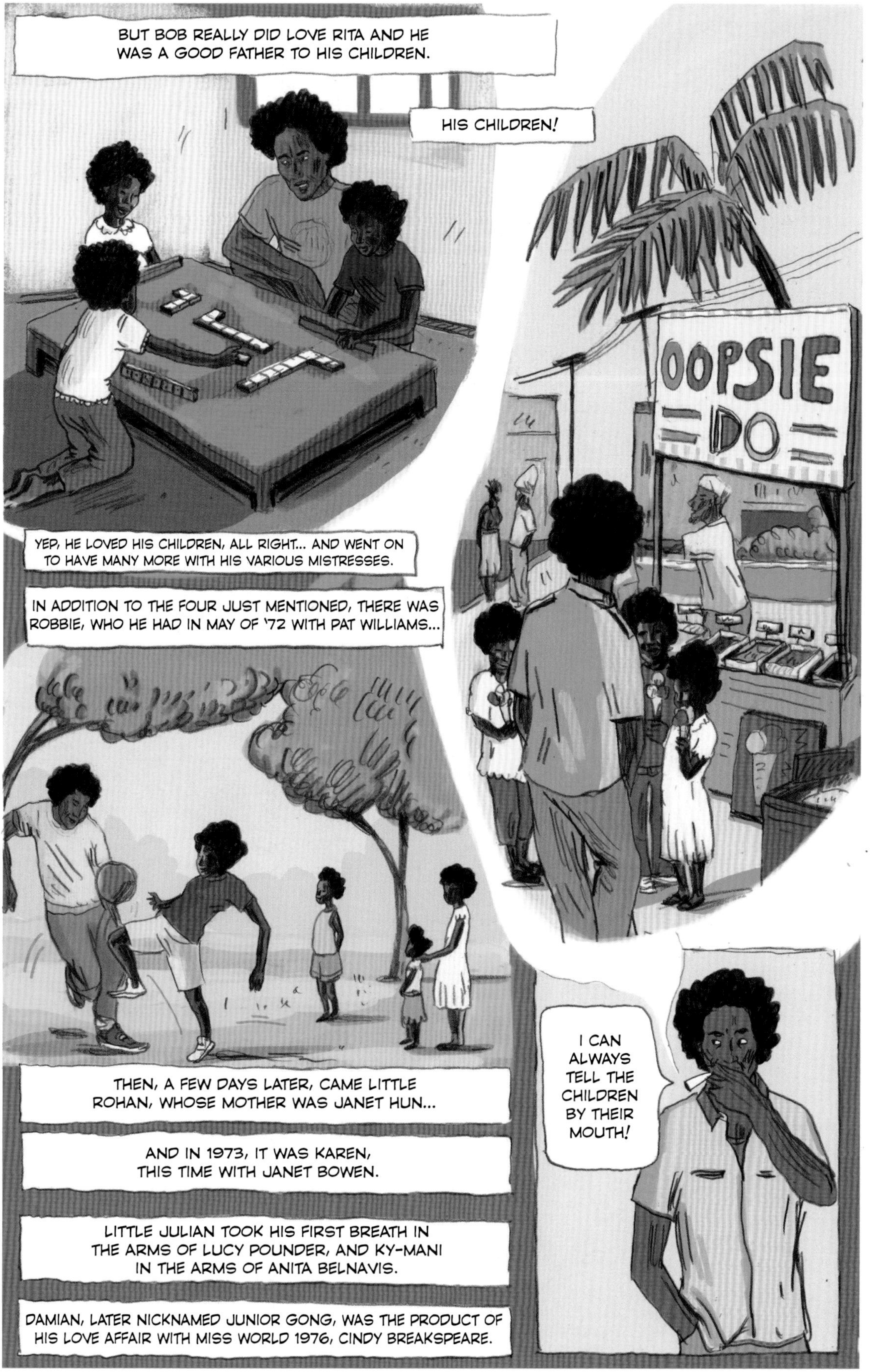
BUT BOB REALLY DID LOVE RITA AND HE WAS A GOOD FATHER TO HIS CHILDREN.
HIS CHILDREN!
YEP, HE LOVED HIS CHILDREN, ALL RIGHT... AND WENT ON TO HAVE MANY MORE WITH HIS VARIOUS MISTRESSES.
IN ADDITION TO THE FOUR JUST MENTIONED, THERE WAS ROBBIE, WHO HE HAD IN MAY OF '72 WITH PAT WILLIAMS...
OOPSIE DO
THEN, A FEW DAYS LATER, CAME LITTLE ROHAN, WHOSE MOTHER WAS JANET HUN...
AND IN 1973, IT WAS KAREN, THIS TIME WITH JANET BOWEN.
LITTLE JULIAN TOOK HIS FIRST BREATH IN THE ARMS OF LUCY POUNDER, AND KY-MANI IN THE ARMS OF ANITA BELNAVIS.
DAMIAN, LATER NICKNAMED JUNIOR GONG, WAS THE PRODUCT OF HIS LOVE AFFAIR WITH MISS WORLD 1976, CINDY BREAKSPEARE.
I CAN ALWAYS TELL THE CHILDREN BY THEIR MOUTH!

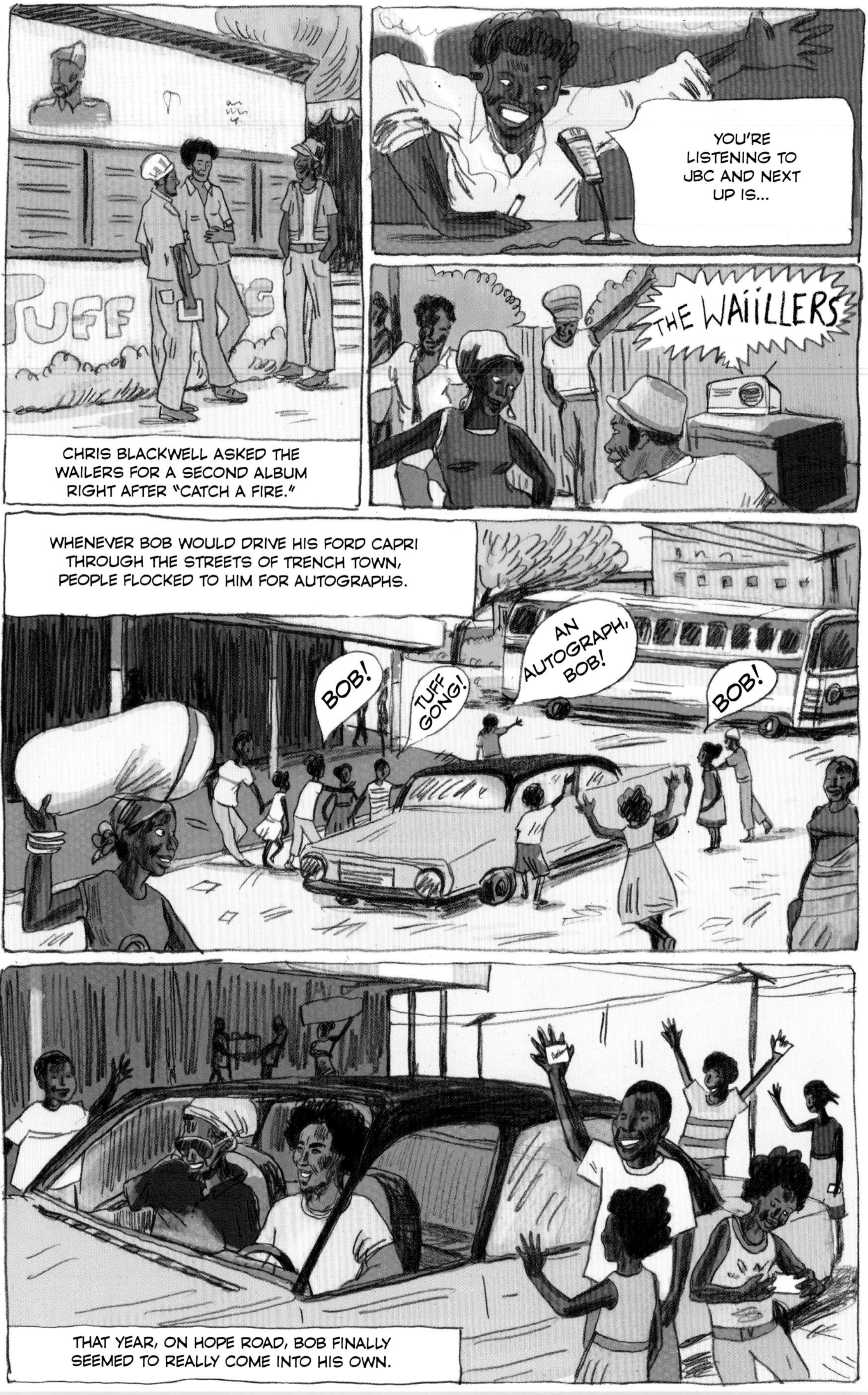
CHRIS BLACKWELL ASKED THE WAILERS FOR A SECOND ALBUM RIGHT AFTER "CATCH A FIRE."
YOU'RE LISTENING TO JBC AND NEXT UP IS...
THE WAIILLERS
WHENEVER BOB WOULD DRIVE HIS FORD CAPRI THROUGH THE STREETS OF TRENCH TOWN, PEOPLE FLOCKED TO HIM FOR AUTOGRAPHS.
BOB!
TUFF GONG!
AN AUTOGRAPH, BOB!
BOB!
THAT YEAR, ON HOPE ROAD, BOB FINALLY SEEMED TO REALLY COME INTO HIS OWN.

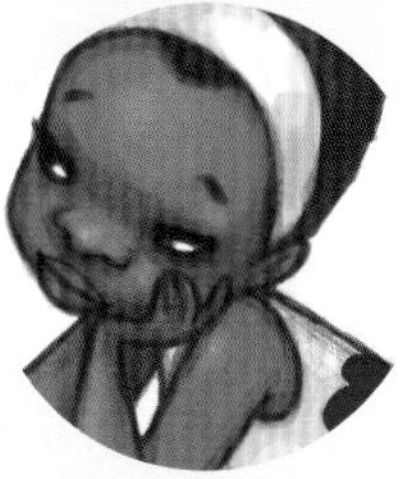

Bob Marley, Rita... and all the other women

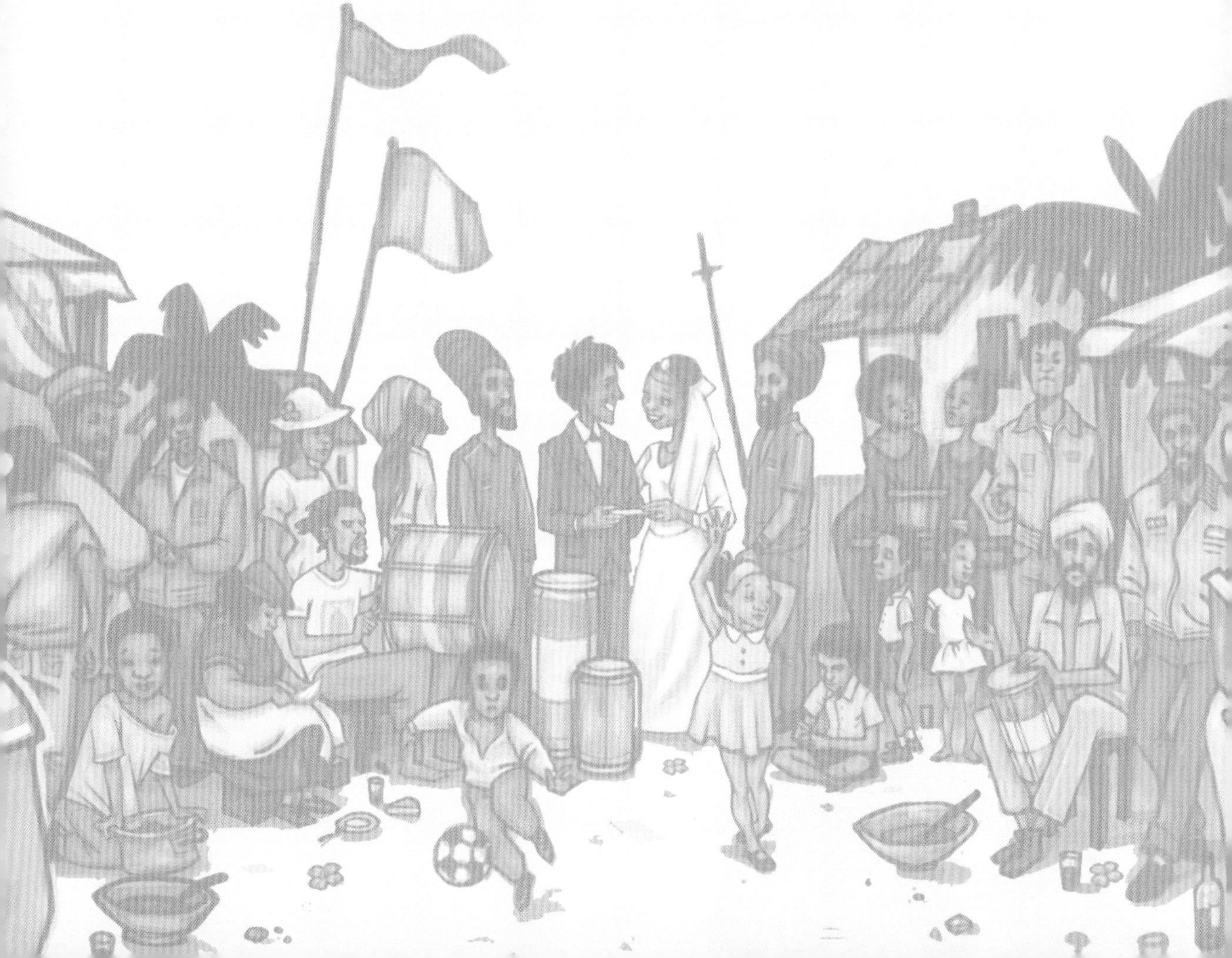

While Bob Marley officially acknowledged paternity of eleven children, it's harder to keep track of his mistresses… An incorrigible ladies' man, he devoted his love songs to some of his conquests but remained married to Rita Anderson for fifteen years.

After the release of Catch A Fire in 1973, Bob Marley spent several years living in the villa of his producer Chris Blackwell, on the aptly named Hope Road. It was their first hit album and the future seemed bright with promise! Even though Trenchtown, the ghetto he grew up in, was just a few miles away, the villa was a radical change of scenery. A beautiful house with a garden and a rehearsal studio—what more could a man possibly want? His wife, Rita, lived a little further away on the coast with their three children: Cedella, David (who went by Ziggy) and Stephen, as well as little Sharon, whom Cedella had from a previous relationship and whom Bob adopted. During that time period, Bob Marley lived the good life, and we're not just talking music and weed... The artist also had many romantic liaisons, most notably with Jamaican actress and photographer Esther Anderson. She gave the world a few famous pictures of Bob Marley, namely the one on the cover of Burnin', the second album produced by Island Records. At least Bob remained faithful to his producer, if not to his wife... And this was hardly unprecedented behavior.

It's not easy being the wife of a legend.

Indeed, Bob Marley had already had a number of extra-marital affairs. In the spring of 1972, he had achieved the feat of becoming a father three times in just a few weeks! To wit: barely had Rita given birth to Stephen, that Pat Williams, an old girlfriend of his, gave birth to Robert (aka Robbie), with little Rohan following in his footsteps a few days later, born of mother Janet Hunt, another mistress of Bob. One year later, in London, another Janet gave birth to baby Karen. And the list goes on. All in all, Bob Marley recognized paternity of eleven children from seven different women. But rumor has it, he fathered a good twenty offspring! The criteria he used to determine paternity? Whether or not the child spoke out of the corner of his mouth, as he later told his friend Diane Jobson, who was also his attorney. Not exactly the most convincing argument... But at least

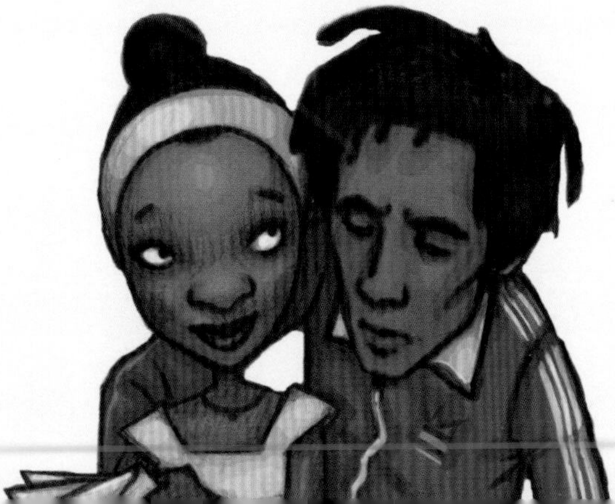

it didn't stop his children from singing! Sure enough, a good number of Marley's children went into music. In 1979, four of his blood childeren, Cedella, Ziggy, Stephen and Sharon, started a band called The Melody Makers, which later became Ziggy and the Melody Makers, before the eldest of the Marley boys pursued a solo career—successfully so, since to date he has received no less than five Grammy Awards in the Best Reggae Album category.

Another musician who went on to achieve fame is Damian Marley, who performs under the stage name Junior Gong, i.e. the son of Tuff Gong, the nickname Bob Marley once used for himself and which referred to the founder of the Rastafari movement, Leonard Percival Howell, aka The Gong. Born in 1978, Damian is the son of Cindy Breakspeare, a jazz musician and model who was elected Miss World 1976. It was with her in mind that Bob Marley sang "I want to give you some love," in "Turn Your Lights Low," and she was also the woman to inspire the beautiful declaration of love in "Satisfy My Soul:" "When you hold me tight, you make me feel all right... You satisfy my soul." His love for that woman still haunted him when he asks in the famous refrain: "Is this love that I'm feeling?" However, their romance was not without its share of problems for the singer, for while they did live together in London, Cindy Breakspeare had

her own career. "I don't wanna wait in vain for your love," worries Bob Marley, who goes on to sing "Tears in my eyes burn, while I'm waiting for my turn," in the moving 1977 "Waitin' in Vain." Those feelings, however, didn't stop him from heading back to Jamaica a few months later, where he moved on to new conquests...

During that whole time, and despite the singer's many love affairs, Rita and Bob Marley remained married. They said "I do" in 1966 and it never occurred to either one to get a divorce. In 2012, at a big reggae festival in France, Rita told several reporters that she had accepted her husband's infidelities: "Our mission to share our music was more important." Lest we forget, in the beginning, Rita Anderson and her I-Threes vocal group were Bob Marley's backup singers. From that moment forward, she remained at the musician's side through thick and thin, sharing in his first defeats and in his resounding successes while raising their six children. In her mind, she was "more than a wife" to him, and became "A mother, a guide." For audiences around the world though, she is first and foremost the woman the singer consoles in one of his most unforgettable songs, which countless millions have sung along to: "No woman no cry."

The Sheriff Died Tonight

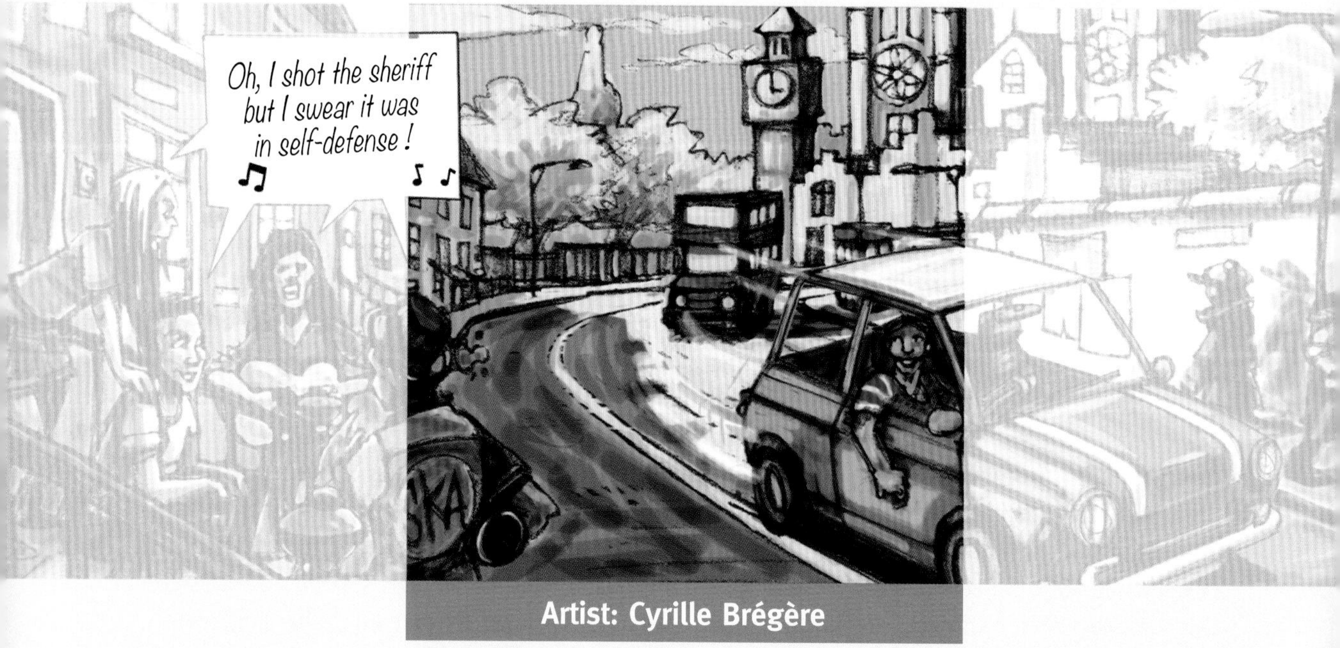
Oh, I shot the sheriff but I swear it was in self-defense !
SKA

Artist: Cyrille Brégère

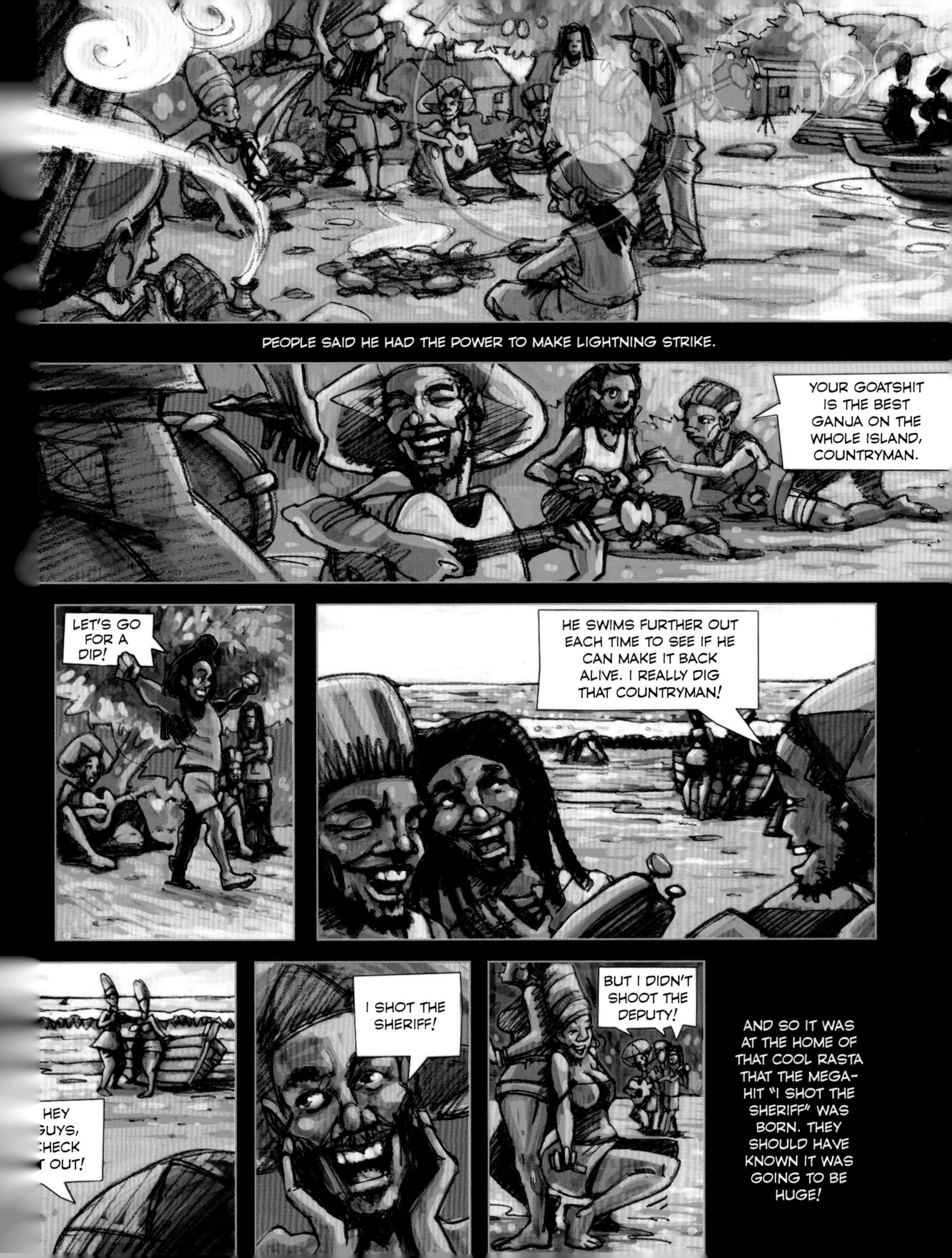
PEOPLE SAID HE HAD THE POWER TO MAKE LIGHTNING STRIKE.
YOUR GOATSHIT IS THE BEST GANJA ON THE WHOLE ISLAND, COUNTRYMAN.
LET'S GO FOR A DIP!
HE SWIMS FURTHER OUT EACH TIME TO SEE IF HE CAN MAKE IT BACK ALIVE. I REALLY DIG THAT COUNTRYMAN!
HEY GUYS, CHECK T OUT!
I SHOT THE SHERIFF!
BUT I DIDN'T SHOOT THE DEPUTY!
AND SO IT WAS AT THE HOME OF THAT COOL RASTA THAT THE MEGA-HIT "I SHOT THE SHERIFF" WAS BORN. THEY SHOULD HAVE KNOWN IT WAS GOING TO BE HUGE!

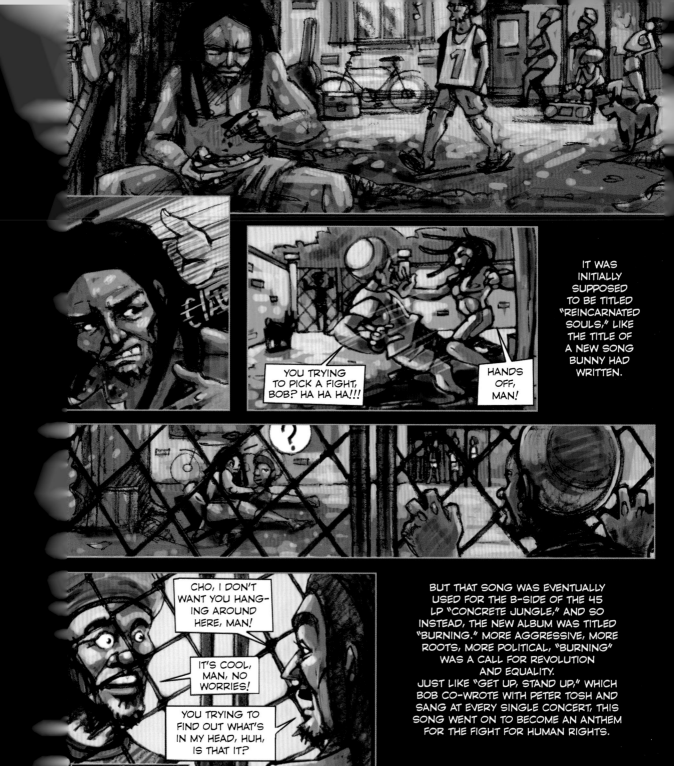

IT WAS INITIALLY SUPPOSED TO BE TITLED "REINCARNATED SOULS," LIKE THE TITLE OF A NEW SONG BUNNY HAD WRITTEN.

YOU TRYING TO PICK A FIGHT, BOB? HA HA HA!!!

HANDS OFF, MAN!

CHO, I DON'T WANT YOU HANGING AROUND HERE, MAN!

IT'S COOL, MAN, NO WORRIES!

YOU TRYING TO FIND OUT WHAT'S IN MY HEAD, HUH, IS THAT IT?

WELL WHY DON'T YOU JUST ASK ME?

BUT THAT SONG WAS EVENTUALLY USED FOR THE B-SIDE OF THE 45 LP "CONCRETE JUNGLE," AND SO INSTEAD, THE NEW ALBUM WAS TITLED "BURNING." MORE AGGRESSIVE, MORE ROOTS, MORE POLITICAL, "BURNING" WAS A CALL FOR REVOLUTION AND EQUALITY.
JUST LIKE "GET UP, STAND UP," WHICH BOB CO-WROTE WITH PETER TOSH AND SANG AT EVERY SINGLE CONCERT, THIS SONG WENT ON TO BECOME AN ANTHEM FOR THE FIGHT FOR HUMAN RIGHTS.

I'LL TELL YOU: IT'S JAH!!!

*ERIC CLAPTON DID A COVER OF "I

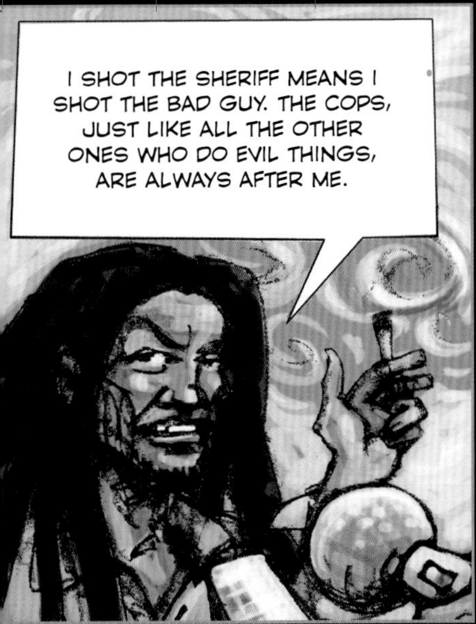
I SHOT THE SHERIFF MEANS I SHOT THE BAD GUY. THE COPS, JUST LIKE ALL THE OTHER ONES WHO DO EVIL THINGS, ARE ALWAYS AFTER ME.

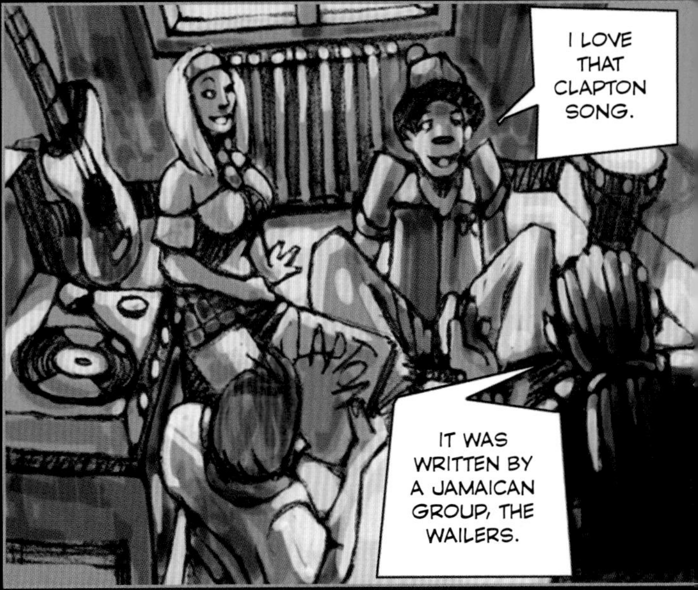
I LOVE THAT CLAPTON SONG.
IT WAS WRITTEN BY A JAMAICAN GROUP, THE WAILERS.

FROM THEN ON, THE WAILERS BECAME A HOUSEHOLD NAME.

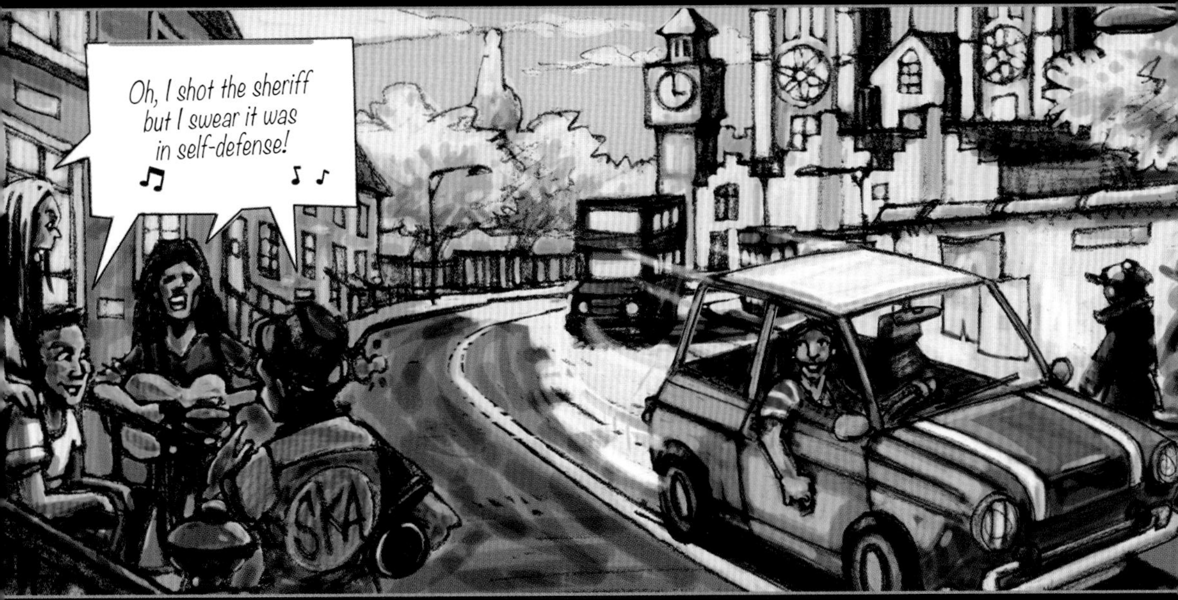
Oh, I shot the sheriff but I swear it was in self-defense!
SKA

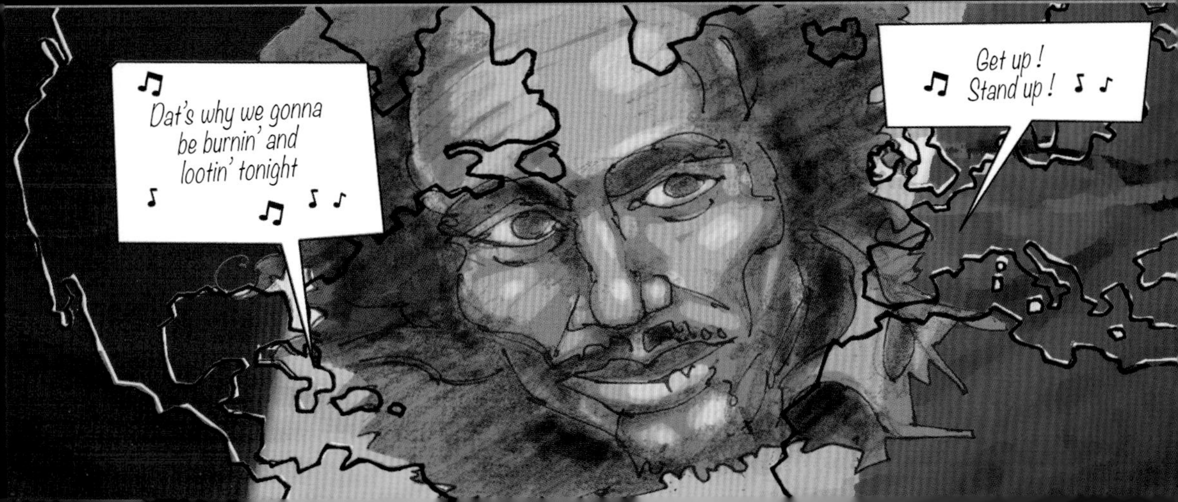
Dat's why we gonna be burnin' and lootin' tonight
Get up ! Stand up !

Around the World

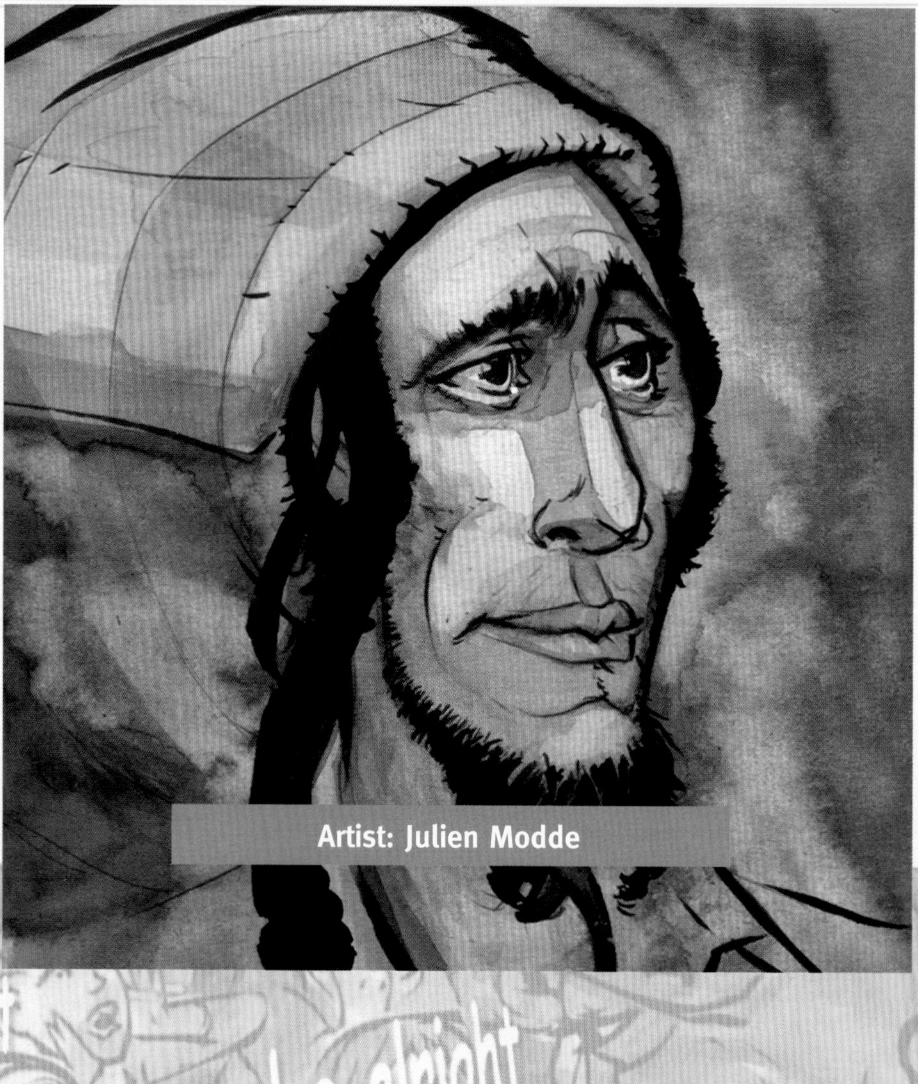

Artist: Julien Modde

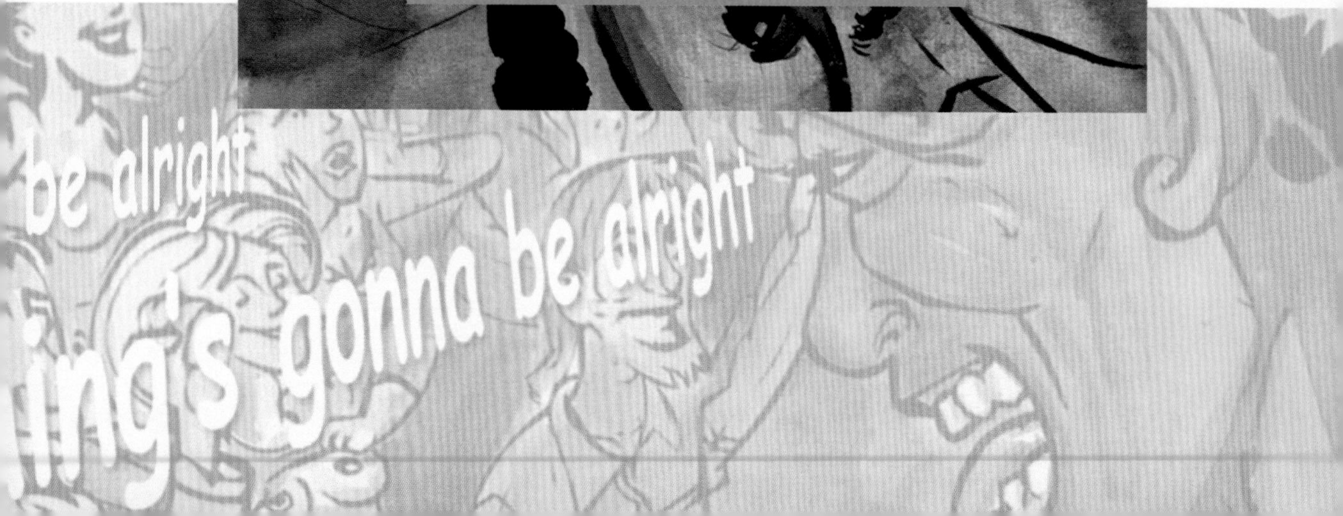
be alright
ing's gonna be alright

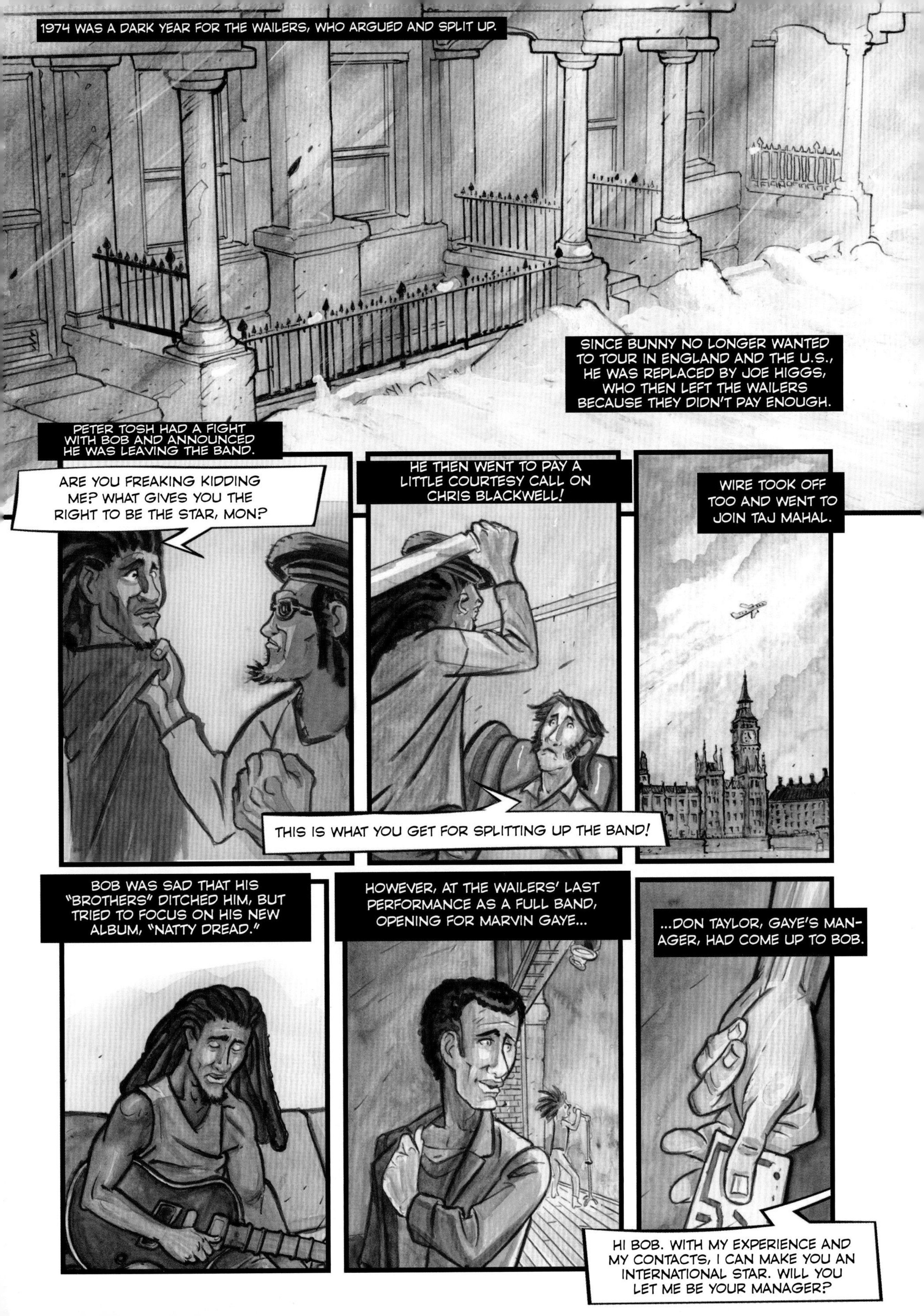
1974 WAS A DARK YEAR FOR THE WAILERS, WHO ARGUED AND SPLIT UP.
SINCE BUNNY NO LONGER WANTED TO TOUR IN ENGLAND AND THE U.S., HE WAS REPLACED BY JOE HIGGS, WHO THEN LEFT THE WAILERS BECAUSE THEY DIDN'T PAY ENOUGH.
PETER TOSH HAD A FIGHT WITH BOB AND ANNOUNCED HE WAS LEAVING THE BAND.
ARE YOU FREAKING KIDDING ME? WHAT GIVES YOU THE RIGHT TO BE THE STAR, MON?
HE THEN WENT TO PAY A LITTLE COURTESY CALL ON CHRIS BLACKWELL!
THIS IS WHAT YOU GET FOR SPLITTING UP THE BAND!
WIRE TOOK OFF TOO AND WENT TO JOIN TAJ MAHAL.
BOB WAS SAD THAT HIS "BROTHERS" DITCHED HIM, BUT TRIED TO FOCUS ON HIS NEW ALBUM, "NATTY DREAD."
HOWEVER, AT THE WAILERS' LAST PERFORMANCE AS A FULL BAND, OPENING FOR MARVIN GAYE...
...DON TAYLOR, GAYE'S MANAGER, HAD COME UP TO BOB.
HI BOB. WITH MY EXPERIENCE AND MY CONTACTS, I CAN MAKE YOU AN INTERNATIONAL STAR. WILL YOU LET ME BE YOUR MANAGER?

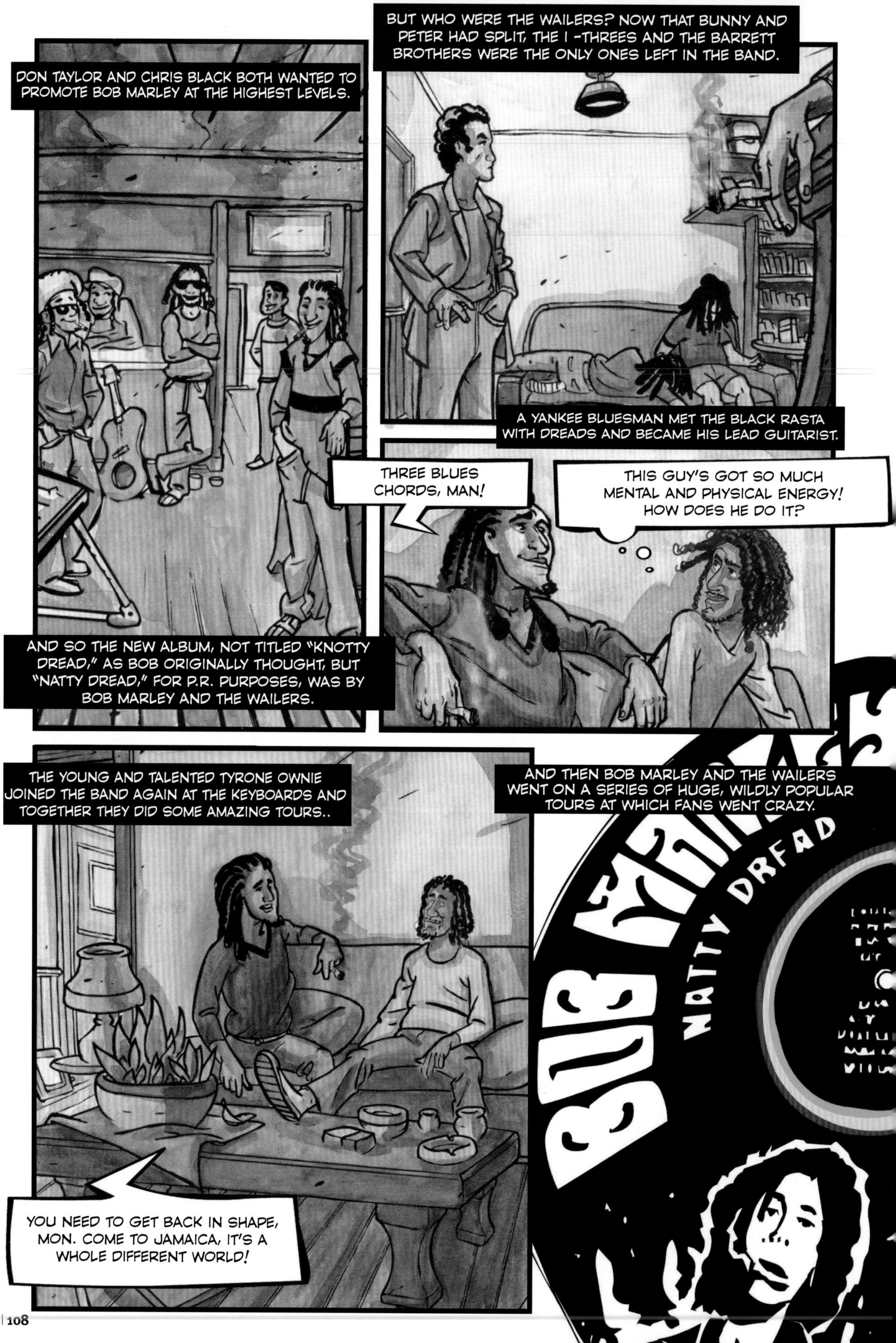
DON TAYLOR AND CHRIS BLACK BOTH WANTED TO PROMOTE BOB MARLEY AT THE HIGHEST LEVELS.
AND SO THE NEW ALBUM, NOT TITLED "KNOTTY DREAD," AS BOB ORIGINALLY THOUGHT, BUT "NATTY DREAD," FOR P.R. PURPOSES, WAS BY BOB MARLEY AND THE WAILERS.
BUT WHO WERE THE WAILERS? NOW THAT BUNNY AND PETER HAD SPLIT, THE I -THREES AND THE BARRETT BROTHERS WERE THE ONLY ONES LEFT IN THE BAND.
A YANKEE BLUESMAN MET THE BLACK RASTA WITH DREADS AND BECAME HIS LEAD GUITARIST.
THREE BLUES CHORDS, MAN!
THIS GUY'S GOT SO MUCH MENTAL AND PHYSICAL ENERGY! HOW DOES HE DO IT?
THE YOUNG AND TALENTED TYRONE OWNIE JOINED THE BAND AGAIN AT THE KEYBOARDS AND TOGETHER THEY DID SOME AMAZING TOURS..
YOU NEED TO GET BACK IN SHAPE, MON. COME TO JAMAICA, IT'S A WHOLE DIFFERENT WORLD!
AND THEN BOB MARLEY AND THE WAILERS WENT ON A SERIES OF HUGE, WILDLY POPULAR TOURS AT WHICH FANS WENT CRAZY.
NATTY DREAD

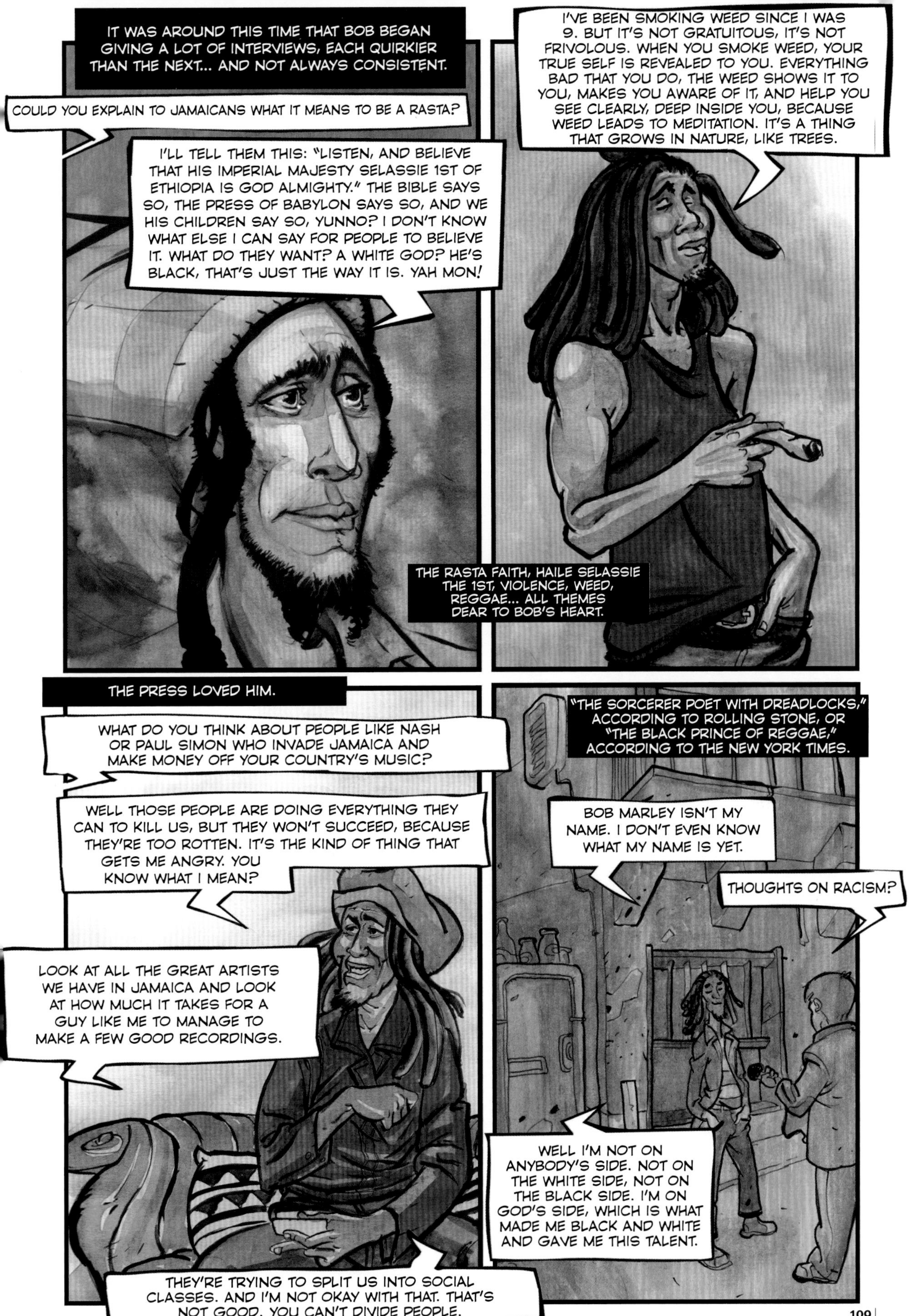
IT WAS AROUND THIS TIME THAT BOB BEGAN GIVING A LOT OF INTERVIEWS, EACH QUIRKIER THAN THE NEXT... AND NOT ALWAYS CONSISTENT.
COULD YOU EXPLAIN TO JAMAICANS WHAT IT MEANS TO BE A RASTA?
I'LL TELL THEM THIS: "LISTEN, AND BELIEVE THAT HIS IMPERIAL MAJESTY SELASSIE 1ST OF ETHIOPIA IS GOD ALMIGHTY." THE BIBLE SAYS SO, THE PRESS OF BABYLON SAYS SO, AND WE HIS CHILDREN SAY SO, YUNNO? I DON'T KNOW WHAT ELSE I CAN SAY FOR PEOPLE TO BELIEVE IT. WHAT DO THEY WANT? A WHITE GOD? HE'S BLACK, THAT'S JUST THE WAY IT IS. YAH MON!
I'VE BEEN SMOKING WEED SINCE I WAS 9. BUT IT'S NOT GRATUITOUS, IT'S NOT FRIVOLOUS. WHEN YOU SMOKE WEED, YOUR TRUE SELF IS REVEALED TO YOU. EVERYTHING BAD THAT YOU DO, THE WEED SHOWS IT TO YOU, MAKES YOU AWARE OF IT, AND HELP YOU SEE CLEARLY, DEEP INSIDE YOU, BECAUSE WEED LEADS TO MEDITATION. IT'S A THING THAT GROWS IN NATURE, LIKE TREES.
THE RASTA FAITH, HAILE SELASSIE THE 1ST, VIOLENCE, WEED, REGGAE... ALL THEMES DEAR TO BOB'S HEART.
THE PRESS LOVED HIM.
WHAT DO YOU THINK ABOUT PEOPLE LIKE NASH OR PAUL SIMON WHO INVADE JAMAICA AND MAKE MONEY OFF YOUR COUNTRY'S MUSIC?
WELL THOSE PEOPLE ARE DOING EVERYTHING THEY CAN TO KILL US, BUT THEY WON'T SUCCEED, BECAUSE THEY'RE TOO ROTTEN. IT'S THE KIND OF THING THAT GETS ME ANGRY. YOU KNOW WHAT I MEAN?
LOOK AT ALL THE GREAT ARTISTS WE HAVE IN JAMAICA AND LOOK AT HOW MUCH IT TAKES FOR A GUY LIKE ME TO MANAGE TO MAKE A FEW GOOD RECORDINGS.
THEY'RE TRYING TO SPLIT US INTO SOCIAL CLASSES. AND I'M NOT OKAY WITH THAT. THAT'S NOT GOOD. YOU CAN'T DIVIDE PEOPLE.
"THE SORCERER POET WITH DREADLOCKS," ACCORDING TO ROLLING STONE, OR "THE BLACK PRINCE OF REGGAE," ACCORDING TO THE NEW YORK TIMES.
BOB MARLEY ISN'T MY NAME. I DON'T EVEN KNOW WHAT MY NAME IS YET.
THOUGHTS ON RACISM?
WELL I'M NOT ON ANYBODY'S SIDE. NOT ON THE WHITE SIDE, NOT ON THE BLACK SIDE. I'M ON GOD'S SIDE, WHICH IS WHAT MADE ME BLACK AND WHITE AND GAVE ME THIS TALENT.

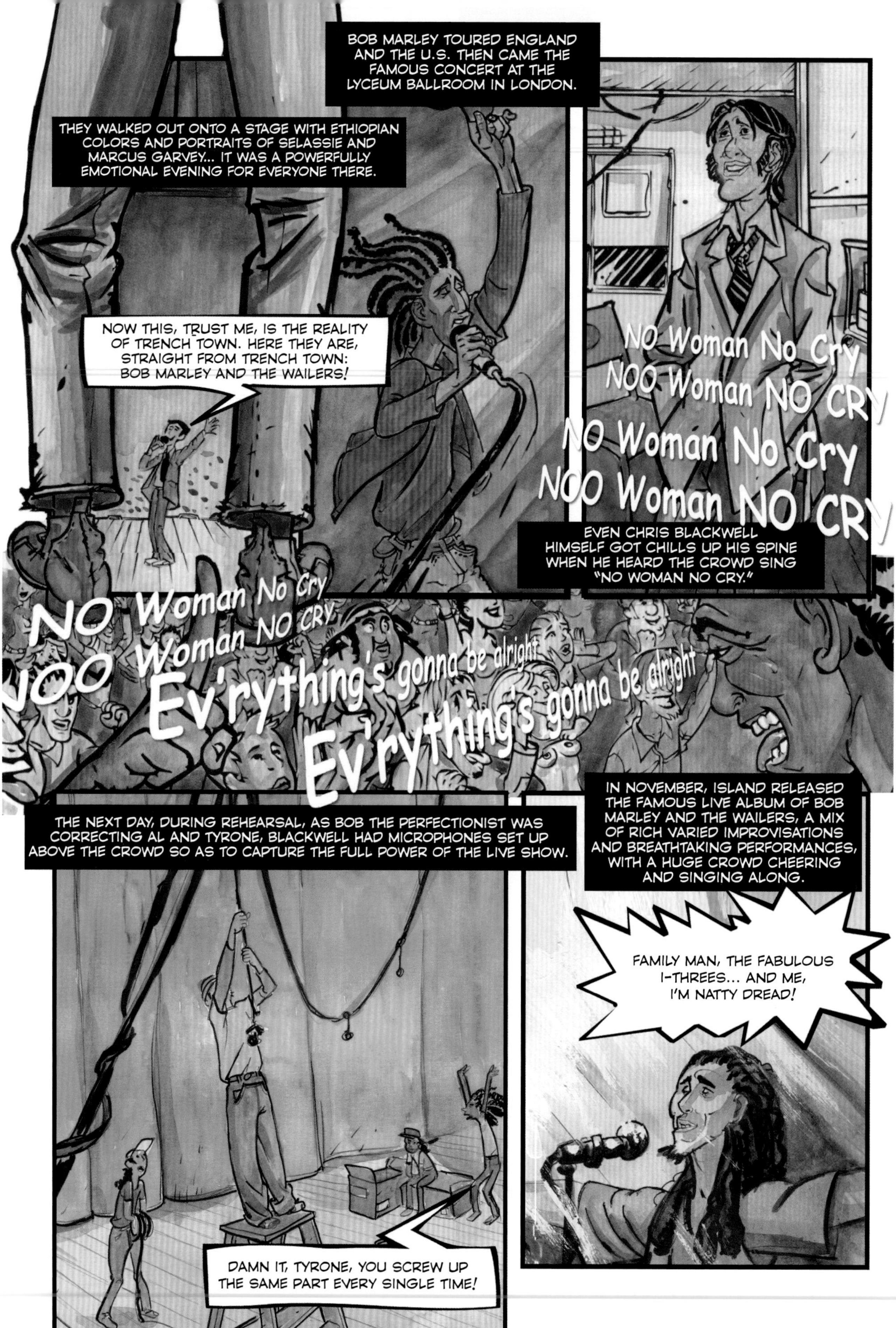

BOB MARLEY TOURED ENGLAND AND THE U.S. THEN CAME THE FAMOUS CONCERT AT THE LYCEUM BALLROOM IN LONDON.
THEY WALKED OUT ONTO A STAGE WITH ETHIOPIAN COLORS AND PORTRAITS OF SELASSIE AND MARCUS GARVEY... IT WAS A POWERFULLY EMOTIONAL EVENING FOR EVERYONE THERE.
NOW THIS, TRUST ME, IS THE REALITY OF TRENCH TOWN. HERE THEY ARE, STRAIGHT FROM TRENCH TOWN: BOB MARLEY AND THE WAILERS!
NO Woman No Cry
NOO Woman NO CRY
NO Woman No Cry
NOO Woman NO CRY
EVEN CHRIS BLACKWELL HIMSELF GOT CHILLS UP HIS SPINE WHEN HE HEARD THE CROWD SING "NO WOMAN NO CRY."
NO Woman No Cry
NOO Woman NO CRY
Ev'rything's gonna be alright
Ev'rything's gonna be alright
THE NEXT DAY, DURING REHEARSAL, AS BOB THE PERFECTIONIST WAS CORRECTING AL AND TYRONE, BLACKWELL HAD MICROPHONES SET UP ABOVE THE CROWD SO AS TO CAPTURE THE FULL POWER OF THE LIVE SHOW.
DAMN IT, TYRONE, YOU SCREW UP THE SAME PART EVERY SINGLE TIME!
IN NOVEMBER, ISLAND RELEASED THE FAMOUS LIVE ALBUM OF BOB MARLEY AND THE WAILERS, A MIX OF RICH VARIED IMPROVISATIONS AND BREATHTAKING PERFORMANCES, WITH A HUGE CROWD CHEERING AND SINGING ALONG.
FAMILY MAN, THE FABULOUS I-THREES... AND ME, I'M NATTY DREAD!

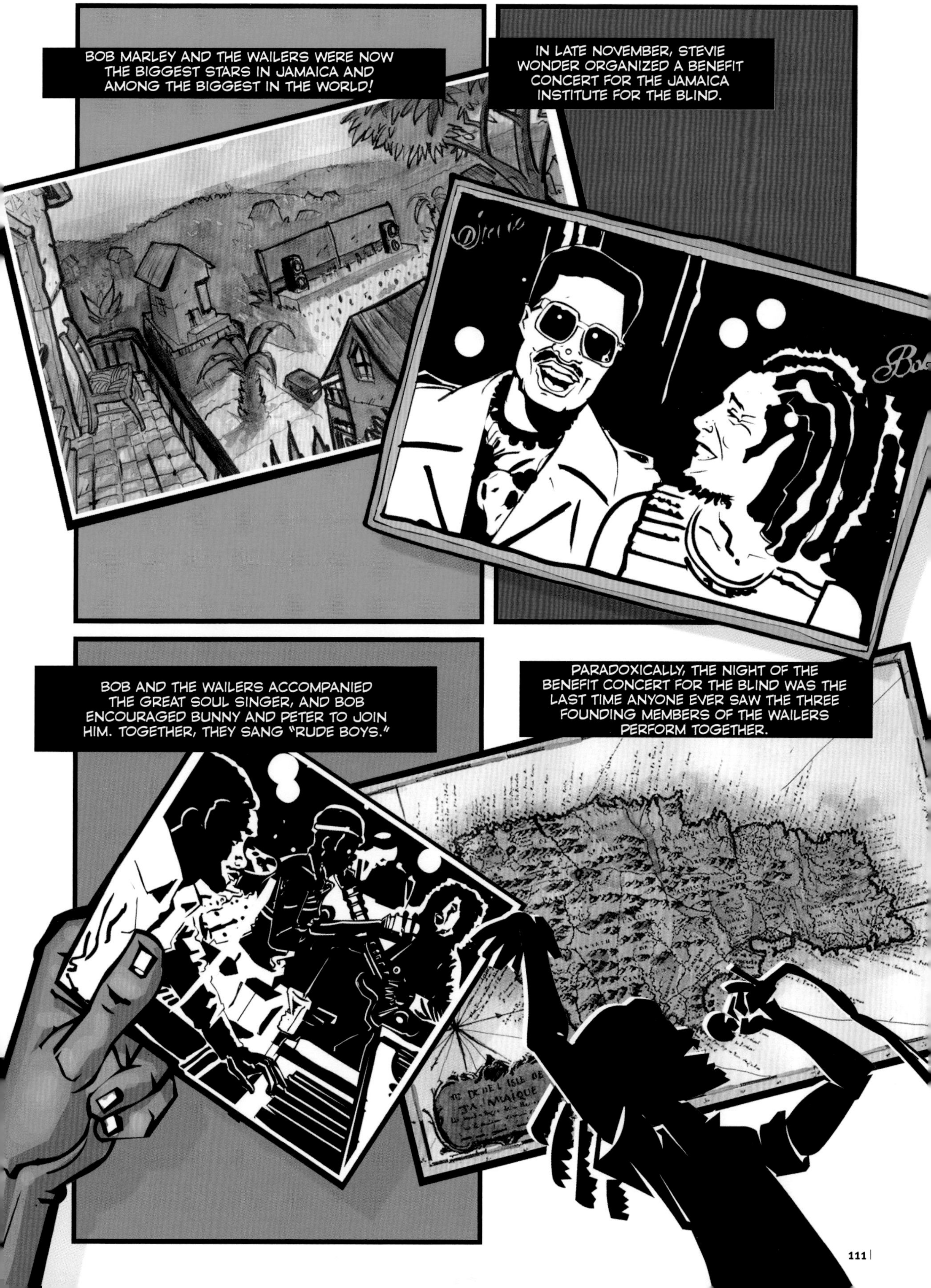
BOB MARLEY AND THE WAILERS WERE NOW THE BIGGEST STARS IN JAMAICA AND AMONG THE BIGGEST IN THE WORLD!
IN LATE NOVEMBER, STEVIE WONDER ORGANIZED A BENEFIT CONCERT FOR THE JAMAICA INSTITUTE FOR THE BLIND.
BOB AND THE WAILERS ACCOMPANIED THE GREAT SOUL SINGER, AND BOB ENCOURAGED BUNNY AND PETER TO JOIN HIM. TOGETHER, THEY SANG "RUDE BOYS."
PARADOXICALLY, THE NIGHT OF THE BENEFIT CONCERT FOR THE BLIND WAS THE LAST TIME ANYONE EVER SAW THE THREE FOUNDING MEMBERS OF THE WAILERS PERFORM TOGETHER.

Panic in the Hen House

Artist: Moh

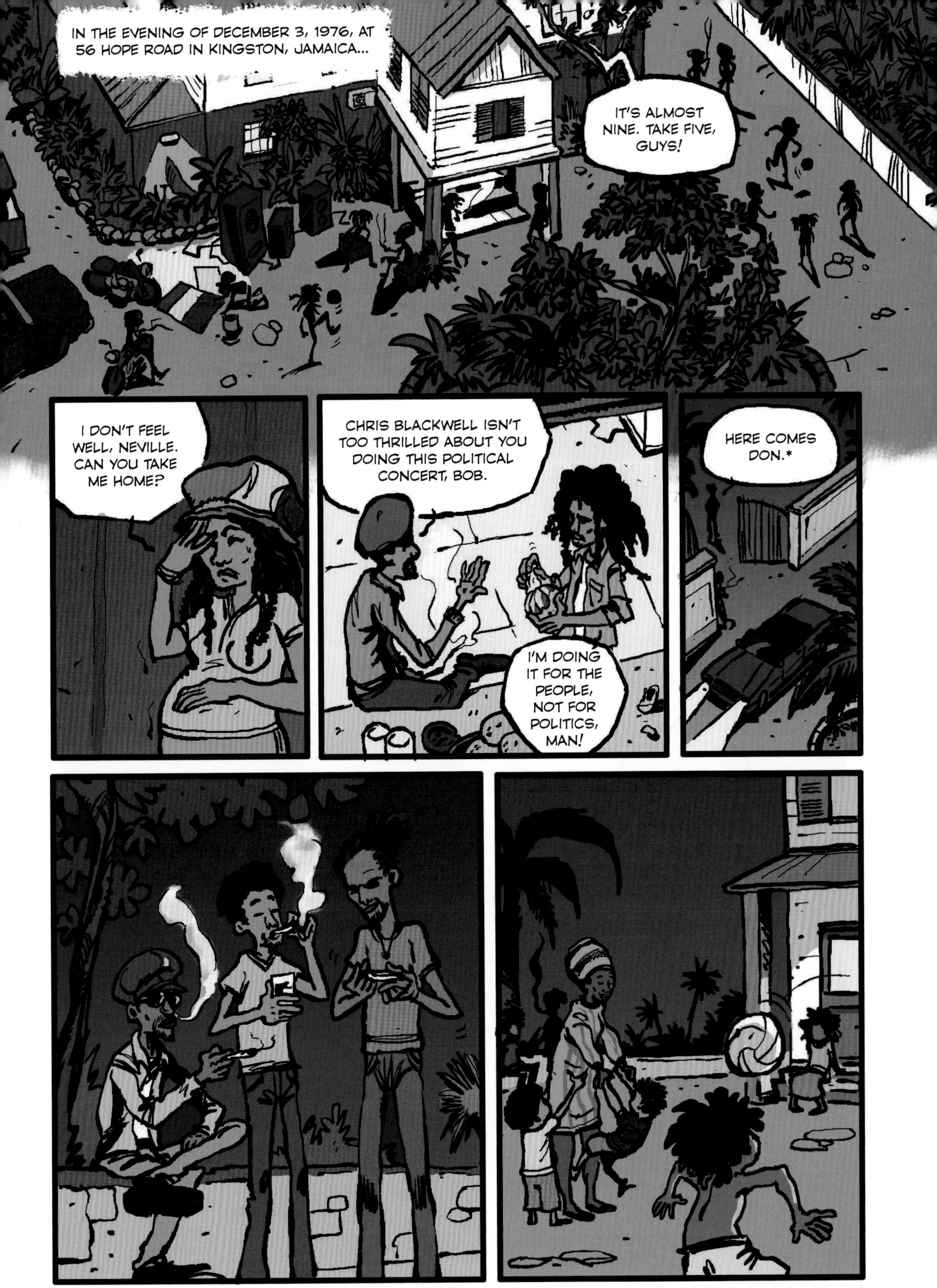
IN THE EVENING OF DECEMBER 3, 1976, AT 56 HOPE ROAD IN KINGSTON, JAMAICA...
IT'S ALMOST NINE. TAKE FIVE, GUYS!
I DON'T FEEL WELL, NEVILLE. CAN YOU TAKE ME HOME?
CHRIS BLACKWELL ISN'T TOO THRILLED ABOUT YOU DOING THIS POLITICAL CONCERT, BOB.
I'M DOING IT FOR THE PEOPLE, NOT FOR POLITICS, MAN!
HERE COMES DON.*

*DON TAYLOR, THEIR MANAGER.

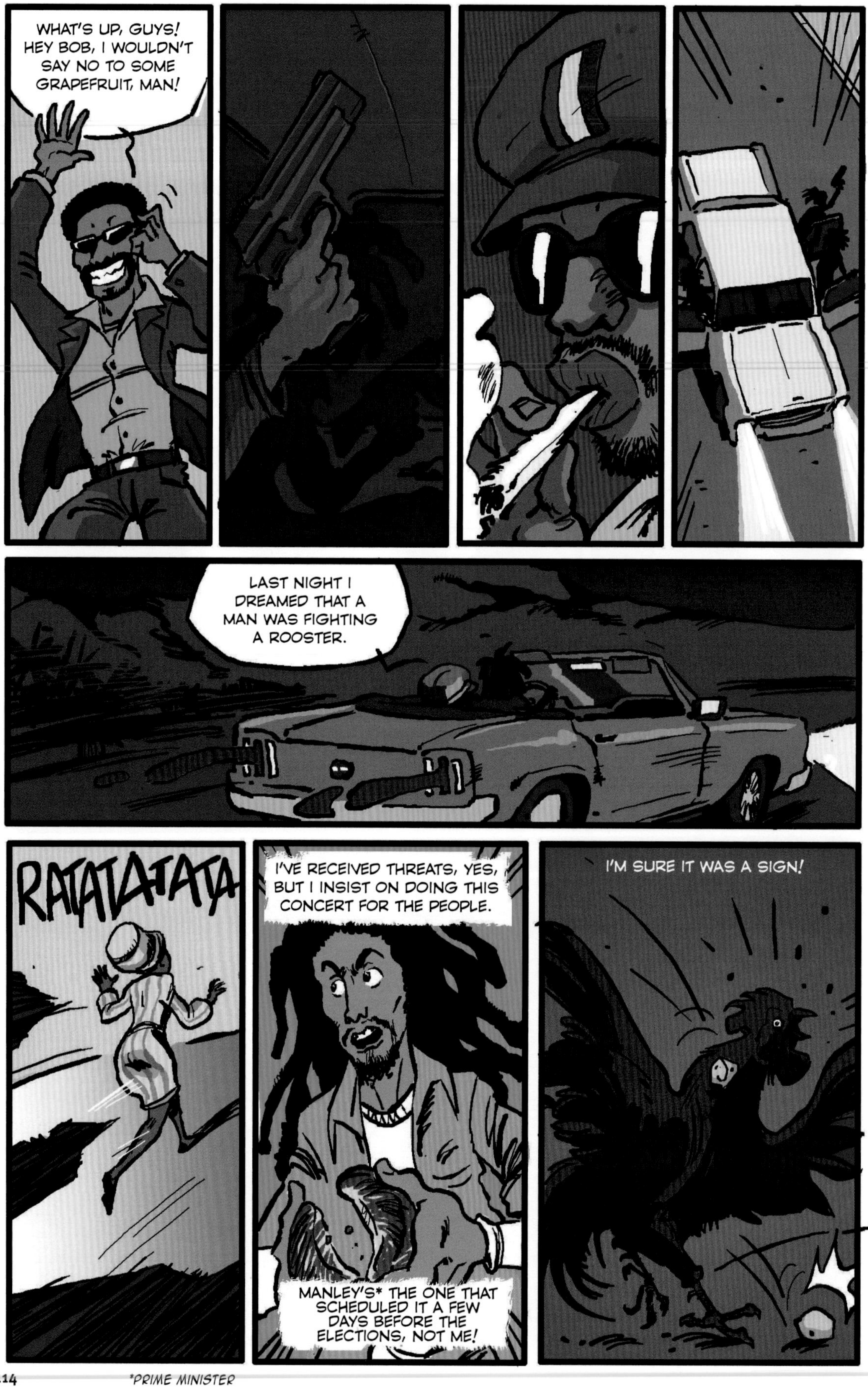
WHAT'S UP, GUYS! HEY BOB, I WOULDN'T SAY NO TO SOME GRAPEFRUIT, MAN!
LAST NIGHT I DREAMED THAT A MAN WAS FIGHTING A ROOSTER.
RATATATATA
I'VE RECEIVED THREATS, YES, BUT I INSIST ON DOING THIS CONCERT FOR THE PEOPLE.
MANLEY'S* THE ONE THAT SCHEDULED IT A FEW DAYS BEFORE THE ELECTIONS, NOT ME!
I'M SURE IT WAS A SIGN!

*PRIME MINISTER

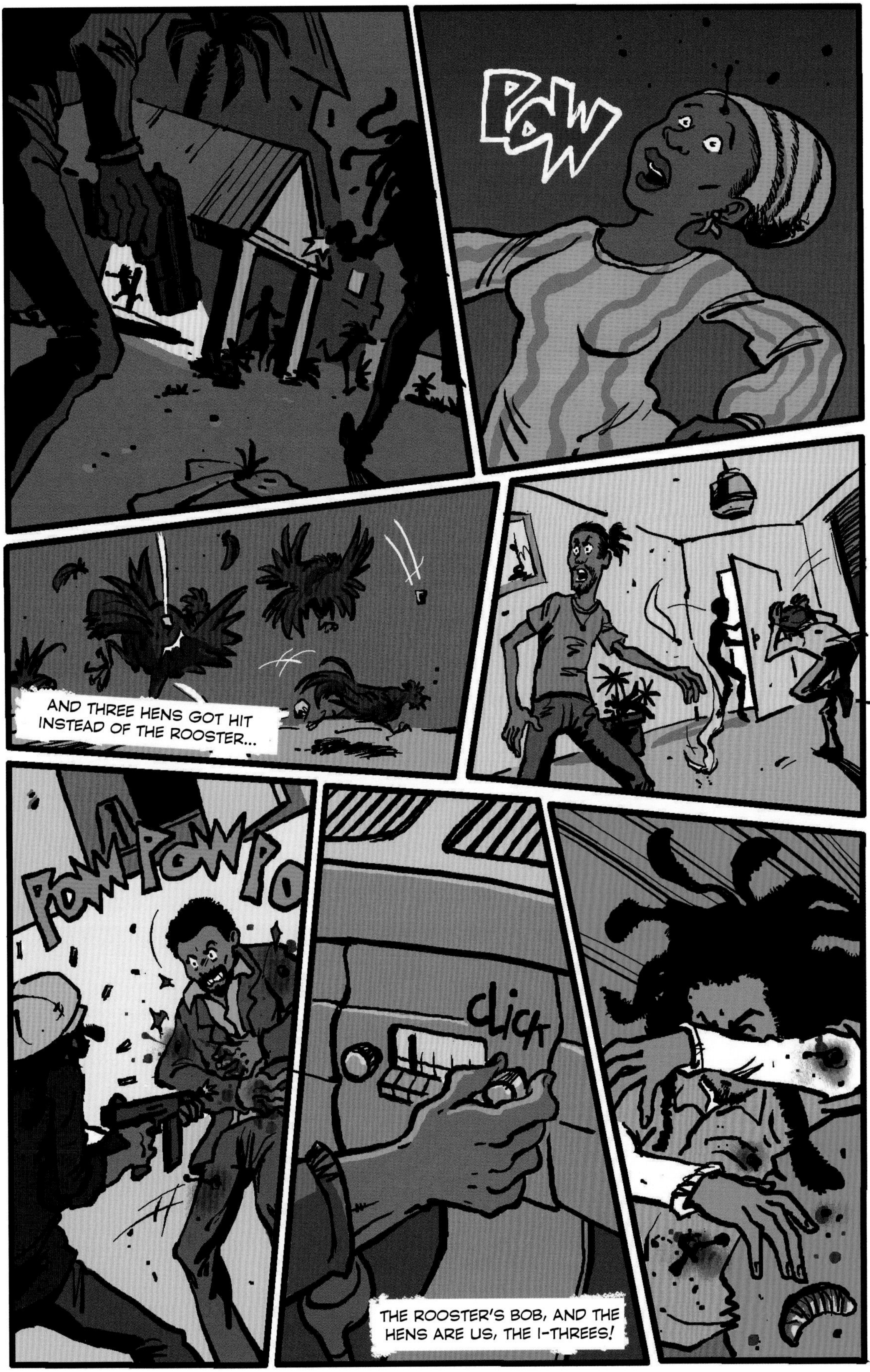
POW
AND THREE HENS GOT HIT INSTEAD OF THE ROOSTER...
POW POW PO
CLICK
THE ROOSTER'S BOB, AND THE HENS ARE US, THE I-THREES!

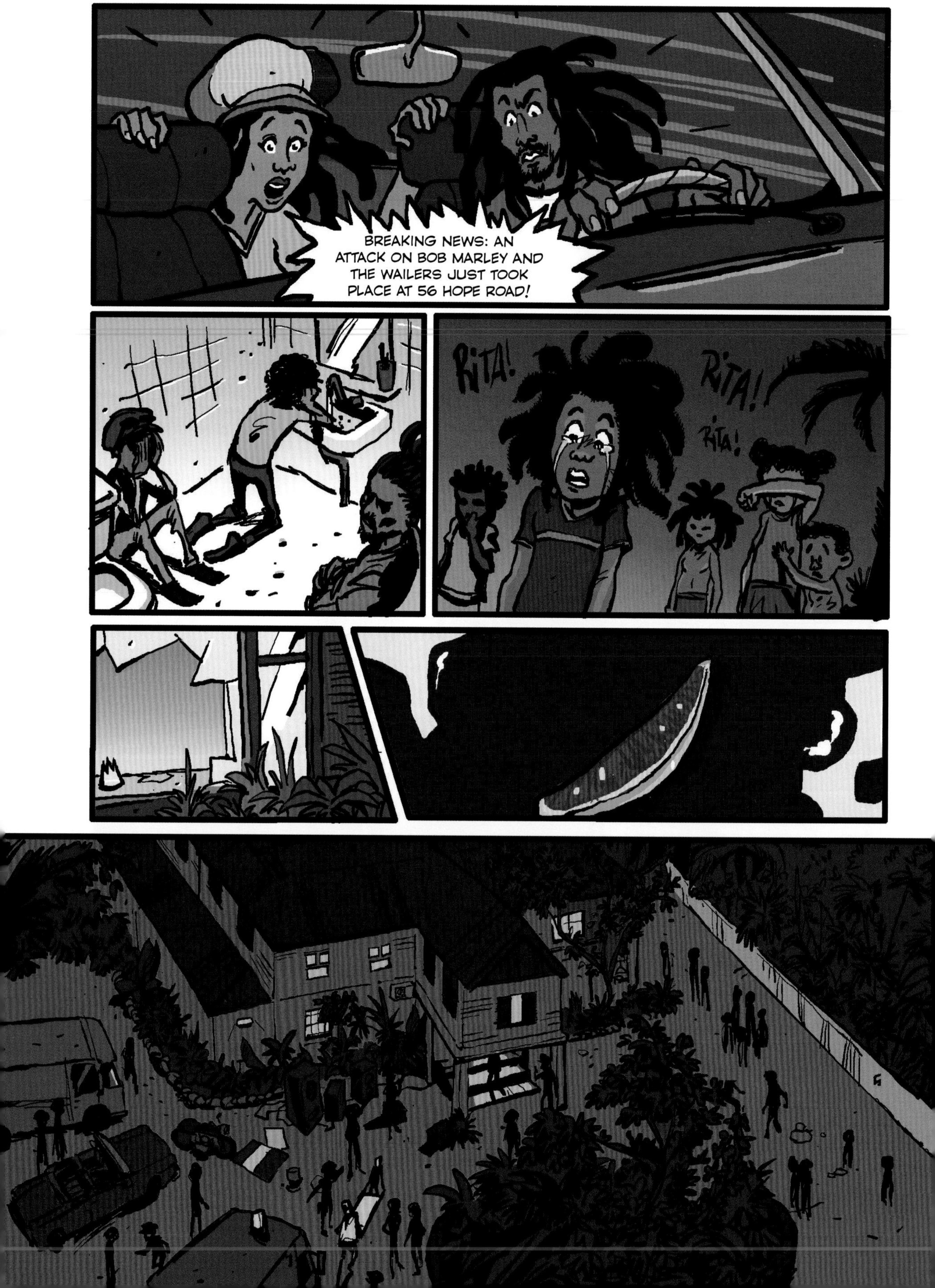

BREAKING NEWS: AN ATTACK ON BOB MARLEY AND THE WAILERS JUST TOOK PLACE AT 56 HOPE ROAD!
RITA!
RITA!
RITA!

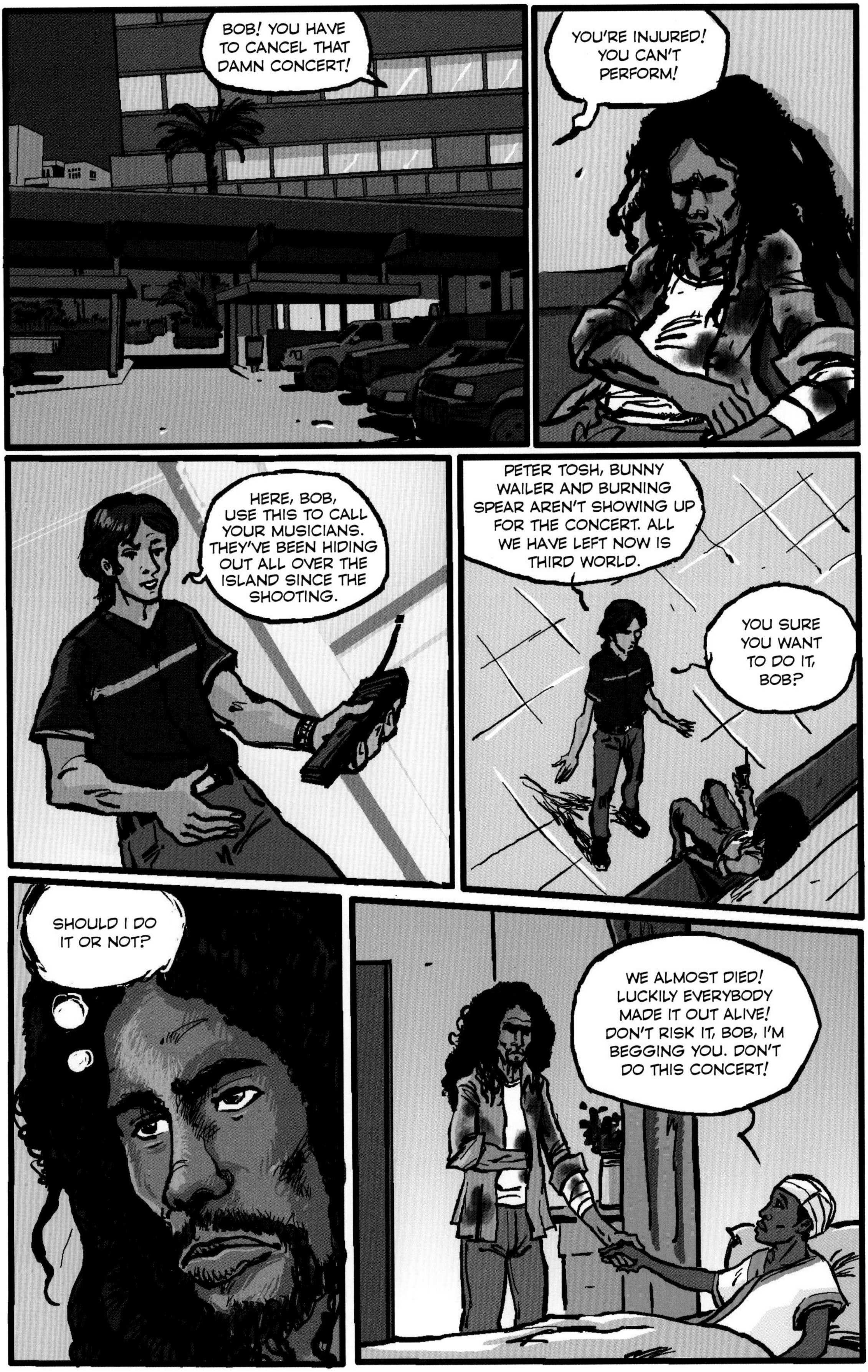
BOB! YOU HAVE TO CANCEL THAT DAMN CONCERT!
YOU'RE INJURED! YOU CAN'T PERFORM!
HERE, BOB, USE THIS TO CALL YOUR MUSICIANS. THEY'VE BEEN HIDING OUT ALL OVER THE ISLAND SINCE THE SHOOTING.
PETER TOSH, BUNNY WAILER AND BURNING SPEAR AREN'T SHOWING UP FOR THE CONCERT. ALL WE HAVE LEFT NOW IS THIRD WORLD.
YOU SURE YOU WANT TO DO IT, BOB?
SHOULD I DO IT OR NOT?
WE ALMOST DIED! LUCKILY EVERYBODY MADE IT OUT ALIVE! DON'T RISK IT, BOB, I'M BEGGING YOU. DON'T DO THIS CONCERT!

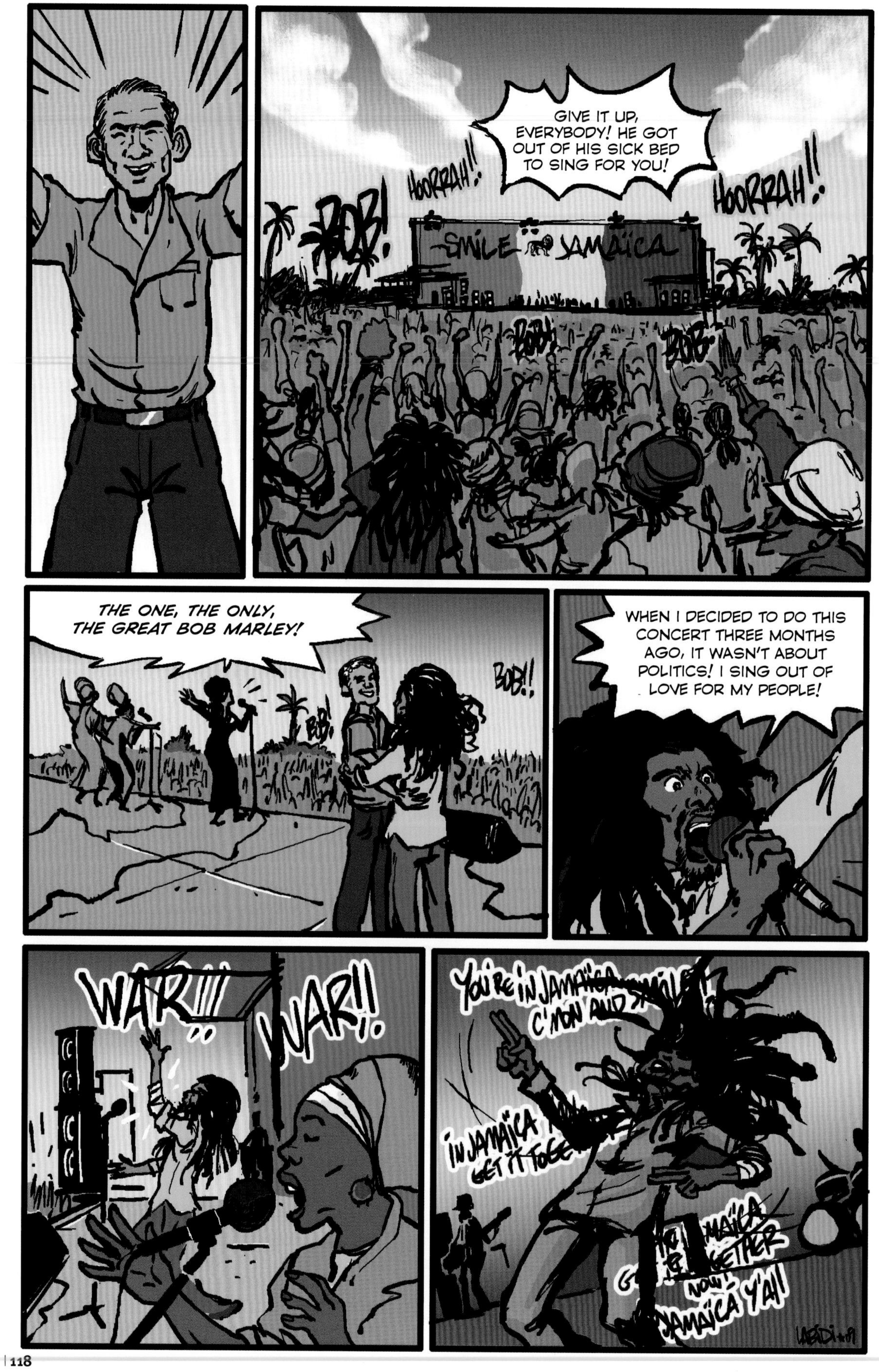
GIVE IT UP, EVERYBODY! HE GOT OUT OF HIS SICK BED TO SING FOR YOU!
HOORRAH!!
BOB!
SMILE JAMAICA
HOORRAH!!
BOB
BOB
THE ONE, THE ONLY, THE GREAT BOB MARLEY!
BOB!
BOB!!
WHEN I DECIDED TO DO THIS CONCERT THREE MONTHS AGO, IT WASN'T ABOUT POLITICS! I SING OUT OF LOVE FOR MY PEOPLE!
WAR!!
WAR!!
C'MON AND
IN JAMAICA
NOW
JAMAICA Y'ALL

The Price
of Fame

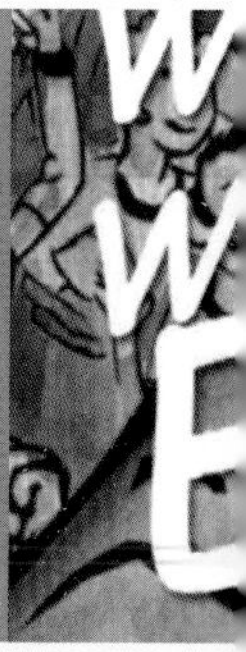

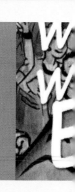

Now the figurehead of the Rasta movement, Bob Marley gave voice to the oppressed through his songs. But fame also made him a target: in 1976, he was the victim of attempted murder while in Jamaica, a country divided by political rivalries.

Who would have ever thought that a cowboy story would cause such a stir? In 1974, when Eric Clapton decided to do a cover of "I Shot the Sheriff," a song from the Wailers' second album, Burnin', he had no idea what a coup that was. For indeed, after a promising beginning, the English guitarist's career had slowed down since, hampered by his addiction to heroine and alcohol. But thanks to that song, Clapton managed not only to give his career a boost, but also to propel Bob Marley onto the international scene: in other words, a double score. Sweet!

From that moment forward, despite tensions between the band members, they came out with one hit after another. Bob Marley became a symbol of the protest movement and fight for justice. The famous "Get Up, Stand Up" calls on everyone to stand up for their rights and not give up the fight, while "Crazy Baldheads" goes as far as threatening to "chase those crazy Baldheads out of town." Reggae gradually became the music of the oppressed and resonated with the Rastafari movement that the singer with the dreadlocks now embodied.

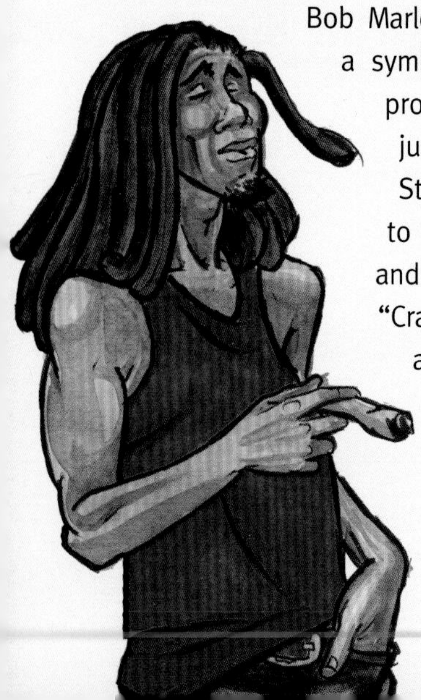

Ethiopia is a holy land for Rastas.

A true and distinctive Rasta characteristic, that hairstyle is said to emulate the one worn by the elite Ethiopian soldiers, known as the Mountain Lions—either that or it was inspired by the long locks of the god Shiva. The Rastafari faith does draw from both African tradition, from which it borrows the sound of the drums, and Hinduism, mainly in terms of their diet. Add to that a sprinkle of Catholicism (reading the Bible) and a few drops of revolutionary Marxism, and the result is the singular mix of beliefs known as Rastafari. That's what it means to be a Rastafari. In terms of the name itself, the term comes from the name of Ethiopian emperor Haile Selassie before his coronation in 1930: Ras Tafari, which means "the lord that will be feared."

For Rastas, who had had a strong presence in Jamaica since the 60s, Haile Selassie was God's envoy on Earth. As for Bob Marley, he considered himself a simple messenger. And it is with that in mind that he put to music a speech the Ethiopian leader gave in 1963 before the U.N. in New York. That song is "War," which expresses the notion of "lasting peace" while

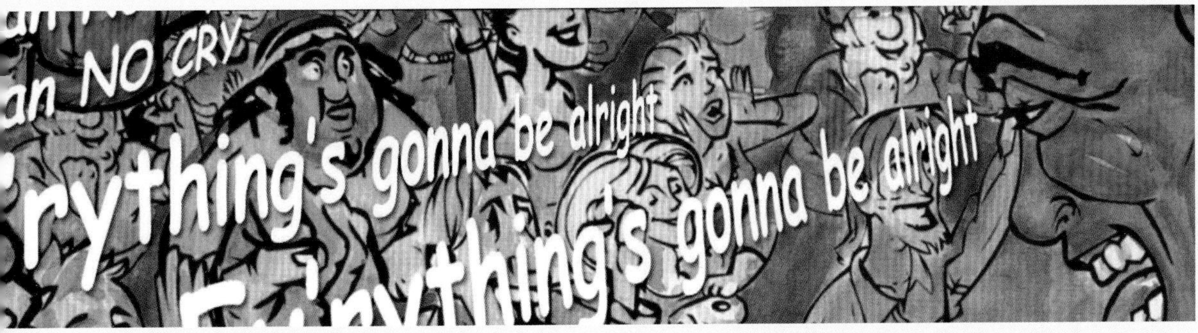
an NO CRY
rything's gonna be alright
rything's gonna be alright

denouncing inequalities between "First class and second class citizens" and racism: "Until the color of a man's skin is of no more significance than the color of his eyes, Me say war."

But the war Bob Marley sings about is an ideological war, made of thoughts and words. His weapon is his music. As he sings in "Trenchtown Rock," "One good thing about music, when it hits you feel no pain." Others use more than just metaphors to make a point, as the artist would learn to his own detriment in 1976, when there was an armed attempt on his life. At that time, while most of the world was frozen by the Cold War, Jamaica was in the throes of a civil war. Elections were coming up, with the two rival parties being the JLP (Jamaican Labor Party), which was conservative and pro-USA, and the PNP (People's National Party), which was pro-Cuba and USSR. In ghettos like Trenchtown, there were fights between rival gangs claiming allegiance to the two parties. While not affiliated with the PNP, Bob Marley agreed to perform at a peace concert that party organized, titled Smile Jamaica. But two days before the event, six armed men, thought to have been sent by the JLP, showed up at Marley's home at 56 Hope Road. They broke into the house in the middle of the night and fired some fifty rounds. Luckily they weren't very good shots, for as implausible as it may sound, Bob Marley was only hit in the chest and the arm. His wife Rita took a bullet to the head, but miraculously, it wasn't fatal.

Many other artists would have bowed out over a lot less. But not Bob Marley, who saw the concert as the opportunity to give an even louder voice to his message of non-violence. When he walked on stage with his bandages singing "War," it was an unforgettable moment in both the musical and political sense. And the audience of 80,000 fans must have given him a big boost of energy, because after announcing that he would only do one song, he ended up giving a performance that lasted an hour and a half. At the end of the concert, he even went as far as miming a duel and showing the audience his wounds. However, once that little moment of bravery had passed, the reality of the attack caught up with Bob Marley, and he went to live in London for a while, far away from the violence in his country but fully determined to keep on singing.

Punky Reggae Party

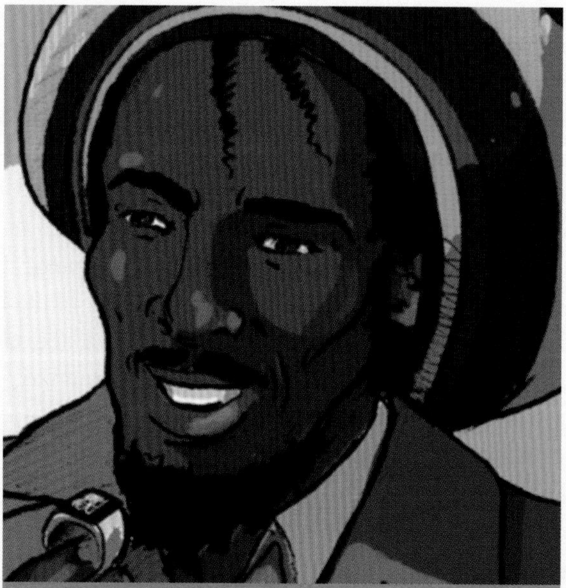

Artist: Armel Ressot

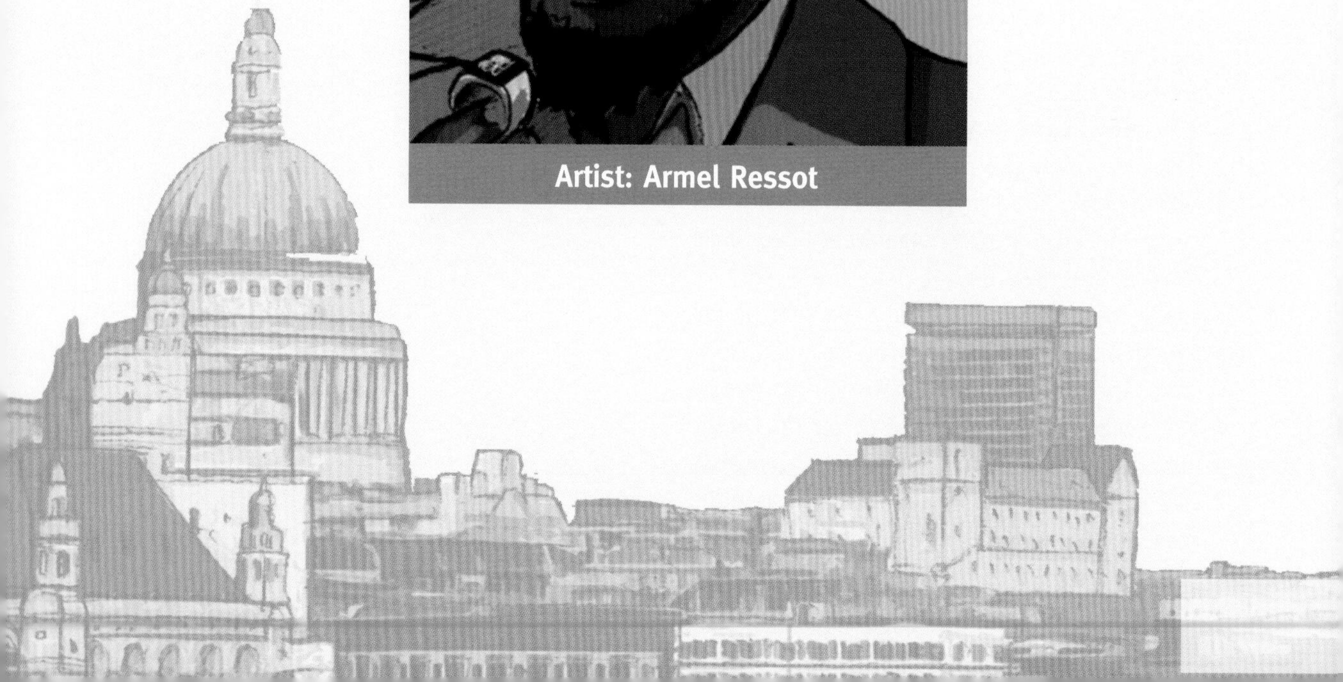

WHEN BOB MARLEY MOVED TO LONDON IN 1977, FOLLOWING THE ATTEMPT ON HIS LIFE, HE BECAME THE DARLING OF THE BRITISH PRESS.

HE HAD GRADUALLY RISEN TO THE RANK OF GLOBAL CELEBRITY.

BUT IT WAS HIS LOVE AFFAIR WITH THE NEW MISS WORLD THAT CAUSED THE BIGGEST MEDIA FRENZY.

THE TIMES

BEAUTY AND THE BEAST

The world's biggest reggae star romantically linked to Miss World, from Jamaica, with whom is expecting a ...d they plan to ...e Damian M...

THE VIBE HAD CHANGED IN LONDON, WHERE WHITE ROCKERS WERE NOW PUNKS.

THOSE VULTURES NEED TO LEAVE BOB THE HELL ALONE!

THIS NEW PROTEST MOVEMENT, WHICH COMBINED ANARCHISM AND NIHILISM, WAS REJECTED BY THE ENGLISH LIKE THE RASTAS ONCE HAD BEEN IN JAMAICA.

HOW RAD WAS THAT WHEN THE SEX PISTOLS SCREAMED FUCK THE QUEEN!

LONDON CALLING TO THE FARAWAY TOWNS

NOW WAR IS DECLARED AND BATTLE COME DOWN

TWO OF THE BIGGEST NAMES IN THIS NEW DEAFENING MUSICAL GENRE WERE THE SEX PISTOLS AND THE CLASH.

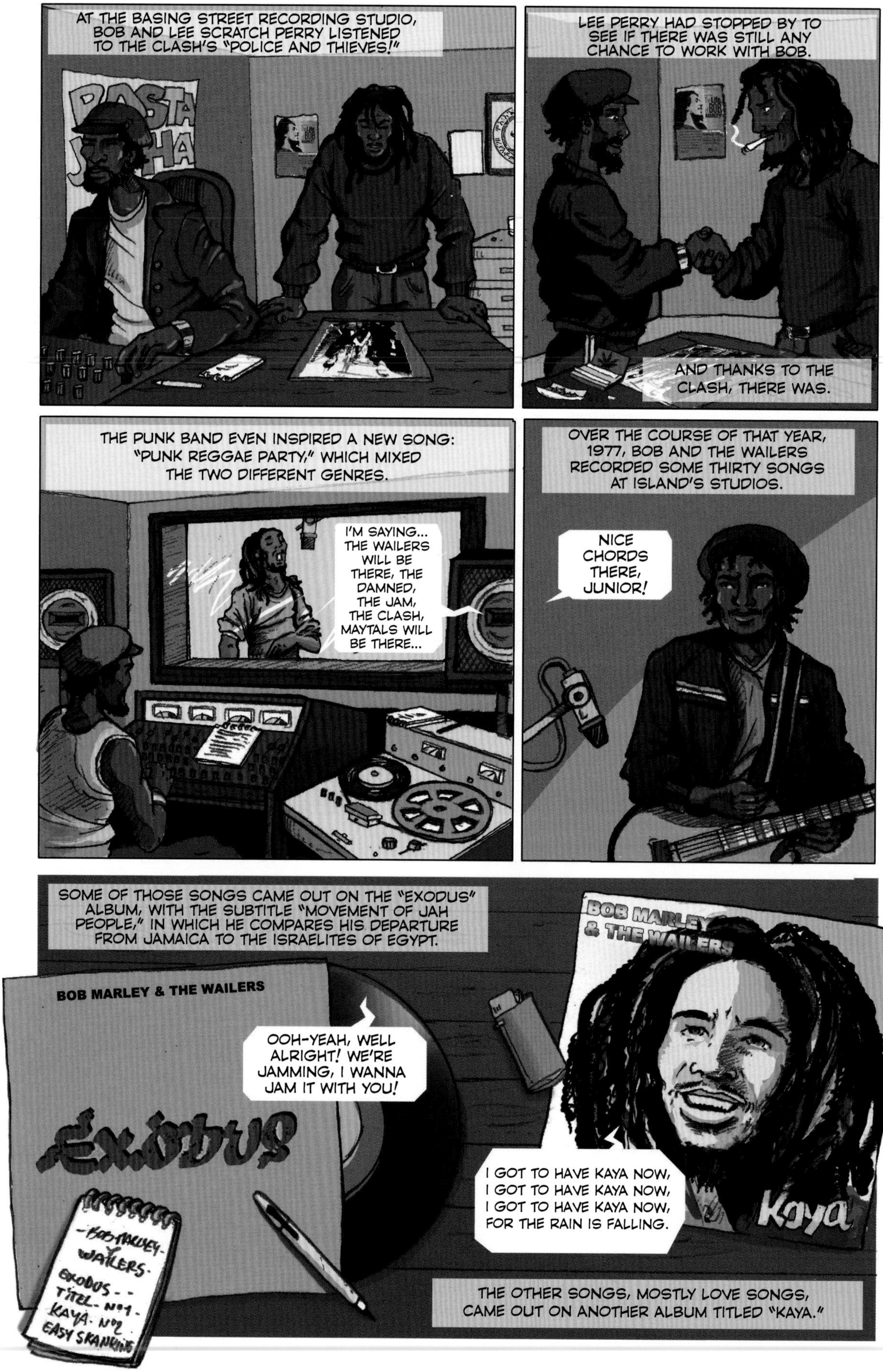
AT THE BASING STREET RECORDING STUDIO, BOB AND LEE SCRATCH PERRY LISTENED TO THE CLASH'S "POLICE AND THIEVES!"
RASTA JAH
LEE PERRY HAD STOPPED BY TO SEE IF THERE WAS STILL ANY CHANCE TO WORK WITH BOB.
AND THANKS TO THE CLASH, THERE WAS.
THE PUNK BAND EVEN INSPIRED A NEW SONG: "PUNK REGGAE PARTY," WHICH MIXED THE TWO DIFFERENT GENRES.
I'M SAYING... THE WAILERS WILL BE THERE, THE DAMNED, THE JAM, THE CLASH, MAYTALS WILL BE THERE...
OVER THE COURSE OF THAT YEAR, 1977, BOB AND THE WAILERS RECORDED SOME THIRTY SONGS AT ISLAND'S STUDIOS.
NICE CHORDS THERE, JUNIOR!
SOME OF THOSE SONGS CAME OUT ON THE "EXODUS" ALBUM, WITH THE SUBTITLE "MOVEMENT OF JAH PEOPLE," IN WHICH HE COMPARES HIS DEPARTURE FROM JAMAICA TO THE ISRAELITES OF EGYPT.
BOB MARLEY & THE WAILERS
EXODUS
OOH-YEAH, WELL ALRIGHT! WE'RE JAMMING, I WANNA JAM IT WITH YOU!
BOB MARLEY & THE WAILERS
I GOT TO HAVE KAYA NOW, I GOT TO HAVE KAYA NOW, I GOT TO HAVE KAYA NOW, FOR THE RAIN IS FALLING.
Kaya
-BOB MARLEY- WAILERS- EXODUS - - TITEL- Nº1 - KAYA- Nº2 EASY SKANKING
THE OTHER SONGS, MOSTLY LOVE SONGS, CAME OUT ON ANOTHER ALBUM TITLED "KAYA."

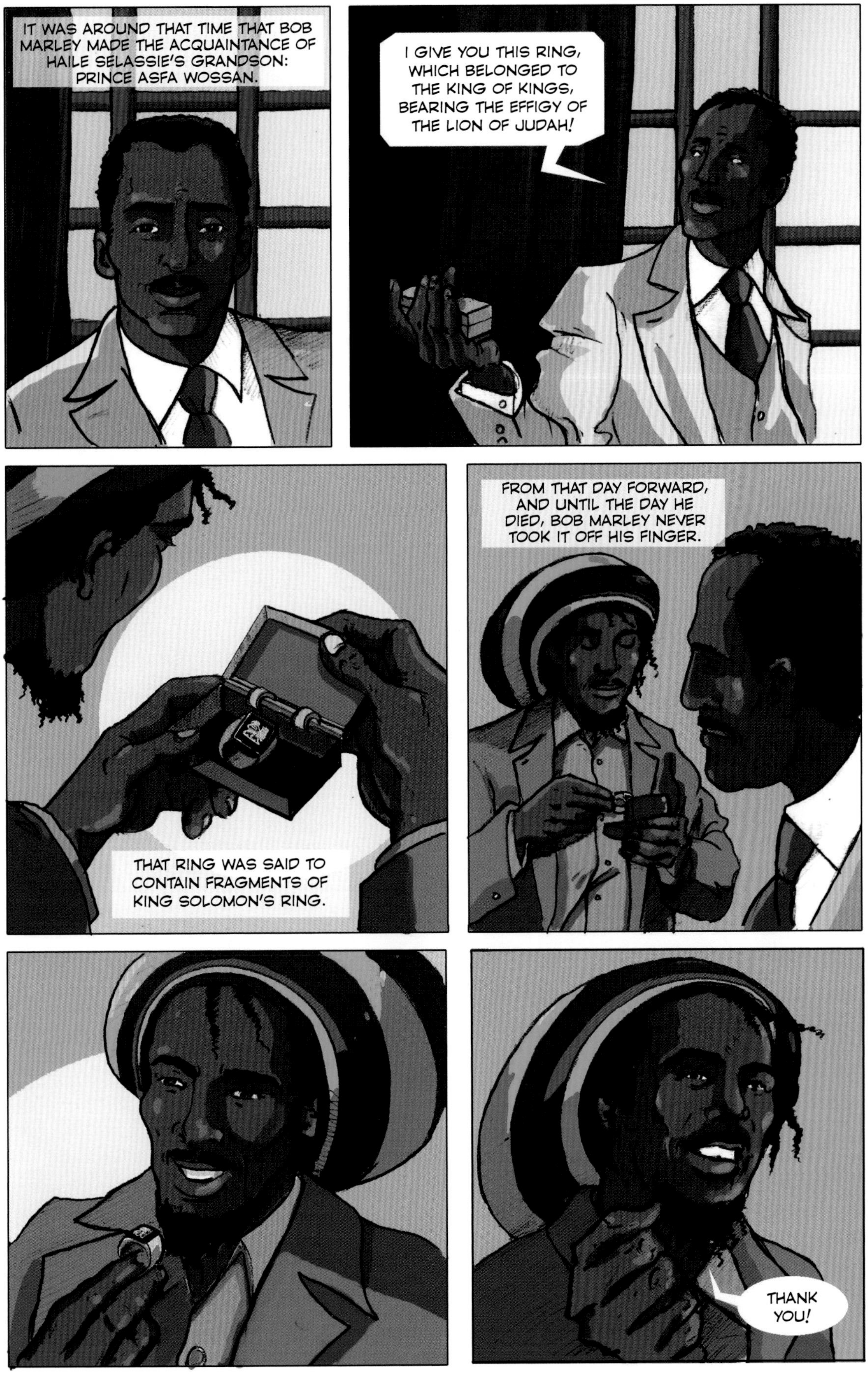
IT WAS AROUND THAT TIME THAT BOB MARLEY MADE THE ACQUAINTANCE OF HAILE SELASSIE'S GRANDSON: PRINCE ASFA WOSSAN.
I GIVE YOU THIS RING, WHICH BELONGED TO THE KING OF KINGS, BEARING THE EFFIGY OF THE LION OF JUDAH!
THAT RING WAS SAID TO CONTAIN FRAGMENTS OF KING SOLOMON'S RING.
FROM THAT DAY FORWARD, AND UNTIL THE DAY HE DIED, BOB MARLEY NEVER TOOK IT OFF HIS FINGER.
THANK YOU!

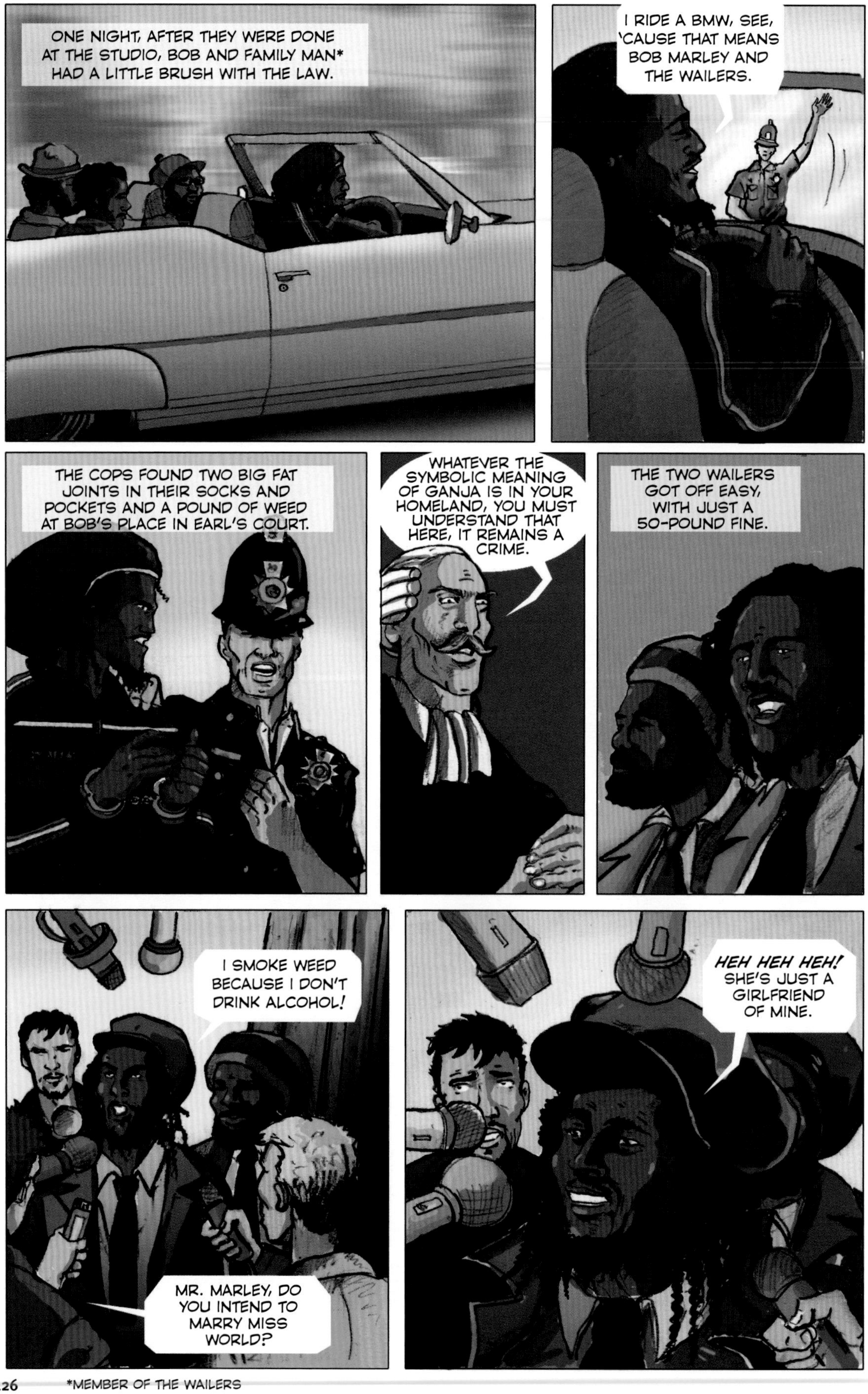
ONE NIGHT, AFTER THEY WERE DONE AT THE STUDIO, BOB AND FAMILY MAN* HAD A LITTLE BRUSH WITH THE LAW.
I RIDE A BMW, SEE, 'CAUSE THAT MEANS BOB MARLEY AND THE WAILERS.
THE COPS FOUND TWO BIG FAT JOINTS IN THEIR SOCKS AND POCKETS AND A POUND OF WEED AT BOB'S PLACE IN EARL'S COURT.
WHATEVER THE SYMBOLIC MEANING OF GANJA IS IN YOUR HOMELAND, YOU MUST UNDERSTAND THAT HERE, IT REMAINS A CRIME.
THE TWO WAILERS GOT OFF EASY, WITH JUST A 50-POUND FINE.
MR. MARLEY, DO YOU INTEND TO MARRY MISS WORLD?
I SMOKE WEED BECAUSE I DON'T DRINK ALCOHOL!
HEH HEH HEH! SHE'S JUST A GIRLFRIEND OF MINE.

*MEMBER OF THE WAILERS

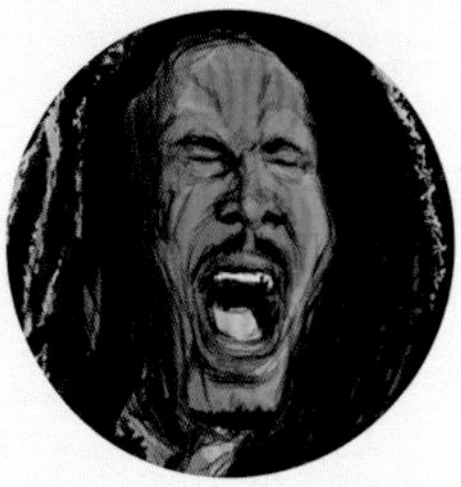

From Exile to Exodus

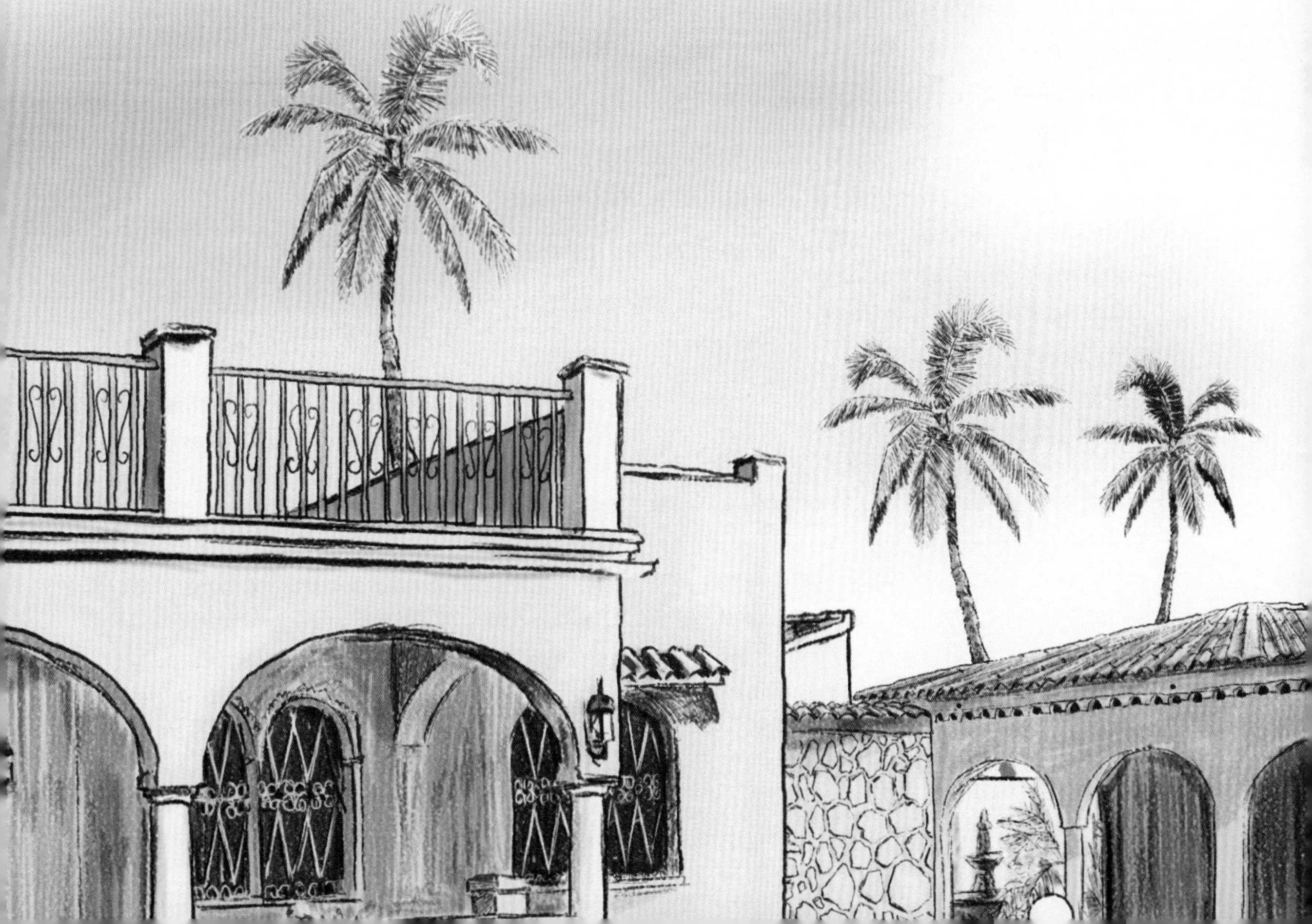

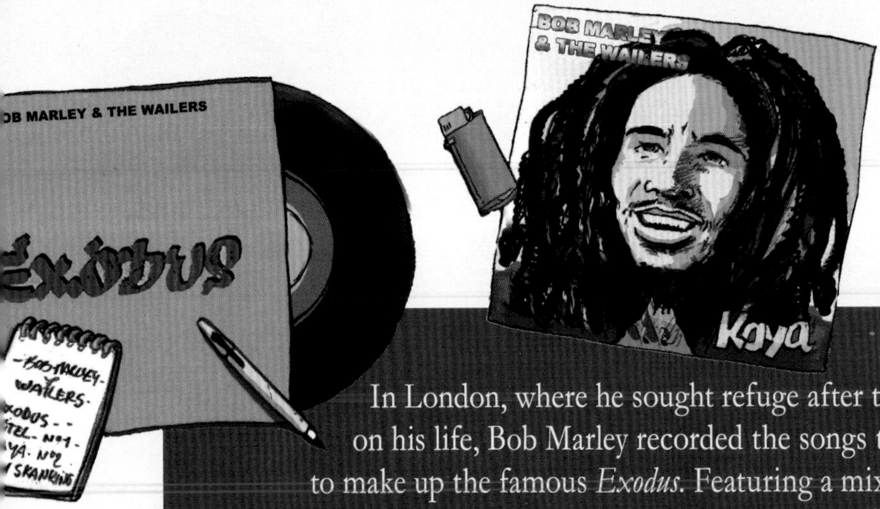
BOB MARLEY & THE WAILERS
Kaya

In London, where he sought refuge after the attempt on his life, Bob Marley recorded the songs that went on to make up the famous *Exodus*. Featuring a mix of love ballads and lyrics denouncing injustice, the reggae album with rock influences calls for a return to roots and tolerance between peoples.

January 1977. After the attempt on his life, Bob Marley and his wife Rita left Jamaica and moved to London. This forced exile had no effect on the singer's creativity—just the opposite, in fact. Some twenty songs were produced in the space of just fourteen months. While some of them had already been written, they needed polishing. For the first time in his career, Bob Marley enjoyed truly professional production facilities. He worked at the Island Records' studios at 22 Saint Peter's Square, in the Hammersmith neighborhood: a basement nicknamed the Fallout Shelter (bomb shelter). Probably a little exaggerated... But in the absence of actual bombs, at least musicians were safe from distraction there. Many productive days were spent there, and as for polishing... they polished, all right! Some songs were done dozens of different ways. They kept the best versions for the album, while alternate versions would be included in the Deluxe editions that came later.

For Bob, this was the *Exodus* period. Double exile. Double exodus.

In addition to Aston and Carlton Barrett, two brothers who played the bass guitar and the drums beautifully, the Wailers band now included Donald Hanson Marvin Kerr Richards Junior, a lead guitar without equal, also from Jamaica, who traded in his extensive name for the more reasonable Junior Marvin. The young man was in high demand and even declined an offer by Stevie Wonder to play with Bob Marley. He contributed some very rock sounds to the reggae band and shined in a few heart-rending guitar solos.

After several months of hard work, ten songs were eventually selected to appear on the first album of this new lineup, Exodus, which came out on June 3, 1977. The title had several different connotations: first, the ship carrying Shoah survivors to the land of Israel thirty years earlier, an adventure that inspired the film by Otto Preminger, starring Paul Newman; but the exodus that the singer, himself living in exile, mainly croons about

is that of the black Diaspora returning to its continent of origin, Africa. "We're leaving Babylon, We're going to our Father land," sings Bob Marley. In Rasta lingo, Babylon refers to colonial power and, in a more general sense, to white Westerners. Alternating between tears of despair and anger, the song asks: "Open your eyes and look within: Are you satisfied (with the life you're living)?" It's a call to "Rule equality, Wipe away transgression, Set the captives free." The song lasts a whopping eight minutes… with "Exodus," Marley certainly took the time to get his message across!

The four other tracks on the A-side of the album feature similar themes: "The Heathen" encourages victims to get back on their feet, while "Guiltiness" warns the oppressors, i.e. the "big fish Who always try to eat down the small fish," that soon "They'll eat the bread of sorrow!" and that they have "Guiltiness pressed on their conscience." And what a better way to call people to action than by evoking famous people who dared to defy authority? That meant putting into one basket the likes of Jesus Christ, Marcus Garvey (the Pan-Africanism activist who, like Bob Marley, was originally from St. Ann) and Paul Bogle (another Jamaican rebel, born before the abolition of slavery and eventually hanged

for defying British settlers). The result was the beautifully put together "So Much Things To Say." And if these historical examples haven't won you over, there's still the terrible threat of the Last Judgment that Bob Marley refers to in "Natural Mystic," where the bass sounds are as loud as the biblical trumpets. However, one can be an activist who denounces injustice while still taking time to enjoy life: the B-side of Exodus is much lighter and features love songs like the gentle ballad "Turn Your Lights Down Low," the joyful "Three Little Birds," and "One Love," a veritable ode to tolerance. Despite the still recent impact of the attempt on his life, "Bob was in love and generally happy; that comes across in that album" his producer Chris Blackwell later said. Either way, the blend of political and romantic material was popular with the audience: Exodus was a huge hit and propelled Bob Marley to the top 20 on American charts for the first time ever. And it wasn't a flash in the pan, either: the album remained at the top of the British charts for over a year. The other songs recorded in London, mainly love longs, were quickly collected into a second album, Kaya, which came out in March of 1978. But the album that remained forever engraved in the collective memory was Exodus, which *Time* declared the best album of the 20th century.

Red Card

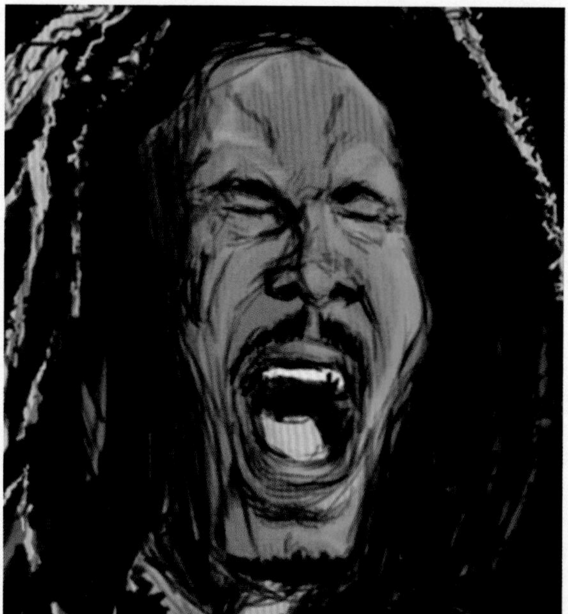

Artist: Lu-K

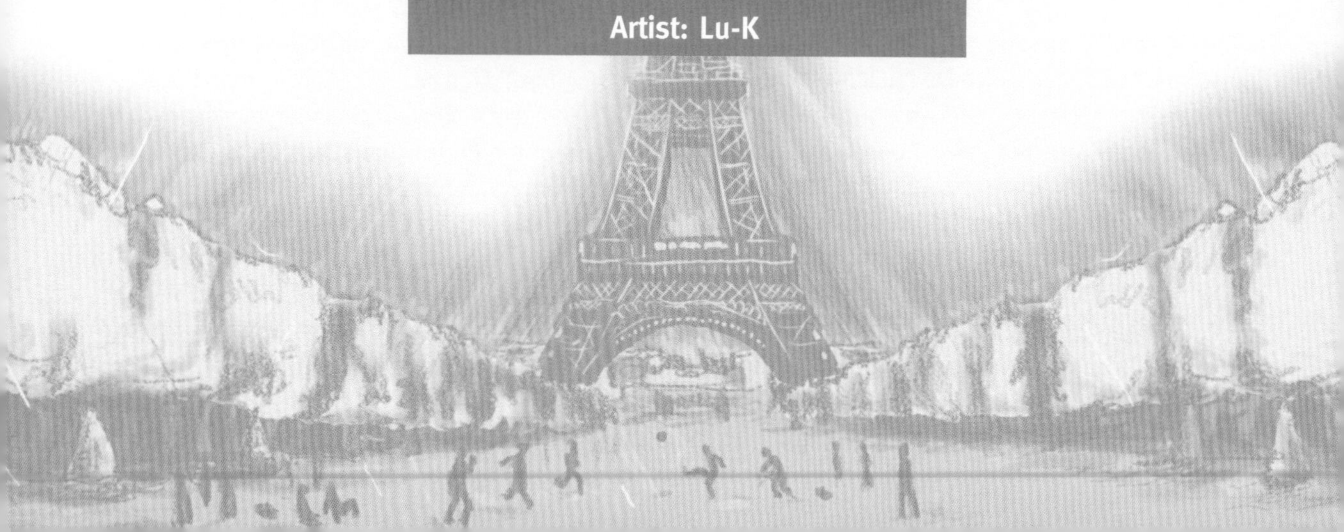

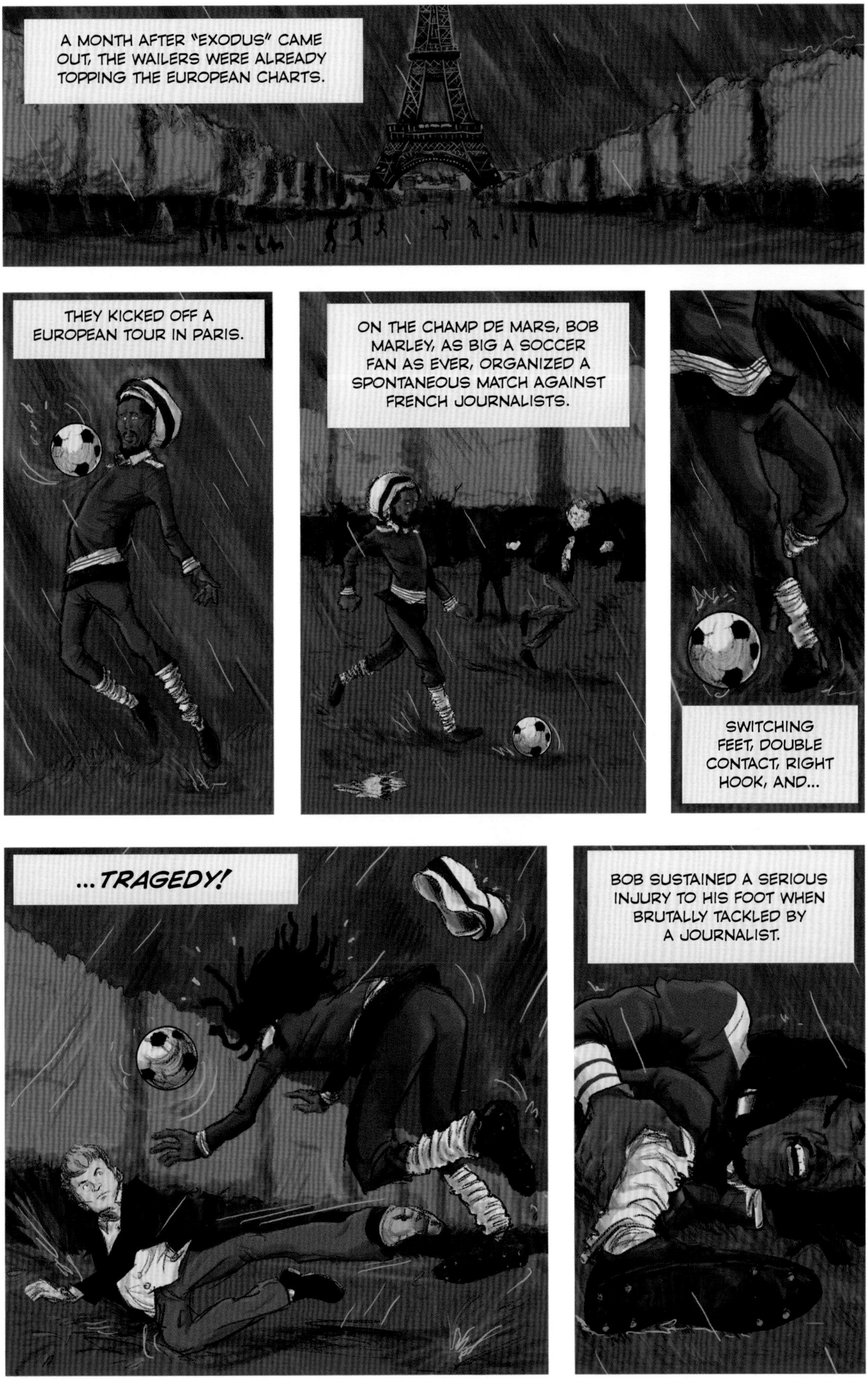
A MONTH AFTER "EXODUS" CAME OUT, THE WAILERS WERE ALREADY TOPPING THE EUROPEAN CHARTS.
THEY KICKED OFF A EUROPEAN TOUR IN PARIS.
ON THE CHAMP DE MARS, BOB MARLEY, AS BIG A SOCCER FAN AS EVER, ORGANIZED A SPONTANEOUS MATCH AGAINST FRENCH JOURNALISTS.
SWITCHING FEET, DOUBLE CONTACT, RIGHT HOOK, AND...
...TRAGEDY!
BOB SUSTAINED A SERIOUS INJURY TO HIS FOOT WHEN BRUTALLY TACKLED BY A JOURNALIST.

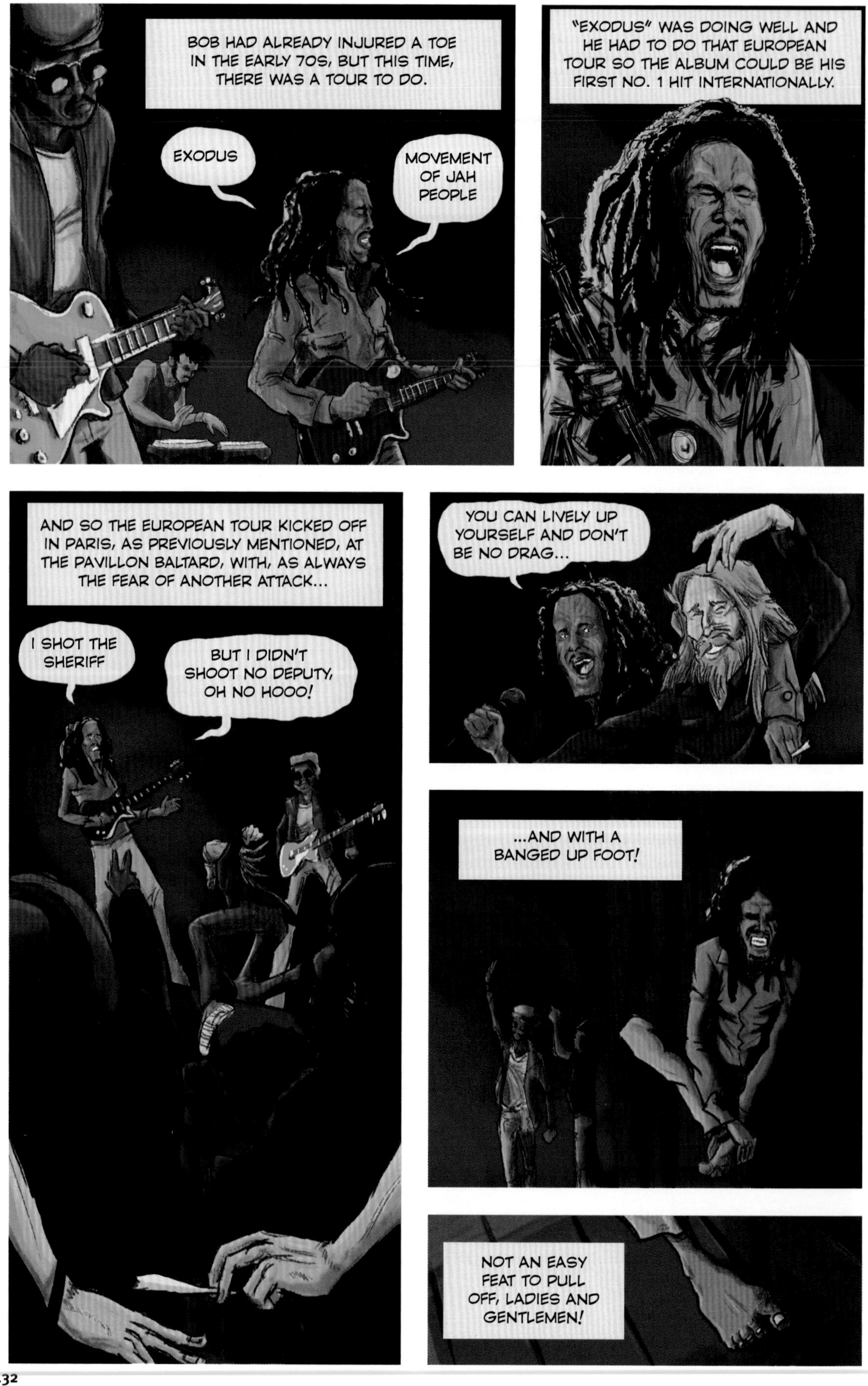
BOB HAD ALREADY INJURED A TOE IN THE EARLY 70S, BUT THIS TIME, THERE WAS A TOUR TO DO.
EXODUS
MOVEMENT OF JAH PEOPLE
"EXODUS" WAS DOING WELL AND HE HAD TO DO THAT EUROPEAN TOUR SO THE ALBUM COULD BE HIS FIRST NO. 1 HIT INTERNATIONALLY.
AND SO THE EUROPEAN TOUR KICKED OFF IN PARIS, AS PREVIOUSLY MENTIONED, AT THE PAVILLON BALTARD, WITH, AS ALWAYS THE FEAR OF ANOTHER ATTACK...
I SHOT THE SHERIFF
BUT I DIDN'T SHOOT NO DEPUTY, OH NO HOOO!
YOU CAN LIVELY UP YOURSELF AND DON'T BE NO DRAG...
...AND WITH A BANGED UP FOOT!
NOT AN EASY FEAT TO PULL OFF, LADIES AND GENTLEMEN!

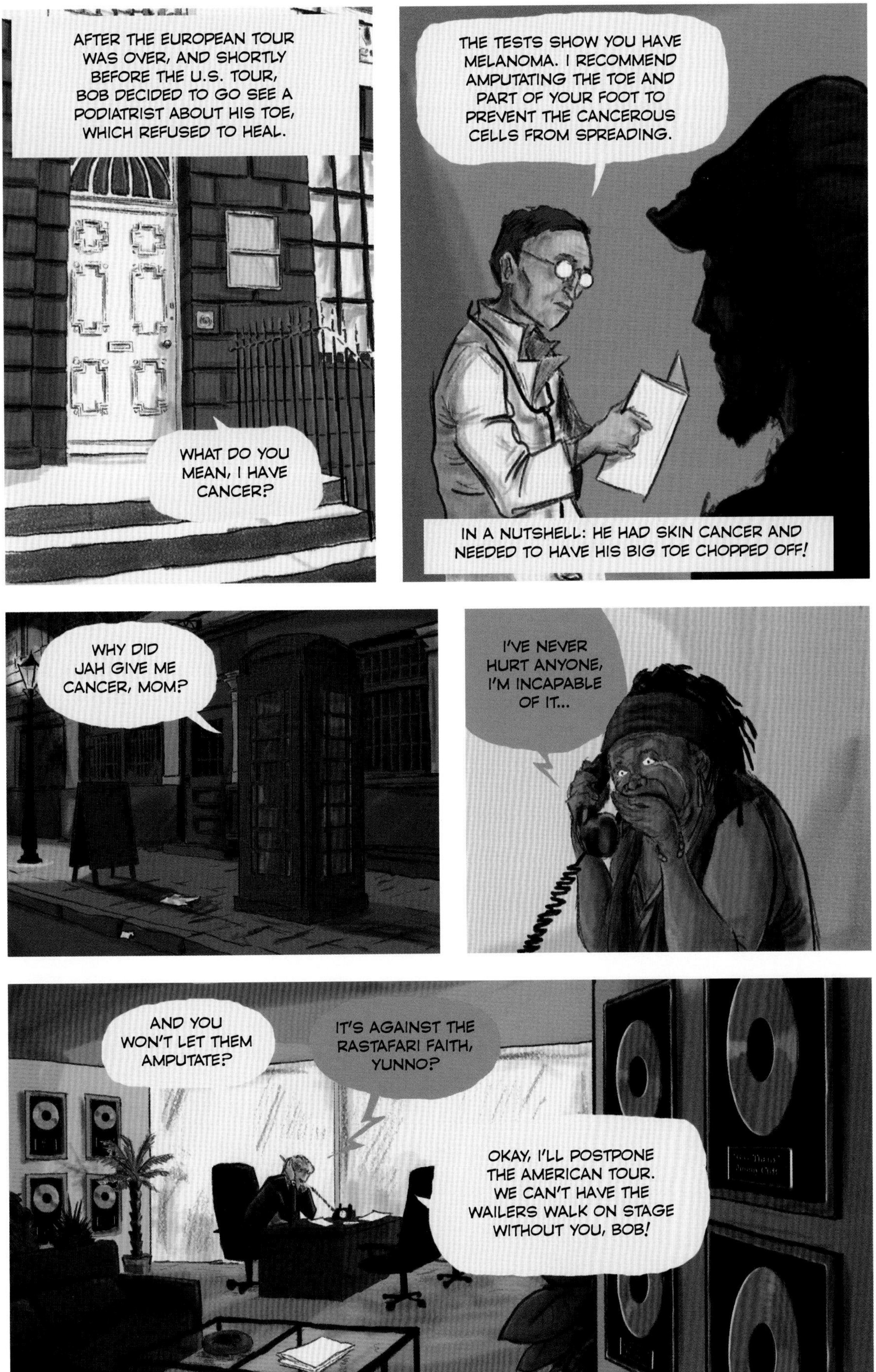
AFTER THE EUROPEAN TOUR WAS OVER, AND SHORTLY BEFORE THE U.S. TOUR, BOB DECIDED TO GO SEE A PODIATRIST ABOUT HIS TOE, WHICH REFUSED TO HEAL.
WHAT DO YOU MEAN, I HAVE CANCER?
THE TESTS SHOW YOU HAVE MELANOMA. I RECOMMEND AMPUTATING THE TOE AND PART OF YOUR FOOT TO PREVENT THE CANCEROUS CELLS FROM SPREADING.
IN A NUTSHELL: HE HAD SKIN CANCER AND NEEDED TO HAVE HIS BIG TOE CHOPPED OFF!
WHY DID JAH GIVE ME CANCER, MOM?
I'VE NEVER HURT ANYONE, I'M INCAPABLE OF IT...
AND YOU WON'T LET THEM AMPUTATE?
IT'S AGAINST THE RASTAFARI FAITH, YUNNO?
OKAY, I'LL POSTPONE THE AMERICAN TOUR. WE CAN'T HAVE THE WAILERS WALK ON STAGE WITHOUT YOU, BOB!

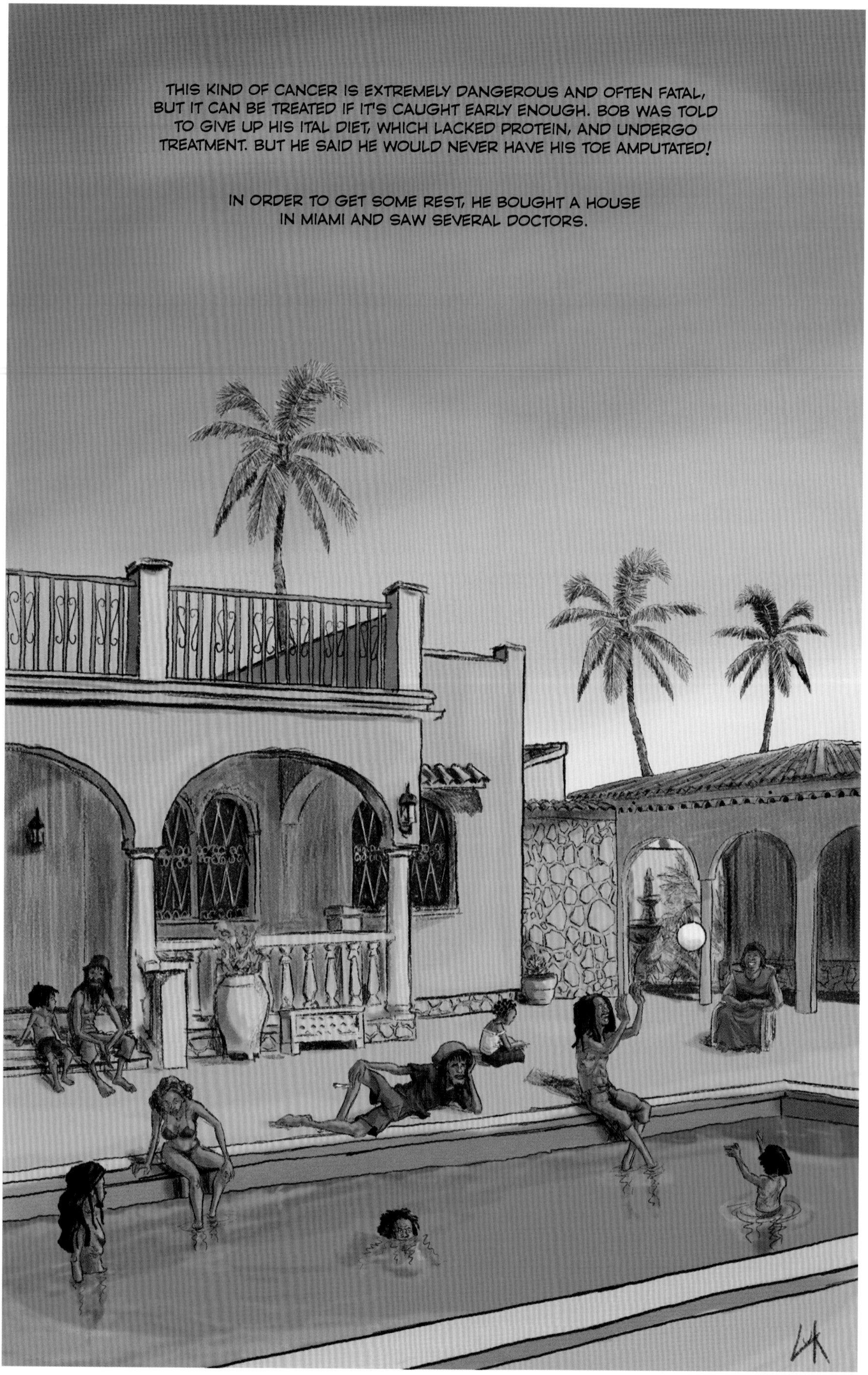
THIS KIND OF CANCER IS EXTREMELY DANGEROUS AND OFTEN FATAL, BUT IT CAN BE TREATED IF IT'S CAUGHT EARLY ENOUGH. BOB WAS TOLD TO GIVE UP HIS ITAL DIET, WHICH LACKED PROTEIN, AND UNDERGO TREATMENT. BUT HE SAID HE WOULD NEVER HAVE HIS TOE AMPUTATED!
IN ORDER TO GET SOME REST, HE BOUGHT A HOUSE IN MIAMI AND SAW SEVERAL DOCTORS.

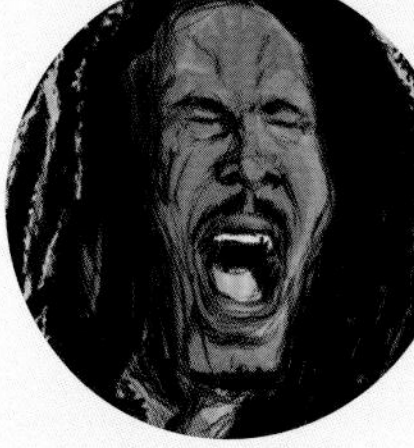

Bob Marley and His Love of Soccer

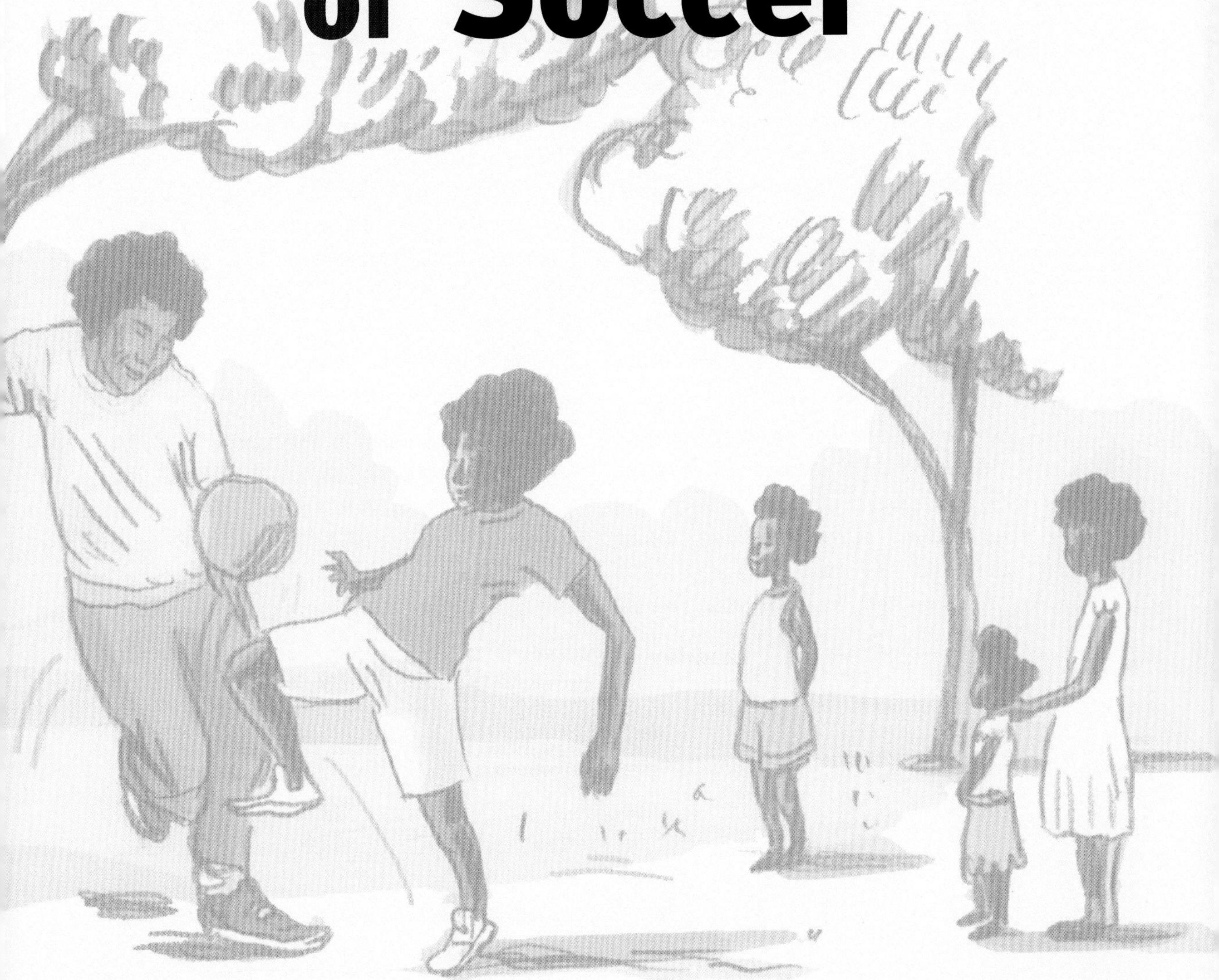

Like many Jamaicans who grew up in the slums, Bob Marley was a big fan of soccer. He practiced every day and loved playing little matches when his concert schedule allowed for it.

Whether he was in Kingston, London, or on tour, Bob Marley spent most of his time with a guitar in his hand: hardly surprising, for a musician. What's a little more surprising is that he spent almost just as much time with a ball bouncing off his foot! For him, soccer was much more than a hobby; it was a true passion. And not a recent one. It all started in Trenchtown: like most other rude boys, young Nesta Marley played in soccer matches between teams from the various different streets. Even though it was a British import from the late 19th century, soccer quickly became super popular in Jamaica—much more than cricket and polo, which have always been considered an aristocratic sport reserved for the upper, wealthier classes.

Over the years, Bob Marley never lost his love of kicking around a soccer ball: he would do it in between rehearsal sessions (or even during), before a concert, during intermission. Basically, any time he had a free moment, he would play. And the other band members certainly weren't about to stop him, quite the contrary: the Wailers were all crazy about soccer, and a member of their entourage, Alan Skip Cole, was a former soccer player with the Jamaican team, a true star that some natives inland compared to the King, i.e. Pelé! A close friend of Bob Marley, the famous forward-center went with him on tour and trained him on a daily basis. "I have two loves," the singer once said, "reggae and soccer." And while music came first, it's because it wasn't as violent, according to Marley, who always tried to make room for both: if there were big soccer matches playing while they were on tour, he arranged for the band to be able to watch them on the tour bus. While on the road, they would also organize friendly games against locals in the various cities on their tour route. And interviews with the press weren't enough for Bob Marley to change his schedule; reporters just had to wait until the game was over, like everybody else!

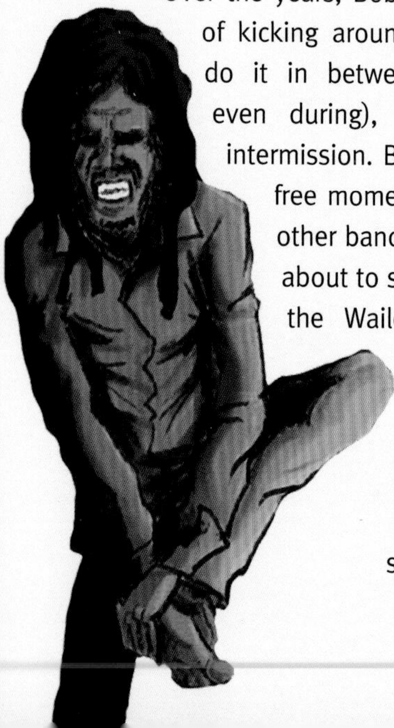

On the Exodus Tour in the spring of 1977, organized so the Wailers could promote the album they recorded in London, they played several such soccer matches, one of which went on to become legendary. The day: May 10. The setting: near the Eiffel Tower. The Wailers played the Polymusclés, a team made up of Parisian showbiz people, including pop singer Herbert Léonard. A few members of the rock music press had been invited to complete the musicians' team. The Polymusclés were brimming with self-confidence, especially when they saw the Jamaicans arrive in old jogging outfits and Rasta beanies with eyes red from the weed they had just smoked. Except that those screwballs were

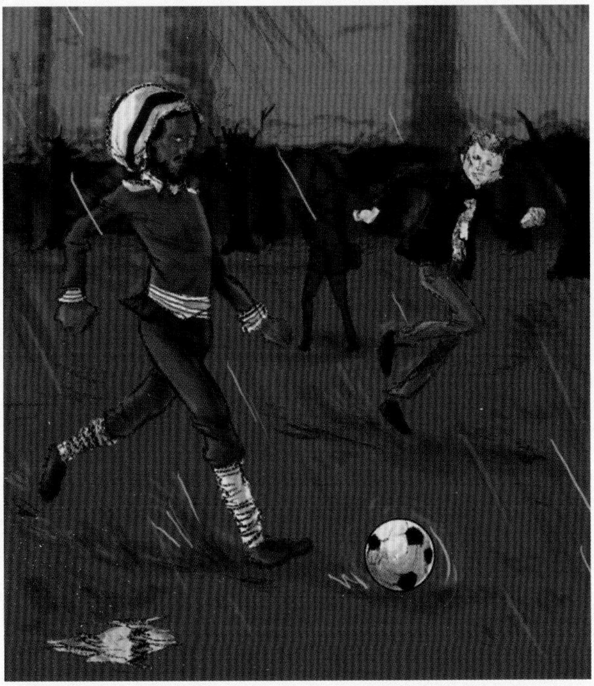

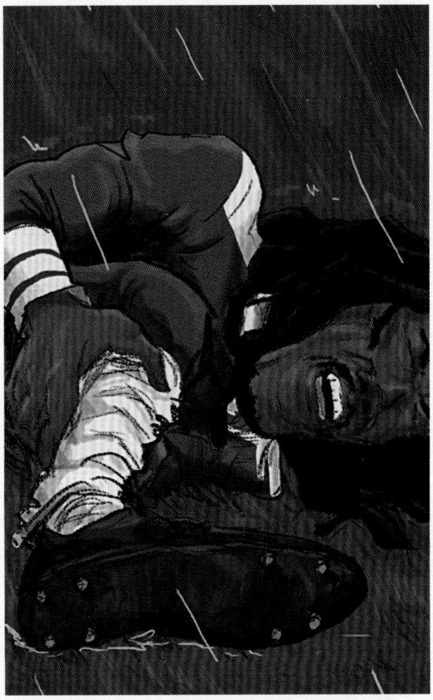

better than they looked! Francis Dordor, then a reporter with Best magazine, admired their instincts and their skills with dummy moves: "Marley was unquestionably talented with the ball. He dribbled it with the dexterity unique to those who, from the favelas of Brazil to the slums of Africa, learned how to play barefoot on rocky fields," he wrote in 1999 in popular cultural magazine Les Inrocks. However, talent does not protect one from injury: the singer was brutally tackled to the ground by an opponent who crushed his toe, which opened up an old wound that hadn't been treated properly. He limped off the field and watched the rest of the match from the sidelines: a spectacular win for The Wailers.

"Soccer is freedom."

Though he was in a lot of pain over the weeks that followed, Bob Marley carried on with the tour, and—unable to resist—with soccer as well. "I need soccer. Soccer is freedom," he was fond of saying. But his wound was still not healing and so, in July of '77, he finally went to see a doctor. The news was not good: he had malignant melanoma, in other words cancer. This time, the rest of the Exodus Tour was canceled. But while Bob Marley agreed to a little forced convalescence, it was out of the question for them to amputate his foot despite his doctor's recommendation, for it was forbidden under Rasta religion. All the singer would agree to was a light ablation and a cleansing of the toe. After resting up for a few months, he was back at it... back on the road, back on the stage, and back on the soccer field. In June of '78, the Kaya Tour, named after the title of the second London album after Exodus, took place at the same time as the World Cup in Argentina. Another good reason to organize friendly local matches! And so on and so forth: in 1980, as a sidebar to a concert, a tournament was organized in a stadium in Fulham, near London, while in Nantes, the Wailers played the Canaris, the champions of France at the time. That year, 100,000 people came to cheer for him in Milan, at the San Siro stadium: highly symbolic since it was in that mythical soccer venue that Bob Marley performed the biggest concert of his life.

Ablaze

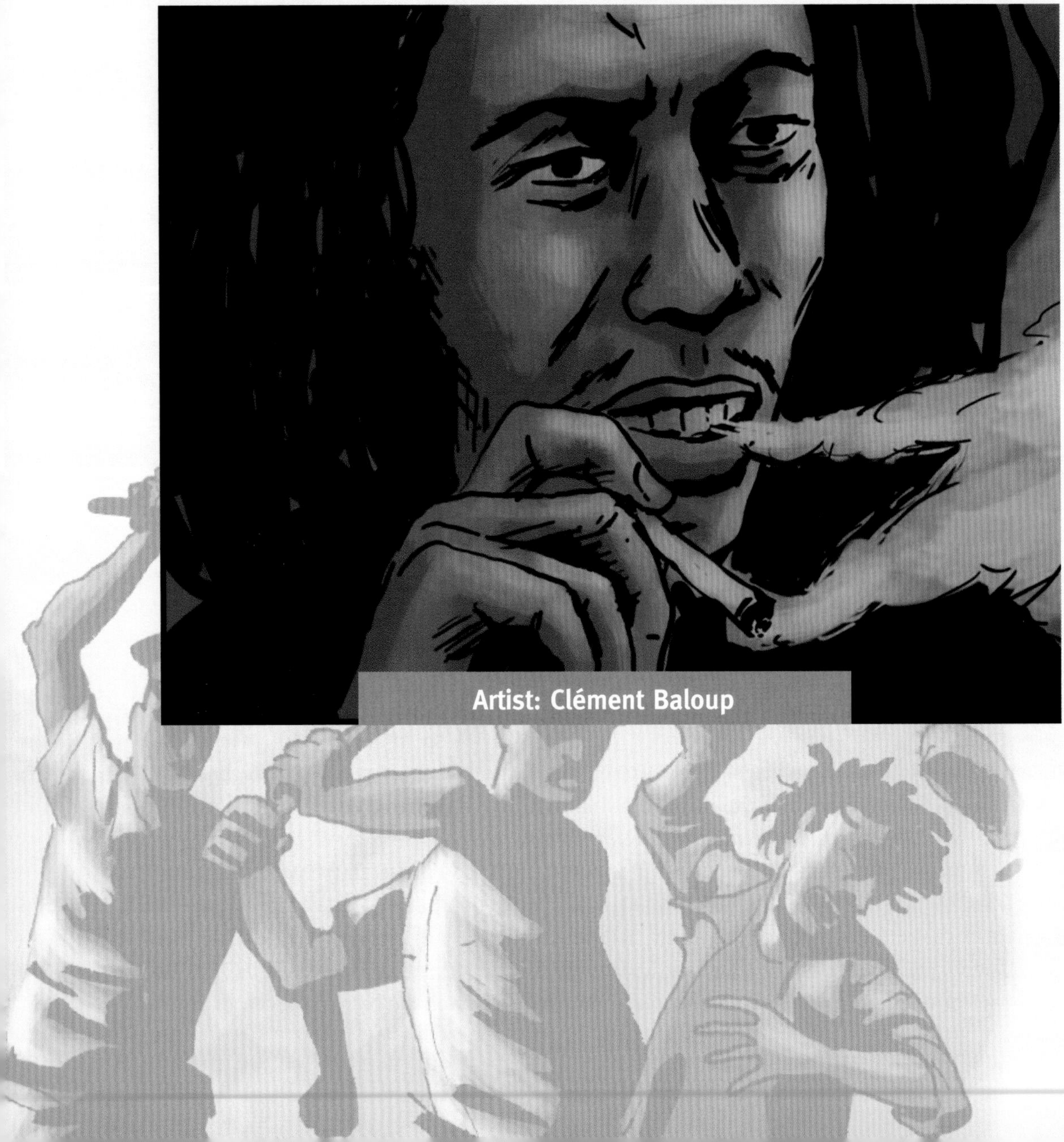

Artist: Clément Baloup

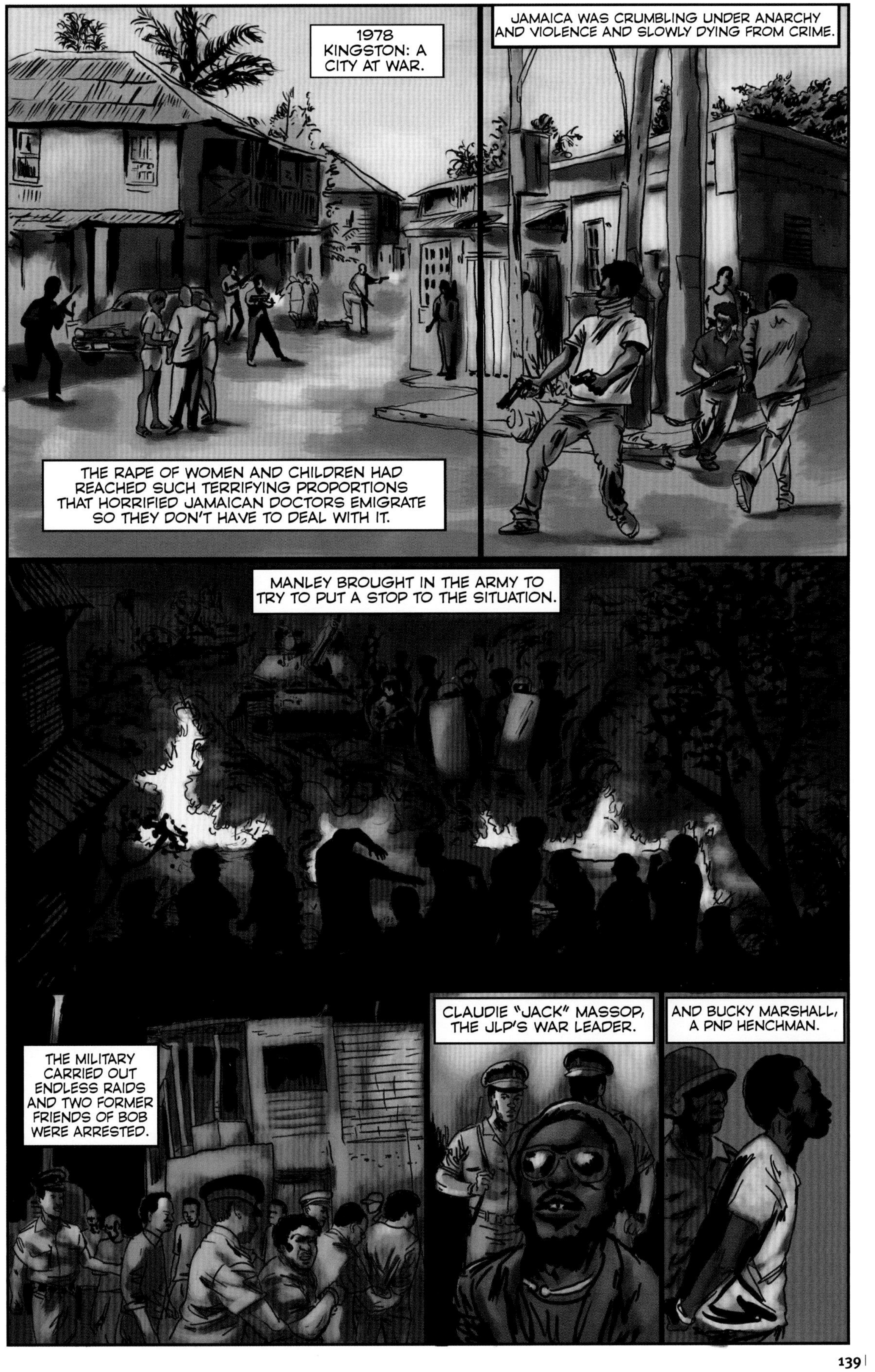
1978
KINGSTON: A CITY AT WAR.
JAMAICA WAS CRUMBLING UNDER ANARCHY AND VIOLENCE AND SLOWLY DYING FROM CRIME.
THE RAPE OF WOMEN AND CHILDREN HAD REACHED SUCH TERRIFYING PROPORTIONS THAT HORRIFIED JAMAICAN DOCTORS EMIGRATE SO THEY DON'T HAVE TO DEAL WITH IT.
MANLEY BROUGHT IN THE ARMY TO TRY TO PUT A STOP TO THE SITUATION.
THE MILITARY CARRIED OUT ENDLESS RAIDS AND TWO FORMER FRIENDS OF BOB WERE ARRESTED.
CLAUDIE "JACK" MASSOP, THE JLP'S WAR LEADER.
AND BUCKY MARSHALL, A PNP HENCHMAN.

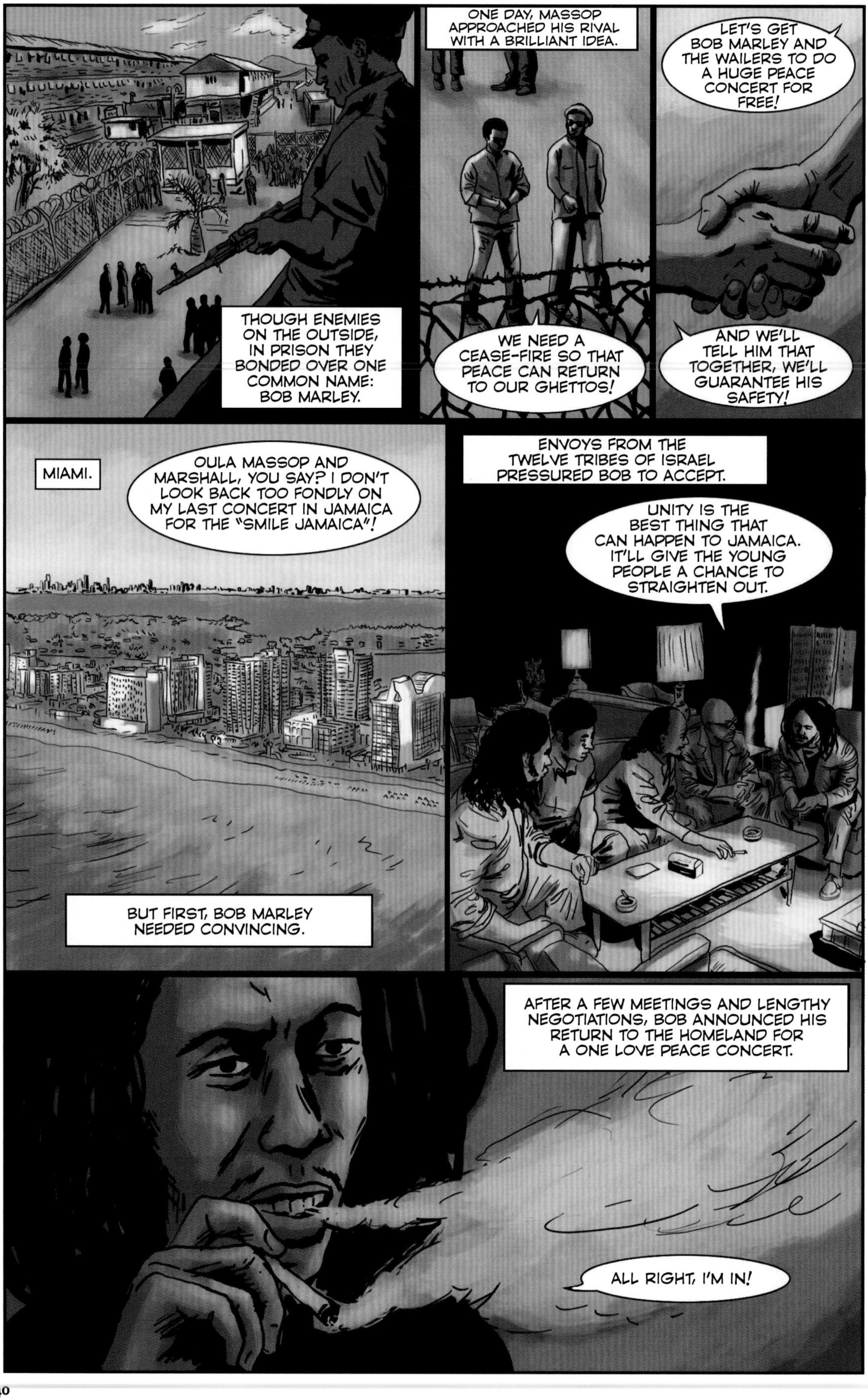
THOUGH ENEMIES ON THE OUTSIDE, IN PRISON THEY BONDED OVER ONE COMMON NAME: BOB MARLEY.
ONE DAY, MASSOP APPROACHED HIS RIVAL WITH A BRILLIANT IDEA.
WE NEED A CEASE-FIRE SO THAT PEACE CAN RETURN TO OUR GHETTOS!
LET'S GET BOB MARLEY AND THE WAILERS TO DO A HUGE PEACE CONCERT FOR FREE!
AND WE'LL TELL HIM THAT TOGETHER, WE'LL GUARANTEE HIS SAFETY!
MIAMI.
OULA MASSOP AND MARSHALL, YOU SAY? I DON'T LOOK BACK TOO FONDLY ON MY LAST CONCERT IN JAMAICA FOR THE "SMILE JAMAICA"!
BUT FIRST, BOB MARLEY NEEDED CONVINCING.
ENVOYS FROM THE TWELVE TRIBES OF ISRAEL PRESSURED BOB TO ACCEPT.
UNITY IS THE BEST THING THAT CAN HAPPEN TO JAMAICA. IT'LL GIVE THE YOUNG PEOPLE A CHANCE TO STRAIGHTEN OUT.
AFTER A FEW MEETINGS AND LENGTHY NEGOTIATIONS, BOB ANNOUNCED HIS RETURN TO THE HOMELAND FOR A ONE LOVE PEACE CONCERT.
ALL RIGHT, I'M IN!

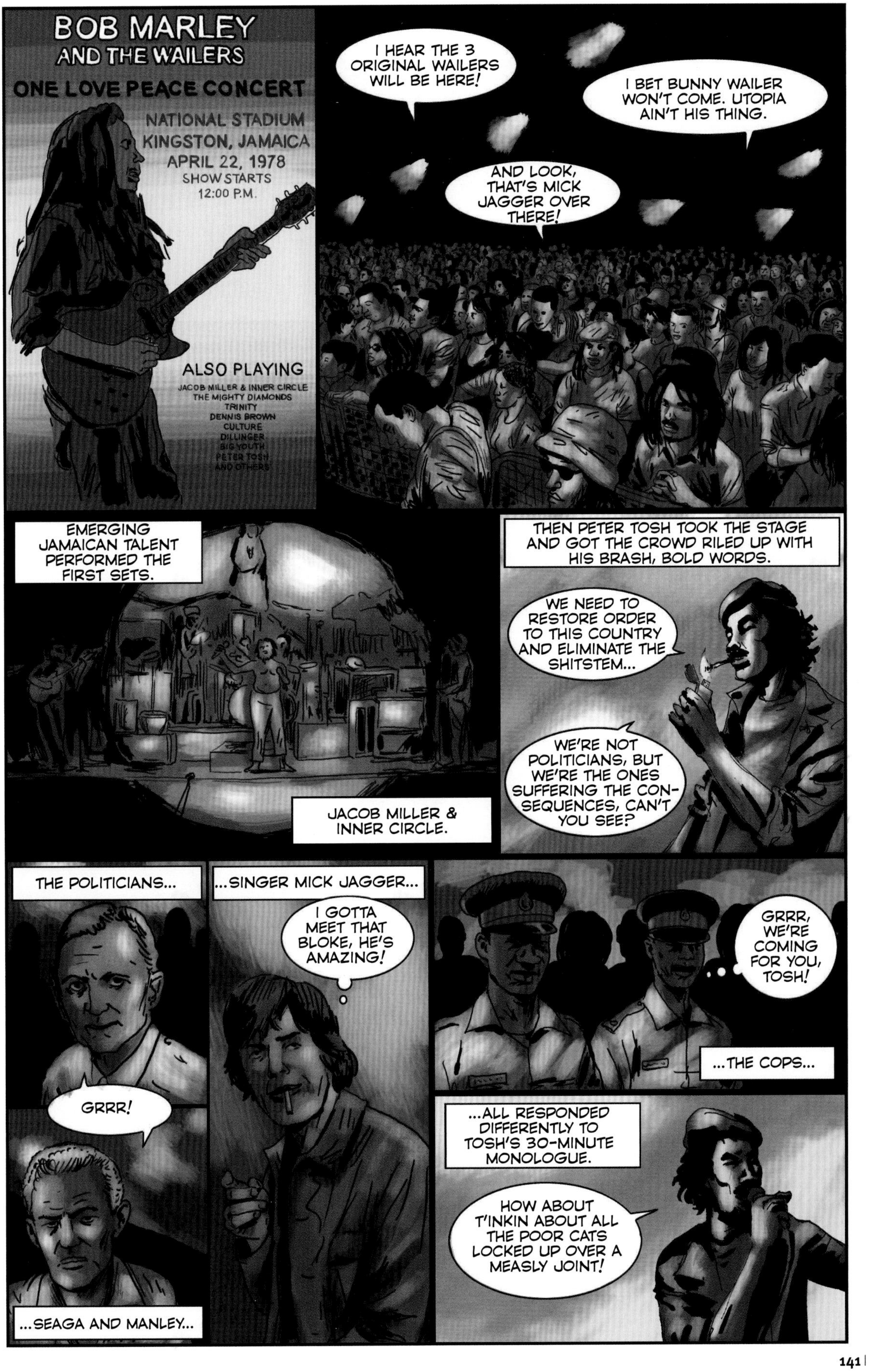
BOB MARLEY
AND THE WAILERS
ONE LOVE PEACE CONCERT
NATIONAL STADIUM
KINGSTON, JAMAICA
APRIL 22, 1978
SHOW STARTS
12:00 P.M.
ALSO PLAYING
JACOB MILLER & INNER CIRCLE
THE MIGHTY DIAMONDS
TRINITY
DENNIS BROWN
CULTURE
DILLINGER
BIG YOUTH
PETER TOSH
AND OTHERS
I HEAR THE 3 ORIGINAL WAILERS WILL BE HERE!
I BET BUNNY WAILER WON'T COME. UTOPIA AIN'T HIS THING.
AND LOOK, THAT'S MICK JAGGER OVER THERE!
EMERGING JAMAICAN TALENT PERFORMED THE FIRST SETS.
JACOB MILLER & INNER CIRCLE.
THEN PETER TOSH TOOK THE STAGE AND GOT THE CROWD RILED UP WITH HIS BRASH, BOLD WORDS.
WE NEED TO RESTORE ORDER TO THIS COUNTRY AND ELIMINATE THE SHITSTEM...
WE'RE NOT POLITICIANS, BUT WE'RE THE ONES SUFFERING THE CON-SEQUENCES, CAN'T YOU SEE?
THE POLITICIANS...
GRRR!
...SEAGA AND MANLEY...
...SINGER MICK JAGGER...
I GOTTA MEET THAT BLOKE, HE'S AMAZING!
GRRR, WE'RE COMING FOR YOU, TOSH!
...THE COPS...
...ALL RESPONDED DIFFERENTLY TO TOSH'S 30-MINUTE MONOLOGUE.
HOW ABOUT T'INKIN ABOUT ALL THE POOR CATS LOCKED UP OVER A MEASLY JOINT!

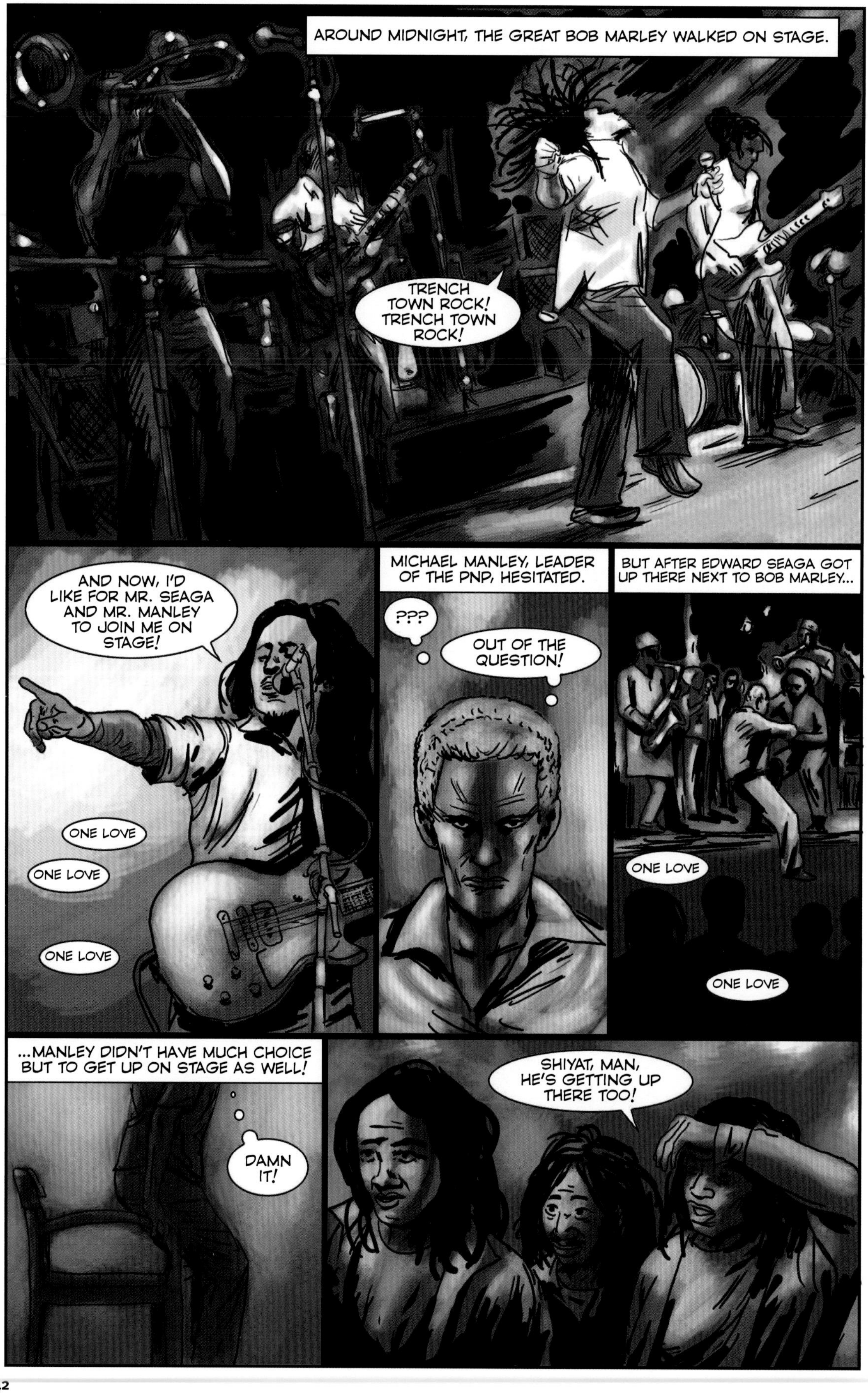
AROUND MIDNIGHT, THE GREAT BOB MARLEY WALKED ON STAGE.
TRENCH TOWN ROCK! TRENCH TOWN ROCK!
AND NOW, I'D LIKE FOR MR. SEAGA AND MR. MANLEY TO JOIN ME ON STAGE!
ONE LOVE
ONE LOVE
ONE LOVE
MICHAEL MANLEY, LEADER OF THE PNP, HESITATED.
???
OUT OF THE QUESTION!
BUT AFTER EDWARD SEAGA GOT UP THERE NEXT TO BOB MARLEY...
ONE LOVE
ONE LOVE
...MANLEY DIDN'T HAVE MUCH CHOICE BUT TO GET UP ON STAGE AS WELL!
DAMN IT!
SHIYAT, MAN, HE'S GETTING UP THERE TOO!

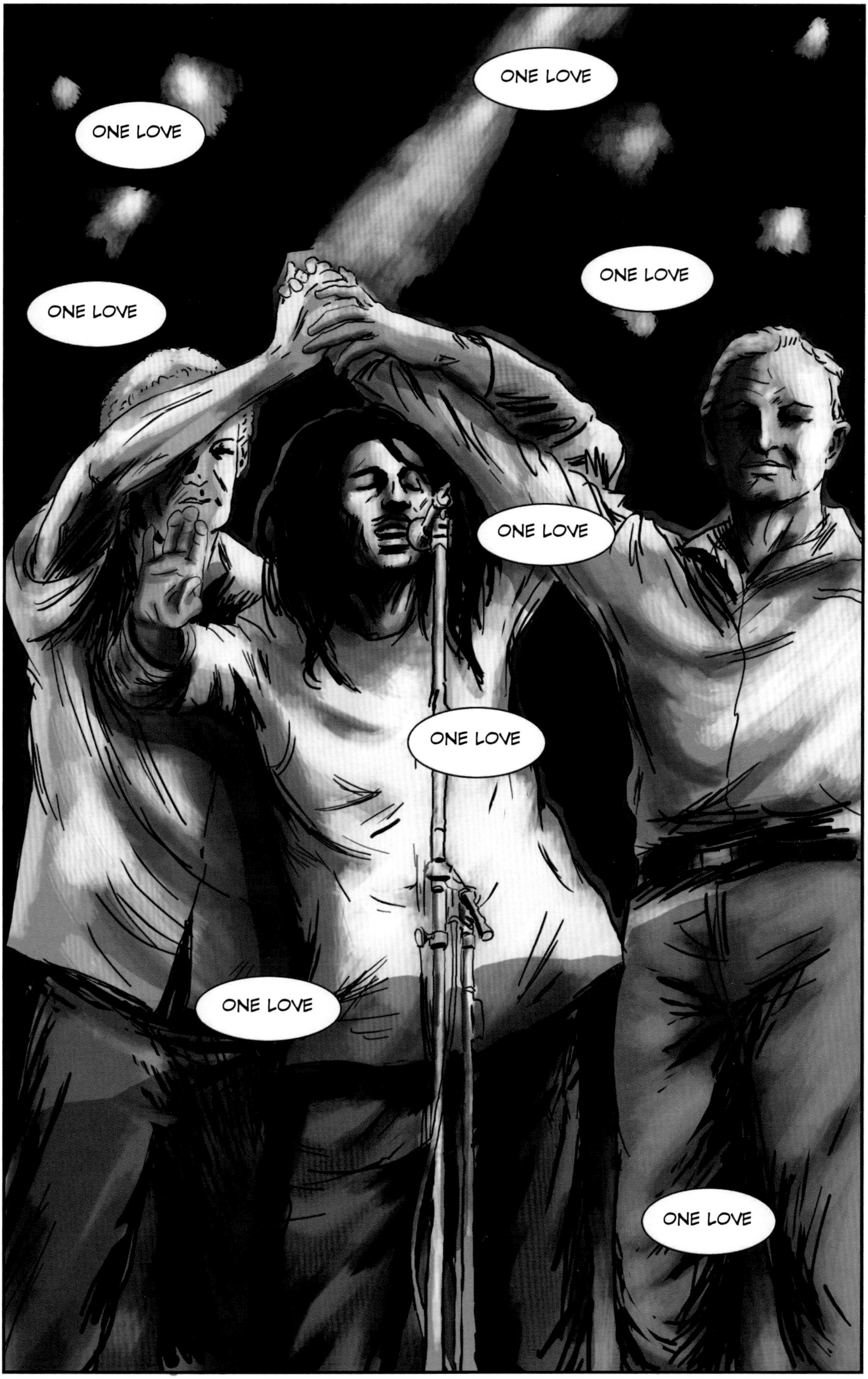
ONE LOVE
ONE LOVE
ONE LOVE
ONE LOVE
ONE LOVE
ONE LOVE
ONE LOVE
ONE LOVE

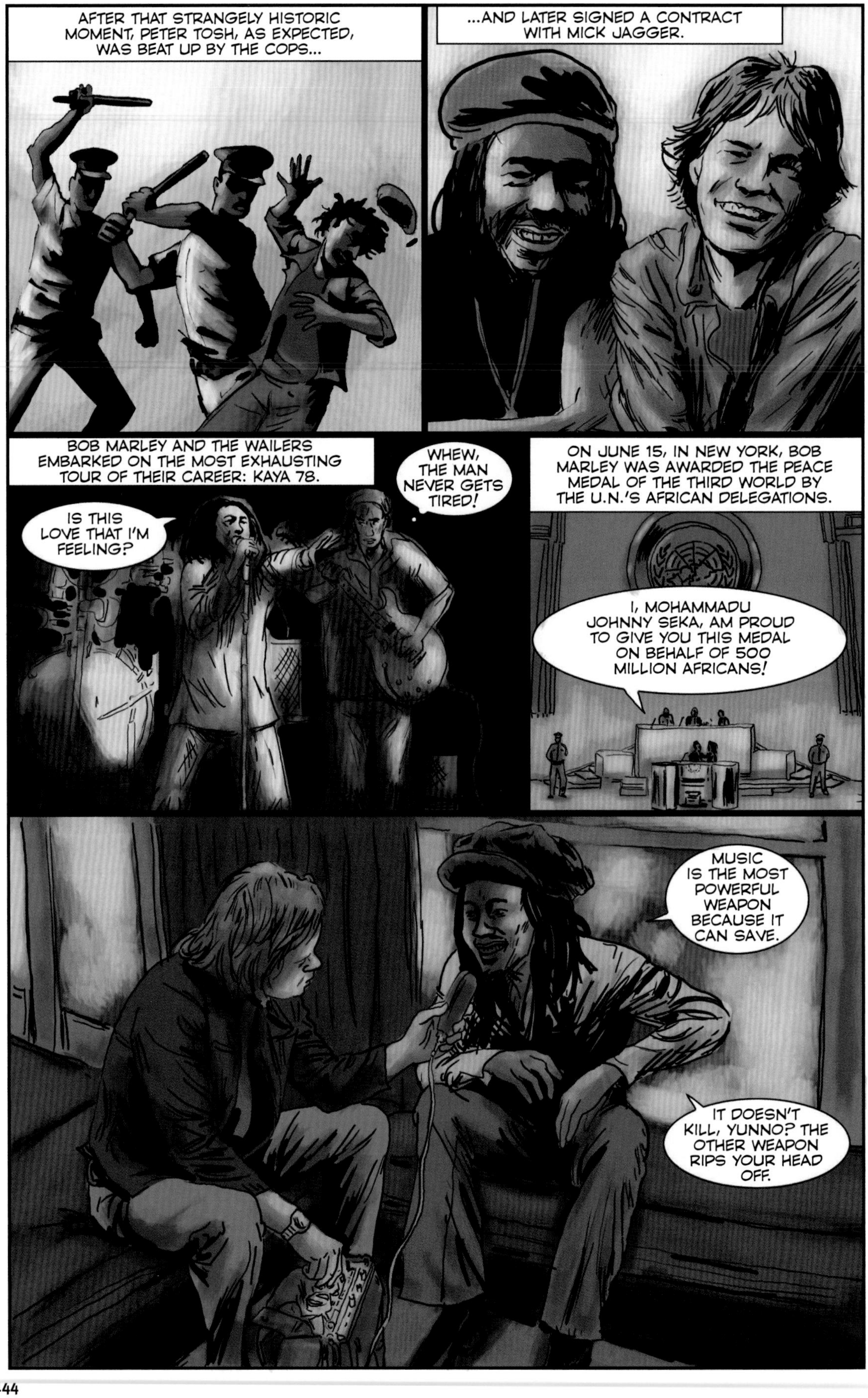
AFTER THAT STRANGELY HISTORIC MOMENT, PETER TOSH, AS EXPECTED, WAS BEAT UP BY THE COPS...
...AND LATER SIGNED A CONTRACT WITH MICK JAGGER.
BOB MARLEY AND THE WAILERS EMBARKED ON THE MOST EXHAUSTING TOUR OF THEIR CAREER: KAYA 78.
IS THIS LOVE THAT I'M FEELING?
WHEW, THE MAN NEVER GETS TIRED!
ON JUNE 15, IN NEW YORK, BOB MARLEY WAS AWARDED THE PEACE MEDAL OF THE THIRD WORLD BY THE U.N.'S AFRICAN DELEGATIONS.
I, MOHAMMADU JOHNNY SEKA, AM PROUD TO GIVE YOU THIS MEDAL ON BEHALF OF 500 MILLION AFRICANS!
MUSIC IS THE MOST POWERFUL WEAPON BECAUSE IT CAN SAVE.
IT DOESN'T KILL, YUNNO? THE OTHER WEAPON RIPS YOUR HEAD OFF.

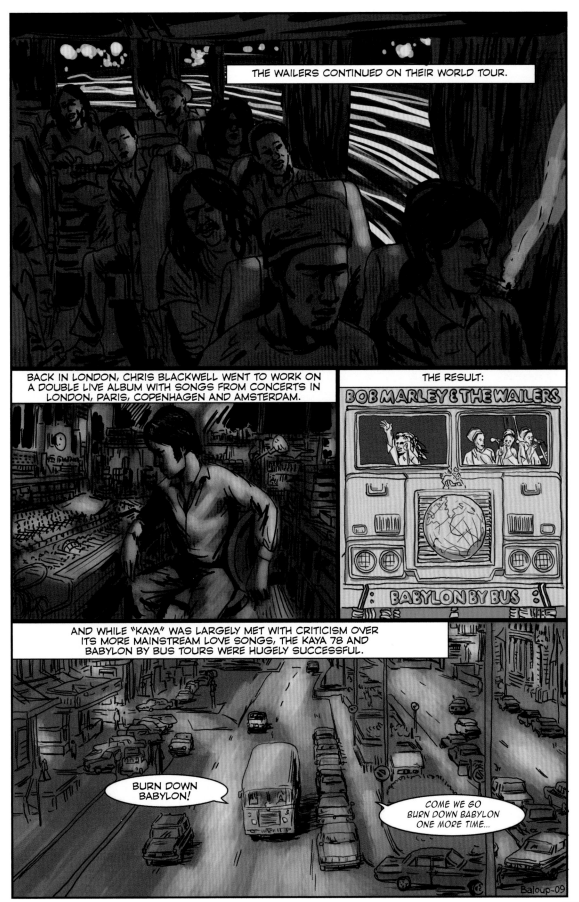

THE WAILERS CONTINUED ON THEIR WORLD TOUR.

BACK IN LONDON, CHRIS BLACKWELL WENT TO WORK ON A DOUBLE LIVE ALBUM WITH SONGS FROM CONCERTS IN LONDON, PARIS, COPENHAGEN AND AMSTERDAM.

THE RESULT:

BOB MARLEY & THE WAILERS

BABYLON BY BUS

AND WHILE "KAYA" WAS LARGELY MET WITH CRITICISM OVER ITS MORE MAINSTREAM LOVE SONGS, THE KAYA 78 AND BABYLON BY BUS TOURS WERE HUGELY SUCCESSFUL.

BURN DOWN BABYLON!

COME WE GO BURN DOWN BABYLON ONE MORE TIME...

Baloup-09

Roots

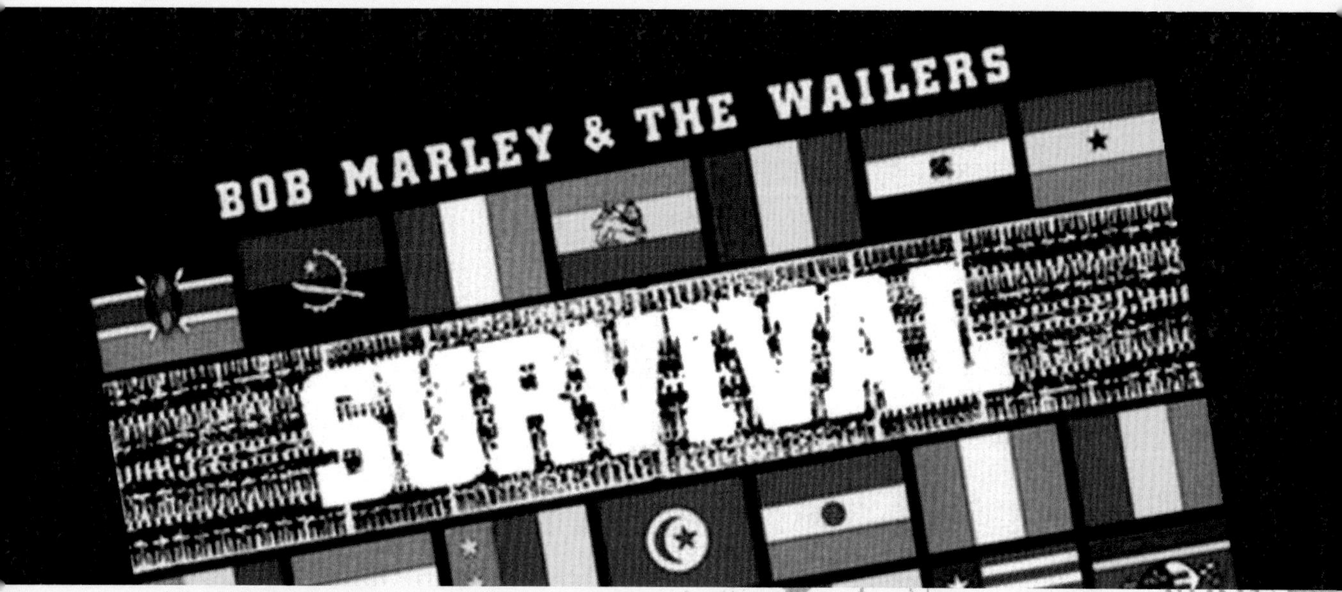
BOB MARLEY & THE WAILERS
SURVIVAL

Artist: Joël Allessandra

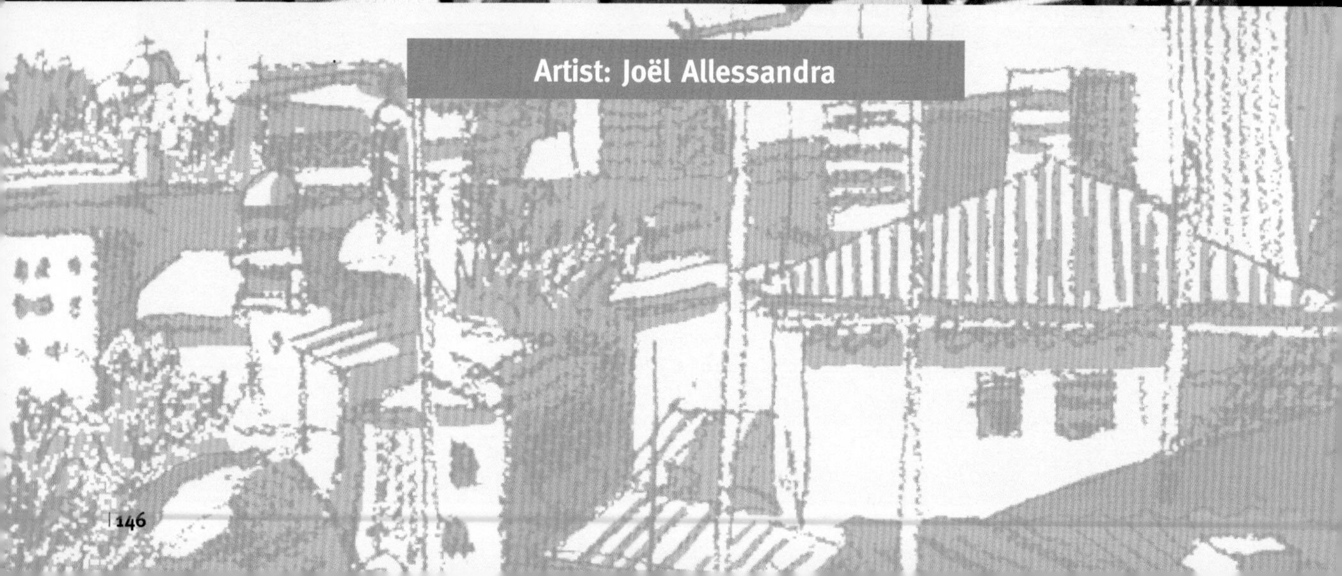

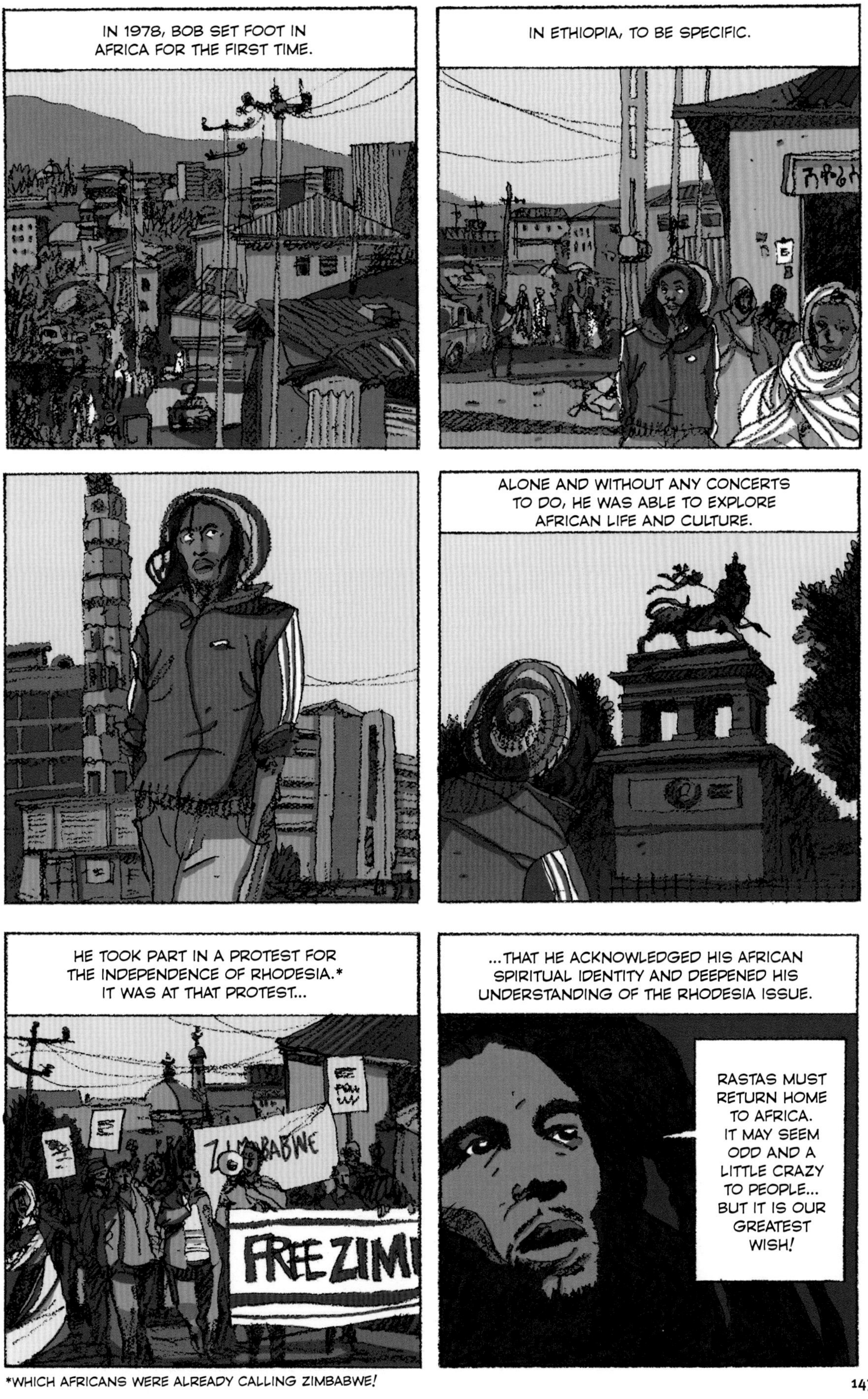
IN 1978, BOB SET FOOT IN AFRICA FOR THE FIRST TIME.
IN ETHIOPIA, TO BE SPECIFIC.
ALONE AND WITHOUT ANY CONCERTS TO DO, HE WAS ABLE TO EXPLORE AFRICAN LIFE AND CULTURE.
HE TOOK PART IN A PROTEST FOR THE INDEPENDENCE OF RHODESIA.* IT WAS AT THAT PROTEST...
ZIMBABWE
FREE ZIM
...THAT HE ACKNOWLEDGED HIS AFRICAN SPIRITUAL IDENTITY AND DEEPENED HIS UNDERSTANDING OF THE RHODESIA ISSUE.
RASTAS MUST RETURN HOME TO AFRICA. IT MAY SEEM ODD AND A LITTLE CRAZY TO PEOPLE... BUT IT IS OUR GREATEST WISH!

*WHICH AFRICANS WERE ALREADY CALLING ZIMBABWE!

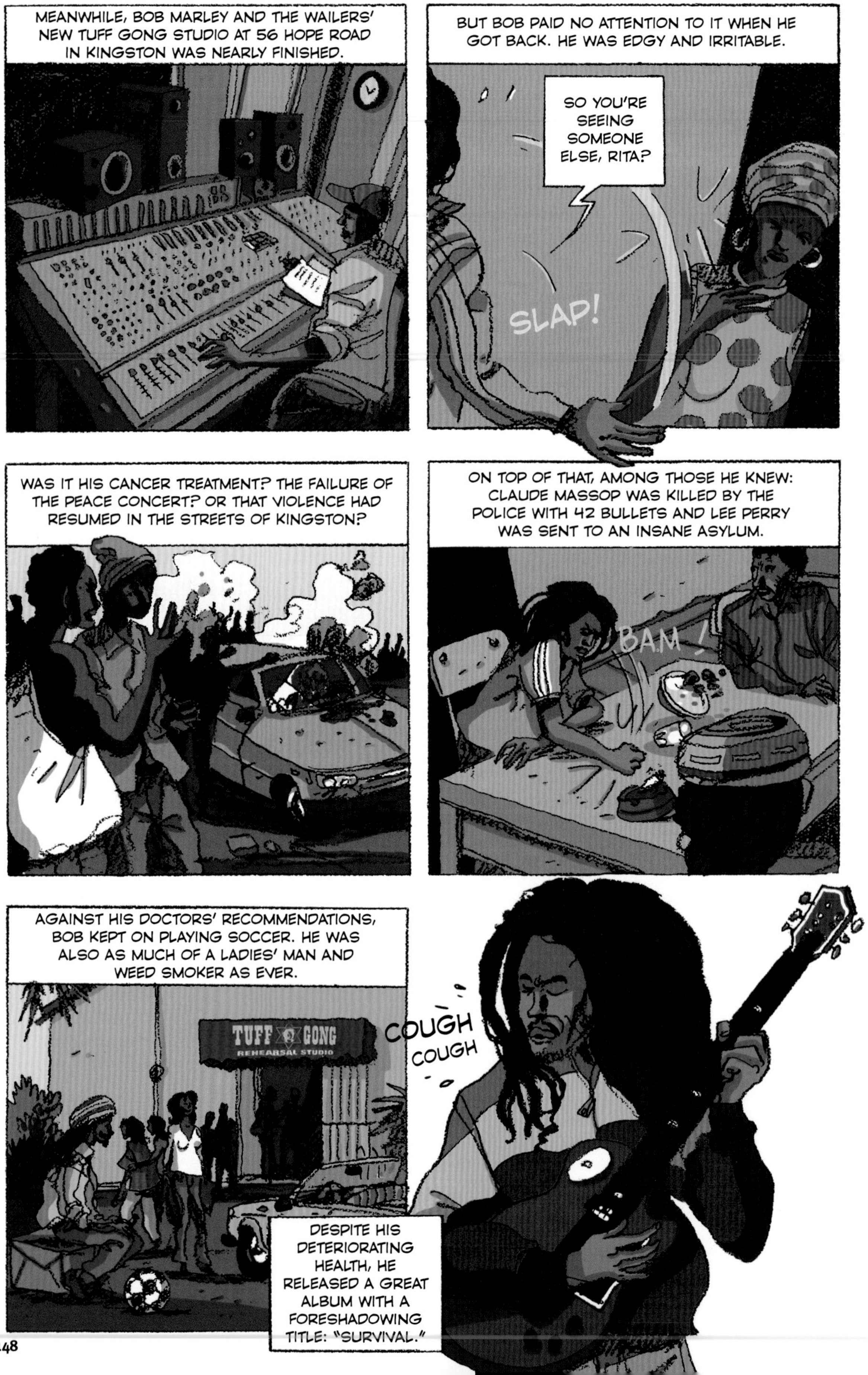

MEANWHILE, BOB MARLEY AND THE WAILERS' NEW TUFF GONG STUDIO AT 56 HOPE ROAD IN KINGSTON WAS NEARLY FINISHED.
BUT BOB PAID NO ATTENTION TO IT WHEN HE GOT BACK. HE WAS EDGY AND IRRITABLE.
SO YOU'RE SEEING SOMEONE ELSE, RITA?
SLAP!
WAS IT HIS CANCER TREATMENT? THE FAILURE OF THE PEACE CONCERT? OR THAT VIOLENCE HAD RESUMED IN THE STREETS OF KINGSTON?
ON TOP OF THAT, AMONG THOSE HE KNEW: CLAUDE MASSOP WAS KILLED BY THE POLICE WITH 42 BULLETS AND LEE PERRY WAS SENT TO AN INSANE ASYLUM.
BAM !
AGAINST HIS DOCTORS' RECOMMENDATIONS, BOB KEPT ON PLAYING SOCCER. HE WAS ALSO AS MUCH OF A LADIES' MAN AND WEED SMOKER AS EVER.
TUFF GONG
REHEARSAL STUDIO
COUGH
COUGH
DESPITE HIS DETERIORATING HEALTH, HE RELEASED A GREAT ALBUM WITH A FORESHADOWING TITLE: "SURVIVAL."

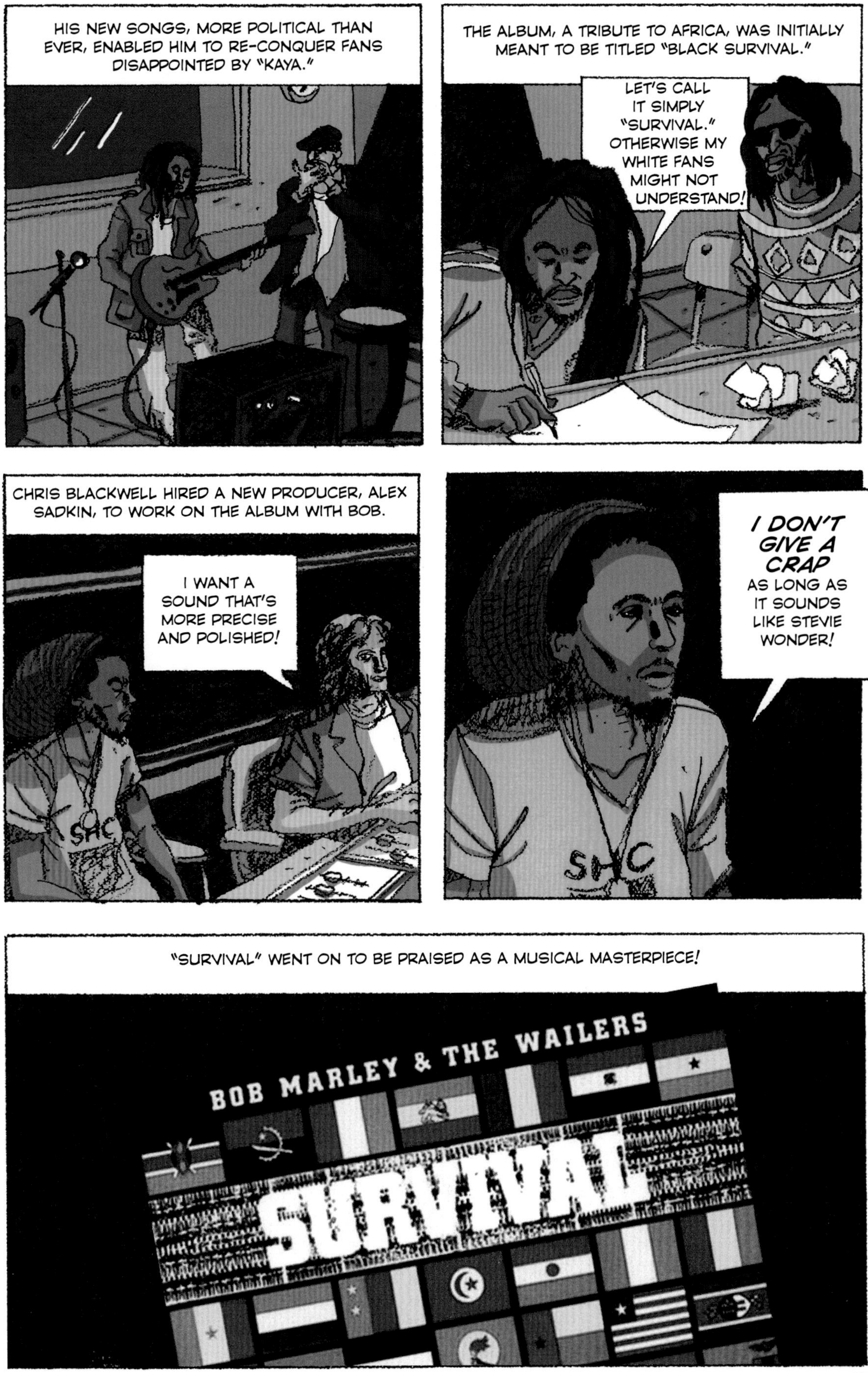
HIS NEW SONGS, MORE POLITICAL THAN EVER, ENABLED HIM TO RE-CONQUER FANS DISAPPOINTED BY "KAYA."
THE ALBUM, A TRIBUTE TO AFRICA, WAS INITIALLY MEANT TO BE TITLED "BLACK SURVIVAL."
LET'S CALL IT SIMPLY "SURVIVAL." OTHERWISE MY WHITE FANS MIGHT NOT UNDERSTAND!
CHRIS BLACKWELL HIRED A NEW PRODUCER, ALEX SADKIN, TO WORK ON THE ALBUM WITH BOB.
I WANT A SOUND THAT'S MORE PRECISE AND POLISHED!
I DON'T GIVE A CRAP AS LONG AS IT SOUNDS LIKE STEVIE WONDER!
"SURVIVAL" WENT ON TO BE PRAISED AS A MUSICAL MASTERPIECE!
BOB MARLEY & THE WAILERS
SURVIVAL

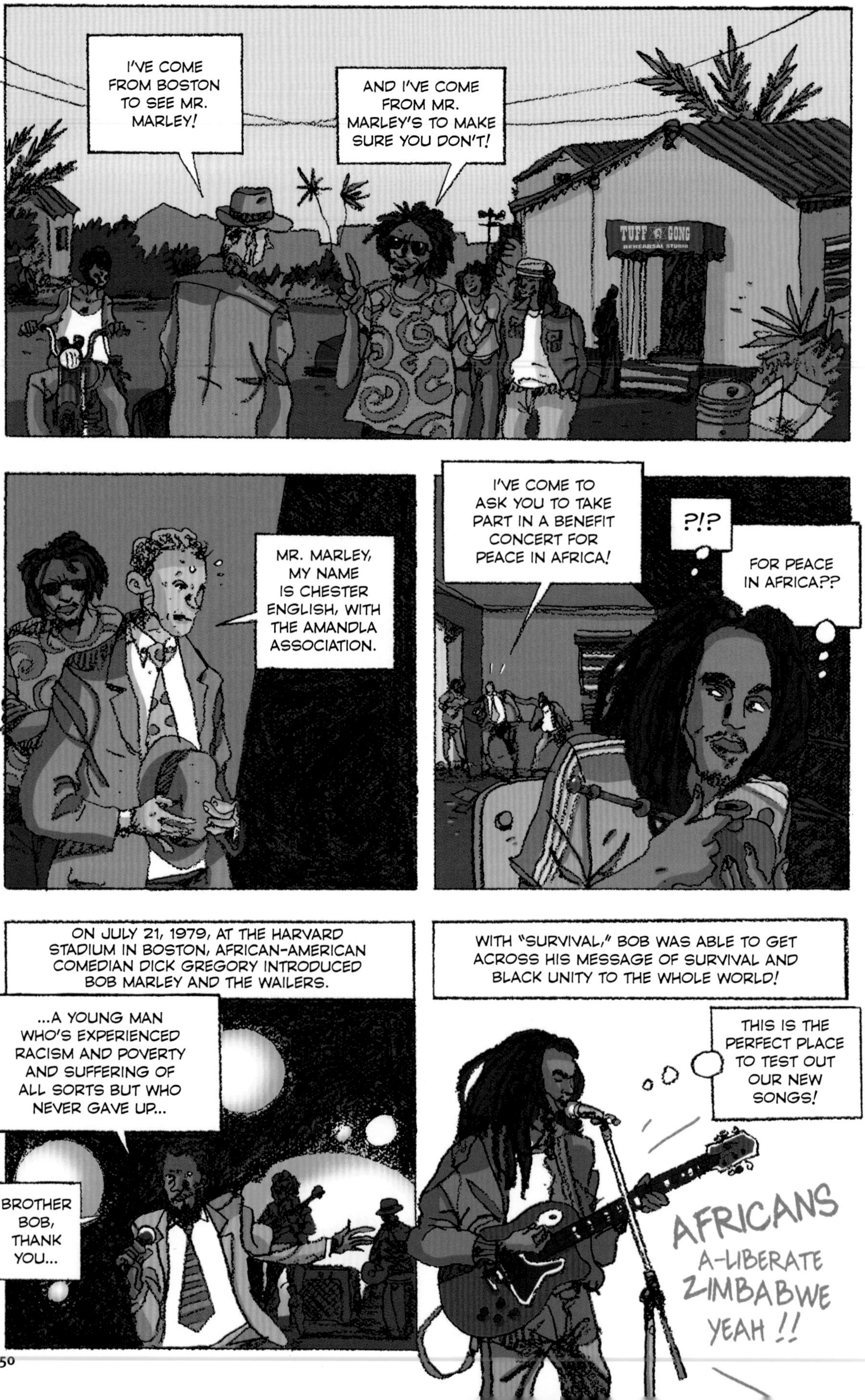

I'VE COME FROM BOSTON TO SEE MR. MARLEY!
AND I'VE COME FROM MR. MARLEY'S TO MAKE SURE YOU DON'T!
TUFF GONG
MR. MARLEY, MY NAME IS CHESTER ENGLISH, WITH THE AMANDLA ASSOCIATION.
I'VE COME TO ASK YOU TO TAKE PART IN A BENEFIT CONCERT FOR PEACE IN AFRICA!
?!?
FOR PEACE IN AFRICA??
ON JULY 21, 1979, AT THE HARVARD STADIUM IN BOSTON, AFRICAN-AMERICAN COMEDIAN DICK GREGORY INTRODUCED BOB MARLEY AND THE WAILERS.
...A YOUNG MAN WHO'S EXPERIENCED RACISM AND POVERTY AND SUFFERING OF ALL SORTS BUT WHO NEVER GAVE UP...
BROTHER BOB, THANK YOU...
WITH "SURVIVAL," BOB WAS ABLE TO GET ACROSS HIS MESSAGE OF SURVIVAL AND BLACK UNITY TO THE WHOLE WORLD!
THIS IS THE PERFECT PLACE TO TEST OUT OUR NEW SONGS!
AFRICANS A-LIBERATE ZIMBABWE YEAH !!

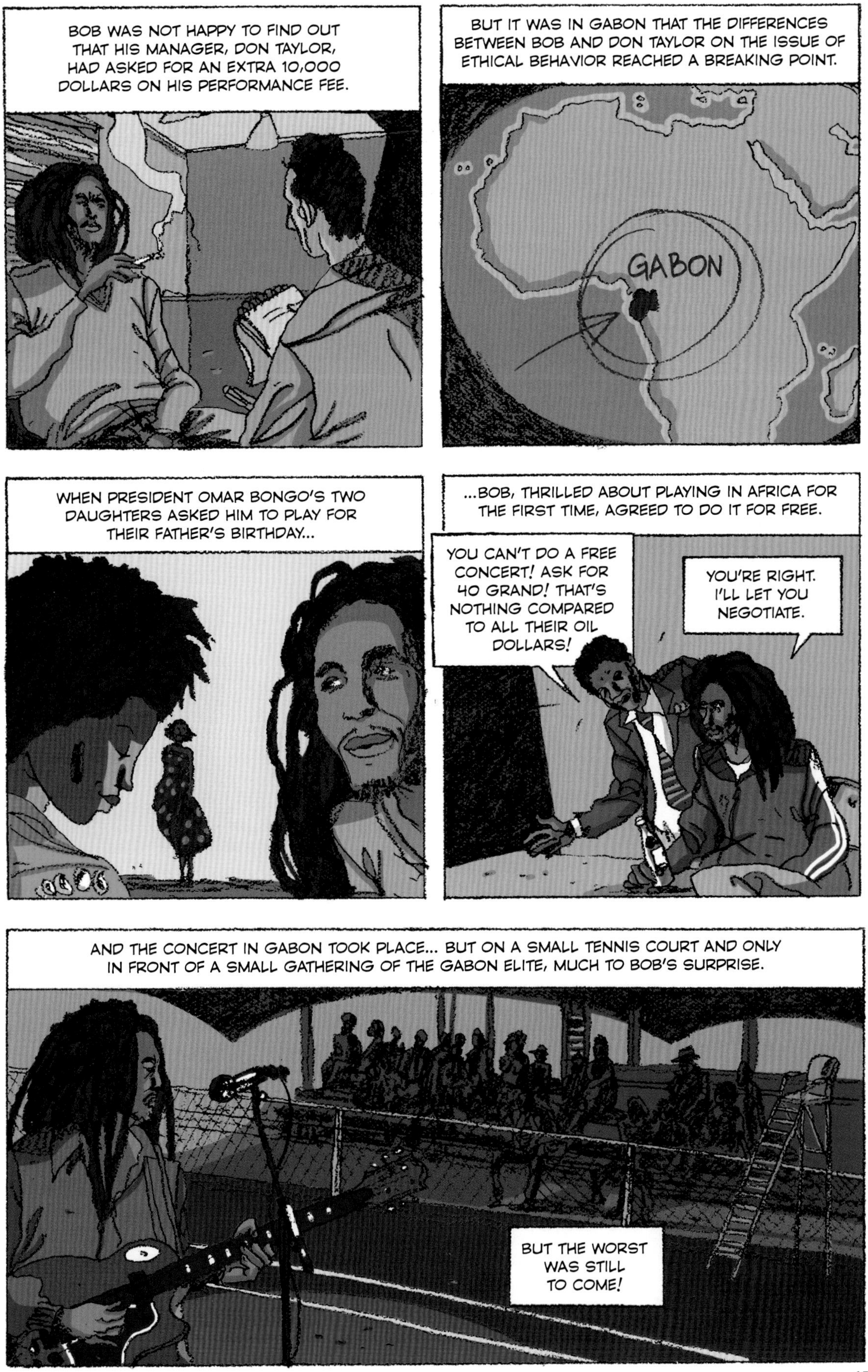
BOB WAS NOT HAPPY TO FIND OUT THAT HIS MANAGER, DON TAYLOR, HAD ASKED FOR AN EXTRA 10,000 DOLLARS ON HIS PERFORMANCE FEE.
BUT IT WAS IN GABON THAT THE DIFFERENCES BETWEEN BOB AND DON TAYLOR ON THE ISSUE OF ETHICAL BEHAVIOR REACHED A BREAKING POINT.
GABON
WHEN PRESIDENT OMAR BONGO'S TWO DAUGHTERS ASKED HIM TO PLAY FOR THEIR FATHER'S BIRTHDAY...
...BOB, THRILLED ABOUT PLAYING IN AFRICA FOR THE FIRST TIME, AGREED TO DO IT FOR FREE.
YOU CAN'T DO A FREE CONCERT! ASK FOR 40 GRAND! THAT'S NOTHING COMPARED TO ALL THEIR OIL DOLLARS!
YOU'RE RIGHT. I'LL LET YOU NEGOTIATE.
AND THE CONCERT IN GABON TOOK PLACE... BUT ON A SMALL TENNIS COURT AND ONLY IN FRONT OF A SMALL GATHERING OF THE GABON ELITE, MUCH TO BOB'S SURPRISE.
BUT THE WORST WAS STILL TO COME!

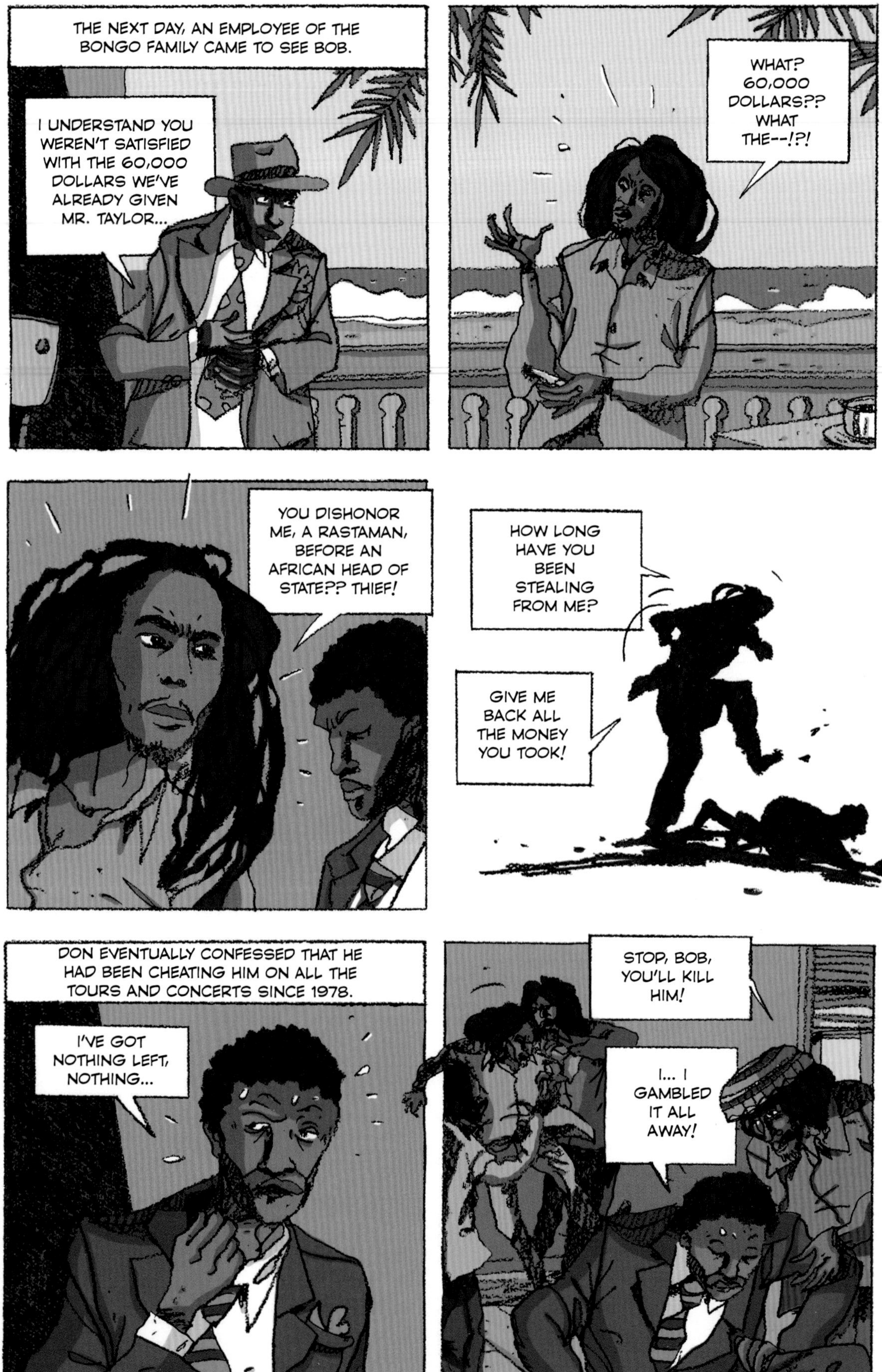
THE NEXT DAY, AN EMPLOYEE OF THE BONGO FAMILY CAME TO SEE BOB.
I UNDERSTAND YOU WEREN'T SATISFIED WITH THE 60,000 DOLLARS WE'VE ALREADY GIVEN MR. TAYLOR...
WHAT? 60,000 DOLLARS?? WHAT THE--!?!
YOU DISHONOR ME, A RASTAMAN, BEFORE AN AFRICAN HEAD OF STATE?? THIEF!
HOW LONG HAVE YOU BEEN STEALING FROM ME?
GIVE ME BACK ALL THE MONEY YOU TOOK!
DON EVENTUALLY CONFESSED THAT HE HAD BEEN CHEATING HIM ON ALL THE TOURS AND CONCERTS SINCE 1978.
I'VE GOT NOTHING LEFT, NOTHING...
STOP, BOB, YOU'LL KILL HIM!
I... I GAMBLED IT ALL AWAY!

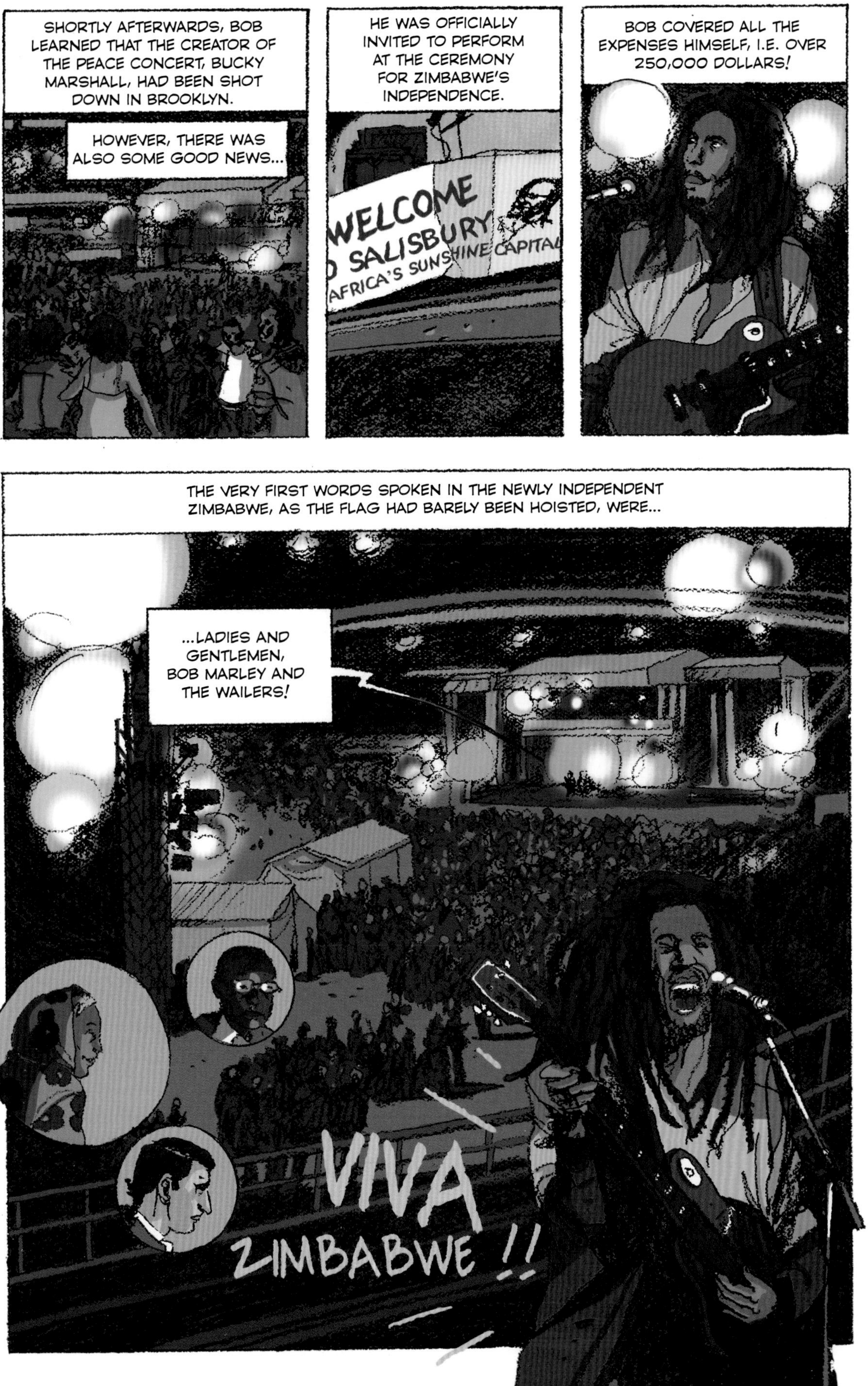
SHORTLY AFTERWARDS, BOB LEARNED THAT THE CREATOR OF THE PEACE CONCERT, BUCKY MARSHALL, HAD BEEN SHOT DOWN IN BROOKLYN.
HOWEVER, THERE WAS ALSO SOME GOOD NEWS...
HE WAS OFFICIALLY INVITED TO PERFORM AT THE CEREMONY FOR ZIMBABWE'S INDEPENDENCE.
WELCOME
O SALISBURY
AFRICA'S SUNSHINE CAPITAL
BOB COVERED ALL THE EXPENSES HIMSELF, I.E. OVER 250,000 DOLLARS!
THE VERY FIRST WORDS SPOKEN IN THE NEWLY INDEPENDENT ZIMBABWE, AS THE FLAG HAD BARELY BEEN HOISTED, WERE...
...LADIES AND GENTLEMEN, BOB MARLEY AND THE WAILERS!
VIVA ZIMBABWE !!

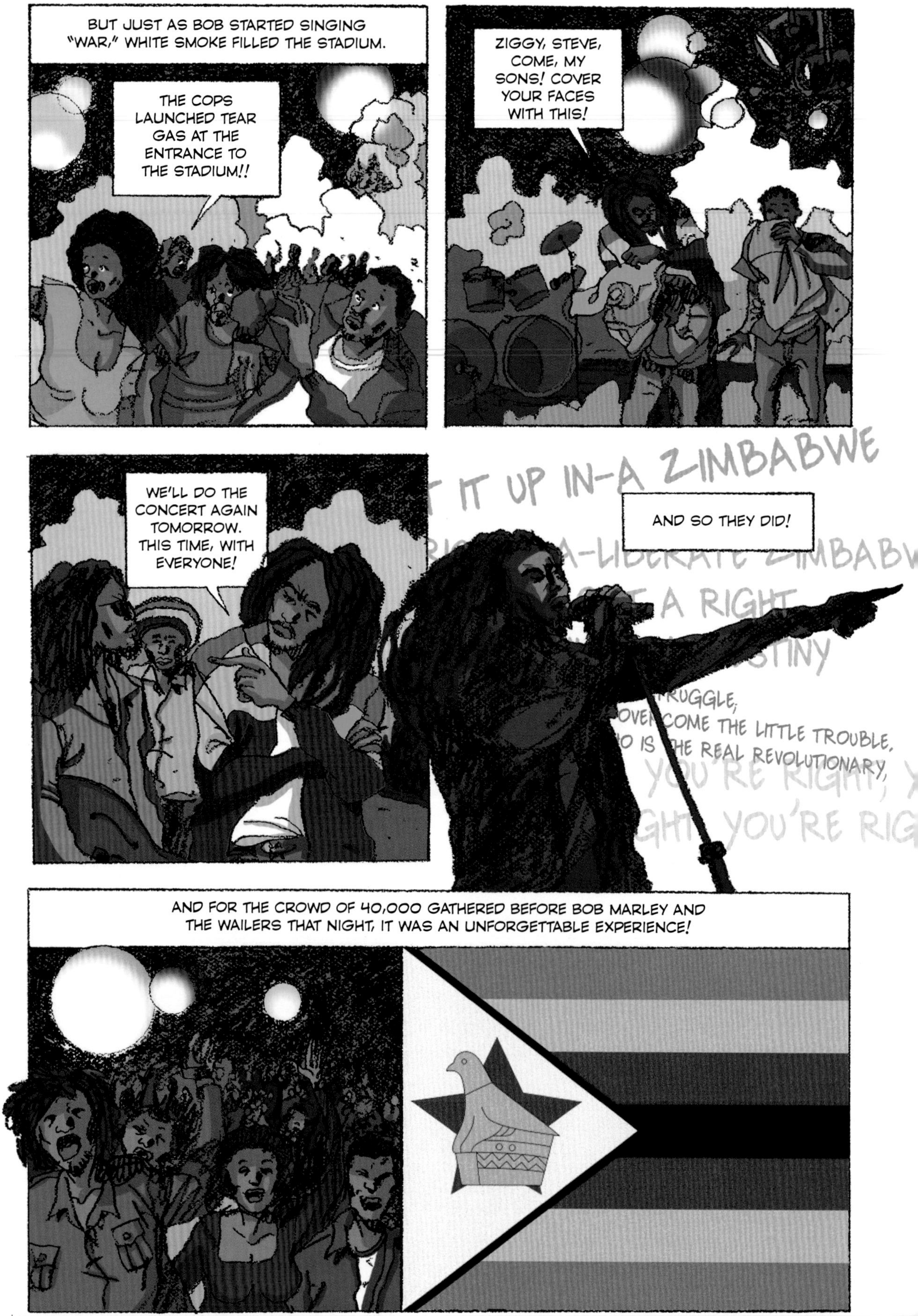
BUT JUST AS BOB STARTED SINGING "WAR," WHITE SMOKE FILLED THE STADIUM.
THE COPS LAUNCHED TEAR GAS AT THE ENTRANCE TO THE STADIUM!!
ZIGGY, STEVE, COME, MY SONS! COVER YOUR FACES WITH THIS!
WE'LL DO THE CONCERT AGAIN TOMORROW. THIS TIME, WITH EVERYONE!
AND SO THEY DID!
IT UP IN-A ZIMBABWE
A RIGHT
COME THE LITTLE TROUBLE,
IS THE REAL REVOLUTIONARY,
AND FOR THE CROWD OF 40,000 GATHERED BEFORE BOB MARLEY AND THE WAILERS THAT NIGHT, IT WAS AN UNFORGETTABLE EXPERIENCE!

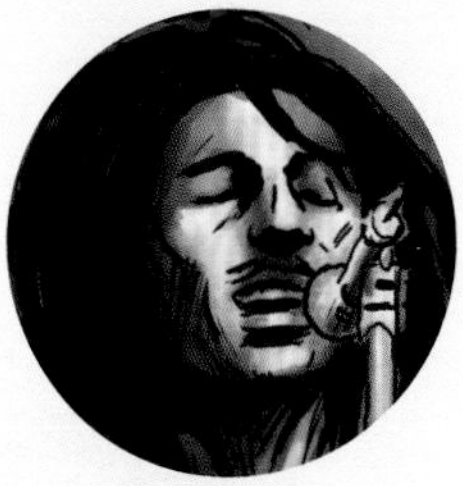

For Peace and Unity Among Peoples

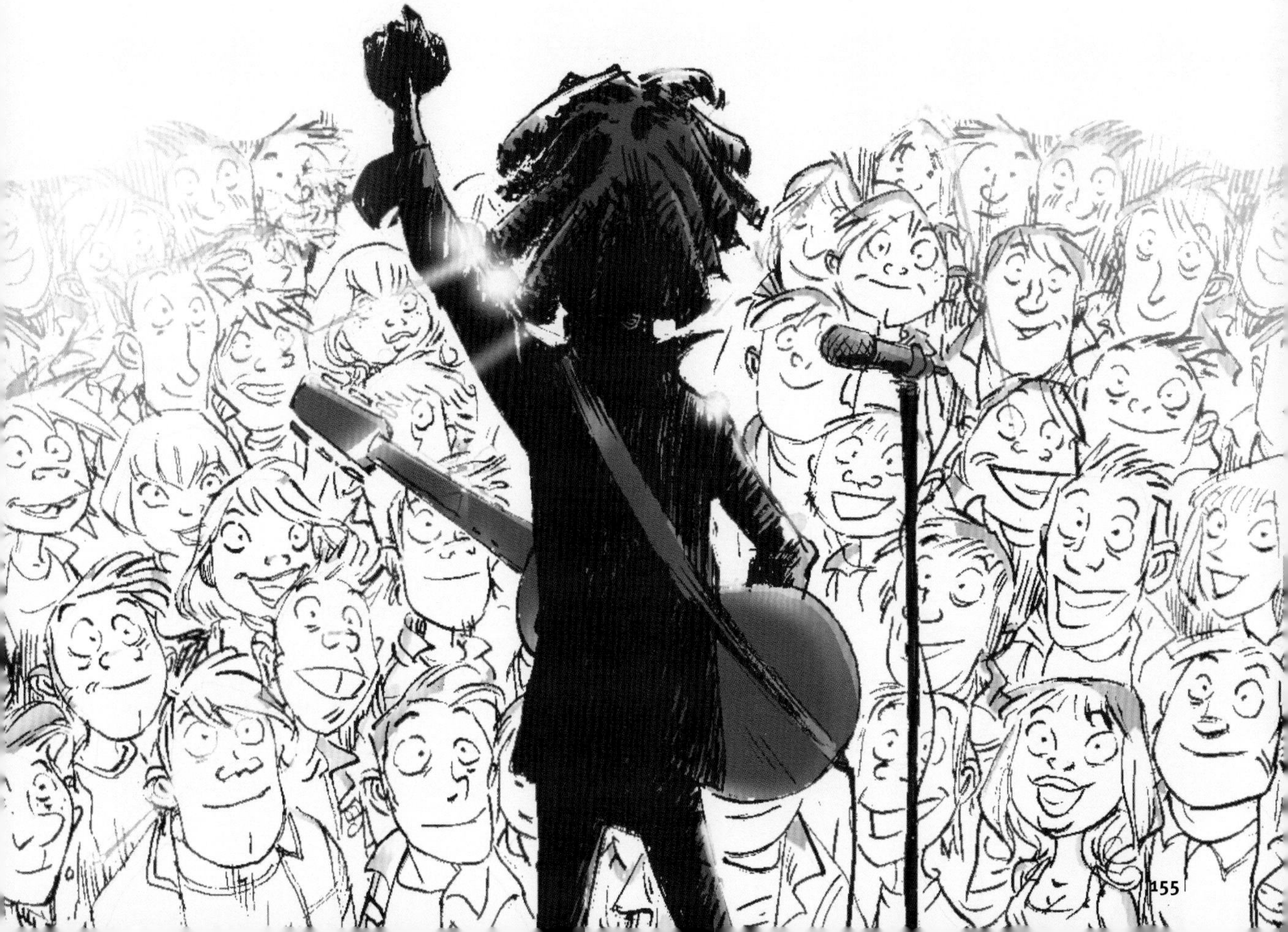

Bob Marley truly believed that "music can set people free," and for the remainder of his days devoted all his energy to defending the values of peace and solidarity, both in his own country and across the African continent.

Two years after the attempt on his life that led him to exile, Bob Marley returned to his native island. He had a good reason to do so: performing at a concert for peace. He was to be the headlining act of a Kingston show that featured fifteen other reggae singers and bands, including Big Youth, Inner Circle and Peter Tosh, who was now pursuing a solo career. After the 1976 Smile Jamaica, here came the One Love Peace Concert, a deafening call for national reconciliation, as the country was still ravaged by civil war, an echo of the Cold War that divided the world into two camps for so long.

On April 22, 1978 at 2 p.m., the stadium opened its doors to some 32,000 fans who had come to watch a show both festive and symbolic. The concert started three and a half hours later. Bob Marley didn't take the stage until a little after midnight. Though weakened by the cancer eating away at him, he was full of energy and so was the audience. The fever pitch had reached its height when the singer called out to the two political leaders in the audience and asked them to join him on stage: Socialist prime minister Michael Manley, member of the PNP (People's National Party) and his opponent from the JLP (Jamaica Labor Party), Edward Seaga. The two rivals were on the campaign trail in view of the upcoming 1980 elections and had made sure not to miss the show, i.e. the opportunity to be seen with the idol and pride of Jamaica! But this they were not expecting... They grudgingly agreed and went to stand on either side of Bob Marley as he joined their hands over his head to the tunes of "Jammin'," a song with a beautiful double meaning. One of the tracks on the Exodus album, it can indeed be interpreted as an invitation to dance and make merry, or as a call to play music together and improvise in order to forget about oppression. For a few minutes, the three men stood there like that before the audience. It was a powerful image and emotions ran high in the audience. But symbolic moments are often all too brief...

On May 21, 1981, Bob Marley entered the Rasta pantheon in heaven.

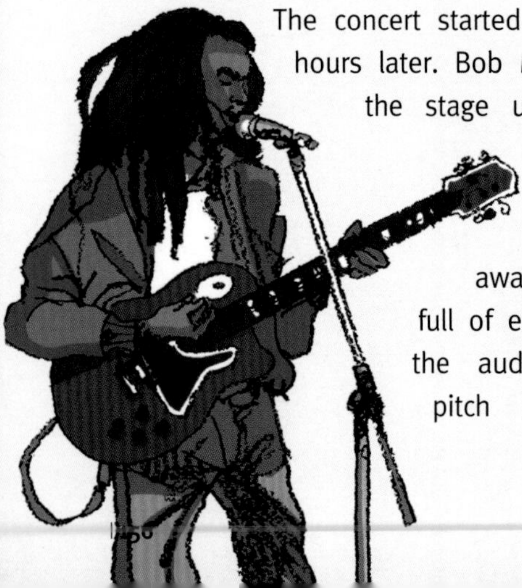

Two months later, when Bob Marley was awarded the U.N.'s peace medal for that gesture, as well as his larger efforts, fighting in the name

of political parties had already resumed in the slums of Kingston, without any real effort by the leaders to try and stop them. In 1980, the elections took place in a climate of violence, ending in the victory of Edward Seaga. In his "Ambush in the Night," a reference to the attack in his home, Bob Marley doesn't try to hide his disappointment or bitterness: "See them fighting for power... Through political strategy, They keep us hungry, And when you gonna get some food, Your brother got to be your enemy, we-e-ell!"

His insistence on solidarity and equality between people didn't just apply to Jamaica but to peoples across the globe, and especially to Africans, whom Bob Marley encouraged to unite in "Africa Unite." He had been preaching that for some time, but it wasn't until 1978 that he first set foot on that continent, "the cornerstone of [his] ancestors," as he called it. First he traveled to Kenya, then to Ethiopia, where he visited the war-ravaged kingdom of Haile Selassie. The emperor had been buried in an anonymous grave, which outraged the singer.

Bob Marley returned to Africa in 1980, to Gabon, at the invitation of Pascaline Bongo, with whom he was involved romantically. The President's daughter asked him to perform at the birthday party for her dictator father. Not exactly his shining moment, but Marley swore he had no idea what kind of regime it was before he accepted. A few months later, he took part in the festivities organized in celebration of the independence of Rhodesia, now called Zimbabwe: a much more politically correct event, as Robert Mugabe was then a Marxist comrade and not yet a despot. Buoyed by the liberation of the last African colony, the singer paid 250,000 dollars out of his own pocket to bring the necessary material to the concert he put on in the capital. The event was such a hit that thousands of people were forced to watch from behind the fence, which they tried to break through. Perhaps understandable, considering it had been twenty years since such a show had taken place in the country! As a result, the police fired tear gas and the audience dispersed in an atmosphere of chaos and confusion while Bob Marley continued to sing. The concert resumed the next day, this time without any rioting. "Every man gotta right to decide his own destiny," proclaims the musician in "Zimbabwe," the piece he dedicated to the fledgling country. And also: "Brother, you're right, you're right, we'll have to fight, We gonna fight for our rights!" Beyond decolonization, he also encourages everyone to "emancipate [themselves] from mental slavery" in "Redemption Song," which came out that same year of 1980: "None but ourselves can free our minds."

All the Way

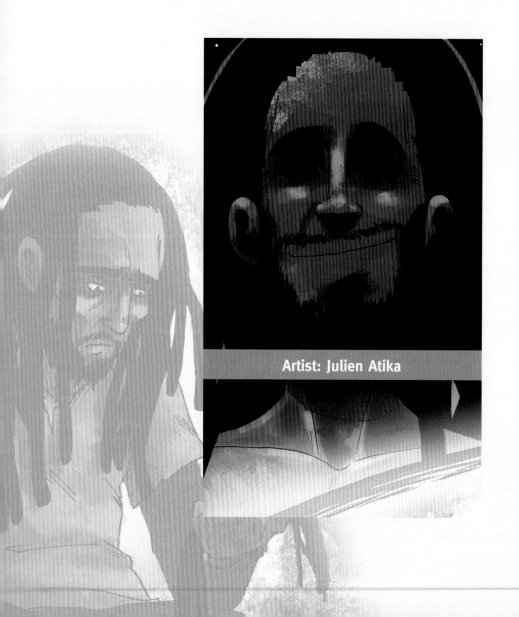

Artist: Julien Atika

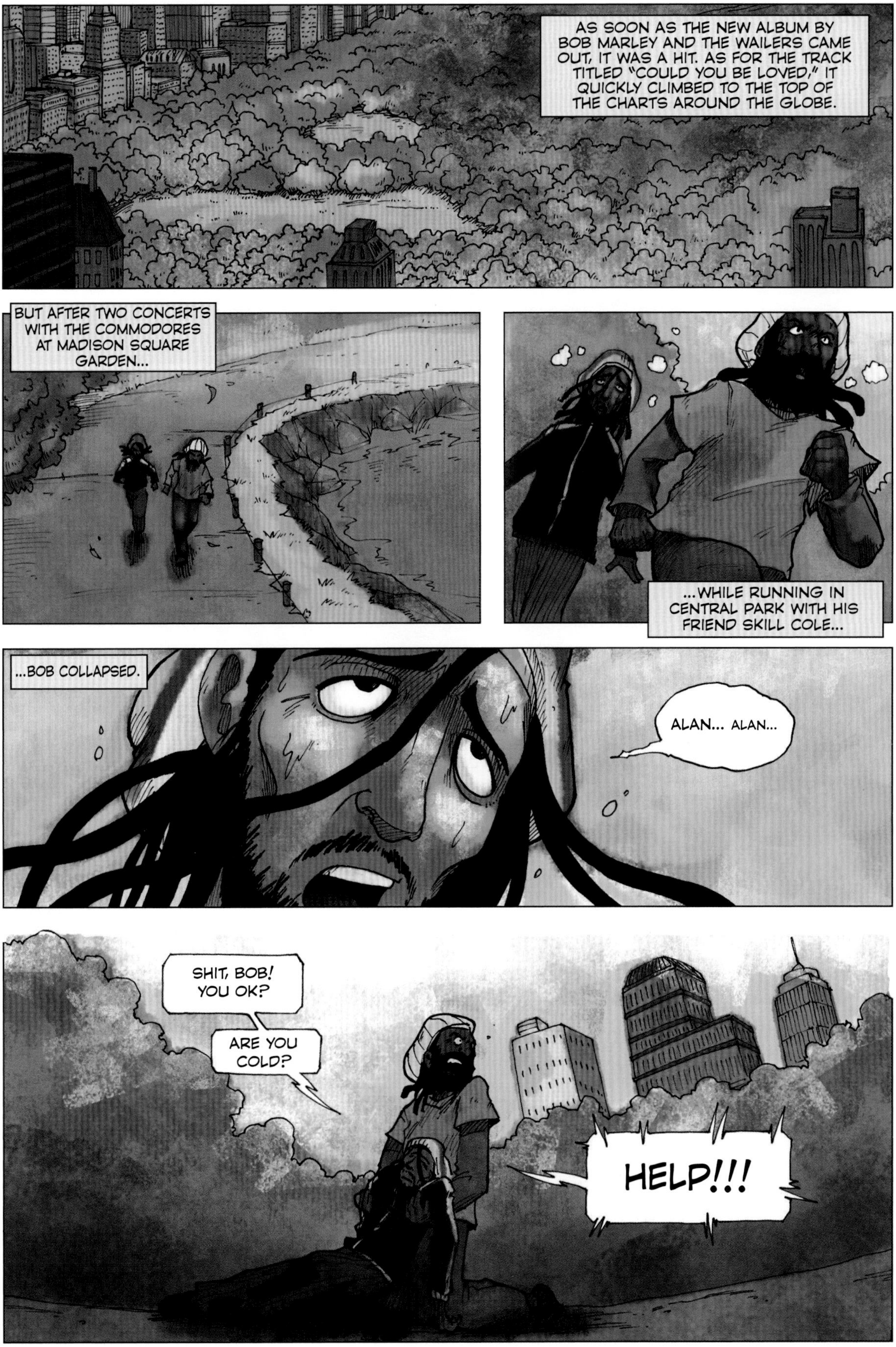
AS SOON AS THE NEW ALBUM BY BOB MARLEY AND THE WAILERS CAME OUT, IT WAS A HIT. AS FOR THE TRACK TITLED "COULD YOU BE LOVED," IT QUICKLY CLIMBED TO THE TOP OF THE CHARTS AROUND THE GLOBE.
BUT AFTER TWO CONCERTS WITH THE COMMODORES AT MADISON SQUARE GARDEN...
...WHILE RUNNING IN CENTRAL PARK WITH HIS FRIEND SKILL COLE...
...BOB COLLAPSED.
ALAN... ALAN...
SHIT, BOB! YOU OK?
ARE YOU COLD?
HELP!!!

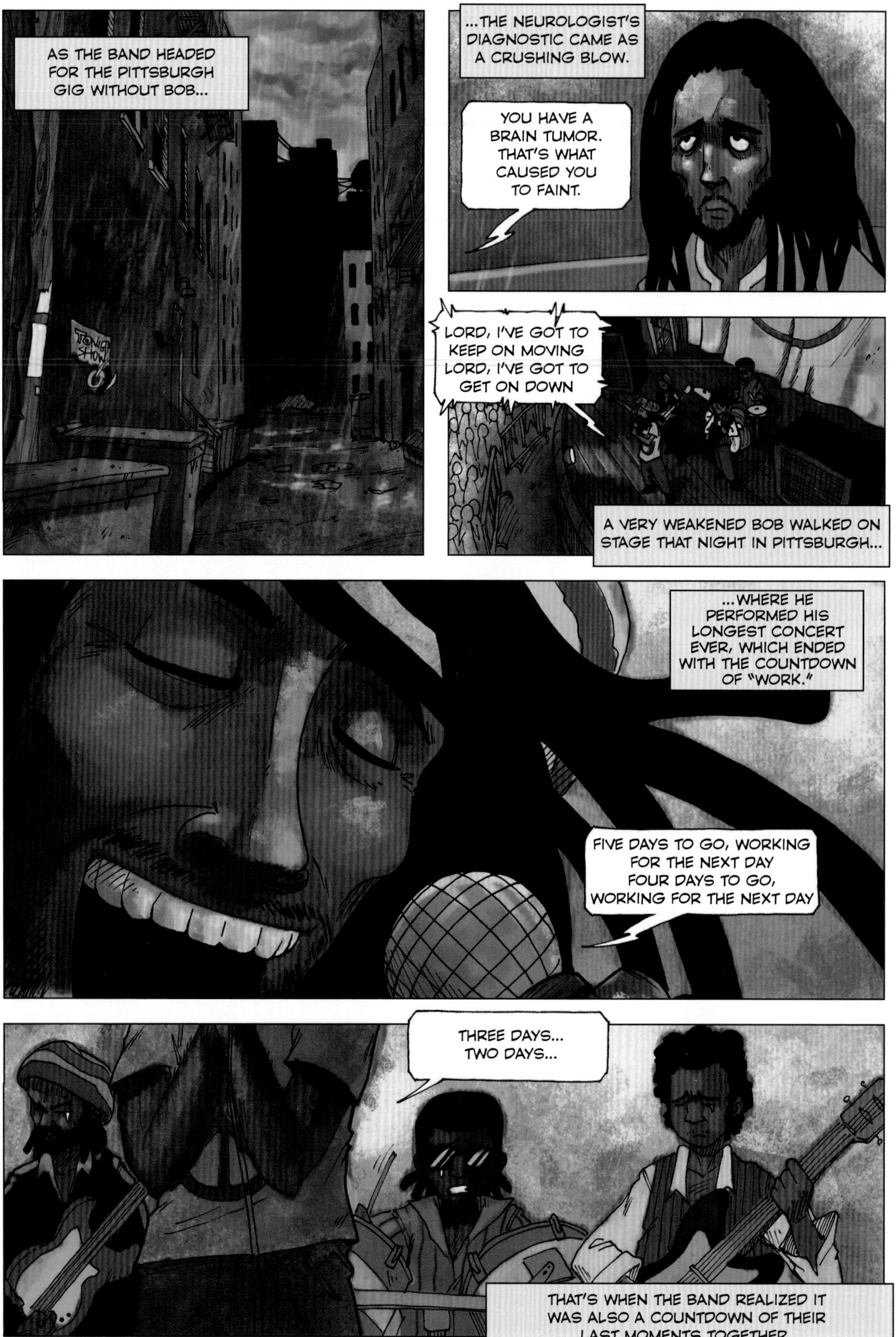
AS THE BAND HEADED FOR THE PITTSBURGH GIG WITHOUT BOB...
TONIGHT SHOW
...THE NEUROLOGIST'S DIAGNOSTIC CAME AS A CRUSHING BLOW.
YOU HAVE A BRAIN TUMOR. THAT'S WHAT CAUSED YOU TO FAINT.
LORD, I'VE GOT TO KEEP ON MOVING LORD, I'VE GOT TO GET ON DOWN
A VERY WEAKENED BOB WALKED ON STAGE THAT NIGHT IN PITTSBURGH...
...WHERE HE PERFORMED HIS LONGEST CONCERT EVER, WHICH ENDED WITH THE COUNTDOWN OF "WORK."
FIVE DAYS TO GO, WORKING FOR THE NEXT DAY FOUR DAYS TO GO, WORKING FOR THE NEXT DAY
THREE DAYS... TWO DAYS...
THAT'S WHEN THE BAND REALIZED IT WAS ALSO A COUNTDOWN OF THEIR LAST MOMENTS TOGETHER.

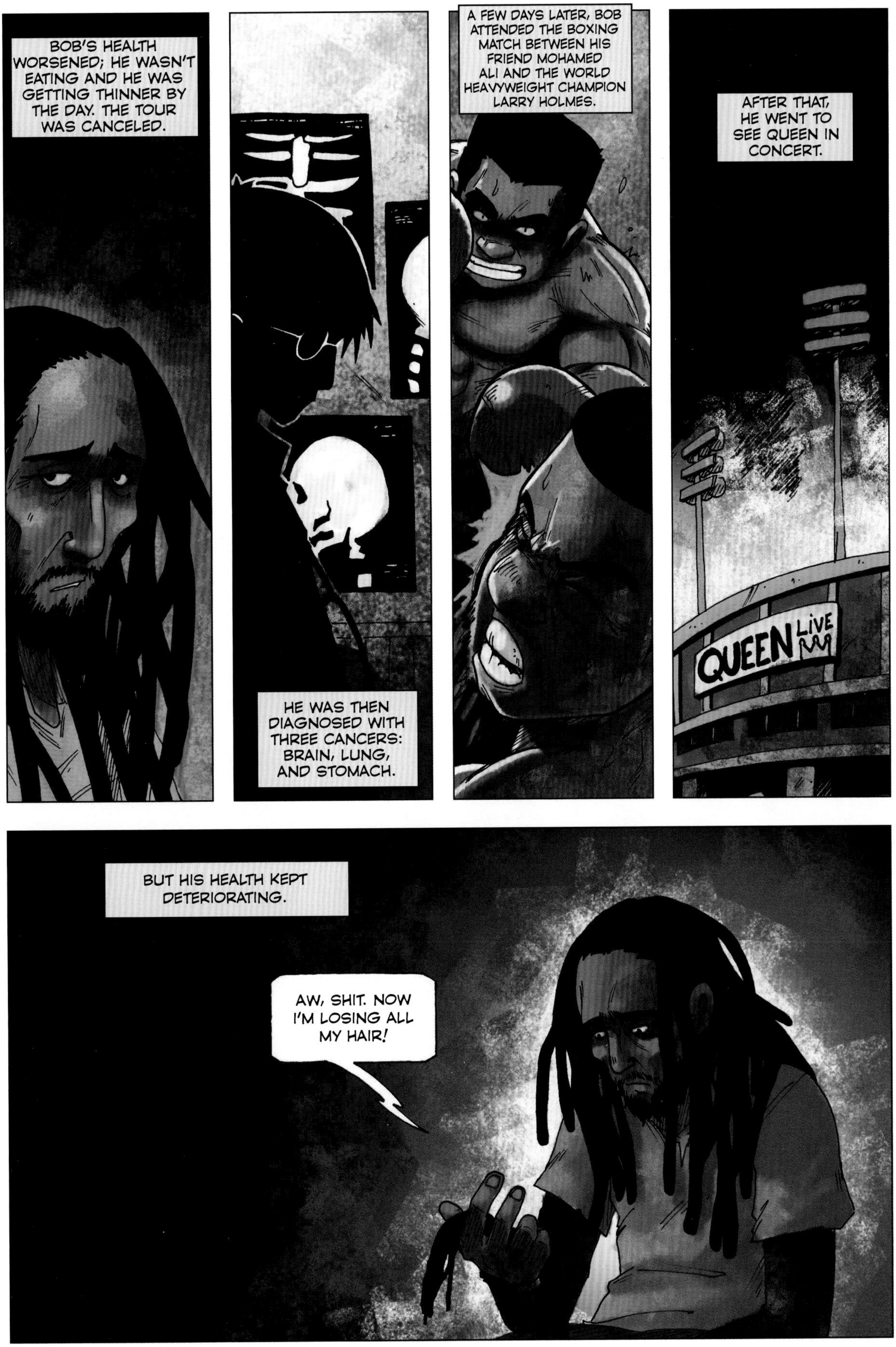
BOB'S HEALTH WORSENED; HE WASN'T EATING AND HE WAS GETTING THINNER BY THE DAY. THE TOUR WAS CANCELED.
HE WAS THEN DIAGNOSED WITH THREE CANCERS: BRAIN, LUNG, AND STOMACH.
A FEW DAYS LATER, BOB ATTENDED THE BOXING MATCH BETWEEN HIS FRIEND MOHAMED ALI AND THE WORLD HEAVYWEIGHT CHAMPION LARRY HOLMES.
AFTER THAT, HE WENT TO SEE QUEEN IN CONCERT.
QUEEN LIVE
BUT HIS HEALTH KEPT DETERIORATING.
AW, SHIT. NOW I'M LOSING ALL MY HAIR!

BOB'S MOTHER WANTED HER SON TO BE BAPTIZED BY THE ETHIOPIAN ORTHODOX CHURCH.

THIS WAS DONE ON NOVEMBER 4, 1980 AT THE WELLINGTON HOTEL.

BOB WAS GIVEN THE NAME BERHANE SELASSIE.

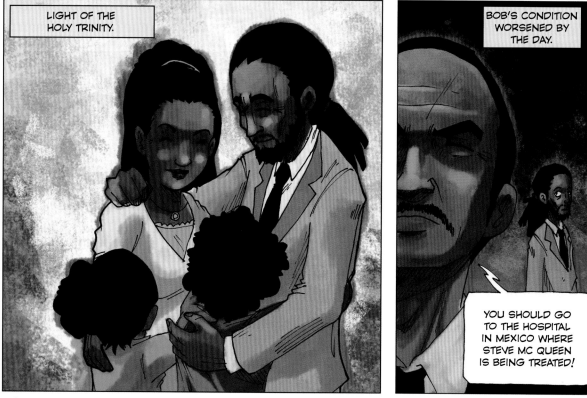

LIGHT OF THE HOLY TRINITY.

BOB'S CONDITION WORSENED BY THE DAY.

YOU SHOULD GO TO THE HOSPITAL IN MEXICO WHERE STEVE MC QUEEN IS BEING TREATED!

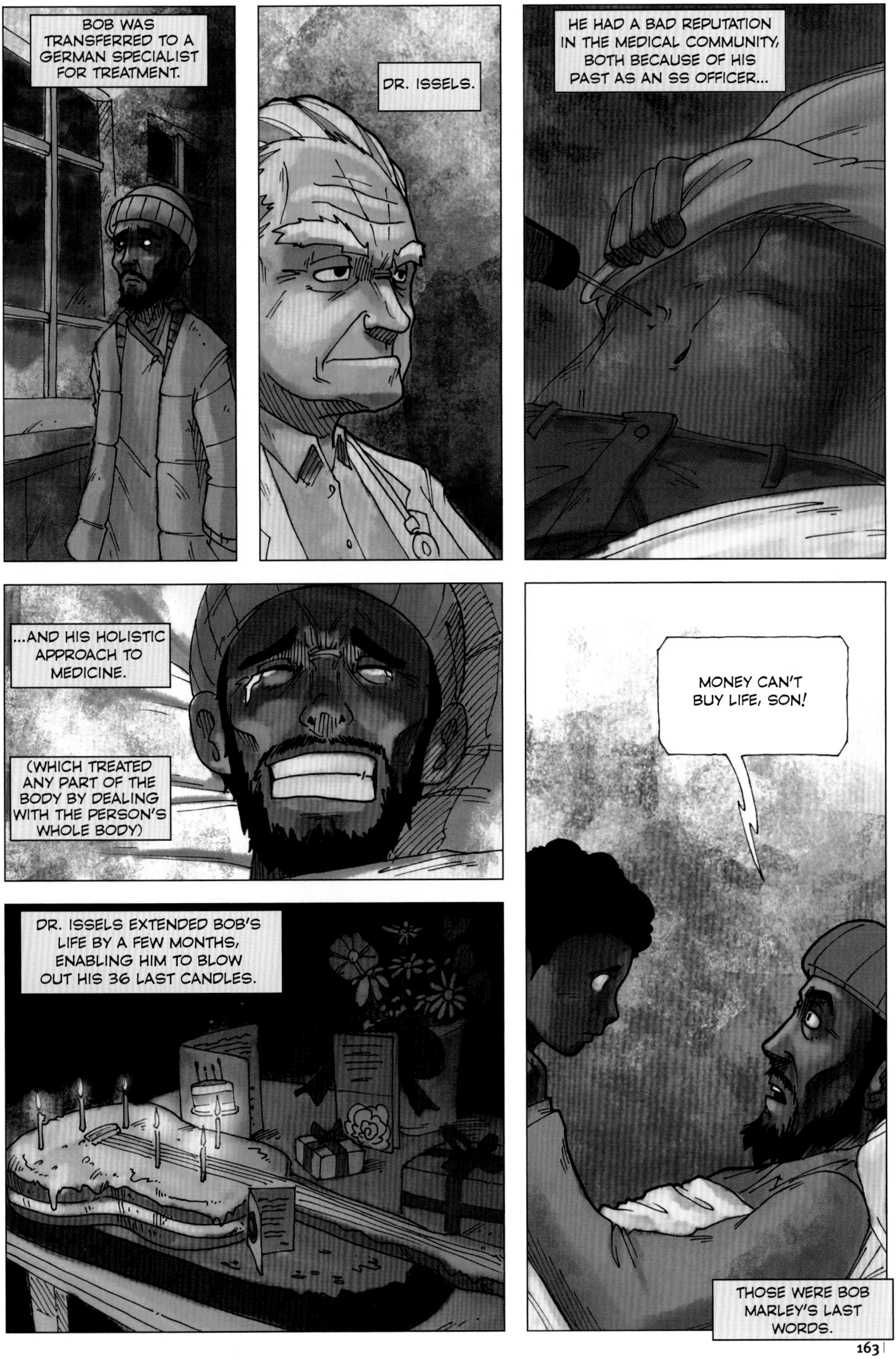
BOB WAS TRANSFERRED TO A GERMAN SPECIALIST FOR TREATMENT.
DR. ISSELS.
HE HAD A BAD REPUTATION IN THE MEDICAL COMMUNITY, BOTH BECAUSE OF HIS PAST AS AN SS OFFICER...
...AND HIS HOLISTIC APPROACH TO MEDICINE.
(WHICH TREATED ANY PART OF THE BODY BY DEALING WITH THE PERSON'S WHOLE BODY)
DR. ISSELS EXTENDED BOB'S LIFE BY A FEW MONTHS, ENABLING HIM TO BLOW OUT HIS 36 LAST CANDLES.
MONEY CAN'T BUY LIFE, SON!
THOSE WERE BOB MARLEY'S LAST WORDS.

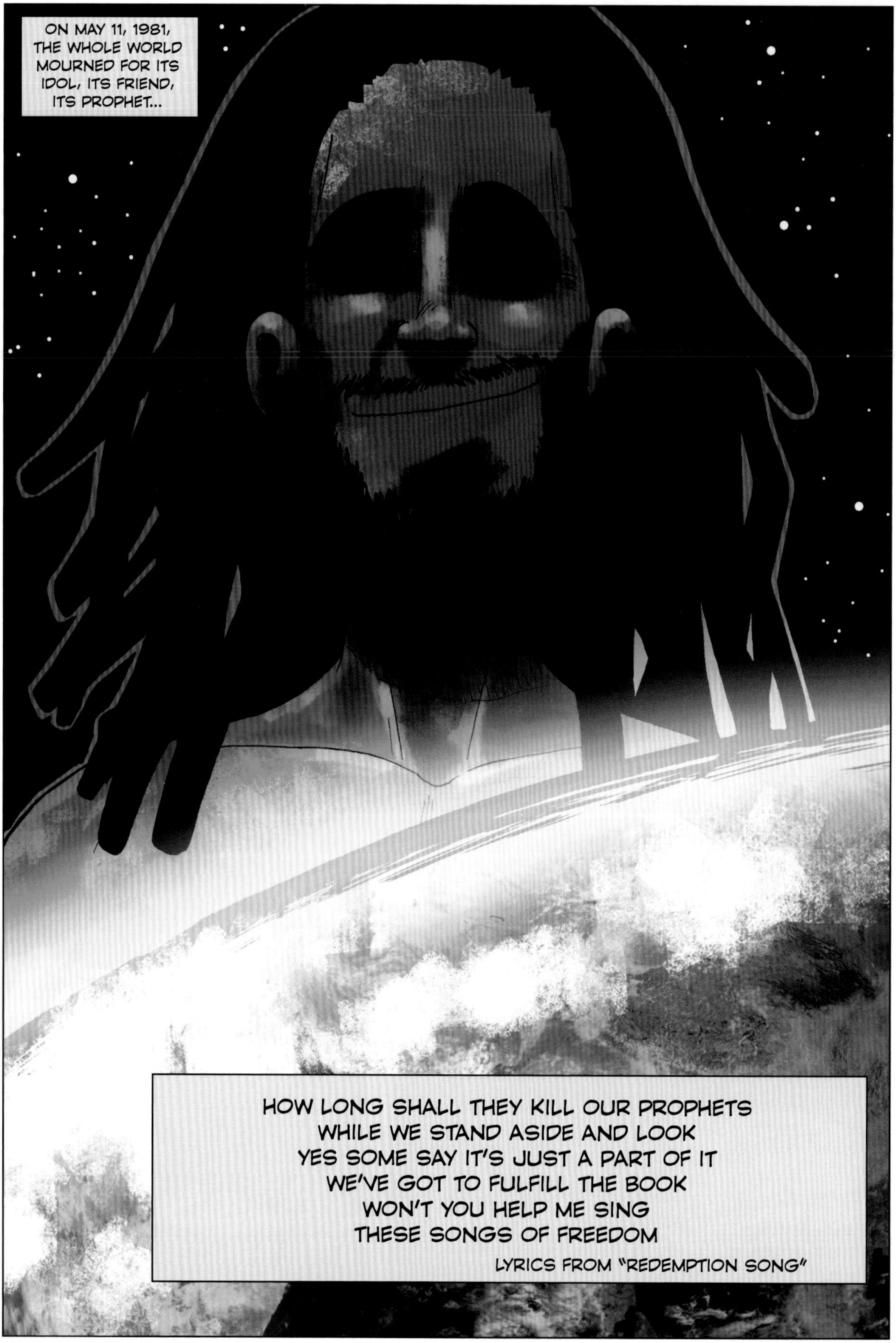
ON MAY 11, 1981, THE WHOLE WORLD MOURNED FOR ITS IDOL, ITS FRIEND, ITS PROPHET...
HOW LONG SHALL THEY KILL OUR PROPHETS
WHILE WE STAND ASIDE AND LOOK
YES SOME SAY IT'S JUST A PART OF IT
WE'VE GOT TO FULFILL THE BOOK
WON'T YOU HELP ME SING
THESE SONGS OF FREEDOM
LYRICS FROM "REDEMPTION SONG"

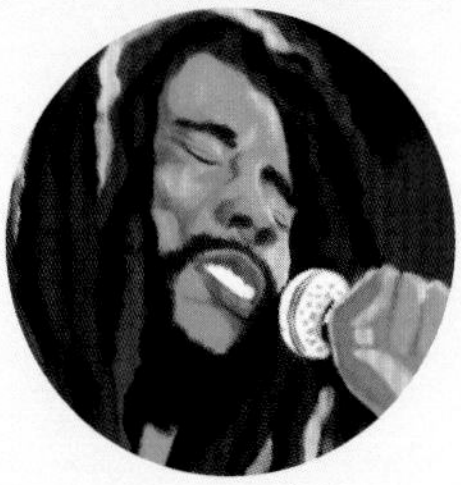

Death of the "Pope of Reggae"

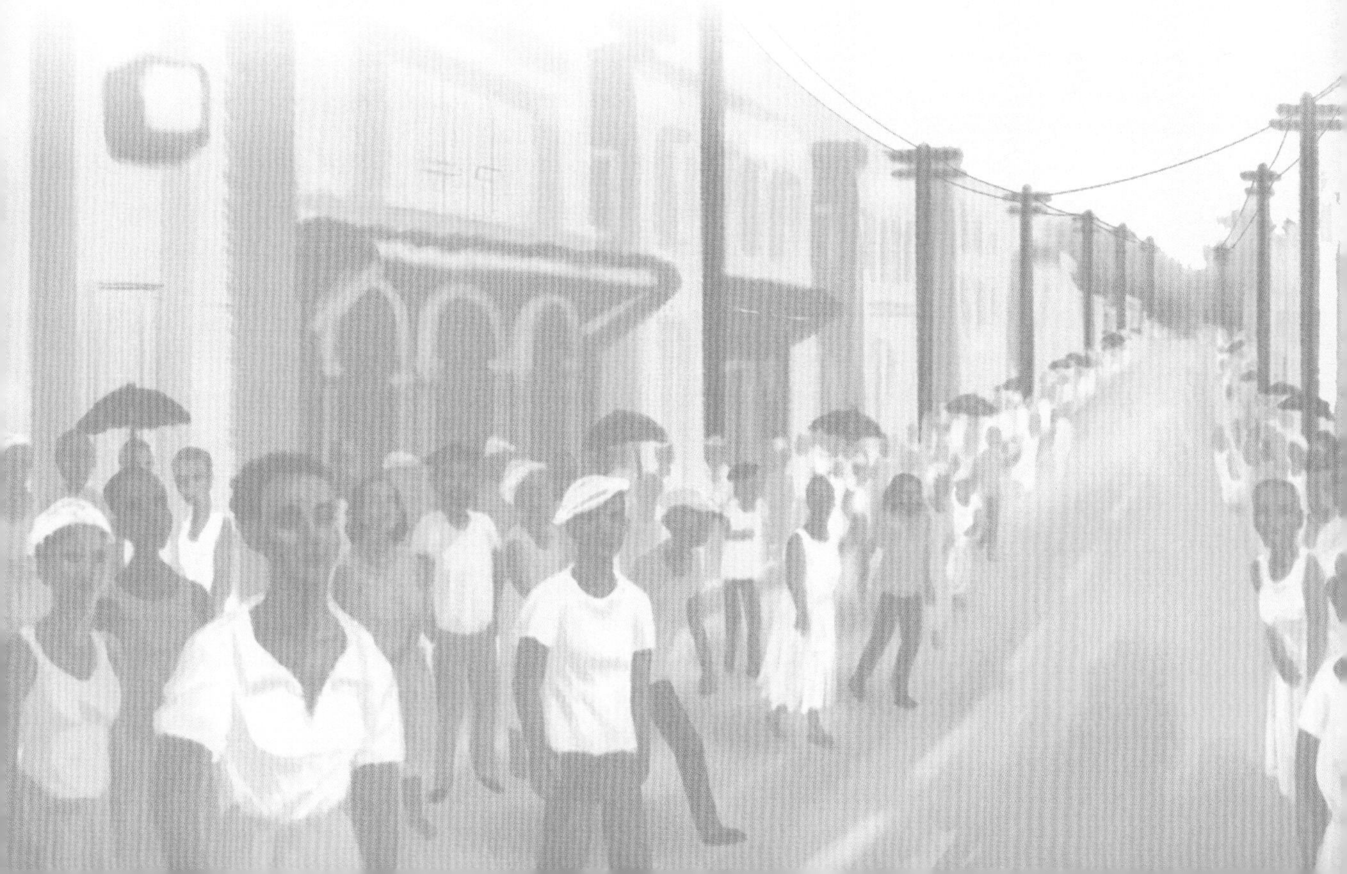

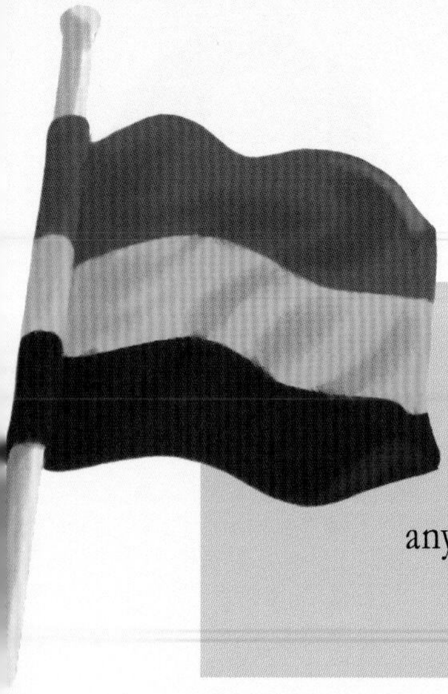

At the pinnacle of success and fame, Bob Marley embarked on his last tour in 1980, which lasted until his body wouldn't let him get up on stage anymore. When he died the following year, he left his world the legacy of his music and a message for posterity.

Despite the cancer that was making him weaker by the day, Bob Marley never stopped performing in his last year. If anything, he put on even more concerts. He was now a global star and played for fans around the world, be it in Kingston at the Reggae Sunsplash festival, in New Zealand for the Maori, or in the U.S., Europe, and Japan.

In 1980, he gave the world *Uprising*, the eighth and last album the singer released in his lifetime, recorded as always with the Wailers. It was a more intimate album than his last one, the very political *Survival*, despite the brightly colored cover picturing Bob Marley in front of a rising sun, his arms outstretched and his fists clenched. A posture of prayer or of revolt? Either way, his political message is still present on the album, as in the ironic "Real Situation," which evokes the war: "Well, it seems like total destruction the only solution." But it was another track, with disco beats, that quickly became a hit and made the album one as well: the famous "Could You Be Loved."

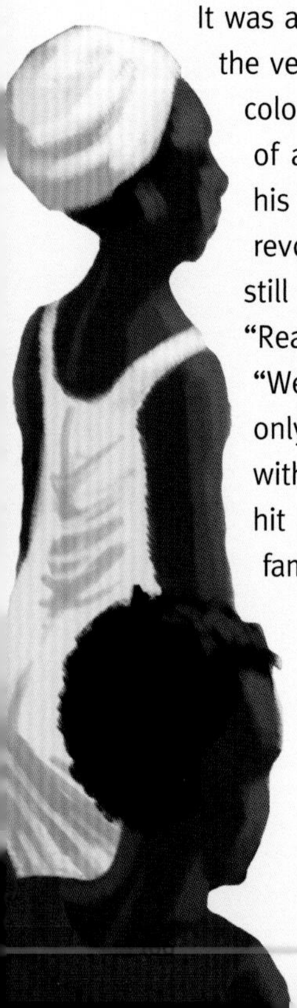

The tour kicked off with a bang. First stop, the Hallenstadion in Zurich, Switzerland, then the hippodrome in Munich, Germany. By the time the band arrived in France, the album had already gone gold, with more than 100,000 copies sold. Needless to say, they didn't have a problem filling seats! The shows in Lille, Bordeaux, Orléans, Nantes and Dijon all attracted an audience of 10,000, while in Paris, 50,000 fans came to listen to him at Le Bourget. Enough to cause quite a few traffic jams on the highway, and to inspire a wisecrack from Coluche, a comedian running for president at the time: he remarked that "the pope of reggae" had attracted twice as many fans than those who had gathered at the same venue a few weeks earlier to see Pope John Paul II. "I wonder if reggae isn't overtaking religion," he added.

Bob Marley himself was modest about his celebrity status. In an interview a few months later, he used a metaphor to explain his way of dealing with fame: "I keep my head in bandages so it doesn't get too big." In his view, it's the message he fought to communicate that made him so popular: "the truth, as well as the determination to stay alive and survive." Words all the more poignant given that the singer was growing thinner by the day. But the show must go on, as Freddie Mercury once said, and the Uprising Tour continued. After a summer in Europe, the Jamaicans arrived in the U.S., fully determined to reach the black

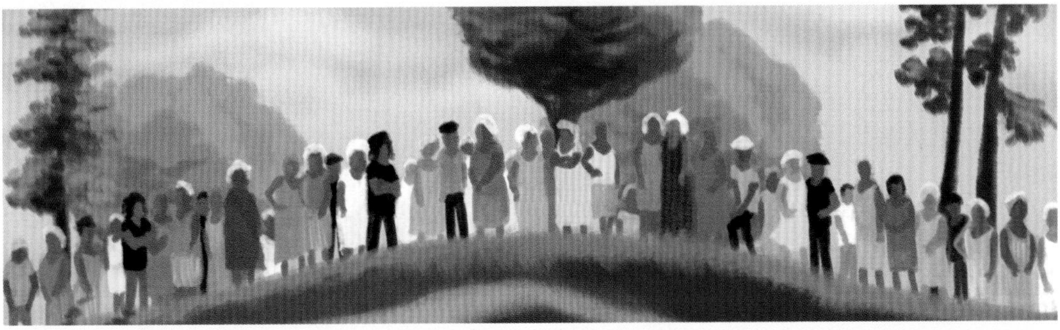

community in particular. They put on concerts in Boston, Rhode Island and New York. But then on September 21, while jogging in Central Park with his friend Alan Skip Cole, Bob Marley fell to the ground and passed out. Despite feeling extremely weak, he walked on stage two days later at the Stanley Theater in Pittsburgh. That sold-out concert was recorded. It would be Bob Marley's last, first sold as a pirated copy before the official edition, *Live Forever*, was released in 2011. The musicians came back on stage for several encores, but the rest of the U.S. tour was canceled: there was no longer denying that the cancer had spread to Marley's entire body.

The singer's doctors found five tumors in him: three in the brain, one in the lungs, and one in the stomach. They gave him two months to live. Bob Marley then traveled to Germany to undergo treatment with Dr. Josef Issels, a controversial physician who advocated for alternative treatments to fight cancer. There is no way of knowing whether it was due to the treatment or to Bob Marley's incredible inner strength, but the fact is that he survived seven months—at the cost, however, of tremendous suffering. At last, on May 11, 1981, nearly four years to the day after the famous soccer match in which his toe was crushed, Bob Marley passed away at Miami's Cedars of Lebanon Hospital. He was given a state funeral in Jamaica, after which the artist was laid to rest on a hill in his native village with a guitar, a Bible and a soccer ball.

The posthumous album *Confrontation* came out in 1983, followed by the greatest hits album *Legend* in 1994. While Bob Marley met with success during his lifetime, that compilation album smashed all his previous records, with 25 million copies sold to date. But beyond reggae, it was his life's journey, his political message and his aura that made Bob Marley an icon the world will never forget.

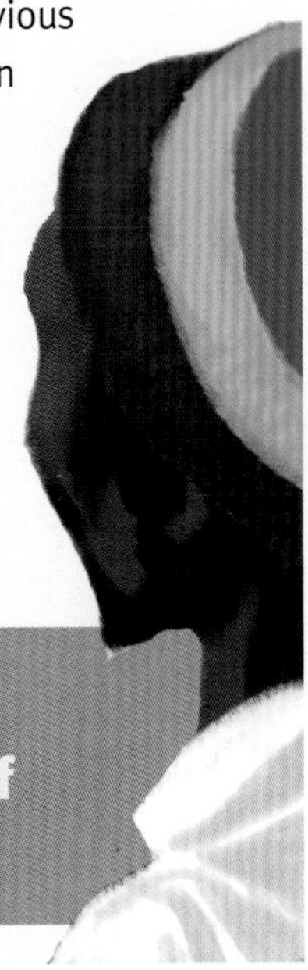

" My life matters not to me, it's the life of others that matters. My life only matters if it can be of service to a lot of people."

Now What?

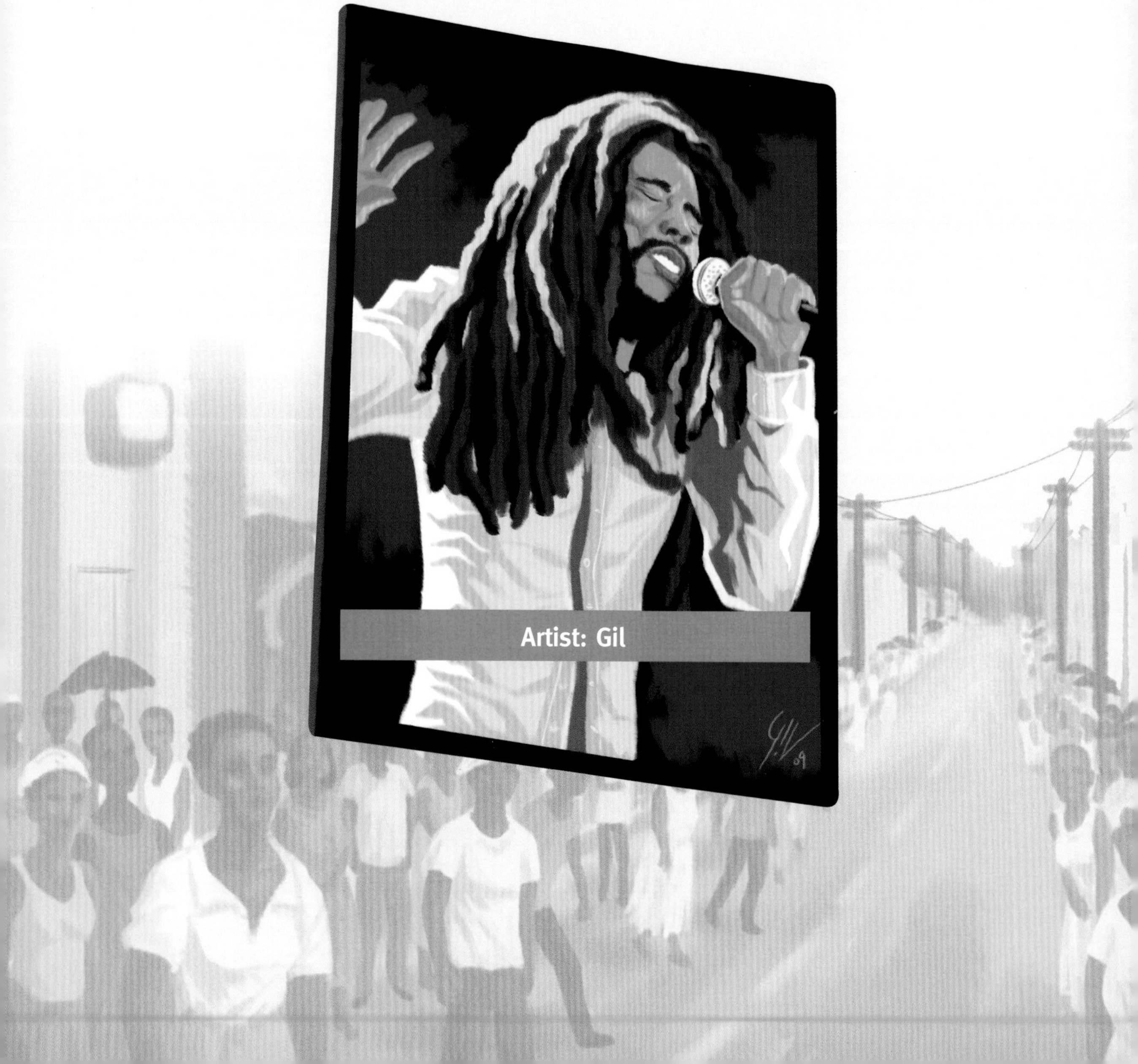

Artist: Gil

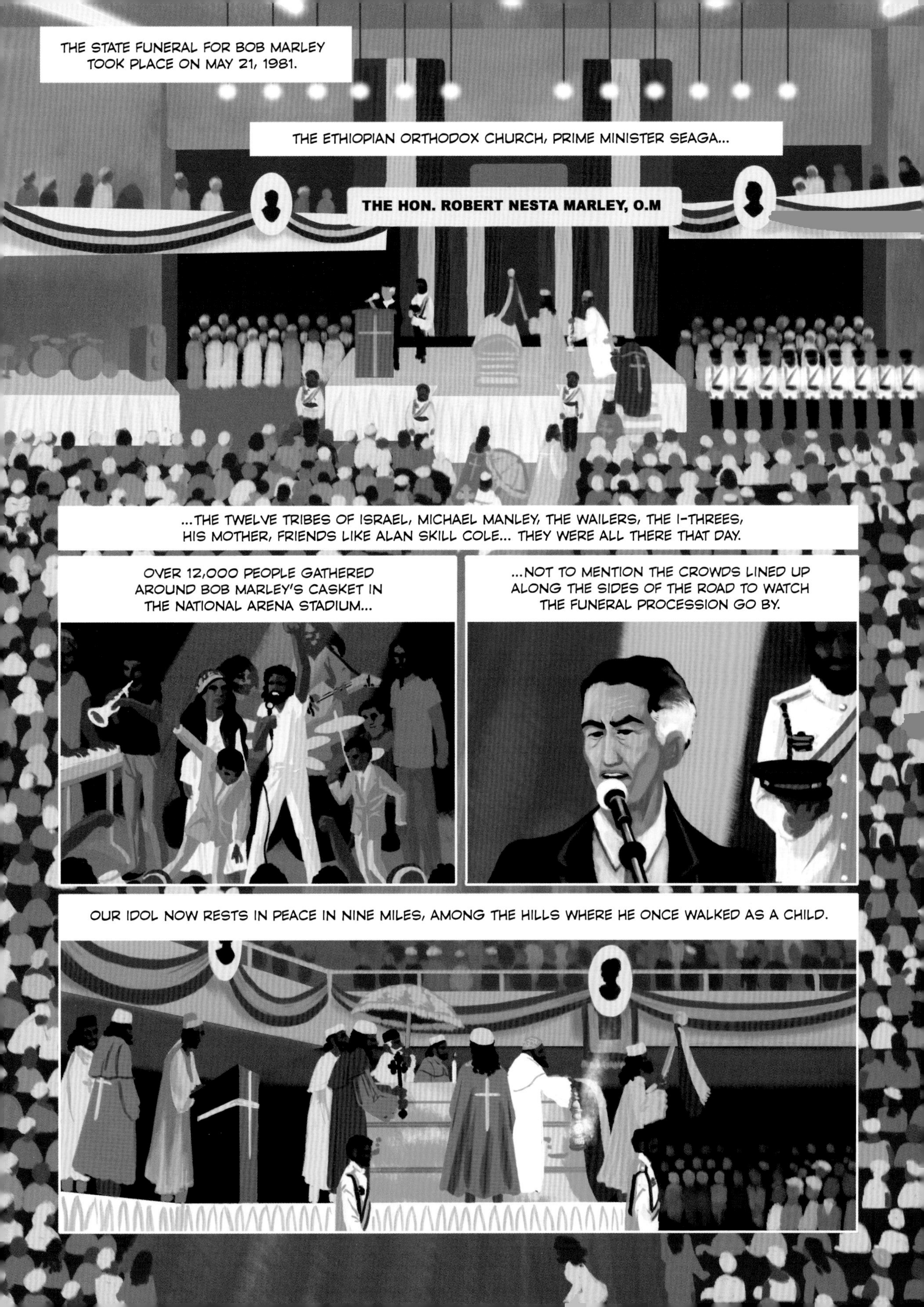
THE STATE FUNERAL FOR BOB MARLEY TOOK PLACE ON MAY 21, 1981.
THE ETHIOPIAN ORTHODOX CHURCH, PRIME MINISTER SEAGA...
THE HON. ROBERT NESTA MARLEY, O.M
...THE TWELVE TRIBES OF ISRAEL, MICHAEL MANLEY, THE WAILERS, THE I-THREES, HIS MOTHER, FRIENDS LIKE ALAN SKILL COLE... THEY WERE ALL THERE THAT DAY.
OVER 12,000 PEOPLE GATHERED AROUND BOB MARLEY'S CASKET IN THE NATIONAL ARENA STADIUM...
...NOT TO MENTION THE CROWDS LINED UP ALONG THE SIDES OF THE ROAD TO WATCH THE FUNERAL PROCESSION GO BY.
OUR IDOL NOW RESTS IN PEACE IN NINE MILES, AMONG THE HILLS WHERE HE ONCE WALKED AS A CHILD.

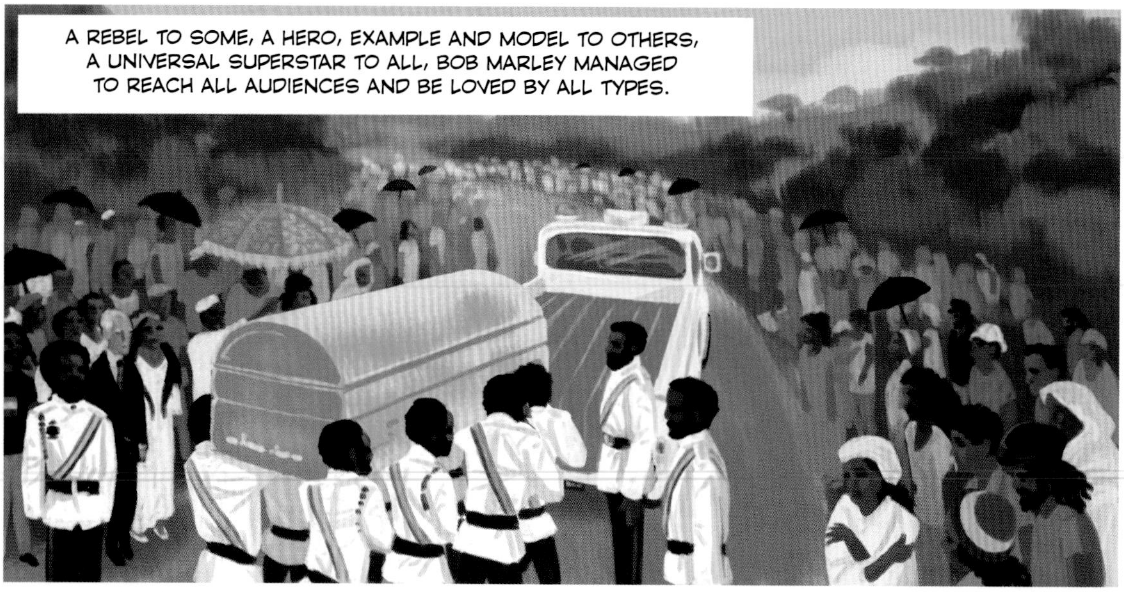
A REBEL TO SOME, A HERO, EXAMPLE AND MODEL TO OTHERS, A UNIVERSAL SUPERSTAR TO ALL, BOB MARLEY MANAGED TO REACH ALL AUDIENCES AND BE LOVED BY ALL TYPES.

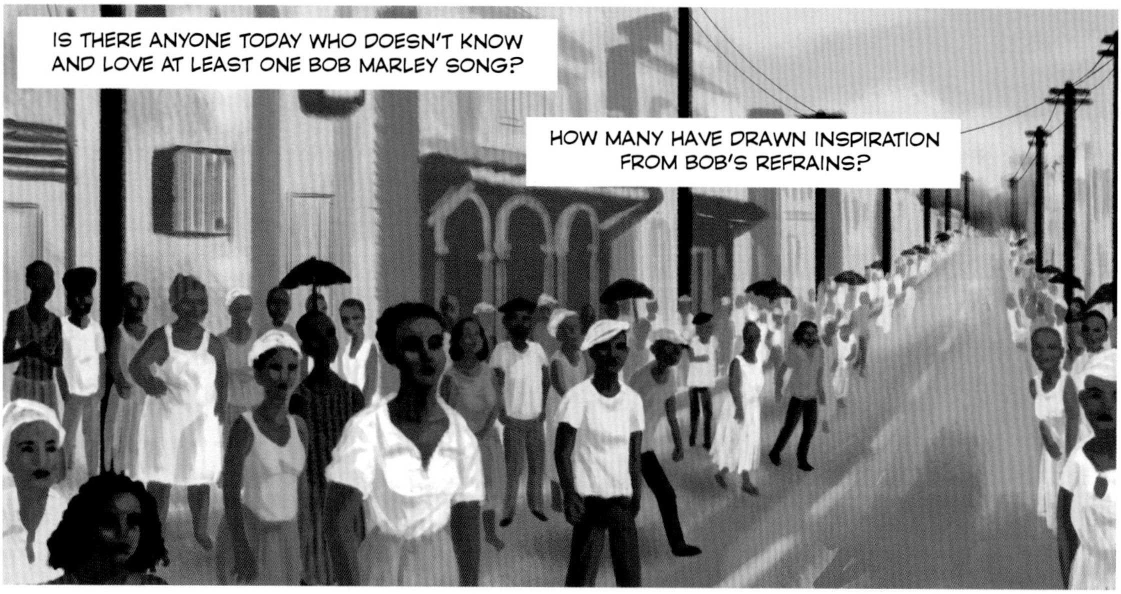
IS THERE ANYONE TODAY WHO DOESN'T KNOW AND LOVE AT LEAST ONE BOB MARLEY SONG?
HOW MANY HAVE DRAWN INSPIRATION FROM BOB'S REFRAINS?

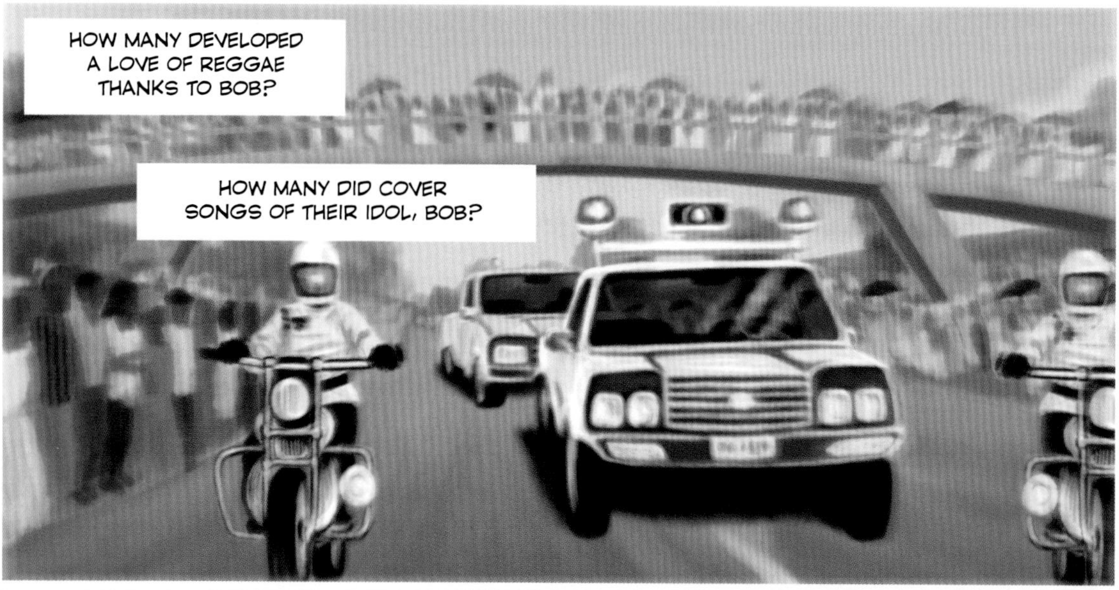
HOW MANY DEVELOPED A LOVE OF REGGAE THANKS TO BOB?
HOW MANY DID COVER SONGS OF THEIR IDOL, BOB?

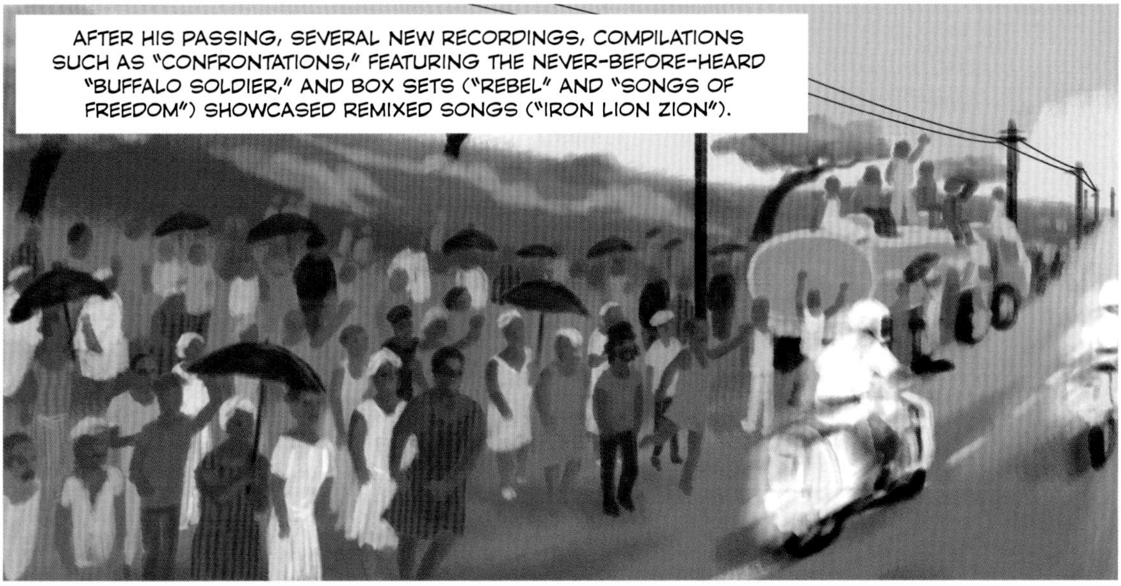
AFTER HIS PASSING, SEVERAL NEW RECORDINGS, COMPILATIONS SUCH AS "CONFRONTATIONS," FEATURING THE NEVER-BEFORE-HEARD "BUFFALO SOLDIER," AND BOX SETS ("REBEL" AND "SONGS OF FREEDOM") SHOWCASED REMIXED SONGS ("IRON LION ZION").

THE BIGGEST OF THOSE WAS THE GREATEST HITS ALBUM "LEGEND," WHICH HAS SOLD OVER 25 MILLION COPIES...

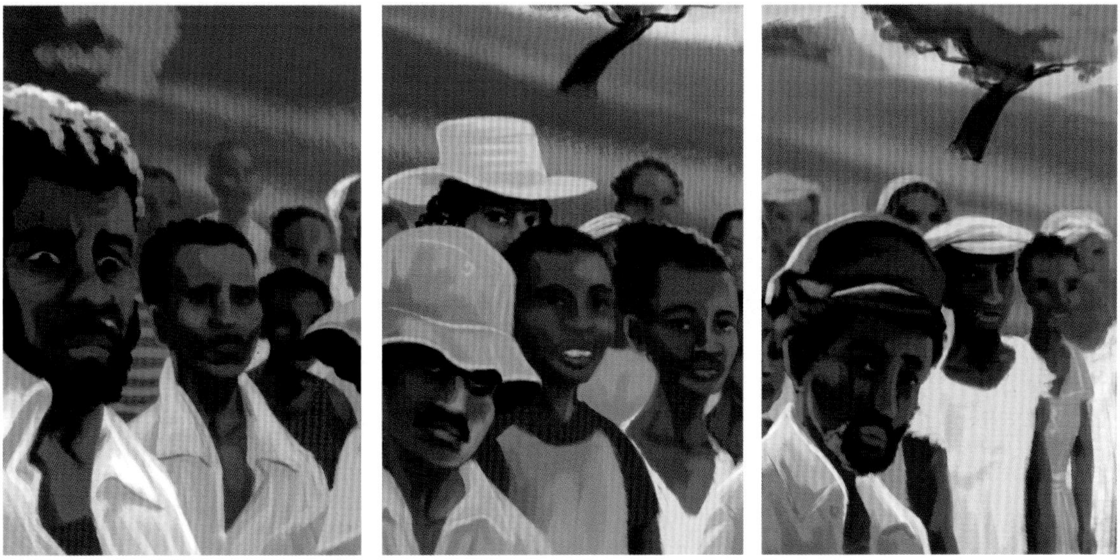

...OUTPERFORMING SOME OF THE GREATEST ALBUMS OF ALL TIME, INCLUDING THE BEATLES' "SGT. PEPPER'S LONELY HEARTS CLUB BAND" AND PINK FLOYD'S "DARK SIDE OF THE MOON."

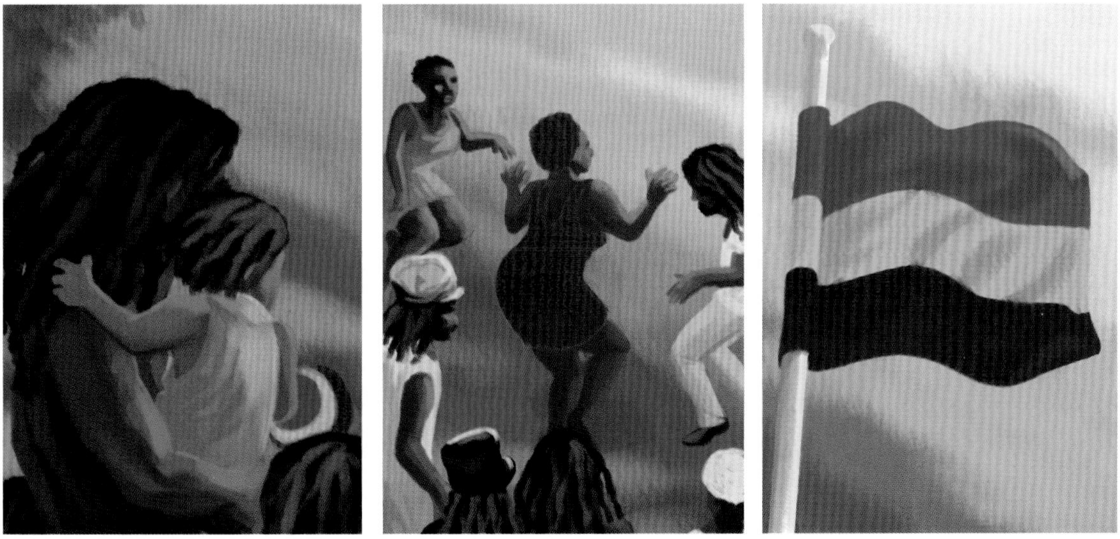

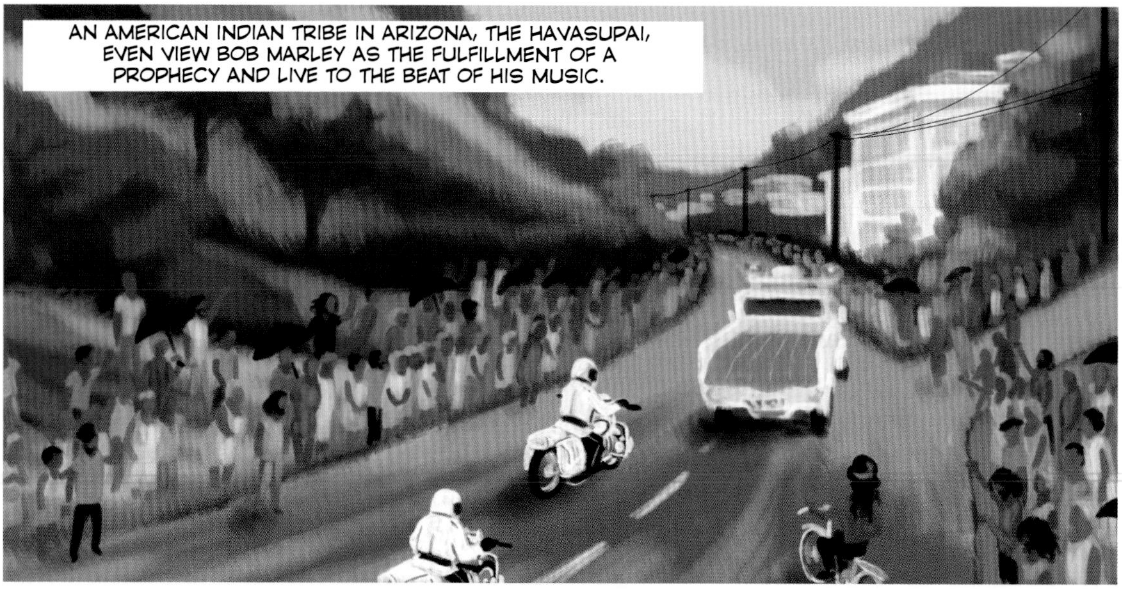
AN AMERICAN INDIAN TRIBE IN ARIZONA, THE HAVASUPAI, EVEN VIEW BOB MARLEY AS THE FULFILLMENT OF A PROPHECY AND LIVE TO THE BEAT OF HIS MUSIC.

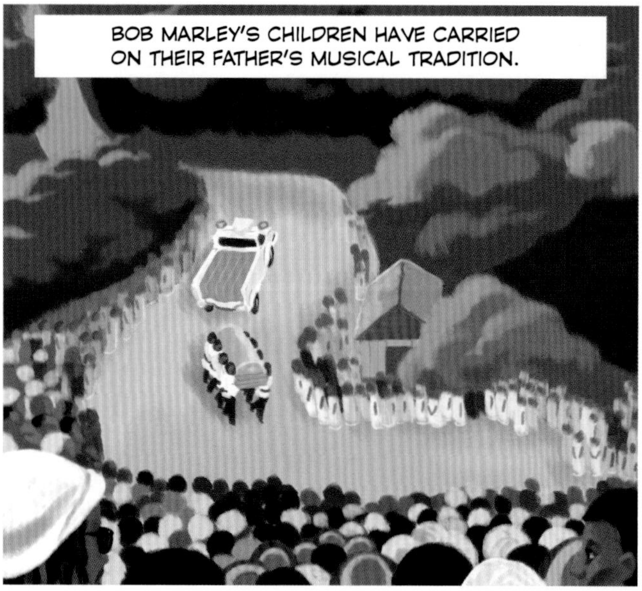
BOB MARLEY'S CHILDREN HAVE CARRIED ON THEIR FATHER'S MUSICAL TRADITION.

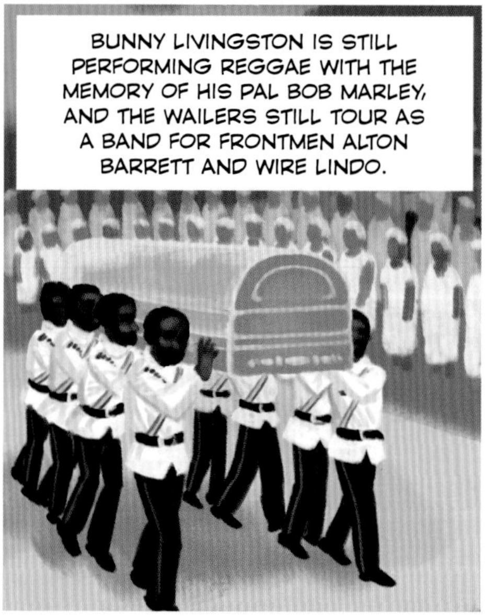
BUNNY LIVINGSTON IS STILL PERFORMING REGGAE WITH THE MEMORY OF HIS PAL BOB MARLEY, AND THE WAILERS STILL TOUR AS A BAND FOR FRONTMEN ALTON BARRETT AND WIRE LINDO.

WHEN AMNESTY INTERNATIONAL ORGANIZED A WORLD TOUR IN 1988, ALL THE BIGGEST STARS OF ROCK (STING, BRUCE SPRINGSTEEN, U2 AND OTHERS) WOULD START AND END THEIR CONCERTS WITH "GET UP STAND UP."

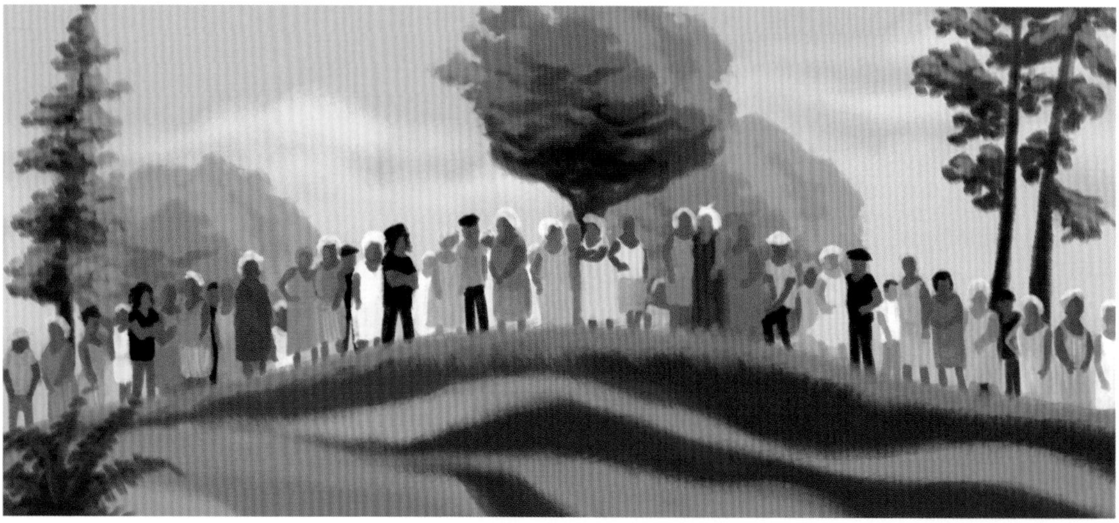

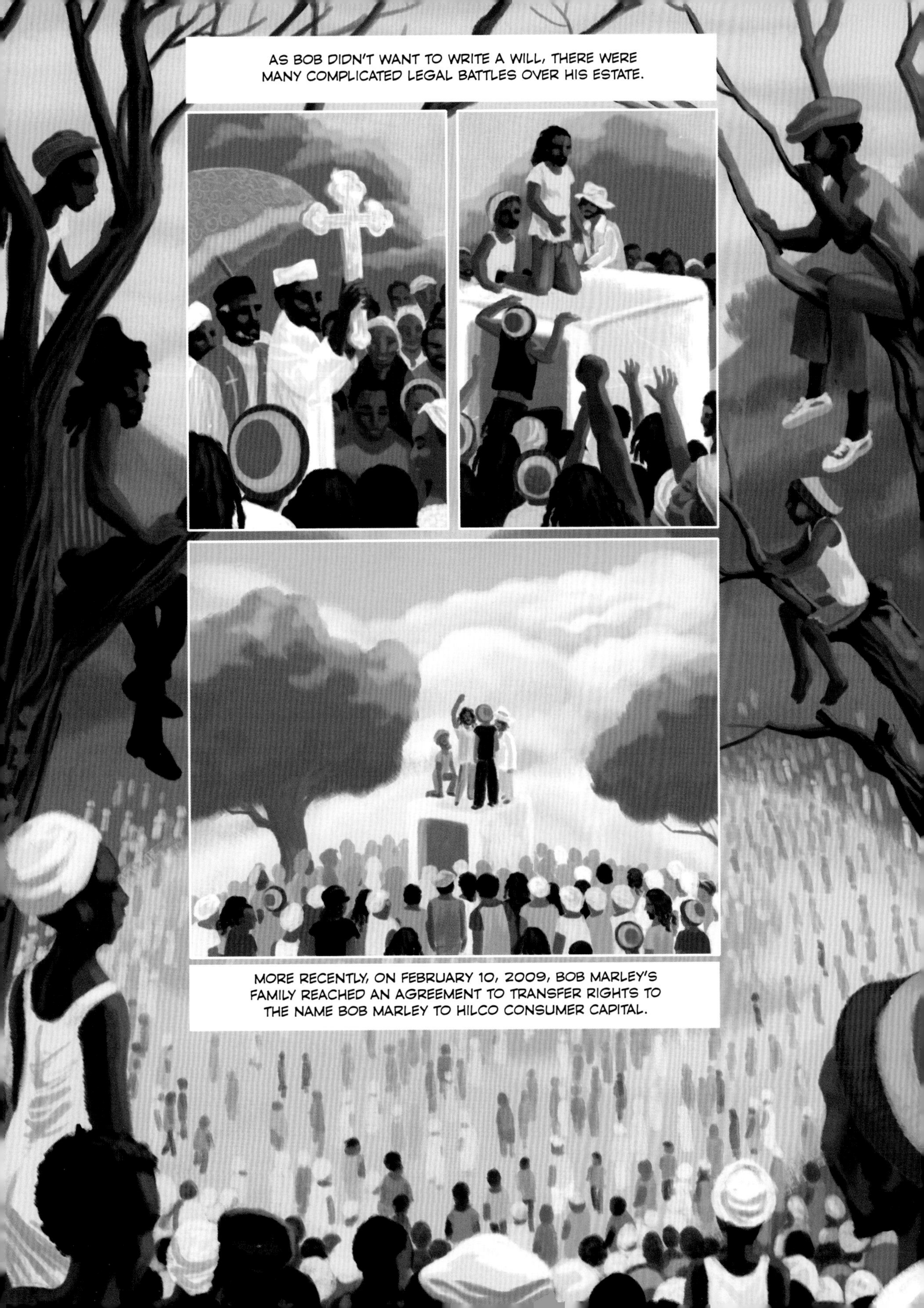
AS BOB DIDN'T WANT TO WRITE A WILL, THERE WERE MANY COMPLICATED LEGAL BATTLES OVER HIS ESTATE.
MORE RECENTLY, ON FEBRUARY 10, 2009, BOB MARLEY'S FAMILY REACHED AN AGREEMENT TO TRANSFER RIGHTS TO THE NAME BOB MARLEY TO HILCO CONSUMER CAPITAL.

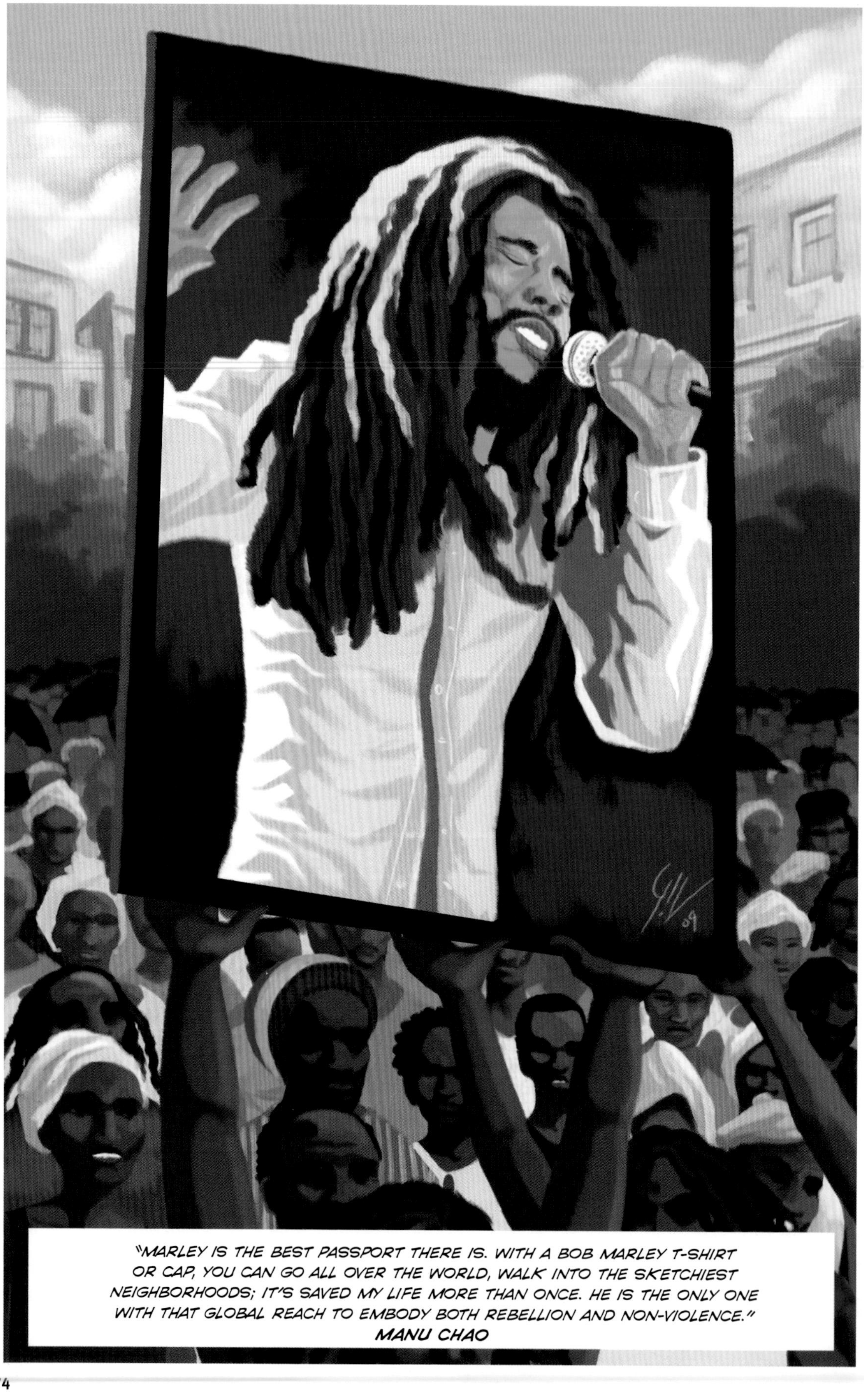
"MARLEY IS THE BEST PASSPORT THERE IS. WITH A BOB MARLEY T-SHIRT OR CAP, YOU CAN GO ALL OVER THE WORLD, WALK INTO THE SKETCHIEST NEIGHBORHOODS; IT'S SAVED MY LIFE MORE THAN ONCE. HE IS THE ONLY ONE WITH THAT GLOBAL REACH TO EMBODY BOTH REBELLION AND NON-VIOLENCE."
MANU CHAO

Further Reading

Soul Rebel: An Intimate Portrait of Bob Marley in Jamaica and Beyond, by David Burnette;
Insight Editions; 2009. A beautiful collection of photos by the acclaimed Time photojournalist.

Bob Marley by Stephen Davis; Schenkman Books; Revised edition, 1988.
One of the earlier biographies. "Easily the best book about Bob Marley." –Rolling Stone

No Woman No Cry: My Life with Bob Marley, by Rita Marley; Hachette Books; 2013.
An intimate and honest portrayal by Bob's wife, Rita.

Bob Marley: The Untold Story by Chris Salewicz; Farrar, Straus and Giroux, 2011. Critically acclaimed
biography with never-before-seen material by the author of the bestselling biography of *Joe Strummer,*
Redemption Son. "The definitive account of the man and the myth." –The Independent

Catch a Fire: The Life of Bob Marley, by Timothy White; Holt Paperbacks: Revised edition, 2006.
Considered THE classic biography. "Probably the finest biography ever written about a popular
musician." –San Francisco Chronicle

Interview with David Frick of *Rolling Stone Magazine*
http://www.bobmarley.com/media/videos/interviews-docs/interview-with-david-frick-of-rolling-stone
magazine-1978/ One of the rare interviews with the reggae legend.

Studio albums

The Wailing Wailers (Studio One; 1965)

Soul Rebels (Trojan; 1970)

Soul Revolution (Maroon, Upsetter; 1971)

The Best of The Wailers (Beverley's; 1971)

Catch a Fire (Island Records; 1973)

Burnin' (Island Records; 1973)

Natty Dread (Island Records; 1974)

Rastaman Vibration (Tuff Gong; 1976)

Exodus (Island Records; 1977)

Kaya (Island Records; 1978)

Survival (Island Records / Tuff Gong; 1979)

Uprising (Tuff Gong / Island Records; 1980)

Confrontation (Tuff Gong / Island Records; 1983)

Legend (Island Records; 1984; compilation and
top-selling reggae album of all time)

Live albums

Live! (Island Records; 1975)
Babylon by Bus (Tuff Gong / Island; 1978)

Also available from NBM Comics Biographies:
The Beatles in Comics
The Rolling Stones in Comics
Billie Holiday, by Munoz and Sampayo
"Presents glaring flashes of Holiday's songs and life, with stark, striking art that jazz lovers will appreciate."
-Library Journal
Elvis
"As a coffee table art book, Le Henanff's work is a lush success."
-Publishers Weekly
Glenn Gould, a Life Off Tempo
"Hums along in pace with its virtuoso subject."
-Toronto Globe & Mail

We have many more bios and
over 200 graphic novels
See more at:
NBMPUB.COM

NBM
160 Broadway, Suite 700, East Wing
New York, NY 10038
Catalog upon request

THE
BEATLES
in comics
nbm

The
ROLLING
STONES
in comics
nbm

MUÑOZ & SAMPAYO
BILLIE HOLIDAY
nbm

Elvis
nbm

SANDRINE REVEL
GLENN
GOULD
A LIFE OFF TEMPO
nbm

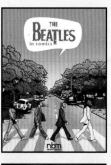

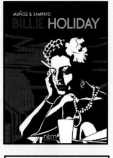

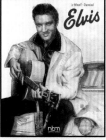

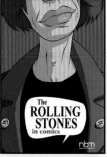

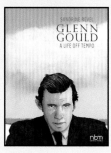